A Different Voice, A Different Song

A Different Voice, A Different Song

Reclaiming Community through the Natural Voice and World Song

Caroline Bithell

Oxford University Press is a department of the University of Oxford.
It furthers the University's objective of excellence in research, scholarship,
and education by publishing worldwide.

Oxford New York
Auckland Cape Town Dar es Salaam Hong Kong Karachi
Kuala Lumpur Madrid Melbourne Mexico City Nairobi
New Delhi Shanghai Taipei Toronto

With offices in
Argentina Austria Brazil Chile Czech Republic France Greece
Guatemala Hungary Italy Japan Poland Portugal Singapore
South Korea Switzerland Thailand Turkey Ukraine Vietnam

Oxford is a registered trademark of Oxford University Press
in the UK and certain other countries.

Published in the United States of America by
Oxford University Press
198 Madison Avenue, New York, NY 10016

© Oxford University Press 2014

All rights reserved. No part of this publication may be reproduced, stored in
a retrieval system, or transmitted, in any form or by any means, without the prior
permission in writing of Oxford University Press, or as expressly permitted by law,
by license, or under terms agreed with the appropriate reproduction rights organization.
Inquiries concerning reproduction outside the scope of the above should be sent to the
Rights Department, Oxford University Press, at the address above.

You must not circulate this work in any other form
and you must impose this same condition on any acquirer.

Library of Congress Cataloging-in-Publication Data

Bithell, Caroline, 1957–
A different voice, a different song : reclaiming community through the natural voice
and world song / Caroline Bithell.
  pages cm
Includes bibliographical references and index.
ISBN 978-0-19-935454-2 (hardback)—ISBN 978-0-19-935455-9 (pbk.)—
ISBN 978-0-19-935456-6 (online file)—ISBN 978-0-19-935457-3
(electronic text) 1. Natural voice singing. 2. Singing—Social aspects. I. Title.
  MT820.B57 2014
  782.5—dc23

9 8 7 6 5 4 3 2 1
Printed in the United States of America
on acid-free paper

For Ruben

CONTENTS

List of Illustrations   xi
Acknowledgements   xiii
About the Companion Website   xvii
List of Illustrations on the Companion Website   xix
List of Video Tracks on the Companion Website   xxi

Introduction   1
1. The Natural Voice, Community Choirs, and World Song:
   Setting the Scene   10
       Singing for Water   10
       The Bigger Picture: Definitions and Perspectives   16
           Singing in the Spotlight   19
       Research Contexts: Surveying the Literature   21
           Voice and Voicework   21
           Singing and Choirs   22
           Community Music and Community Music Therapy   25
           Ethnomusicology and World Musics in Education   28
           Musical Tourism   30
       Digging Deeper: Themes, Issues, and Concepts   30
           Networks, Scenes, and Movements   31
           Global Flows, Cosmopolitan Cultures, and Transnational
               Connections   33
           World Music, Cultural Appropriation, and Intercultural
               Engagement   37
           The Politics of Participation and the Art of Celebration   39
       Dancing in the Streets   42
2. In Search of the Natural Voice   45
       The Original Instrument   45
       Frankie Armstrong and the Natural Voice Practitioners'
           Network   47
           The NVPN Philosophy and Concepts of Music in Society   47

    The Giving Voice Project, Theatrical Roots, and the Natural Voice in
        Performance   55
        Kristin Linklater and Michele George   56
        Alfred Wolfsohn and Roy Hart   58
        Jerzy Grotowski and Włodzimierz Staniewski   60
        Giving Voice as Culture and Community   61
    A Meeting of Worlds: Giving Voice and the Natural Voice
        Network   63
    The Natural Voice in Perspective   65
3. Natural Voice Practitioners and Their Journeys: Histories and
   Connections   69
    A Gathering of the Natural Voice Clan   69
    The Roads That Lead to the Natural Voice   72
        Frankie's Singing Journey   73
    Meetings with Voice Practitioners: Contexts and Continuities   78
        Musical Lives   79
        The Folk Connection   81
        The Political Connection   83
        The Theatre Connection   84
        The Classical Connection   86
        The Community Music Connection   87
        The Therapy Connection   89
        The Circle Dance, Summer Camp, and Alternative Community
            Connection   92
        The World Music Connection   96
    The NVPN as Community of Practice   99
4. From Principles to Practice: The Culture of Natural Voice Choirs and
   Workshops   107
    If You Can Talk, You Can Sing   107
    Working with the Voice   109
    Preparing to Sing: The Function of Warm-Up Exercises   110
        Arriving and Tuning In   111
        Voice, Body, Breath, Mind   113
        Paving the Way for Singing in Style   116
        How Times Have Changed   118
    The Aural Method: Teaching and Learning by Ear   120
    Repertoire: Songs from the Oral Tradition   123
        Resources for Teachers   127
    Expanding Horizons   130
    Of Learning and Living   134
5. Singing the Songs of Others   140
    A World of Song   140
    The Attraction of Songs from Elsewhere   142

  Entering New Sound Worlds *143*
  Entering the Lives of Others *147*
   Deeper Resonances: Lost Pasts and Present Yearnings *149*
 The Politics of Unintelligibility *152*
  Songs from Taizé *155*
  Text and Meaning in the Vernacular *157*
  Vocables in Georgian Song *158*
 Ours or Theirs? Of Boundaries and Crossings *160*

6. Performing the Other: Appropriations and Transformations *165*
 Framing Intercultural Encounters *165*
 The African American Continuum and Gospel's Global
  Journeys *169*
 Back to Africa *173*
  Songs and Dances from South Africa *178*
  Songs of the Aka and Baka *181*
 Balkan Bridges *184*
 Gifts from Georgia *189*
 Authenticity, Alterity, and Possession *200*

7. Singing Communities: The World of Community Choirs *206*
 Singing in the Streets *206*
 Choirs, Choirs Everywhere *209*
  Choirs in the British Media *209*
   Amateur Choirs in Britain: Social and Political Legacies *214*
   International Perspectives: Building Bridges through Song *217*
   Locating the Community Choir: Worlds within Worlds *219*
 The Choir in the Community and the Community in the Choir *223*
 Singing, Health, and Happiness *233*
 The Place of Performance *241*
 Opening Doors *247*

8. Scenes from the Global Village: Singing Camps and Travels *252*
 The Singing Village *252*
 Reclaiming Paradise: Of Fields, Festivals, and Foreign Shores *256*
  Tapping into the Festival Current *257*
  Theorising Travel and Tourism *259*
 A Village in a Field: The Unicorn Natural Voice Camp *263*
  The Unicorn Experience *264*
  The Unicorn Repertoire *265*
  The Unicorn Community *270*
 Choirs on the Move *273*
 The Village on the Move: Village Harmony's Overseas Camps *276*
  Village Harmony in Corsica *278*
  Village Harmony in Bosnia *281*
  Village Harmony and Other Travels in Georgia *284*
 Of Refashioning Identities and Living Differently *287*

9. The Voice of the Future   294
    Gathering the Threads   294
    Fallacies and Other Truths   299
    A Quiet Revolution   308
    A River of Music   312

Appendix: NVPN Philosophy and Working Principles   315
References   317
Index   335

LIST OF ILLUSTRATIONS

1.1	Sing for Water at the Thames Festival	11
1.2	Sing for Water choir	12
3.1	Frankie Armstrong	74
6.1	Edisher Garakanidze leading a Georgian workshop	192
7.1	East Lancs Clarion Community Choir	207
7.2	Bolton Clarion Choir	215
7.3	Bangor Community Choir	228
7.4	Proposing a toast at a Georgian *supra*	232
7.5	Tony Backhouse leading a gospel workshop	246
8.1	Houses with towers, Ushguli	254
8.2	Village houses and gardens, Ushguli	254
8.3	Songmasters Gigo Chamgeliani and Murad and Givi Pirtskhelani	255
8.4	Givi Pirtskhelani at the Feast of Limkheri	256
8.5	The Diamond Choir and Rough Diamonds	276
8.6	Village Harmony with Omer Probić	284

ACKNOWLEDGEMENTS

This book could not have been written without the willing collaboration and practical support of a great number of individuals and organisations whose contributions it is my pleasure to acknowledge here. Conducting the research has been an intense, intriguing, salutary, and life-affirming experience. I have had the privilege of joining thousands of singers in all manner of settings, from musty community halls and damp British streets to Caucasian mountain villages and the stages of London's Cultural Olympiad. These singers have, for the most part, been "ordinary" people, technically "amateurs"; among them have been some of the most vibrant, generous, committed—and indeed musical—people I could ever wish to meet. I have also had the honour of working with leading lights from the international voice world and with a host of traditional singing specialists from different parts of the globe. Among my happiest memories are the long hours spent travelling across Georgia and Bosnia with fellow singing enthusiasts from different countries who quickly became friends, as did our hosts and teachers in the places we visited. Song-filled residential workshops and gatherings in rambling old mansions come a close second. While many of those who have accompanied me on this journey are named in these pages, many more remain anonymous. Thank you, all of you, for the inspiration, companionship, and hospitality along the way.

I am especially indebted to the scores of people who agreed to extensive interviews and to those who responded (again, often at length) to my questionnaire surveys. These include members of or participants at events organised by the Natural Voice Practitioners' Network, Village Harmony, Unicorn Camps, and Giving Voice/The Centre for Performance Research. In addition, many choirs across the UK welcomed me into their rehearsals, and choir leaders and members often welcomed me into their homes as well. In particular, I would like to thank the following interviewees for graciously sharing their stories, insights, and reflections, whether personal or professional: Zaka Aman, Stephanie Anderson, Frankie Armstrong, Madge Bray, Polly Bolton, John Bowker, Ali Burns, Bernard Burns, Geoff Burton, David Burbidge, Helen Chadwick, Ann Chamberlayne, Nina Chandler, Nickomo and Rasullah Clarke, Annie Cockburn, Daniel Cohen, Gideon Crevoshay, Sian Croose, Patty Cuyler,

Anita Daulne, Sally Davies, Colin and Ann Douglas, Pauline Down, Rosie Elkinton, Nicoletta Freedman, Katherina Garratt-Adams, Michele George, Jules Gibb, Lucy Gibson, Larry Gordon, Katie Griffiths, Sarah Harman, Michael Harper, Sue Harris, Su Hart, Bill Henderson, Moira Hill, Liz Hodgson, Chris Hoskins, Dee Jarlett, Bruce Knight, Anthony Johnston, Joseph Jordania, Frank Kane, Carl Linich, Pete Linnett, Becca Linton, Gareth Malone, Kirsty Martin, Imke McMurtrie, Joan Mills, Fiona Mills-Carlyon, Ketevan Mindorashvili, Nana Mzhavanadze, Kate O'Connell, Sue Parlby, Shergil Pirtskhelani, Nick Prater, Fran Priest, Irene Railley, James MacDonald Reid, Linda Roast, Chris Rowbury, Jackie Roxborough, Frank Rozelaar-Green, Cath Saunt, Bev Sedley, Polina Shepherd, Kate Shrubsall, Yvette Staelens, Janet Stansfeld, Dessi Stefanova, Mollie Stone, Olu Taiwo, Mark Thomas, Hannah Rose Tristram, Rusudan Tsurtsumia, David Tugwell, Tamta Turmanidze, Candy Verney, Teresa Verney, Tijana Vignjević, Roz Walker, Margaret Walton, Jane Wells, Rowena Whitehead, Derek Wilcox, Hilary Wilson, Jenn Woodward, Tony Wrench, Lynn Yule, and Nato Zumbadze. Together, these and others provided me with far more material than would fit between these covers. There is more to come...

Thank you, too, to those who allowed me to film their performances and informal musical interactions and subsequently agreed to allow me to include extracts from my video collection on the book's companion website. In addition to those featured in the recordings, I am grateful to the following event organisers for accommodating me and smoothing my way: Ali Burns (NVPN annual gatherings), Helen Chadwick, Roxane Smith, and the WaterAid team (Sing for Water, Thames Festival), Jules Gibb (Sing for Water North), Angela Gracey (National Street Choirs Festival, Bury), Patty Cuyler (Village Harmony camp, Georgia), Madge Bray (Lakhushdi trip), and Rusudan Tsurtsumia (International Symposium on Traditional Polyphony, Tbilisi).

It would have been impossible to complete the book itself without the Research Fellowship awarded by the Leverhulme Trust which, in tandem with a semester of institutional leave granted by the University of Manchester, gave me an entire year free of other commitments during which I was able to devote my full attention to this project. Two Small Research Grants from the British Academy and a travel grant from the Music and Letters Trust helped fund earlier phases of fieldwork that paved the way for the book (as well as resulting in other more modest outputs). For all of these I am profoundly thankful.

At Oxford University Press I have benefitted from the expert guidance of executive editor Suzanne Ryan and the ever cheerful and efficient work of editorial assistants Jessen O'Brien, Lisbeth Redfield, and of editor Norm Hirschy, who oversaw the construction of the companion website. I am especially grateful for the detailed commentaries offered by OUP's anonymous readers. Their astute and constructive critiques have contributed significantly to the shape taken by the final manuscript. I have also benefitted from the questioning, advice, and encouragement of colleagues at a series of conferences and research seminars where I presented aspects of this research in its earlier stages: my thanks in particular to those who engaged with my presentations at conferences organised by the Society for Ethnomusicology in Atlanta and at Wesleyan University, the International Council for Traditional Music in St. John's, Newfoundland, and the ICTM study group Mediterranean Music Studies in Malta, and—here in the UK—my guest lectures and research papers at the universities of Newcastle, Edinburgh, and Manchester, King's College London, and the Institute of Musical Research, University of London.

Special thanks are due to my daughter Chloe, who took many of the photographs featured in the book and on the companion website and also acted as expert proofreader. Throughout the project's long gestation, she was a source of sound and ever-patient advice while keeping me fed and watered as I navigated the peaks and troughs of the writing process. Sue Biddle transcribed many of the recorded interviews. Frankie Armstrong read and commented on the entire manuscript: I have greatly valued her enthusiasm and support.

Among those who nurtured my own love of singing, a special mention goes to Sian Ellis Williams, an extraordinarily gifted, energetic, and dedicated music teacher who on joining the staff of Flint High School launched not one but several choirs and introduced us to musical gems from many different times and places. Later, Helen Chadwick, Joan Mills, and Edisher Garakanidze (perhaps unwittingly) provided more stepping-stones that helped me forge my own path and eventually led to this book. Thanks, too, to my parents, Auriol and Peter Bithell, whose readiness to drive halfway across the country to look after three small children allowed me to attend some of the formative events of the 1980s that have now found their way into these pages. At times they wondered what exactly I was up to: here is the answer.

At the heart of this project lies the pioneering work of Frankie Armstrong, members of the Natural Voice Practitioners' Network, and others treading parallel paths in the world of community music-making, both here in the UK and elsewhere in the world. I hope this book will be useful to them, in part as a history of the movement they have helped to shape. I have endeavoured to double-check all factual data and ensure that relevant details are as up-to-date as possible at the time of going to press. I apologise for any oversights, errors, or omissions.

A final thank you to the thousands of singers out there who have gladdened my heart every step of the way. Long may your voices ring!

ABOUT THE COMPANION WEBSITE

www.oup.com/us/adifferentvoiceadifferentsong

Username: Music3
Password: Book3234

Readers are invited to visit the book's companion website, where they will find a wealth of illustrative materials and additional resources. A wide selection of original colour photographs and video clips serve as illustration for events and practices discussed in detail in the book (see lists on the pages that follow). These are cued in the text with the icons 🖼 and ▶ respectively.

The following resources can also be found on the website.

LINKS TO YOUTUBE, VIMEO, AND PODCASTS

Listed here are links to a further selection of video clips of choir performances posted on YouTube and Vimeo, together with links to short films and trailers referred to in the book. Since it is not possible to vouch for the long-term stability of clips on social media, these are not cued directly in the text although some are referenced in the endnotes.

WHO'S WHO: PRACTITIONERS FEATURED IN THE BOOK

This set of sixty-six short biographical entries is provided to help the reader keep track of the part played by individuals who put in more than a fleeting appearance in the book and to point to further information by providing links to personal websites where available.

COMMUNITY CHOIRS: SELECT WEBOGRAPHY

Listed here are the websites and blogs of a small but representative selection of choirs from among those featured in the book. These websites carry a range of materials, which may include photo galleries, sound and video files, repertoire lists, songsheets, events listings and posters, introductions to choir members, short concert reports and testimonials, details of rehearsals and fees, and other practical information for prospective members. Some also include an online shop.

ORGANISATIONS, PROJECTS, AND EVENTS: WEBOGRAPHY

This listing provides links to the websites of many of the organisations, projects, and events referred to in the book. These host a range of useful resources, including events listings, databases (of choirs, practitioners, recordings, etc.), newsletters, short films, podcasts, research reports, guidelines, training opportunities, extensive holdings of archival materials, and links to YouTube channels, Facebook, and other social media sites. Some also include an online shop.

SONGBOOKS AND OTHER RESOURCES FOR CHOIR LEADERS

This listing includes details of a wealth of resources for community choir and workshop leaders, most of which are referred to in the book. These include songbooks, teaching CDs and DVDs, and online resources.

LIST OF ILLUSTRATIONS ON THE COMPANION WEBSITE

01.01	Sing for Water at the Thames Festival
01.02	Sing for Water choir
01.03	Roxane Smith conducts Sing for Water choir
01.04	Michael Harper conducts Sing for Water choir
01.05	Stephen Taberner conducts Sing for Water choir
01.06	Una May Olomolaiye and Sing for Water choir
01.07	A flourish of scarves
01.08	The Lovenotes
01.09	Helen Chadwick and Mouthful
03.01	Frankie Armstrong
07.01	Banner at National Street Choirs Festival
07.02	Banner at National Street Choirs Festival
07.03	Rehearsing for mass sing at National Street Choirs Festival
07.04	Eleanor Hill and mass choir at National Street Choirs Festival
07.05	East Lancs Clarion Community Choir at National Street Choirs Festival
07.06	Exaltation of Larks at National Street Choirs Festival
07.07	Manchester Community Choir at National Street Choirs Festival
07.08	Bury Art Gallery
07.09	Clarion cycling club posters
07.10	Clarion cycling club and choirs posters
07.11	Bolton Clarion Choir with East Lancs Clarion Choir at Working Class Movement Library
07.12	Bangor Community Choir on carnival day
07.13	Proposing a toast at a Georgian *supra*

07.14	Maspindzeli sing at a *supra*
07.15	Tony Backhouse leading a gospel workshop
08.01	Village houses, Lakhushdi
08.02	Houses with towers, Ushguli
08.03	View of Mount Shkhara, Ushguli
08.04	Cluster of towers, Ushguli
08.05	Lamaria church, Ushguli
08.06	Village houses and gardens, Ushguli
08.07	Village house, Lakhushdi
08.08	Songmasters Gigo Chamgeliani and Murad and Givi Pirtskhelani
08.09	Givi Pirtskhelani at the Feast of Limkheri
08.10	Gigo Chamgeliani and Givi Pirtskhelani at the Feast of Limkheri
08.11	Irina Nonikashvili explains toasting ritual
08.12	The Diamond Choir and Rough Diamonds
08.13	Jean-Etienne Langiani teaching at Village Harmony Corsican camp
08.14	Frank Kane teaching at Village Harmony Corsican camp
08.15	Gîte at Canari
08.16	View from Canari
08.17	Poster for Village Harmony concert in Bosnia
08.18	Village Harmony with Omer Probić in Bosnia
08.19	Ushguli and Mount Shkhara
08.20	Trek on horseback, Ushguli
08.21	Georgian instruments and song words
08.22	Chuniri lesson
08.23	Drying tobacco in Qvashta
08.24	Church near Sighnaghi
08.25	Monastery of Davit-Gareja
08.26	*Supra* with dancing
08.27	Song-learning in Lakhushdi
08.28	Song-learning in Lakhushdi
08.29	Preparing herbs, Lakhushdi

LIST OF VIDEO TRACKS ON THE COMPANION WEBSITE

01.01	Sing for Water choir singing "Kaki Lambe"
01.02	Sing for Water choir singing "Hamba Kancane"
03.01	Kathy Bullock talking about spirituals
03.02	Kathy Bullock working on a blues scale
03.03	Singing "Everything Will Be Alright" at NVPN annual gathering
04.01	Helen Chadwick leading a warm-up
04.02	Gitika Partington leading a warm-up
04.03	Kirsty Martin leading a warm-up
04.04	Frankie Armstrong talking about speech and song
04.05	Frankie Armstrong demonstrating hoeing exercise
04.06	Polina Shepherd teaching "Ya Na Kamushke Sizhu"
04.07	Polina Shepherd teaching "Ne Zhurit'sa Khloptsi"
04.08	Alice Robin teaching "My Home Is Far Away"
04.09	Olwyn Pearce, Jacqui Ford, Jules Gibb, and Eleanor Hill co-conducting "Love Call Me Home"
04.10	Patty Cuyler teaching Corsican "Sanctus"
04.11	Patty Cuyler teaching Corsican "Sanctus"
06.01	Maspindzeli singing "Guruli Mgzavruli"
06.02	Maspindzeli male ensemble singing "Kriste Aghdga"
06.03	Tabuni singing "Irinola"
06.04	Borjghali singing "Tsmindao Ghmerto"
06.05	Thornlie Primary Georgian Choir singing "Iavnana"
06.06	Gorani singing "Imeretian Rider's Song"
07.01	Open Voice Choir singing "Iqude Wema"
07.02	Manchester Community Choir singing "I Am A River"

07.03	Exaltation of Larks singing "Ami Tomake/Go To Sleep"
07.04	Moorvoices and Whitby Community Choir singing "Johnny Has Gone For A Soldier"
07.05	Out Aloud singing "Gentleman Jack"
07.06	Bradford Voices Community Choir singing "Less For More"
08.01	Northern Harmony singing "Az' ukuba"
08.02	Northern Harmony singing "Abre vodenichare"
08.03	Northern Harmony singing "Tamario"
08.04	Village Harmony camp participants rehearsing "Vazhao Dilis Mzis Tskhivo"
08.05	Village Harmony camp participants take a bagpipe lesson
08.06	Village Harmony and friends singing at a *supra*
08.07	Men of Lakhushdi village singing "Lazhghvash"
08.08	Murad Pirtskhelani teaching "Shisha da Gergili"
08.09	"Tsmindao" sung by Lakhushdi men
08.10	"Tsmindao" and making Svan salt
08.11	"Tsmindao" sung by guests and visitors at Feast of Limkheri
08.12	Murad Pirtskhelani, Gigo Chamgeliani, and Givi Pirtskhelani singing at church door
08.13	Post-prandial singing at Feast of Limkheri
08.14	Initiation into traditional toasting rituals

A Different Voice, A Different Song

Introduction

This book is the result of my investigations into a new choral culture that sits at the intersection of two contemporary developments, neither of which has yet been the subject of a full-length critical study. The first is the natural voice movement, associated in the United Kingdom with a thriving network of open-access community choirs, weekend singing workshops, and summer camps. The second is a growing transnational network of amateur singers who participate in multicultural music activity by performing songs from "other" cultures, often travelling to the music's place of origin to learn directly from singers there. In seeking to locate the roots of these phenomena and to explicate the connections between them, this book uncovers the history of a grassroots scene that has been gathering force since the 1970s, with disparate, largely informal, and to some extent countercultural pathways gradually crystallising into a set of more clearly defined networks and initiatives. These have, to varying degrees, established themselves on a firmer footing as part of a culture that has moved closer to the mainstream and now enjoys a more visible public presence. While the natural voice community in the United Kingdom, centred around the Natural Voice Practitioners' Network, serves as my principal focus, connections are made with cognate developments elsewhere in the world (most notably in North America and Australia) and with nexuses of local practice in some of the places where more discrete partnerships have been developed (e.g. in South Africa and the Republic of Georgia).

At the heart of the threads I have sought to unravel is the overriding question of how and why songs from non-Western and folk traditions have provided the lynchpin for the natural voice movement. Aspects of the multifaceted answer to this question are woven throughout my analysis. My inquiries have also yielded interesting and sometimes unexpected perspectives relating to the democratisation of the voice, the politics of participation, the liberatory dimensions of harmony singing, the transformative power of performance, and the potential of music making to sustain community and to contribute to intercultural understanding. At a theoretical level, I engage with topical concerns in ethnomusicology and cultural studies by addressing questions of musical style, identity, and reciprocity in the postcolonial world, offering insights into contemporary cultural processes in which sociopolitical dynamics and musical aesthetics intersect in intriguing ways, and revealing a nuanced web of intersections between the local and global where agency lies with individuals rather than markets. Simultaneously, I offer the book as a contribution to the comparatively sparse scholarly literature in the field of community music. In a recent report compiled for the Arts and Humanities Research Council, George McKay and Ben Higham (2011) identified a dearth of analytical and theoretical work in this field and noted a need for more research into the history and repertoire practice of community music—including authoritative critical overviews and alternative readings—and into relations between community music and cognate practices. In furnishing a full-length ethnography that seeks to marry principles and practice with theoretical insights and interpretations derived from different disciplinary perspectives, as well as to map out a series of intersecting pathways and cross-influences, I hope I have helped to fill this gap. With specific reference to community choirs, Cindy Bell, on the basis of her preliminary investigations in the United States, deduced that "non-auditioned choral groups are prevalent in many churches, but only occasionally found in the community", noting that listings carried on the Vocal Area Network website included only "a handful" of choirs that did not require an audition. This prompted her to ask: "Are there other choirs like these...that operate 'under the radar'? What kind of choirs are they? Who directs them, and what is their repertoire? More importantly, how does a non-auditioned choir sound?" (Bell 2008: 233–234). Again, I hope that this book goes some considerable way to providing answers.

It has been intriguing over the course of my research to see a growing interest in the benefits of singing coming from many different quarters, with the emphasis being placed variously on the potential of singing and of choirs to improve individual health and wellbeing, to build social capital and connect communities, and to celebrate diversity. In some cases these interests are linked with government policies and new national agendas. Whether or not we subscribe to the notion of a "Big Society" with its rhetoric of devolving more power to the people (as promoted by British Prime Minister David Cameron), the natural voice movement, alongside other community music initiatives, would seem to have an important role to play in empowering both individuals and communities.

Like many books, this one has emerged from several strands of interest and activity that have threaded through my own personal and professional life. While not wishing to indulge in unnecessary domestic detail, I should arm the reader with at least a few of the facts that inform my positioning in relation to the material. I grew up in Wales, which, as everyone knew, was "the land of song", and so (naturally) we sang. We sang at home, at school, in church, at Girl Guide camp, and at the eisteddfod. Sometimes we sang in competitions but mostly we sang because that's what you did if you were Welsh (even if, like me, you grew up in a part of Wales that was predominantly English-speaking). While I was still at junior school, my hometown of Flint played host to the National Eisteddfod, and it was there that I first experienced the thrill of singing in a mass choir (in Welsh, of course). We also went on school trips to the International Eisteddfod at nearby Llangollen, where I soaked in the colours and sounds of visiting choirs from around the world. At high school, we were lucky to have a music teacher with boundless energy and vision, who set about establishing not one choir but several (including a folk choir) and who introduced us to repertoire in many different styles and languages.

I was always drawn to songs from distant places, in part because they conjured up pictures of other people in other landscapes, and these were the landscapes I inhabited in my imagination. At a sensory level, I revelled in the different timbres and harmonies, the feel of different languages in my ear and mouth. At an international Boy Scout and Girl Guide camp I attended as a teenager, I spent happy hours exchanging songs with a group of Finnish girls. Only later in life did I realise that I could not, in fact, translate every word of the Welsh folk songs that I sang and traded at that time. There were words I loved—words that made me feel a certain way, words that represented something profound, words that were archived deep in the fibres of my being—but my relationship to them was not, it turned out, tied to their literal, lexical meaning. Perhaps it is because I grew up in this not-quite-bilingual world that singing songs in languages other than my mother tongue did not seem at all unusual. Only much later did it strike me as in any way questionable, and ultimately it was my desire to know more about where the different songs that ended up in my personal repertoire came from and what they "meant", in a more holistic sense, that led me to a career in ethnomusicology.

When I encountered the circle dance scene in the 1980s, I quickly became involved in the musical side of things, tracking down the words to the Balkan songs that formed the core of the dance tunes circulating at that time, and teaching them to a group of friends, initially as part of the project of providing live music for dancing. This endeavour was to be augmented by a series of Bulgarian song and dance workshops that I attended in Bristol, including a weekend led by members of the Bistritsa Grandmothers. Early on in this stage of my journey I also attended a performance at Theatr Clwyd of a show called *The Woman of Thirteen Shirts* by Pauper's Carnival, featuring Vanya Constant, Claire Hughes, and Helen Chadwick. The piece was constructed around the stories attached to thirteen shirts, gleaned from women in different parts of the world; these stories were told with the help of a powerful set of songs, sung *a cappella* in styles that also evoked the places from which the stories (and shirts) came. It was one of those moments when a light turns on and your heart wakes up. Hungry for more, I began to frequent international voice and theatre festivals that offered the opportunity not only to observe performances but also to participate in workshops with the artists. Of particular appeal were the intensive voice workshops, usually spread over several days, that were offered by the Centre for Performance Research and Magdalena Project in Wales and Cirque Divers in Belgium, and it was at these events that I had my first taste of singing Corsican and Georgian songs, for example. By this time I had progressed to leading workshops of my own, as well as coordinating scratch choirs at summer camps. Under the auspices of adult education programmes in my home area, I also ran evening classes with titles like "Sing Out!" and "Songs from Far and Near".

This was all before the days of the Natural Voice Practitioners' Network (NVPN). By the time the NVPN was launched, I had taken a step sideways, returning to academia (in 1993) to pursue a doctor of philosophy degree in ethnomusicology and moving for a while to Corsica, the focus of my fieldwork. I was not, therefore, directly involved in the development of the organisation, even though after completing my PhD and being engaged as a lecturer at Bangor University, I continued to run occasional workshops and, with Pauline Down, established a community choir that was hosted by the university and was loosely related to my ethnomusicology teaching. As I emerged from more than a decade of preoccupation with Corsican music that culminated in my book *Transported by Song* (2007), it suddenly struck me that the decidedly niche world I'd been part of in the 1980s had evolved almost beyond recognition. Not only had the singing branch of this world consolidated its identity with the establishment of the NVPN: natural-voice-related activity had snowballed and community choirs, it seemed, had moved into an entirely different league. My academic interests, meanwhile, had led me to explore multipart singing traditions from many different parts of the world and to consider, from an insider perspective, the social, psychological, and political dimensions of collective singing. I now began to think about how the natural voice approach and the world song impulse fit together. I also realised that I was already in possession of a wealth of materials and contacts that could form the foundation for a new research project—and so this book began to take shape.

Together, the identities and experiences I had accumulated—as insider and outsider, practitioner and academic, advocate and critic—furnished me with the histories, understandings, and questions that underpin this study. The environment in which I grew up fed an enduring fascination with matters of singing and identity, on the one hand, and of language and meaning, on the other. My ethnomusicological training, together with earlier forays into social anthropology and linguistics, provided me with the theoretical and methodological foundations for analysing multipart singing traditions and articulating their significance for both home and adoptive communities. My grounding, both practical and theoretical, in the voluntary arts allowed me to fine-tune my interest in matters of democratisation, empowerment, community building, health and wellbeing, and cultural diversity.

This book, then, takes the form of an ethnography based on long-term, multi-locale fieldwork. I should note that my methodology differs in fundamental ways from that typically adopted by music psychologists, whose investigations into the health benefits of singing, for example, have often involved comparatively short-term projects designed according to the scientific method. With its essentially empirical approach and concern for measurable evidence, the emphasis in such work is on the systematic collection of data (often under laboratory conditions) that may then be analysed and quantified using standardised, validated measures. Results are typically reported in terms of project design, methodology, and statistical analysis, with reference to sample sizes, control groups, standardised scores, significant correlations, and statistical significance. The manner in which the investigation proceeded (including the precise methods by which subjects were selected and experiments conducted) is described in a way that allows the investigation to be replicated by other researchers, who may thereby either validate or dispute the findings. If qualitative material derived from interviews is included, then this, too, is usually subjected to content analysis (using, for example, Interpretative Phenomenological Analysis), leading to the kinds of results that may again be conveyed using graphs and tables or described in term of percentages, in parallel with direct quotation.[1]

My own approach is complementary in being situated firmly within the ethnographic tradition of my home discipline of ethnomusicology (itself closely allied with anthropology). Pride of place, in contemporary ethnography, is given to qualitative data, with a particular interest in the subjective, the experiential, and the insider viewpoint, and with the researcher positioned as alert participant more than detached observer. The resulting text is expected to convey new perspectives and original insights derived from the material, together with interpretations informed by relevant theoretical work. It may also include substantial passages of something akin to what Clifford Geertz (borrowing from Gilbert Ryle) termed "thick description"—a detailed, multi-layered, quasi-novelistic picture-in-words that, in paying attention to the context in which the action takes place, conveys to the reader the experience of "being there" while also pointing to possible "meanings" of the events described. If we concede that culture is to be found, as Geertz proposed, in the webs of significance that we (humankind) spin around ourselves, then its analysis is "not an experimental science in search of law but an interpretative one in search of meaning" (1993: 5). This, essentially, is the nature of my quest.

Throughout my text, then, theoretical discourse and critical analysis is interwoven with thick descriptions of practice, case studies, and quotation from personal interviews. My field is not a single village or even a single country. My subjects are an identifiable community of people, involved in a particular musical culture, but they are spread across a wide catchment area and many are themselves highly mobile within this terrain. They gather, however, around a set of core principles and practices, events and activities, organisations and locations. My task has been to accompany them as they go about their business in the field thereby defined. My primary data is derived from participant-observation at choir rehearsals, performances, workshops, camps, overseas tours, festivals, and symposia, supplemented by extensive and in-depth surveying—via semi-structured, narrative interviews and questionnaires—of voice teachers, choir and workshop leaders, camp and festival organisers, project leaders, and general participants. Events such as the NVPN annual gathering and the Unicorn Natural Voice Camp provided me with the opportunity to carry out multiple interviews with people from different parts of the British Isles. Village Harmony camps in Georgia, Bosnia, and Corsica, like the Giving Voice festivals I attended in Wales and Poland, allowed me to extend my inquiries to participants from other parts of the world. I also made visits of three-to-four days' duration to select parts of the United Kingdom, where I visited weekly choir sessions as a participant-observer, conducted interviews with choir leaders, and spoke with choir members. In a variety of locations I took part in a series of residential workshops that had a more specialised focus, such as Georgian singing or song-writing, together with mass choir gatherings and festivals such as the National Street Choirs Festival and the national Sing for Water event in London. Finally, I attended conferences and symposia on singing-related themes, including the Phenomenon of Singing International Symposium in Newfoundland, the International Symposium on Traditional Polyphony in Georgia, a SEMPRE conference (Society for Education, Music and Psychology Research) on the theme of music, health, and wellbeing hosted by the Sidney De Haan Research Centre at Canterbury University, and two one-day conferences on English folk song and community choirs at Cecil Sharp House in London. Audiovisual illustrations relating to some of these events can be found on the book's companion website.

This brief preamble should have provided a sufficient overall context for the chapters that follow. Chapter 1 takes the form of an extended introduction both to the book's immediate subject matter and to the theoretical perspectives that drive my analysis. I begin by identifying the communities and practices that are that my main focus. I then map out the broader fields within which the histories and practices I describe are positioned, and I familiarise the reader with a set of key concepts and themes that inform my interpretations throughout the book. Reference is made here to pertinent theoretical work in ethnomusicology, social anthropology, political science, and cultural and social theory.

From chapter 2, the book's organisation may be conceived as a series of concentric circles via which the reader is led to an ever-deepening appreciation of the multifaceted ways in which world songs act as the lynchpin for the natural voice movement. At the centre is the concept of the natural voice, around which is gathered a group of practitioners who exemplify diverse musical and professional backgrounds but are united in their adherence to a set of fundamental principles. In chapter 2, then, I set out to unpack the notion of the "natural voice", aided by an examination of the UK-based NVPN (with particular reference to its statement of philosophy and working principles) and an international body of practice brought together under the umbrella of the Giving Voice festival, an initiative of the Centre for Performance Research (which is based in Wales but works with partners worldwide). I also introduce the English folksinger Frankie Armstrong, the main inspiration and driving force behind the NVPN. Chapter 3 explores the singing journeys that have led individual practitioners to the natural voice fold, beginning with the different experiences and insights that have fed into Frankie's distinctive brand of voice work. With further reference to the musical and professional backgrounds of a representative selection of other practitioners based in the United Kingdom, I show how the movement has incorporated perspectives and values from a variety of musical worlds while also being influenced by the sociopolitical currents with which some of its more established members were associated in the 1970s and 1980s. Here, we make brief forays into the worlds of folk revival, experimental theatre, community music, social work, the women's movement, the Campaign for Nuclear Disarmament, circle dance, summer camps, and alternative therapies.

The next circle features repertoire choices and related issues—ranging from styles of teaching and learning to case studies detailing the ways in which particular musical repertoires have travelled. These are considered in a set of three chapters, in which my perspective moves from the general to the specific. Chapter 4 begins by showing how the principles embraced by the NVPN translate into practice. First, I examine the function and rationale of the kind of warm-up sequence that typically opens a choir session or workshop. I continue my analysis of methodology by considering the process of teaching and learning by ear, primarily in terms of practicalities. I then go on to explore the match between the natural voice ethos and songs from the world's oral traditions, together with a summary of the kinds of resources available to community choir leaders. In the final part of the chapter, I offer a more theoretical consideration of the politics of participation. In chapter 5, I pursue in greater depth my investigations into the place of world song in natural voice and community choir circles. I seek to explain why these songs-from-elsewhere play such a prominent part in the repertoire and how they help the movement achieve its broader aims. Drawing on interview and questionnaire responses from choir members as well as voice practitioners, I examine the different orders of attraction associated with songs of varied provenance and the meanings that may be attributed to them in their new environment. Turning to questions of language, I devote the second half of the chapter to an examination of the politics of unintelligibility. Chapter 6 continues this focus on songs from elsewhere through case studies of bodies of repertoire that have proven especially popular: gospel songs, songs from different parts of Africa (in particular, South Africa and the equatorial forest region of central Africa), songs from the Balkans, and Georgian songs. I argue that these more detailed stories of how music travels and how music accomplishes its work invite us to reconsider questions of authenticity, appropriation, and ownership while also attending to the dialogic and transformative potential of intercultural performance.

In the next circle are the singers who perform this repertoire and the contexts—mainly local but also regional and national—in which such performances take place. In Chapter 7, then, I turn to the world of natural-voice-style community choirs, set within the broader context of amateur choirs and choral singing, both contemporary and historical, and of generic considerations of the ways in which singing may be construed in relation to health, happiness, and wellbeing. Particular attention is paid to notions of community and to the ways in which personal rewards intersect with social impact. This part of my discussion includes short, contrasting case studies of Bangor Community Choir (in North Wales) and the London Georgian choir Maspindzeli. I also explore further the dynamics of performance and offer an overview of the varied locations and settings in which community choirs may share their repertoire with the wider community. Additional short case studies include Cambridge-based Good Vibrations choir and its engagement with asylum-seekers at Oakington Immigration Reception Centre.

The final circle extends to the international plane, featuring far-flung destinations to which many singers find their way and from where many of the songs originate. Chapter 8 continues the theme of community but this time in relation to the notion of the global village. The main body of the chapter is devoted to case studies of the Unicorn Natural Voice Camp (held in the South of England) and the overseas singing tours offered by the organisation Village Harmony (with particular reference to Corsica, Bosnia, and Georgia). My analysis of the latter is framed in part by perspectives derived from the critical literature on travel and tourism. Alongside exploring the dynamics of "being there" for tour participants, I attend to the symbolic meanings that may be attached to their presence by the host community. Turning back from this vantage point to face the centre, the reader is able to appreciate the ways in which national and transnational networks contribute to the sustainability of local communities, and vice versa. I end the chapter by revisiting questions of identity in the contemporary world, together with ideas about how the performing arts, and more particularly music, offer themselves as a prime site for experimenting with new ways of being.

Finally, chapter 9 takes the form of an extended conclusion in which I draw together the various threads that have been woven through the book. First, I review a set of key themes and concepts that have reappeared in different guises: finding a voice, participation, performance, community, networks, journeys, liberation, transcendence, empowerment, crossing boundaries, opening doors, liminality, *communitas*, transformation, conviviality, and collective joy. I then elaborate on the ways in which certain fallacies, misconceptions, and assumptions have been challenged or reframed in the worlds we have entered in the course of our journey. I end by reflecting on the broad impact of the trends and initiatives I have described and their potential to contribute to a substantial reconfiguring of ideas about vocal identity and musical sounds, values, and meanings.

NOTE

1. For examples of this approach, see articles in *Psychology of Music*, the journal of the Society for Education, Music and Psychology Research.

CHAPTER 1

The Natural Voice, Community Choirs, and World Song

Setting the Scene

SINGING FOR WATER

It is a Sunday afternoon in early September 2011, and I am on the banks of the River Thames, not far from London's Tower Bridge. The annual Mayor's Thames Festival is in full swing, offering a tempting programme of free outdoor performances and other activities at different sites along the South Bank. Parts of the riverside walkway and some of the open grassy areas that stretch between Tower Bridge and Hungerford Bridge are lined with market stalls offering a colourful variety of global cuisines, clothes, jewellery, artwork, and other handicrafts. The next event to take place at The Scoop—an open-air, amphitheatre-style performance space in front of City Hall—is a performance by the Sing for Water choir. As the crowd builds, the air becomes vibrant with anticipation, curiosity, and goodwill. Soon every place is taken, not only on the wide paved steps around the sunken stage that form the official seating area, but also at the metal balustrade, from which more spectators have an aerial view of the proceedings from the plaza above.

Sixty miles away, England's south coast is being pounded by storms. The skies over London have been ominously overcast, and there have been intermittent showers throughout the morning; but now, as the mass choir of 850 singers takes to the stage, the clouds part and the sun beats down (figure 1.1). The singers, arranged ten or so deep in a huge horseshoe formation, present a wash of variegated colour forming blocks of sky blue (sopranos), purple (altos), turquoise (tenors), and indigo (basses). Some sport scarves, hats, or flowers. The majority appear, in terms of the problematic classifications of the

Figure 1.1 Sing for Water at the Scoop. Thames Festival, London, September 2011.
Source: Photo courtesy of Chloe Grant.

2011 United Kingdom Census, to be "White British". The songs they sing, on the other hand, are drawn from an eclectic palette and hold clues to a web of intriguing connections.

All the songs are in arrangements for at least four voice-parts and are sung *a cappella*. Because the singers perform them from memory, they are free to move with the music while they sing and reach out directly to the crowd. Basic dance steps, swaying, clapping, or arm movements accompany some of the songs. The event's creative directors, Roxane Smith and Michael Harper, conduct most of the pieces (figure 1.2). Not surprisingly, the theme of water is prominent. The choir launches into a rendition of Janice Marie's "Let Love Rain Down", in an arrangement by Dee Jarlett, co-director of Bristol's Gasworks Choir. The anthemic refrain, with its evocation of liberty and justice for all and allusion to the reggae-like mantra of "one love", points to principles embraced by many of the singers gathered here today. "Water Wrinkles" by Morag Carmichael, who is here in the choir, then zooms in to focus on our immediate surroundings, its simple lyric painting a picture of the Thames as it flows under nearby Hammersmith Bridge. It is followed by a rousing rendition, under the direction of guest conductor Stephen Taberner, of "Dato's Mravalzhamier", a variant of the ubiquitous Georgian toasting song whose one-word text *mravalzhamier* may be translated as "may you live a long life" or, more literally, "many years" (roughly equivalent to wishing

Figure 1.2 Sing for Water choir with Roxane Smith conducting. Thames Festival, London, September 2011.
Source: Photo courtesy of Chloe Grant.

someone "many happy returns" on their birthday). The time is now ripe for more active audience participation, and everyone in the crowd becomes part of the show as Stephen teaches a short three-part song, "Seven Steps", to the choir and audience together. The choir then takes us to Nigeria with "Ide Were", a Yoruba song to Ochun, the goddess of love and the river, whose rich harmonic fabric is interwoven with delicate solo lines improvised by Una May Olomolaiye. The next song, "My Mouth", is a composition by Sing for Water's founder, Helen Chadwick; using text by the Turkish poet Fazıl Hüsnü Dağlarca, it is drawn from a larger work, *The Singing Circle*, commissioned by the Royal Opera House. This time, the solo lines are taken by Michael Harper, whose gospel-infused counter-tenor soars above the hymn-like, block harmonies of the choir. Then we return to Africa with the upbeat Zulu song "Ziyamazumekisi" conducted by Una May Olomolaiye, who also sings the solo calls. The set ends triumphantly with the Motown favourite "Dancing in the Street", in an arrangement by Nick Petts (co-director of another Bristol choir, People of Note), with soloist Una May at her most exuberant. With its invitation to people from "across the nation" to come together and dance in the streets, the song is a fitting encapsulation of the spirit of the festival. In a final flourish, the singers produce brightly hued scarves that they wave in the air, forming a multicoloured rainbow, evocative of Desmond Tutu's vision of a post-apartheid Rainbow Nation. With the final reprise of "Ziyamazumekisi", Una May once again directs the audience to join in the singing and move to the beat[1] (🔊▶) see web figures 01.01–01.09 and video tracks 01.01–01.02).

The event we have just witnessed is one of the more public manifestations of a grass-roots movement focused around community singing that has been quietly gathering pace since the 1980s, and that now represents one of the most intriguing and potentially momentous developments in the world of amateur, voluntary, participatory arts in the United Kingdom. The Sing for Water initiative itself is celebrating its tenth anniversary. The brainchild of singer and composer Helen Chadwick, the first Sing for Water concert took place in 2002. The annual London event has since been supplemented by a growing web of local fundraising initiatives, including regional mass sings such as Sing for Water West in Bristol, Sing for Water North in Manchester, and Sing and Swim for Water in Cambridge. Before today's event, the initiative had already raised a total of well over half a million pounds for the charity WaterAid, which brings clean water, sanitation, and hygiene education to communities throughout Africa and Asia—a sum far surpassing Helen's original dream of raising £1,000.[2]

For the curious bystander, today's performance raises a number of questions. Where have these 850 singers come from? How is it possible that—as Roxane mentioned when she introduced the singers—this is the first time these particular individuals have all performed together as a choir? How did they learn these songs in a range of foreign languages that they sing without words or scores? They all look so joyful, so colourful, so energised, so much in their element. Is this something that I, too, can be a part of?

The first question is answered at the end of the performance when Simon Hughes, local Member of Parliament and Chair of the Thames Festival Trust, takes the microphone to run through a list of fifty choirs from across Britain and beyond which are represented here today by at least some of their members. Several identify themselves with reference to their locality; these include Bangor Community Choir, Norwich Community Choir, Crystal Palace Community Choir, Colliers Wood Chorus, Streatham Voices, and the Cardiff Canton Singers, alongside the more suggestive Red Leicester Choir and the quirky-sounding Whitstable Whistlefish. Many others choirs have adopted names that seem to be indicative of their purpose, both musical and social: Get Vocal, Sounds Allowed, Good Vibrations, The Big Heart and Soul Choir, Open Arms, Raised Voices, and Raise the Roof. Still others, such as the Quangle Wangle Choir and Where's the Cake, opt for the whimsical or obtuse. The singers have all been busy over the summer learning the repertoire, some in weekly choir meetings, some in specially arranged day workshops, and others on their own using teaching CDs and scores prepared by Roxane and Michael. Many of them took part in a mass rehearsal yesterday afternoon; others arrived only for the sound check and a somewhat piecemeal run-through early this morning. Most have been sponsored by friends and colleagues, using either the traditional sponsorship forms provided by WaterAid or the online fundraising site Just Giving. Cash donations will also be collected after the performance by WaterAid volunteers dressed as taps and toilets, who will circulate among the crowd carrying buckets. This year alone, the event will raise £33,000.

Some of the singers have been staunch members of their local community choir for fifteen years or more. Others are new recruits, who may have cut their singing teeth in a beginner's group billed as "Singing for the Terrified"; for them, too, Sing for Water may come to represent an annual reunion with singing friends from far and wide, as well as a fundraising venture. Many will have stories about how joining a choir has "changed their life". The majority of the choirs and singing groups to which they belong are directed by members of the Natural Voice Practitioners' Network (NVPN), of which the three UK-based conductors of today's performance—Roxane, Michael, and Una May—are also members. These three are already well known to many of the singers, who have encountered them at other key events in their singing calendar, such as the Unicorn Natural Voice Camp, or at a day workshop in their home area.

If the majority of faces in the choir fall on the Caucasian end of the racial and ethnic spectrum, this is balanced out with this trio of conductors. Michael Harper, a classically trained counter-tenor whose professional credits range from operatic roles to solo recitals, grew up immersed in the spiritual and gospel singing traditions of the African American community in his hometown in Virginia. In parallel with his performance career, he now undertakes projects with community groups and works as a consultant and voice trainer for Youth Music and Sing Up, as well as teaching classical singing. Having been taken into the heart of the natural voice community, he also appears as a guest teacher at the Unicorn Natural Voice Camp. Vocalist and composer Una May Olomolaiye, born in Leeds to Jamaican parents, likewise grew up in the gospel tradition. She performs with the professional *a cappella* group Black Voices and has become a recognised solo voice in the British jazz scene. Her activities in the natural voice world include directing Coventry's WorldSong choir and the Leicester Amika Choir. She has also collected music on her travels in Africa, some of which she has subsequently arranged for choirs. She brings to her work with British choirs a strong improvisatory and rhythmic sensibility, as well as seemingly boundless energy and a natural capacity to tap into people's hidden potential that have made her such a popular teacher. These qualities are shared by Roxane Smith, who, from her home base in rural Wales, leads community choirs in Machynlleth, Aberystwyth, and Dolgellau and runs singing sessions at drug and alcohol rehabilitation centres, as well as workshops for schools, colleges, and youth groups. She, too, is a regular teacher at the Unicorn Natural Voice Camp, and has also worked on mass community choir projects under the auspices of the Centre for Performance Research.³ Joining the team as guest conductor this year is Stephen Taberner. A leading player in the *a cappella* movement in Australia, Stephen is best known in the United Kingdom as the director of the Australian all-male vocal ensemble the Spooky Men's Chorale, which has just completed its 2011 UK tour. Since the Spooky Men grew out of its members' shared passion for Georgian songs, it is fitting that Stephen should have conducted "Mravalzhamier". He, too, is a familiar face to many of today's singers, who attended a Spooky Men concert or workshop elsewhere in the country only a week or two ago.

The Georgian connection can be traced back to the roots of the Sing for Water story. The event's founder, Helen Chadwick, has been fascinated with music from different parts of the world throughout her career as a singer, actress, and composer—a career which spans her early work with Cardiff Laboratory Theatre, her subsequent work at the National Theatre, her recent production *Dalston Songs* (staged at the Royal Opera House's Linbury Theatre), and her performances with her own vocal *a cappella* ensemble, the Helen Chadwick Group. Helen also founded the London Georgian choir, initially known as Songs of the Caucasus and later renamed Maspindzeli, and the first Sing for Water performance consisted entirely of Georgian songs.

Today's programme performed by the mass choir has been punctuated by guest spots featuring the Manchester-based vocal quartet The Lovenotes, with jazz/blues singer Helen Watson. The natural voice connection extends to members of this ensemble too. Jules Gibb is the current Chair of the Natural Voice Practitioners' Network and another stalwart of the Unicorn Natural Voice Camp. Like fellow Lovenotes Faith Watson and Rose Hodgson, Jules also leads choirs and singing groups in and around Greater Manchester, and earlier in the summer she co-organised the first Sing for Water North performance that took place as part of the Manchester Day Parade.

The question "Is this something that I, too, could be part of?" is answered by Helen Chadwick in her opening statement on the "About Sing for Water" page on WaterAid's website: "Sing for Water is all about people creating events under their own banner and in their own way. Anyone who enjoys singing can take part" (http://www.wateraid.org/uk, acc. July 10, 2013). The original happening in London has spawned a growing network of initiatives that now includes events in France, Germany, and Australia, as well as regional Sing for Water performances across Britain; these mass sings take place in city squares or in water-related settings, such as piers and swimming pools. In this sense, what we have just witnessed is only the tip of the iceberg. Sing for Water offers a powerful example of how, to further exploit the water metaphor, a pebble is cast, the ripples spread, the waves gather force, and a trickle turns into a tide.⁴

THE BIGGER PICTURE: DEFINITIONS AND PERSPECTIVES

My opening vignette offers the reader a window onto the musical, social, and political world that is the focus of this book. It also points to some of the themes to be explored in greater depth in the chapters that follow. Many of the individuals and initiatives to which the reader has been introduced will also reappear, sometimes in different guises. Crucially, the Sing for Water story brings together three interrelated components that are central to this study: the natural voice, community choirs, and "world song" (the latter being the shorthand I adopt—by analogy with "world music"—to refer to songs from diverse cultures).

Several references have been made to the concept of the "natural voice": the natural voice community, the Natural Voice Practitioners' Network, and the Unicorn Natural Voice Camp. Broader applications and implications of the term are explored in chapter 2. In the context of the natural voice movement in the United Kingdom, the "natural voice"—which is sometimes also characterised as the "instinctive" or "authentic" voice—refers principally to a voice that is not classically trained. The natural voice philosophy, as articulated in the NVPN mission statement, is based on the belief that "singing is everyone's birthright"—a formulation that resonates with the oft-repeated African saying, "If you can walk, you can dance; if you can talk, you can sing." The NVPN statement continues: "and we are committed to teaching styles that are accepting and inclusive of all, regardless of musical experience and ability" (http://www.naturalvoice.net/, acc. July 10, 2013). The NVPN was founded by a group of voice practitioners who had undertaken a particular style of voice-work training with Frankie Armstrong. Better known to many as an English folksinger, Frankie continues to act as the mentor of the movement. The story of her singing journey and the evolution of her philosophy and practice is one of the threads running through the chapters that follow.

Most of the singers involved in Sing for Water belong to amateur singing collectives that refer to themselves as "community choirs". There are, of course, thousands of amateur choirs across Britain—including choral societies, Welsh male voice choirs, socialist choirs, Gilbert and Sullivan societies, and other types, such as those featured in the 2008 television series *Last Choir Standing*, for instance, and many of these would also see themselves as community choirs. The question of what makes natural-voice-style choirs different from other choirs, and how deep these differences might run, is another prominent thread in my narrative. Natural voice choirs may be defined initially as open-access choirs, in keeping with their fundamental commitment to inclusivity. In contrast to most choral societies or amateur "four-part choirs in the classical tradition" (such as those described in Ruth Finnegan's *The Hidden Musicians*), natural voice choirs do not hold auditions or require the ability to sight-read. Songs are taught by ear and sung *a cappella* and there is far less emphasis on public performance; in fact, some choirs on the NVPN website are listed as "non-performing". The image natural voice choirs present when they do perform is also quite different from that of the type of amateur choir which models itself on professional choirs. Typically, as in the spectacle presented by Sing for Water, the singers are colourfully and informally clad. Rather than standing stiffly in orderly rows, looking down at their music folders, they may be clapping or moving to the beat. There may be a moment in the performance when audience members are invited to join in the singing, which reinforces the message that they, too, might find their niche in such a choir.

The material a natural voice choir performs is also very different from that of a typical choral society, as art music is noticeably absent. As in the Sing for Water set described above, arrangements of Anglo-American popular songs figure prominently in the repertoire of many choirs, together with new material composed specifically for choirs of this kind. Perhaps the most striking feature, though, is the extensive place given to songs from different parts of the globe. Tullia Magrini has commented on the way in which "musics coming from the most different places...find unexpected new listeners, fans, and sometimes performers in the most unlikely places" (2000: 328). Salsa classes and samba bands are now widely available and highly visible leisure activities, easily accessed by the residents of any sizeable British town. More surprising, perhaps, is the number of amateur singers with a working repertory of songs from the oral traditions of places as diverse as the Caucasus, the Balkans, Corsica, Saamiland, Orkney, Cameroon, South Africa, Hawai'i, and the Cook Islands. While in many cases these songs from elsewhere represent one element in an even more eclectic programme, some choirs devote themselves exclusively to this repertoire and may refer to themselves specifically as "world music choirs".

Singing songs from other parts of the world is, of course, nothing new. Some readers may have memories of their days as Girl Guides or Boy Scouts, singing African, Maori, or Native American ("Red Indian") songs around a campfire—songs that served as common currency throughout the movement. International camps also offered opportunities for participants from different countries to share their songs: archival documents accessible via the Pine Tree Web make reference both to campfire songs and to folk songs sung by Boy Scouts of different nations at the World Scout Jamboree.[5] Pete Seeger and the Weavers, Joan Baez, and other singers associated with the North American folk revival popularised such songs as "Tzena, Tzena, Tzena" (a song in Hebrew written by Issachar Miron and Jehiel Hagges), "Wimoweh" (based on the South African song "Mbube", first recorded by Solomon Linda's Evening Birds in 1939), the Cuban "Guantanamera" (of disputed authorship), and "Gracias a la Vida" (by Chilean singer-songwriter Violeta Parra). Such songs often assumed anthemic status, and were sung by sympathisers the world over as a statement of solidarity with those striving for peace and democracy. Songs from South Africa in particular have long been popular with Britain's political choirs, and songs from the African American spiritual and gospel traditions have established themselves in the repertory of many Welsh male voice choirs, together with perennial favourites like the Russian song "Kalinka".

What we have witnessed in recent years, however, is a dramatic broadening of the constituency for a vast selection of lesser-known songs in more complex arrangements, aided by greater accessibility and ease of dissemination of these songs via new media. Drawn from the more authentic musical realities of contemporary cultures, these songs are of a different order from the token African, Japanese, or Spanish songs found in school songbooks, and from the arranged folk songs with piano accompaniment brought together in national songbooks. Even more remarkable is the extent to which these songs have become part of people's day-to-day lives and identities, as opposed to occupying the space apart that is the summer camp or concert stage.

The weekend workshops and voice camps attended by many of the singers involved in the natural voice and community choir network typically share the key features summarised above. In these settings, singers may be exposed to more intensive or exploratory work, often delving deeply into the music of one particular culture under the guidance of a native teacher. Again, allowance is made for singers with differing degrees of musical competence, and teaching and learning by ear is the norm. This fundamental emphasis on oral transmission is of central significance. In bypassing musical literacy, the movement challenges fundamental assumptions, conventions, and power relations that underpin many areas of musical activity (including music education) in Britain and in other parts of what is commonly designated "the West".

The choirs and individuals who inhabit this world typically have a strong outward-facing stance that impels them to explore new realms of experience and to make new connections beyond their immediate community. This in turn allows them to contribute to improving not only their own quality of life but also that of other people in other places. While my central focus is on networks of singing activity in the British Isles, my study also follows some of the singers as they venture out—literally as well as metaphorically—into the wider world, where they establish mutually rewarding musical alliances with singers in other cultures that, in some cases, develop into profound, long-term relationships. At this point, the natural voice world intersects with a growing transnational community of singers from different countries who likewise participate in multicultural music activity by learning and performing songs from places where singing plays a more prominent and "natural" role in community life. Some of these other global travellers will also put in appearances later in this book.

Interestingly, since I began this research, singing has come to enjoy a higher public profile here in Britain, owing in part to the introduction of government-backed initiatives designed to bring singing back into everyday life. In 2007, the Labour government launched its National Singing Programme. Composer, broadcaster, and music educator Howard Goodall was appointed National Ambassador for Singing, his brief being to direct a four-year programme called Sing Up. With an initial budget of £40 million, Sing Up aimed to make every British primary school a "singing school". Also in 2007, the then Mayor of London, Ken Livingston, launched the five-year Sing London scheme with the goal of "getting the whole of London singing" in time for the Olympics in 2012. The project's first large-scale event, a ten-day festival held that same year, offered Londoners the opportunity to be "united in collective song—all kinds of people singing all kinds of music in all kinds of places" (http://www.singlondon.org/about-us/our-history, acc. July 10, 2013). Natural voice practitioners are among those who have found work as part of these programmes.

Increased attention has also been paid to the health benefits of singing; short journalistic reports on this topic now regularly find their way into national and local news media. Most recently, this interest has been fuelled by the initiatives of the Sidney De Haan Research Centre for Arts and Health (founded in 2004 at Canterbury Christ Church University), whose mission is to carry out scientific research into "the potential value of music, and other participative arts activities, in the promotion of well-being and health of individuals and communities" and, more particularly, to provide the research evidence base for establishing "Singing on Prescription" (http://www.canterbury.ac.uk/Research/Centres/SDHR/Home.aspx, acc. July 10, 2013.) The centre's activities and outputs include a systematic review of a body of non-clinical research on singing and health; a cross-national survey of choral singers in Australia, England, and Germany; and evaluations of the Silver Song Club Project, run by Sing For Your Life Ltd., which promotes community singing groups for older people.[6] Related initiatives include Singing Hospitals, an international network for the promotion of singing in health-care settings, and Singing for the Brain, a project established by Chreanne Montgomery-Smith under the auspices of the Alzheimer's Society. The latter gained national attention via *The Alzheimer's Choir*, a widely acclaimed documentary film featuring members of the Bristol Singing for the Brain group (made up of Alzheimer's sufferers and their spouses) that was aired in 2009 as part of the BBC2 Wonderland series.

Choirs, meanwhile, have become something of a fetish as far as the British media is concerned. The television channel BBC2 has screened several runs of the reality TV series *The Choir*, featuring classically trained choirmaster Gareth Malone attempting to knock into shape a makeshift choir formed of sometimes reluctant individuals from, for example, an unpromising comprehensive school or a down-at-heel housing estate, most with little or no singing experience, to meet the deadline for a high-profile performance in a prestigious setting such as London's Royal Albert Hall or the World Choir Games in China. In the summer of 2008, a primetime Saturday evening slot on BBC1 was allocated to a new series, *Last Choir Standing*, which operated according to the knockout principle, with entrants in the earlier rounds being accepted or rejected by a panel of celebrity judges and the finalists being systematically voted off the programme by viewers. Another programme entitled *The Choir* is an established Sunday-evening feature on BBC Radio 3. Introduced by Welsh singer Aled Jones (who, as a young boy, was catapulted to fame as the voice of the theme song to *The Snowman*[7]), this programme has showcased many different kinds of choir, from established classical chorales and cathedral choirs to visiting ensembles from the Republic of Georgia.

The racy introduction to the first episode of *Last Choir Standing* impressed upon viewers the useful fact that Britain now had more choirs than fish and chip shops. This flurry of media activity might lead us to believe that the barriers to universal participation have largely been removed. Certainly, at first sight, spectacles such as *Last Choir Standing* seem to represent a significant move towards the democratisation of singing. Anyone can have a go and, at least in the later stages of the selection process, the public help determine the winner. Many in the natural voice and community music world, however, are unsettled by an underlying ethos that remains antithetical to the principle of empowerment these communities hold so sacred. Series such as *The Choir* and *Last Choir Standing* may have served to popularise amateur singing, but for their critics they continue to embody much that is wrong with the way in which singing is conventionally taught and, more crucially, the way in which individual singers may be judged, demoralised, and, ultimately, excluded.

Series such as *The X-Factor* go even further in reinforcing many of the same timeworn values and preconceptions. Entrants aspire to a position of stardom that allows them to occupy centre-stage and bask in the limelight, while also enjoying newfound personal wealth and winning lucrative recording contracts. They can do this, however, only at the expense of the other contestants who must suffer rejection. This format results in deep disappointment, resentment, and the shattering of dreams, many of which were patently unrealistic in the first place, and it all takes place on a very public stage, witnessed by millions. Although some of the hopefuls who fall by the wayside have gained the sympathy of many viewers, who now share their disappointment at losing, others become the butt of ridicule; scenes of their humiliation may even be engineered by the production team because this is part of the recipe for drawing huge numbers of viewers to cut-price reality TV.

Manifestations such as *Sing for Water*, together with the ever-expanding network of local choirs on which they draw, continue to offer an alternative model outside the competitive framework and to provide a home for singers whose goals are primarily interpersonal and experiential rather than individualistic and competitive. These singers are not chasing media-fuelled dreams of fame and fortune. Having found their voices, they are using them to draw attention not to themselves but to issues in the wider world that matter to them. And in their choice of songs, they go some way, at least, towards embracing and giving voice to the multicultural society that Britain has now become.

RESEARCH CONTEXTS: SURVEYING THE LITERATURE

The various trends that are brought together in my triad of the natural voice, community choirs, and world song have not yet been comprehensively documented or theorised, in part because they have thus far operated largely beneath the radar. Here I present a brief overview of relevant literature, identifying some of the landmark texts that continue to serve as points of reference, alongside more recent publications that stake out the contemporary state of the field and identify its current concerns and debates. The reader is directed to the bibliographies of these latter works for more extensive references to the most recent research. I engage with further bodies of literature in the following section of this chapter, where I dig deeper into the semiotic fields of more discrete themes and concepts.

Voice and Voicework

A work that is perhaps the closest to this book in terms of its immediate subject matter is Frankie Armstrong and Jenny Pearson's edited volume *Well-Tuned Women: Growing Strong Through Voicework* (2000). Presenting itself as "an essential guide for all those interested in liberating themselves through song, speech and sound" (back cover), the book is a collection of accounts by female voice practitioners of their personal vocal journeys. Among them are a number of current NVPN members, alongside others to be encountered in these pages, including Kristin Linklater, Michele George, and Ysaye Barnwell. In the course of telling their stories, some contributors examine the suppression of the female voice and the effects of social conditioning on women's vocal expression; others consider political and therapeutic uses of the voice and the use of the voice in self-defence. Frankie Armstrong's autobiography, *As Far as the Eye Can Sing*, offers a more detailed account of her own vocal journey and has helped underpin my telling of her story in chapter 3.

Explicit reference to the natural voice is found in the title of Kristin Linklater's handbook, *Freeing the Natural Voice* (1976, revised edition 2006), of which we shall hear more in chapter 2. Here, Linklater advances her philosophy of the human voice in the context of performance and offers her recipe for freeing the voice from the physical and psychological blocks by which it is often inhibited. Built around a progression of practical exercises, the book offers a programme to be followed over a period of several months. Aimed primarily at actors, the book also can be found on the shelves of some NVPN members. There are other brands of voice work or vocal coaching that on the surface would seem to share a common language with the natural voice movement but which, on closer inspection, turn out to be aimed at a different clientele, with rather different aspirations. Some are designed primarily for professional singers or aspiring pop stars; others belong in the tradition of the human growth movement or have healing or therapy as their prime goal; and some position themselves in relation to the corporate world. Tellingly, *Set Your Voice Free* by Roger Love carries an endorsement on its front cover from John Gray, author of *Men Are from Mars, Women Are from Venus*. Written, we are told, by "America's foremost vocal coach" who lists among his clients the Beach Boys, the Jacksons, Chicago, Phish, and Hanson, the book also sets out to appeal to those who yearn to "turn [their] dreams of singing into reality" or "dazzle potential clients with dynamic presentations". Love tells readers: "I'd like to show you how to find your true voice, the voice that is as rich and full and beautiful and exciting as you are" (1999: 4). One of the most notable features of books like this is that the social or community dimension is virtually absent, their focus being squarely on achieving personal success.

The titles of two further books have recourse to the concept of the "naked" voice. In *The Naked Voice: A Wholistic Approach to Singing*, W. Stephen Smith (professor of voice at the Juilliard School of Music in New York City) explains how his work is designed "to help singers...strip away the encumbrances that keep them from revealing their essential, 'naked voice'", in the process of which they "uncover their truest, most authentic selves" (2007: 3). Chloë Goodchild's *The Naked Voice: A Singer's Journey to the Spirit of Sound* tells the story of another journey of personal discovery through voice. Goodchild calls her brand of voice work the Naked Voice, with the tagline "transforming our lives through the power of sound". Here, "the naked voice" is characterised as "that original voice inside you, prior to your personality voice and social conditioning...the mouthpiece of your soul, the messenger of your true Self" (http://thenakedvoice.com/, acc. July 19, 2013). These diverse approaches are, at least, united in their view that vocal exploration can be a tool for individual transformation and in the conviction that there is, in some sense, something that might be conceived of (albeit problematically) as a "natural", "naked", or "authentic" voice.

Singing and Choirs

The literature on choral music is more substantial and has seen some interesting additions in recent years. Karen Ahlquist's *Chorus and Community* (2006) brings together a selection of case studies of choirs, choruses, and vocal ensembles from across time and across the world, investigating them not only as musical entities but also as groups of people coming together for social, political, and religious purposes.[8] The understanding of both "chorus" and "community" here is quite loose, and the highly divergent nature of the genres and styles under consideration is evident on the book's companion CD. The chorus is presented—in rather general terms—as a tool for "communicat[ing] a variety of messages to serve a variety of needs" (Ahlquist 2006: 1). A surprising number of the chapters take the form of historical studies of such subjects as the connections between music and morality in nineteenth-century England, choral singing in German-speaking Europe in the nineteenth century, the Fisk Jubilee Singers' tour to Holland in 1877, choral music among Russian Mennonites in the early 1900s, choral circles in early Soviet workers' clubs in the 1920s, and a history of a chorus associated with the International Ladies' Garment Workers' Union in Pennsylvania. In several chapters, the focus is less on the choir itself and more on the work of a (male) pioneer: John Curwen in Britain, Hall Johnson in the United States, and Kornelius Neufeld in Russia. Other chapters offer contemporary case studies of union and lesbian, gay, transgender, bisexual (LGTB) choruses in the United States and of the reinvention of the Jewish People's Philharmonic Chorus in New York. The ethnomusicological case studies include one by Bernard Lortat-Jacob, who writes about Sardinian lay brotherhoods, and one by Gregory Barz, who focuses on a Lutheran choir in Tanzania. Barz engages perhaps most closely with notions of community as he unpacks the different ways in which the *kwaya* functions as a musical and social community on multiple levels.[9]

Some interesting insights may also be gleaned from accounts written by choir members. In *Imperfect Harmony: Finding Happiness Singing with Others* (2013), Stacy Horn reflects on almost thirty years of singing with the Choral Society of Grace Church in New York and the central role this played in her life. The choir she writes about may be different to those I am concerned with here—its members undergo auditions, read music, and perform the great choral classics—but she is nonetheless concerned with similar questions. What compels us to sing? Why does communal singing comfort and uplift us when the rest of our life may be marred by disappointment, pain, and loss? Singing in the choir week after week, Horn writes, is "like exercising joy" (15). She also delves into the history of choral singing in the United States and into the recent literature on what the back cover blurb refers to as "the new science of singing", with reference to singing and the brain.

Amanda Lohrey, in her extended essay "The Clear Voice Suddenly Singing" (1998), writes of her time with a small community singing group in the Tasmanian city of Hobart. Singing again emerges as a route to ecstasy, prompting her to more deeply probe the question: What is the secret of the human voice? Lohrey's story offers a useful window onto the *a cappella* renaissance that has been building in Australia since the late 1980s; in this respect, it offers a closer parallel to the natural voice world. In both Lohrey's and Horn's accounts, themes of personal transcendence and of the choir as community stand out as central concerns.

Additional studies of individual choirs are scattered somewhat unpredictably across a range of journals and other edited volumes. These reflect a number of different lines of enquiry with a variety of countries represented. One prominent line of enquiry is the investigation of the therapeutic effects of singing in the context of health challenges or trauma on, for example, adults with cancer (Young 2009), people with eating disorders (Pavlakou 2009), dementia sufferers (Davidson and Fedele 2011), and in response to adverse life events (Von Lob et al. 2010). Other studies focus on the benefits of choir singing for marginalised, isolated, or hard-to-reach groups, such as prison inmates (Cohen 2009; Roma 2010; Silber 2005), homeless men (Bailey and Davidson 2002, 2005), and the elderly (Bungay et al. 2010; Li and Southcott 2012). Discussion of the social aspects of singing tends to be prominent in such works, together with an exploration of personal rewards, such as increased self-esteem, sense of purpose, and general well being.[10] A smaller number of studies have taken a comparative, cross-national, or cross-cultural approach (e.g. Clift et al. 2008a; Clift and Hancox 2010; Louhivuori et al. 2005). Still others have investigated the social and psychological benefits of choir membership with reference to diasporic or immigrant communities (Li and Southcott 2012; Southcott and Joseph 2013; Wood 2010).[11]

The collection *Where Music Helps: Community Music Therapy in Action and Reflection* (Stige et al. 2010a) features a handful of chapters on choirs and singing groups: a group in East London for adults with mental health problems, a choir for adults with physical disabilities in Israel, a children's choir in South Africa, and a senior choir in rural Western Norway. The latter book (which is written from the perspective of music therapy) also includes valuable reflections on how music may be said to create community and on the place of performance in the context of groups set up primarily for social or therapeutic reasons: these are among the key questions I pursue in chapter 7.[12] Studies such as these provide a counterbalance to studies that have focused on more conventional choral traditions whose raison d'être is primarily musical. The majority of the choirs included in the cross-national survey conducted by Clift et al., for example, are choral societies that perform "major choral works from the Western Classical repertoire from the 15th to 20th Centuries" (2008a: 3). We are told that "many participants in the study have had long experience of involvement in choral singing, and many have had singing lessons and can play an instrument. In addition, very few of the respondents were told as children that they could not sing" (10). In their conclusions, the authors note: "This is not to say that adults with little or no previous experience of singing might not find it enjoyable and beneficial if they were to have the opportunity and encouragement to participate in their local communities" (11). In the present study, I reveal that such a world has, in fact, long existed, and that such participation (as manifested by Sing for Water) already reaches far beyond local communities.

Community Music and Community Music Therapy

The scholarly literature on community music making in Britain has, until recently, been relatively sparse. Ruth Finnegan's *The Hidden Musicians: Music-Making in an English Town* (1989) stands out as a landmark in the field. Finnegan documents the diversity of amateur musical activity in the English town of Milton Keynes in the early 1980s. The book's title alludes to the unseen, taken-for-granted, behind-the-scenes work that sustains the wealth of musical activity that the research revealed. Although it focuses on a narrow geographical area, Finnegan's study ranges widely among classical orchestras and choirs, amateur operatic societies, brass bands, folk groups, jazz ensembles, rock bands, pop groups, country and western outfits, ceilidh bands, and church music. The groundbreaking nature of her study lay in its insistence on the value and integrity of grass-roots musical traditions. Crucially, Finnegan argued: "Once one starts thinking not about 'the best' but about what people actually *do*... then it becomes evident that there are in fact several musics, not just one, and that no one of them is self-evidently superior to the others. In Milton Keynes... there are several *different* musical worlds, often little understood by each other yet each having its own contrasting conventions about the proper modes of learning, transmission, composition or performance" (1989: 6). This is precisely the perspective I adopt in my own study.

Anthony Everitt's *Joining In: An Investigation into Participatory Music in the UK* (1997), a report commissioned by the Gulbenkian Foundation and described as the "first-ever account of participation in music in the United Kingdom", represented another landmark. Here, Everitt sets out the principles and politics of participatory music making and offers an insight into the range of instrumental playing and singing that is found in the community, as opposed to on the concert stage. Stephanie Pitts offers variations on the theme in *Valuing Musical Participation* (2005), in which she explores the motivations, values, and experiences of participants in a variety of musical settings—a school, a university, a residential summer school, and two music festivals—with the aim of elaborating a broader theoretical perspective on the way in which music contributes to social and personal fulfilment.

Barbershop singing is an interesting example of a bounded musical community that has attracted attention from sociologists as well as musicologists and ethnomusicologists. Sociologist Robert A. Stebbins, in *The Barbershop*

Singer: Inside the Social World of a Musical Hobby (1996), also focuses on the dynamics of participation, exploring the distinctive lifestyles enjoyed by "barbershoppers" and the rewards they derive from "the barbershop experience". Stebbins considers barbershop singing as an example of a serious leisure pursuit, and describes a world in which local clubs intersect with umbrella groups in the form of national societies, associations, or federations (a model that might also be applied to the natural voice world). In *The British Barbershopper: A Study in Socio-Musical Values* (2005), Liz Garnett (writing as a musicologist and a participant-observer) examines barbershop singing as "a distinctive and under-documented facet of Britain's musical landscape" (1), a "hidden" music, overshadowed by the greater scholarly attention paid to barbershop singing in the United states and Canada. With a particular interest (which I share) in theorising "the ways in which musical style and cultural discourses interact in the formation of identity" (2), Garnett builds on Judith Butler's notion of identity as performative and Anthony Giddens's thesis that each individual is engaged in an ongoing narrative that establishes and maintains a sense of self. She also seeks to unpack what she terms "the processes both of the social mediation of musical meanings and the musical mediation of social meanings" (2). Gage Averill—writing this time about barbershop singing in the United States in *Four Parts, No Waiting: A Social History of American Barbershop Harmony* (2003)—shares a perception of sound structure as social structure. Alongside sociability, participation, and a concern for leisure, Averill identifies service to the community as another value associated with barbershop singing; he also refers to the themes of innocence, alienation, and redemption that lie at the core of the barbershop revival. All of these concepts will find some resonance in our journeys across the natural voice landscape. Especially rewarding is Averill's chapter "Romancing the Tone: Song, Sound, and Significance in Barbershop Harmony", in which he attends in some detail to the emphasis on expanded sound and the thrill the singers derive from the phenomenon of "ringing" chords. Among the aficionados of Balkan and Georgian music to be encountered in later chapters, we will likewise find the notion that particular harmonic configurations lead to euphoric peak experiences.

In the context of community music as both discipline and profession, Lee Higgins' *Community Music: In Theory and Practice* (2012) traces the development of community music in the United Kingdom from the 1960s, when it first began to emerge as a sub-strand of the community arts and community cultural development movement. Describing community music workers as "dreamers" and "boundary-walkers" who derive a "position of strength" from inhabiting the margins and "continu[ing] to challenge through innovation and resistance" (6), Higgins goes on to elaborate a theoretical framework that includes concepts of hospitality, friendship, facilitation, participation, cultural democracy, and diversity. The book also includes reviews of practice, including several case studies of community music projects. Noting the way in which community music has traditionally concerned itself with musical activity outside educational settings and formal, statutory institutions, Higgins characterises its practitioners as "skilled music leaders, who facilitate group music-making experiences in environments that do not have set curricula" (2012: 4). Many skilled leaders of this kind who are active in the natural voice world are encountered in chapter 3.

A newfound international perspective is reflected in *Community Music Today* (Veblen et al. 2013). Hailed by one reviewer as "by far the most comprehensive analysis of community music from around the world in its breadth, depth, and gloriously dynamic diversity" (back cover), the collection presents perspectives from an international cohort of contributors who pay equal attention to theory and practice. Community music is understood comparatively loosely as embracing "formal, informal, nonformal, incidental, and accidental happenings" (back cover). The book includes overviews of community music in North America, the United Kingdom, the Nordic countries, Africa, East Asia, and Australia and New Zealand. It also offers case studies of community music activity in a variety of settings; among them we again find a few concerned with community choirs or choruses (in this case, in the United States and Canada). The material assembled in the *International Journal of Community Music* (under the editorship of Lee Higgins and published since 2008 by Intellect, having had an online presence since 2004) is likewise international in its reach and eclectic in the kind of work represented. In the United Kingdom, meanwhile, shorter articles, reports, and news items are brought together in *Sounding Board*, the quarterly magazine of the organisation Sound Sense.

In his foreword to *Community Music Today* as well as in his own monograph, Higgins links the new injection of energy and interest that community music has enjoyed since 2000 with advances in cognate fields—in this case the increased visibility of applied ethnomusicology, community music therapy, and cultural diversity in music education—which have changed the landscape of musical discourse. The community music therapy movement has, as its name suggests, sought to reinvigorate discussions of music in relation to community from the perspective of music therapy and at the same time to put "culture" more firmly on the music therapy map. In so doing, it has moved closer to the Scandinavian tradition of music therapy, in which culture and community have long been within the frame. A key text here (pre-dating *Where Music Helps*, discussed above, but featuring some of the same authors) is the foundational volume *Community Music Therapy* (Pavlicevic and Ansdell 2004). This book's fourteen contributors—who include music therapists working in Norway, Germany, Israel, South Africa, and the United States alongside several UK-based practitioners—set out to rethink both "music" and "community" and to offer readers "a new way of considering music therapy in more culturally, socially and politically sensitive ways" (back cover).[13] Of particular interest here is the shift away from a conception of music therapy as a method that employs music as treatment for a specific problem or condition to a broader conception of an intervention that harnesses music as part of a health and wellbeing approach. In this respect, community music therapy shares common ground with contemporary understandings of community music.

Ethnomusicology and World Musics in Education

Where it is defined in terms of professional practice, community music is still conceptualised as an act of intervention, whereby a trained practitioner facilitates music making among a group of participants, usually in the context of a funded project. Across the globe, an immeasurable amount of communal music making takes place without any such facilitator, and this, too—as in the local worlds described by Finnegan, Pitts, and our trio of barbershop commentators—offers important insights into the workings of communities defined by particular musical practices. The field of ethnomusicology is, of course, awash with full-length studies of this kind of music making. Typically combining ethnographic documentation with interpretation and theoretical critique, accounts of specific musical traditions add to our understanding, not only of what musical communities exist in the world (what they look and sound like, what they do), but also of how such communities function, at a deeper level, and how music itself does its work in social, psychological, and cultural terms.

Book-length studies of contemporary vocal traditions with a particular focus on multipart singing include Veit Erlmann's *The Early Social History of Zulu Migrant Workers' Choirs in South Africa* (1990) and *Nightsong: Performance, Power, and Practice in South Africa* (1996a), Jane Sugarman's *Engendering Song: Singing and Subjectivity at Prespa Albanian Weddings* (1997), Bernard Lortat-Jacob's *Chants de Passion: Au Coeur d'une Confrérie de Sardaigne* (1998), and my own book, *Transported by Song: Corsican Voices from Oral Tradition to World Stage* (2007). Here it will suffice to highlight just a few additional themes for the reader to keep in mind. Erlmann is especially concerned with the part played by the South African choral genre *isicathamiya* in the lives of its performers and with the meaning of performance as a social act offering a space for embodying alternative identities and imagined orders that may not be possible in day-to-day life; in Erlmann's analysis, meaning does not reside "in the music" but is rather "produced in the ever-shifting interaction between actors, interpreters, and performers" (1996a: 102). The central premise underpinning Lortat-Jacob's discussion of the musical traditions of Sardinian confraternities in *Chants de Passion* is that "acoustic harmony results directly from social harmony and cannot exist without it" (1998: 10). A similar insistence on "the two-way interaction between aesthetic and social considerations" provides the framework for Sugarman's work on singing in Prespa Albanian communities (1997: 22). In *Transported by Song*, I devote a chapter to exploring the subjective experience (for Corsican singers) of singing in harmony and singing with others, together with notions of collective singing as a kind of "intoxication" that has both transcendental and therapeutic properties.

An established classic among ethnographies with singing at their heart is Anthony Seeger's *Why Suyá Sing: A Musical Anthropology of an Amazonian People* (1987; reissued 2004). Of particular interest to us here is that the Suyá people of Brazil, among whom Seeger lived in the 1980s, routinely sang songs in a variety of Indian languages they did not understand and were "generally uninterested in translations" (2004: 19). All songs, Seeger tells us, "were said to come from *outside* Suyá society" (52, my emphasis), and some were learned directly from "foreigners".[14] Here, the answer to "why?" lies in part in the belief that "by taking and performing other groups' songs, the Suyá incorporated some of those groups' power and knowledge into their own community" (58–59). Here we may note not only that singing other people's songs was in this case perfectly normal but also that what was being transmitted or "taken" was more than simply the songs themselves. The Suyá, meanwhile, share the belief that songs transform humans and make them euphoric.

With regard to the consumption of world music away from its place of origin, there now exists a substantial body of critical literature, with contributions from scholars in the fields of ethnomusicology, popular music, and cultural studies. For the most part, however, these works are concerned with the commercial products of the global music industry, and they focus on questions of economics and power relations, often aligning themselves with the discourse of cultural imperialism (discussed later in this chapter). Comparatively little attention has been paid to those who seek to actively participate in music cultures not their own. A notable exception is Mirjana Laušević's *Balkan Fascination: Creating an Alternative Music Culture in America* (2006), a study inspired by the author's realisation that the majority of people who not only danced to but also played and sang Balkan songs and dance tunes in the United States were not (as she had initially assumed) immigrants from Balkan countries like herself but WASPs (White Anglo-Saxon Protestants). We will return in chapter 6 to Laušević's analysis of the layers of meaning that Balkan songs assumed for their American exponents.

Other volumes have addressed the teaching of world music traditions in educational settings. The contributors to Ted Solís's *Performing Ethnomusicology: Teaching and Representation in World Music Ensembles* (2004) consider world music ensembles (mainly instrumental) in universities (mainly in the United States). Several of the studies in this collection offer valuable perspectives on issues of authenticity, to which we will return in chapter 6. Huib Schippers's *Facing the Music: Shaping Music Education from a Global Perspective*

(2010) also draws its examples largely from instrumental traditions. It links developments in ethnomusicology and the rise of world music with the project of increasing cultural diversity in music education, in another exploration of the dynamics of teaching and learning music "out of context". Schippers insists that we should view this phenomenon in a positive light: "The West now has the opportunity to come full circle in its interaction with other music cultures, from knowing only one culture, to exploration, to domination, to exoticism, to tolerance, to acceptance, to inclusion in a new and diverse reality" (2010: xvii–xviii).

Musical Tourism

Finally, parts of my analysis also articulate with the literature on cultural tourism in ways that will be elucidated in chapter 8. With specific regard to musical tourism, my work complements that of Chris Gibson and John Connell (*Music and Tourism: On the Road Again*, 2005) by turning the spotlight on small-scale, collaborative, ethically aware musical encounters that are quite different from the more passively consumed product manufactured by a profit-driven industry that might characterise musical pilgrimages to Liverpool, Nashville, or New Orleans, for example, and from the mass invasion—often uninvited and affording no meaningful exchange with local people—of a remote island identified as the "perfect" location for a global dance party. In so doing, it also responds to Martin Stokes's call for "more nuanced ethnographic research...taking into account at least some of the motivations of actors and agents in tourist encounters and exchanges and the specificities of music as a form of social engagement" (1999: 141).

DIGGING DEEPER: THEMES, ISSUES, AND CONCEPTS

From my focus on the natural voice, community choir, and world song triad, there emerges a set of broader themes and concerns that demand more in-depth critical appraisal and offer the scope for more nuanced theorisation. Some will be introduced and elaborated in the course of my analysis; others warrant an initial exposition as part of this introductory chapter. Central themes that will recur in different contexts include the transformative power of music, the politics of participation, music as social capital, and music as a tool for intercultural engagement. While my conceptual frameworks rest primarily on my home discipline of ethnomusicology, I also draw on theoretical perspectives from social anthropology, political science, and cultural and social theory (including cultural studies and postcolonial studies). A series of studies on ritual, community, and the multiculturalism–cosmopolitanism nexus—again emanating from a range of academic disciplines—have also informed my thinking and helped lend explanatory power to my findings.

Networks, Scenes, and Movements

The "network" descriptor as used by the Natural Voice Practitioners' Network seems an apt one for defining a loose-knit community whose members share a basic philosophy and set of working principles. Apart from the website, the tools of this network include a newsletter, an email dialogue list, an annual gathering and other joint events, and use of similar teaching resources (many produced by NVPN members). The singers who attend the choirs, workshops, and other events organised under the NVPN umbrella, and who also come together at national events like Sing for Water, may likewise be seen as part of a network, although at this level there is no body to which one may sign up as a member beyond one's own choir. Events on the periphery—including one-off day or weekend workshops—may also include people who arrive independently with no prior association with the natural voice world. Some may be involved with other musical networks or have professional reasons for attending (a local school teacher, for example). For others, it may simply be a day out, booked on a whim. Their contact with the network will be transitory, but attendees will still have been exposed to a certain way of working with a certain type of repertoire, and they may be inspired to seek out similar events in the future.

Specialised events, such as those devoted to Georgian singing, may draw their clientele from a smaller pool of singers who are not necessarily active in the wider natural voice network (that is, they may not belong to a choir, or be involved in Sing for Water, or attend summer camps), but who are prepared to travel further afield to pursue their particular passion. These singers may form a more circumscribed network which (as in the Georgian example) has its own email circulation list and other social media connections, together with a common repertoire. Some of the most dedicated may also travel together to the source of the music, thereby accumulating a set of shared experiences and memories as well as friends in the host culture. At this level, concepts denoting transnational groupings become more useful.

The wider world that includes the outer circles of natural-voice-related activity, where the network that defines itself in terms of natural voice overlaps with related networks that have other ways of defining themselves (the community music network, for example), may perhaps best be viewed as "scenes". As described by Richard Peterson and Andy Bennett in their introduction to *Music Scenes*, the "scene" concept has been adopted as a theoretical model for research into the production, performance, and reception of a type of popular music that "focuses on situations where performers, support facilities, and fans come together to collectively create music for their own enjoyment" (2004: 3). A "scene" in this sense, with its informal or do-it-yourself overtones, may be contrasted with the multinational music industry as an operation involving a comparatively small number of people creating off-the-peg music products for mass markets. One modification to this definition must be made if we are to view the natural voice world as a scene. There are no fans in the conventional sense here: the followers are almost exclusively direct participants in, rather than observers or consumers of, the action that occupies centre-stage.

Peterson and Bennett go on to distinguish three different types of scene. A *local scene* "corresponds most closely with the original notion of a scene as clustered around a specific geographic focus". A *translocal scene* is made up of "widely scattered local scenes drawn into regular communication around a distinctive form of music and lifestyle". Finally, a *virtual scene* denotes a "newly emergent formation in which people scattered across great physical spaces create the sense of scene via fanzines and, increasingly, through the Internet" (2007: 6–7). These distinctions and the kind of layering they suggest also form a useful backdrop for my later analysis.

In some writings, as Peterson and Bennett note, "scene" is used more or less interchangeably with "community". The latter, however, is used in so many other senses that it becomes less useful as a referent for a more specialised manifestation without further qualification. Here, I occasionally speak of "the natural voice community" when referring to the body of people involved in the broader "scene", reserving "network" mainly for those times when I am referring more specifically to the NVPN. Peterson and Bennett's formulation of the scene concept draws on Pierre Bourdieu's (1984) definition of the "field" and Howard Becker's (1982) idea of "art worlds". While "field" as used by Bourdieu may be productive as an analytical concept, I find it less inviting for my present purposes, not least because of its overlap with the notion of conducting research "in the field", as well as its use in common parlance to refer to broader social structures, as in "the field of education". If I use the formulation "art worlds" or the related "music worlds", I do so in a broad sense rather than in the more specific terms of Becker's definition, where "art world" encompasses the range of professions and activities that support the production of works of art as part of an explicit argument about the fallacy of artistic autonomy.

To the extent that the majority of the NVPN membership shows a strong commitment to a shared ethos or ideology and to a set of fundamental principles that inform and define its practice, this network also has elements of a movement. It has a message that it wishes to spread and, in presenting an alternative to more mainstream, institutional offerings and in challenging widespread assumptions and orthodoxies that some of its members may view as misguided, it possesses some features suggestive of a subculture or counterculture. It also has, in Frankie Armstrong, a visionary founder and charismatic leader, evocative of the "burning souls" who are often found at the forefront of social movements, including music revivals. Through her pioneering work, Frankie has contributed to developments beyond the United Kingdom as well—in particular, she has been an important influence in the *a cappella* movement in Australia. Like other movements, such as America's civil rights movement or the international women's movement, the natural voice endeavour has also moved in from the margins to make its contribution to a process of social change.

Global Flows, Cosmopolitan Cultures, and Transnational Connections

An interesting body of work presents itself for the theorisation of the transnational groupings alluded to above, helping to shed light not only on the ways in which such formations function but also how they may be seen to relate to broader geopolitical trends and to theories of postmodernism, globalisation, and cosmopolitanism. Here I briefly revisit a selection of seminal or representative texts, giving priority to those theories and concepts that will be of most use to us in the analysis that is to follow.

Much has been written about the postmodern condition and the opportunities, as well as the threats and disillusions, that it presents to its subjects. Postmodernism is typically portrayed as the age of diversity, plurality, hybridity, and creolisation, with their attendant complexities, ambiguities, and impurities. For critics such as Fredric Jameson, the postmodern experience is one of fragmentation which reduces cultural expression to acts of pastiche or bricolage (see Jameson 1998). The past is relentlessly mined as a source of symbols and quotations, but it is a past that has lost its logic and linearity. Deracinated from the old historical certainties and the positivist "grand narratives of progress, expansion and enlightenment" (Featherstone 2005: 167) that they produced, the postmodern consciousness may be more democratic, but it is also more schizophrenic. The absolutes and universals that belonged to the triumph of modernism no longer have validity in a world where essentialising and totalising tendencies are seen as antithetical to a respect for the diversity of ideas as well as cultures. Truths have become partial and open to contestation; every story is allowed its own validity. Difference may now be celebrated, but at the same time, it is commodified: the much-vaunted global village is also a global bazaar that cannot remain independent of the free-market economy. As Glenn Jordan and Chris Weedon express it: "The 'Post-Modern Age' is the age of diversity, choice and the proliferation of tastes. Virtually anything I can imagine, seek or desire is available in the international capitalist market place" (1995: 149). Clearly, this brings opportunities that may also have negative effects as "things", both tangible and intangible, are appropriated and decontextualised, sometimes to the detriment of their maker or place of origin.

Postmodernism also repositions individual subjects as active agents who, rather than inheriting an identity that is fixed and monolithic, construct multiple, fluid identities out of the many possibilities that are now within reach. In this sense, identity is performative. Stuart Hall has spoken of identities as a "process of becoming rather than being", and as being more about "routes" (where we are going) than "roots" (where we have come from) (1996: 4). While this opens up a world of endless possibility, it may also result in disorientation or a sense of being adrift. A sub-strand of the postmodern story is that of the disenchantment and nostalgia that, virus-like, have infected the contemporary Western world. Since the 1960s, accounts have multiplied of how the perceived loss of roots and soul in an increasingly secular, industrialised, institutionalised, and materialistic world has given birth to revival movements seeking to revitalise local rituals and reclaim cultural heritage, thereby restoring a sense of community. To these are added tales of how many in the West have been inspired to turn anew to other, more "traditional" societies that appear to them still to inhabit a kind of golden age and to possess the keys to a more natural, organic, or holistic brand of health, happiness, and wisdom.

Underpinning the postmodern turn are powerful and seemingly relentless processes of globalisation and these, too, have been exhaustively documented and widely theorised. The more normative formulations of globalisation need not detain us here, except to note that their inadequacies have also been hotly debated. As many critics have reminded us, interconnectedness among peoples and cultures is hardly a new phenomenon: processes of interaction and exchange have always been a part of human life. At the same time, much of what is brought under the "global" banner is not, strictly speaking, global at all, even if in the common parlance the term "globalisation" has been used, as Ulf Hannerz puts it, "to describe just about any process that crosses state boundaries" (1996: 6). Hannerz argues for "transnationalism" as a term that is both more accurate and more productive. This he qualifies by stressing that transnationalism does not come with the assumption that we are talking about nations or states as corporate actors. Rather, "in the transnational arena, the actors may now be individuals, groups, movements", as well as business enterprises (ibid.).

The "trans" prefix appears again in the concept of "transculturality", which is Wolfgang Welsch's preferred alternative to multiculturality. Multiculturalism may appear progressive, he argues, insofar as it embraces the goals of tolerance and understanding, but "its all too traditional understanding of cultures threatens to engender regressive tendencies which by appealing to a particularistic cultural identity lead to ghettoisation or cultural fundamentalism". In practice, "lifestyles no longer end at the borders of national cultures, but go beyond these" (1999: 197). Transculturality points to "a multi-meshed and inclusive, not separatist and exclusive, understanding of culture" (200). For similar reasons, David Hollinger has made a case for a perspective he terms "postethnic". He defines postethnicity as "the critical renewal of cosmopolitanism in the context of today's greater sensitivity to roots"—a sensitivity that nonetheless avoids viewing the world as no more than a multiplicity of ethnocentrisms. This renewal has found expression in labels such as "rooted cosmopolitanism", "cosmopolitan patriotism", and "critical cosmopolitanism" that distinguish themselves from cosmopolitanism of the classical kind with its notion of "citizens of the world" who were "proudly rootless" (2005: 5).

To aid the project of theorising what he refers to as "fundamental disjunctures between economy, culture, and politics", Arjun Appadurai proposes five dimensions of "global cultural flows" that serve as the building blocks of "imagined worlds": ethnoscapes, mediascapes, technoscapes, financescapes, and ideoscapes (1996: 33). Of these, ethnoscapes (dealing with the unprecedented movement of peoples in today's shifting landscapes), mediascapes (referring to the widespread production and dissemination of information and images), and technoscapes (the high-speed movement of new technologies across once impenetrable boundaries) are of most use to us here. Taking up the theme of the deterritorialisation of culture and highlighting the "profoundly interactive" nature of contemporary ethnoscapes, Appadurai argues that the "ethno" in ethnography has taken on "a slippery, nonlocalized quality, to which the descriptive practices of anthropology will have to respond" (48). "What a new style of ethnography can do," he goes on to say, "is to capture the impact of deterritorialization on the imaginative resources of lived, local experiences" (152). This is precisely one of my central aims in the present study.

As we prepare to examine more directly the small-scale networks and groupings of individuals who are brought together by shared musical enthusiasms, we find a further set of potentially useful concepts in ethnomusicological and anthropological texts. Thomas Turino, in *Music as Social Life*, introduces the notion of "cultural formations". These may take the form of "smaller nested cultural formations", but they may also straddle national borders. He goes on to identify three prominent trans-state cultural formations: *immigrant communities, diasporas*, and *cosmopolitan formations* (2008: 117). It is the last of these that are of service to us here. "Like diasporas," Turino writes, "*cosmopolitan cultural formations* involve prominent constellations of habits that are shared among widely dispersed groups in countries around the world; but unlike diasporas, cosmopolitan formations are not traced to any particular homeland" (118).

Mark Slobin has adopted the term "interculture" to refer to "the far-flung, expansive reach of musical forces that cross frontiers" (1993: 61). Of the three types of interculture he visualises—*industrial, diasporic*, and *affinity*—it is affinity interculture that is most relevant to the case in hand. In Slobin's analysis, industrial interculture produces the commodified music system that is often portrayed, as he puts it, as "a corporate octopus whose tentacles stretch menacingly across the world, dominating local scenes and choking off competition" (ibid.). Affinity interculture has a far more benign face. The groups it produces, which he memorably characterises as "charmed circles of like-minded music-makers drawn magnetically to a certain genre that creates strong expressive bonding", serve as "nuclei for free-floating units of our social atmosphere, points of orientation for weary travelers looking for a cultural home" (98). The grass-roots, subcultural undertones of this characterisation make it doubly suited to the kinds of musical networks that concern us here.

Tullia Magrini draws on John Blacking's concept of "sound groups", "formed by people who choose a certain music mainly because they identify a part of themselves with the values they connect with that music" (2000: 329). Again, while such groups may coincide with ethnic, generational, or social groups within a given society they may also be transnational, and, crucially, they remain open, acting as voluntary communities of consent (as opposed to prescribed communities of descent). In a similar way, Veit Erlmann adapts Kant's notion of the "aesthetic community...that forms and undoes itself on the basis of taste", applying this to "all those social formations—the loose affiliations, groupings, neo-tribes, and cult groups of free-floating individuals—that are not anchored in rigid structures of control, habitus and filiation" (1998: 12). Elsewhere, he writes of how world music styles "become demarcators of community through the forging of affective links between dispersed places" (1993: 12).

Hannerz, meanwhile, draws attention to an important distinction between cosmopolitans and tourists, building on Paul Theroux's proposal that many people's travel choices are motivated by the notion of "home plus" (Spain, for example, representing—for Northern Europeans—home plus sun). "But the plus," Hannerz goes on, "often has nothing to do with alien systems of meaning, and a lot to do with facts of nature, such as nice beaches," making tourism largely a spectator sport. Cosmopolitans, by contrast, "tend to want to immerse themselves in other cultures...they want to be participants" (1996: 104–105).

In terms of the foregoing definitions, the more adventurous subjects in my study offer a prime example of cosmopolitan individuals who belong to transnational formations in the shape of affinity groups that themselves engage in transcultural activity. To explain how and why these particular groups and networks have formed, how they operate, and what impact they have is part of my objective. In this regard, I see myself—like Hannerz—as "an anthropologist of transnational life" (12), whose aim is to "look at the coherence of the world in terms of interactions, relationships, and networks" (7). Working at the intersection of the personal and political, the local and global, I thus hope to contribute to broader debates about cultural processes in a post-ethnic world.

World Music, Cultural Appropriation, and Intercultural Engagement

World music as a field (rather than an object) takes on some of the characteristics of postmodernism as summarised above, with musics from different places circulating via quasi-global channels and often being reconfigured in new combinations. Developments in media and technology, as well as markets, have resulted in what Steven Feld terms "the total portability, transportability, and transmutability of any and all sonic environments" (1994a: 259). Viewed positively, new opportunities have opened the door to new kinds of agency, creativity, and self-determination. From a more critical perspective, music is at best dislocated from its original functions and meanings as it takes on a new life elsewhere; at worst, it becomes part of a pastiche or fusion where the surrounding discourse of salvage, respect, and collaboration takes precedence over the quality of the musical product, and that discourse itself does not always stand up well to scrutiny.

The commodification of otherness is inevitably overcast by the shadows of racism and exploitation, prompting unfavourable comparison with historical processes of exploration and colonisation that were accompanied by rampant expropriation of raw materials—not to mention people—to swell the coffers and satisfy the desires of the so-called civilised world. For this reason, it is almost impossible to talk about world music without addressing issues of power, ownership, control, and representation. Much ink has been spent on cases of Western pop musicians appropriating exotic sounds to revitalise their professional careers; artists such as Peter Gabriel, Paul Simon, Ry Cooder, Brian Eno, and David Byrne have come under fire for employing, in Carol Muller's words, "a rhetoric of saving, recovering, and consigning to places of safe-keeping lost performances of 'others' silenced or devalued by external forces of modernity" (2002: 420), whilst engaging in the kind of activity that others have referred to as blatant theft.[15]

Metaphors relating to eating, and more specifically cannibalism, abound in the critical literature on postmodernism and cultural appropriation. John Storey draws attention, for example, to Fredric Jameson's frequent references to the "random cannibalization" of a postmodernism that "feeds vampirically on the past" (Storey 2003: 65–67), and Deborah Root—in a book entitled *Cannibal Culture*—alludes to "the consumption of the Other as a source of violence, passion, and spirituality" (1996: back cover). World music becomes one more object of the West's insatiable appetite. It is interesting to note the presence of culinary imagery in more positive representations of world music as well—as, for example, in the *Tower Guide to... World Music*, where its use explicitly embodies the "natural–versus–manufactured" discourse: "Just as Asian, Latin, Mediterranean and African restaurants have immeasurably improved the British palate, world music offers [a] rich, varied, fat-free alternative to the stodgy musical diet [Britain] seems stuck on" (cited in Murphy

2007: 53). This, too, struggles to remain free of imperialist associations but at the same time it reminds us that the appropriation of recipes and foodstuffs has engendered comparatively little angst. Many imports from elsewhere have long been accepted—unproblematically—as part of the contemporary British way of life. Not only does today's Britain have more choirs than chip shops; it also undoubtedly has more curry houses.

Reebee Garofolo is among those who have criticised the standard models of cultural imperialism that assume the corruption of "organic" cultures by the "manufactured" cultures of the West for their tendency to privilege the role of external forces, and to conflate economic power and cultural effects and, in so doing, to neglect the creative dimensions of popular consumption (see Garofolo 1993). Timothy Taylor has taken issue with the preoccupation with postmodernism-as-style, preferring to focus on postmodernity-as-moment and to examine the manner in which "different sounds are mobilized for a vast array of reasons, but, perhaps most often, as a way of constructing and/or solidifying new identities" (1997: 203).[16] In more down-to-earth terms, Peter Martin reminds us that "detailed empirical investigations of real people in real situations tend to reveal a rather different picture from that painted by the 'grand theorists' of mass culture" (2006: 69).

In my own investigation of the world song phenomenon, I am concerned principally with the lived experience of seemingly ordinary people-who-sing who, unlike some of the magpie-like impresarios from the popular music world, are not motivated by the prospect of personal success or economic gain. In describing how these singers are on a mission, not simply to acquire new repertory, but also to explore different ways of using their voice, of being with others, and of engaging with the world-out-there, I seek to shift the emphasis away from the songs themselves as material commodities that might be gifted, traded, borrowed, or pilfered and to pay more attention to processes of creativity, engagement, and empowerment. I also show how the more dedicated travellers to be encountered in these pages are motivated by a strong desire to reconnect the sounds they have grown to love with their source, to experience something of the reality of the people and places to which they naturally belong, and—perhaps most importantly—to "give something back".

As we zoom in to the case in hand, the adoption of "foreign" songs by British and other non-native choirs does raise intriguing questions of a different order. Why do songs from other cultures play such a prominent part in the natural voice scene? Why do so many non-native singers identify so strongly with the music of Georgia, Cameroon, or other more "exotic" cultures? Why do they prefer to sing in languages they do not speak? What does this say about the relationship between music and identity? In the teaching process, what exactly gets transmitted or translated? How might we describe and theorise the cognitive, empirical, and interpersonal processes involved in learning unfamiliar singing styles? How far do the experiences of non-native students map on to conceptualisations of music making in the culture of origin? These are among the questions to which I give detailed consideration in later chapters.

The Politics of Participation and the Art of Celebration

Christopher Small's notion of "musicking", as set out in his book *Musicking: The Meanings of Performing and Listening* (1998), has struck a chord with many readers in both scholarly and lay circles. Small's basic premise is that "music is not a thing at all but an activity, something that people do" (1998: 2). Hence his proposal of the verb "to music", for which he offers the definition: "to take part, in any capacity, in a musical performance, whether by performing, by listening, by rehearsing or practicing, by providing material for performance (what is called composing), or by dancing" (9). The notion of "taking part" is central. "Whatever it is we are doing," Small insists, "we are all doing it together"—and here "we" may be stretched to include others outside the space of the performance itself, such as ticket collectors, piano movers, roadies, and cleaners. In this sense, Small's "musicking" is not too dissimilar to Becker's "art worlds". The act of "musicking" is further characterised as "a ritual through which all the participants explore and celebrate the relationships that constitute their social identity" (back cover).

The themes of ritual, celebration, and identity construction recur in other key works on musical participation, such as Thomas Turino's *Music as Social Life: The Politics of Participation* (2008), which offers an eloquent exposition of the ways in which music is socially meaningful. Turino's central thesis shares something of the spirit of Small's musicking in its proposal that "*music* is not a unitary art form, but rather . . . this term refers to fundamentally distinct types of activities that fulfil different needs and ways of being human" (2008: 1). He distinguishes two fields of real-time performance, which he designates *participatory* and *presentational.* The power of his analytical paradigm rests on his insistence that participatory performance—the preferred mode in many parts of the world—should not be viewed as in some way second-best to presentational performance representing the ideal to which one should aspire. Rather, each kind of performance should be seen to operate according to a different set of values and principles and to fulfil different functions.

Crucially, participatory performance is viewed as "a particular field of activity in which stylized sound and motion are conceptualized most importantly as heightened social interaction" (28). Making music in this way "leads to a special kind of concentration on the other people one is interacting with through sound and motion and on the activity in itself and for itself. This heightened concentration on the other participants is one reason that participatory music-dance is such a strong force for social bonding" (29). Compared with the other musical fields that Turino identifies (presentational, high fidelity, and studio audio art), participatory performance is the most democratic, least competitive, and least hierarchical, and does not therefore "fit well with the broader cultural values of the capitalist-cosmopolitan formation, where competition and hierarchy are prominent and profit making is often a primary goal" (35). This in itself is one reason why participatory activities exist "beneath the radar of mainstream official and popular attention in staunchly capitalist societies" (36).

The notion of social bonding is central to the work of Robert Putnam, whose best-selling *Bowling Alone: The Collapse and Revival of American Community* (2000) offered a compelling account of the decline of social capital in America, as evidenced by the dramatic decrease, from the late 1960s, in the numbers of people joining civic associations, social clubs, churches, and unions. At the same time, people were spending less time with friends and family and giving less money to charity, trends that were exacerbated by factors ranging from the rise of television to urban sprawl. The term "social capital" as employed by Putnam refers to social networks and the norms of reciprocity and trust that are among their by-products. The cardinal insight of the social capital thesis—as Robert Putnam and Lewis Feldstein explain in a later volume, *Better Together: Restoring the American Community* (2003)—is that "social networks have real value both for the people in those networks...as well as for bystanders", with an ever-widening circle reaping rewards via a trickle-down effect (2003: 2). A healthy accumulation of social capital is also, in Putnam's analysis, a prerequisite of a properly functioning democracy.

Putnam further distinguishes two basic types of social capital, which he calls *bonding* and *bridging*. Networks of the bonding kind connect people "who are similar in crucial respects" and tend to be inward-looking, whereas those of the bridging kind bring together different types of people and tend to be outward-looking. The former are characterised as "a kind of sociological Super Glue" and the latter "a sociological WD-40" (Putnam and Feldstein 2003: 2).[17] Because of the introverted nature of bonding social capital, a society possessing this type alone will see its citizens "segregated into mutually hostile camps", as in Belfast, Beirut, or Bosnia (the examples given by Putnam). A pluralist democracy depends on a healthy dose of bridging social capital that requires people to embrace heterogeneity by transcending their social, political, and professional identities and connecting with others who are unlike themselves. Perhaps not surprisingly, Putnam refers to active involvement in, rather than passive consumption of, the arts as a means of generating social capital, and identifies art as being "especially useful in transcending conventional social barriers". He also makes explicit reference to singing as one of the leisure activities that brings people together and increases their social capital. "Singing together," he observes, "does not require shared ideology or shared social or ethnic provenance" (2000: 411).

The theoretical basis for Barbara Ehrenreich's arguments in her book *Dancing in the Streets: A History of Collective Joy* (2007) chimes in many ways with that of Putnam, with at least some of the attributes of social capital resurfacing in the more appealing guise of collective joy or ecstasy. Adopting a turn of phrase coined by French theorist Guy Debord, Ehrenreich characterises the present age as "the society of the spectacle",[18] where "instead of generating their own collective pleasures, people absorb, or consume, the spectacles of commercial entertainment, nationalist rituals, and the consumer culture, with its endless advertisements for the pleasure of individual ownership" (2007: 250). This kind of top-down spectacle, with its power to control and exclude, finds its healthier antithesis in festivity, where "the music invites everyone to the dance" and "shared food briefly undermines the privilege of class", enabling us to "step out of our assigned roles and statuses... and into a brief utopia defined by egalitarianism, creativity, and mutual love" (253).

Commenting on the extent to which the loss of "community" has been both lamented and theorised, Ehrenreich argues that "the loss of *ecstatic* pleasure, of the kind once routinely generated by rituals involving dancing, music, and so on, deserves the same attention accorded to *community* and to be equally mourned" (19). In her analysis, the capacity for collective joy is deeply encoded in our fundamental makeup as human beings but, because of its emancipatory qualities, is viewed by those in power as a threat to their authority. "At some point," Ehrenreich writes in the opening sentence of her chapter "Killing Carnival: Reformation and Repression", "in town after town throughout the northern Christian world, the music stops" (97). The "ecstatic possibility", already banished from the churches, was now driven from the streets and squares as well.

This widespread repression of festivity was seen by Max Weber, as Ehrenreich goes on to note, as a by-product of capitalism, which demanded that the middle classes learn to defer gratification while the lower classes had to be transformed into "a disciplined, factory-ready, working class" faced with "the new necessity of showing up for work sober and on time, six days a week" (100). Holidays had no place in a system whose only concern was to maximise productivity and profit. Capitalism went hand-in-hand with Protestantism, which (as Ehrenreich notes) Weber describes in *The Protestant Ethic* as "descend[ing] like a frost on the life of 'Merrie Old England'" (101). This in turn had negative consequences for individual as well as social well being: Ehrenreich sees a direct link between the decline of festivity, and hence opportunities for the expression of collective joy, and the rise of melancholy or depression that from the seventeenth century took on epidemic proportions. This interpretation adds even greater urgency to the project of reclaiming the right to joy.

DANCING IN THE STREETS

All these activities—singing, dancing, feasting, celebrating, and making merry—lie at the heart of the Thames Festival, where this chapter began. In his introductory note in the 2011 programme booklet, director Adrian Evans wrote: "The Thames Festival celebrates London and the iconic river at its heart...by dancing in the streets, feasting on bridges, racing on the river and playing at the water's edge." On the first day of the festival, Southwark Bridge was transformed into a giant banqueting space to host the Feast on the Bridge, with long rows of trestle tables—punctuated from time to time by food and drink stalls—lining each side of the closed-off road and visitors invited to "eat, drink, dance and make merry". Further opportunities to dance in the streets were offered by the Al Fresco Tango workshop and dance programme at The Scoop on Saturday and the rolling programme of live bands and DJs that kept people on their feet at the Lady Luck Jive Stage near the Southbank Centre on Sunday. When the Sing for Water choir belted out its Motown number and members of the audience at The Scoop rose in response to the injunction to "dance in the streets", other festival-goers across the site were already in full swing.

As I write these words, news drops onto my Facebook page of a more spontaneous outbreak of singing and dancing in Totnes, a small market town in southwest England. I follow the link to a short film that has been posted on YouTube.[19] The credits tell me that it is the eleventh of November, a date traditionally celebrated as Armistice or Remembrance Day, commemorating the end of the First World War and remembering the millions who lost their lives. This year it is 11/11/11, a synchronicity that is being marked by other kinds of grass-roots happenings in different parts of the world. The Totnes "moment" has been inspired by Alex Hanley's vision of mass breakouts of flash-mob dancing in celebration of the interconnectedness of all life on earth and has been co-created by a small team that includes three natural voice practitioners, Roz Walker, Helen Yeomans, and Susie Prater, alongside Susannah Darling Khan, co-director of the School of Movement Medicine. Members of three local community choirs, Global Harmony, Glorious Chorus, and Tula Mama, feature among those who have gathered at the market square—in the rain—to perform a dance routine set to the South African song "Bambalela", meaning "Never Give Up!" Curious onlookers begin to clap their hands and move to the beat, passing vehicles sound their horns, and a wave of umbrellas dances above the crowd.

NOTES
1. The video tracks on the companion website are taken from Sing for Water 2012, which I was able to film. They feature extracts from a comparable set of songs.
2. By December 2012, the running total, according to WaterAid's records, was £672,719. This did not include receipts from events held in Australia or other

donations from choirs and individuals who have chosen WaterAid as their nominated charity for initiatives additional to those billed specifically as Sing for Water events.
3. Here and in other parts of the book, details about individual practitioners may relate to the times and events being described rather than being current at the time of writing. Up-to-date details (current as of August 2013) are given in the biographical listing on the companion website.
4. When this book went to press, a short video compilation titled *Sing for Water 2008 Trailer* was still available online at http://www.youtube.com/watch?v=BEolWXnGKVo.
5. See http://www.pinetreeweb.com, acc. July 10, 2013. The first World Scout Jamboree was held in London in 1920. Subsequent jamborees (which take place roughly every four years) were in Denmark, Hungary, the Netherlands, France, and Austria. Since the late 1950s, locations have included the Philippines, Japan, Australia, Chile, and Thailand.
6. At a local level, the centre has worked in partnership with the Eastern and Coastal Kent Primary Care Trust, Kent and Medway NHS and Social Care Partnership Trust, and Sussex Partnership NHS Foundation Trust to promote the role of music and arts in healthcare and health promotion.
7. *The Snowman* is an animated film made in 1982 by Dianne Jackson, based on the children's picture book by Raymond Briggs. Now a classic, it is an indispensable part of Christmas television programming in the UK. The film's theme song, "Walking in the Air" (sung by Aled Jones), was written by Howard Blake.
8. The endnotes to the chapters in Alquist 2006 are a source of further references to writings on choral music.
9. It seems incongruous that a choir with one of the most colourful sounds—the *Kwaya ya Upendo* that is the subject of Barz's chapter—should appear on the front cover in a black and white image, its members, standing on the steps of the Azania Front Lutheran Cathedral in Dar es Salaam, clad in ankle-length dark robes with white trim and holding their music books, presenting the archetypal image of the church choir. This is a far cry—in visual terms, at least—from the singers who grace my own cover.
10. A more extensive review of the literature on music in relation to health and wellbeing is included in chapter 7.
11. Also relevant to a cross-cultural approach to music and health is new work that is now being brought together under the umbrella of medical ethnomusicology, introduced in *The Oxford Handbook of Medical Ethnomusicology* (Koen 2009).
12. See especially Gary Ansell's chapters, "Belonging through Musicing: Explorations of Musical Community" and "Where Performing Helps: Processes and Affordances of Performance in Community Music Therapy".
13. This sociocultural move is reflected in the titles of two other key volumes, *Culture-Centered Music Therapy* (Stige 2002) and *Contemporary Voices in Music Therapy: Communication, Culture, and Community* (Kenny and Stige 2002).
14. In the mythic past, songs were also learned from jaguars, mice, enemies who lived underground, and Suyá in the process of being transformed into animals. By the time of Seeger's work, visiting anthropologists had also been added to this list.
15. Among other critiques of these trends, see especially Feld 1994b, 2000a, and 2000b. For broader discussions of cultural appropriation not confined to music, see Marcus and Myers 1995; Ziff and Rao 1997.

16. For other critiques of the cultural imperialism stance, see e.g. Appadurai 1990.
17. The terminology of bridging and bonding was first introduced by Ross Gittell and Avis Vidal (1998).
18. *Society of the Spectacle* is the title of Debord's now-classic book, first published in 1968.
19. http://www.youtube.com/watch?v=_6vWOX3FCuM, acc. November 16, 2011.

CHAPTER 2

In Search of the Natural Voice

THE ORIGINAL INSTRUMENT

How might we begin to describe the voice? Where is it located? What is it made of? What does it say?

The voice is a musical instrument we are all born with. We carry it with us, unseen, wherever we go. It may be suppressed or temporarily silenced, but it cannot be mislaid. Unlike our material possessions, it cannot be confiscated or stolen. We may be stripped of all that we own, but our voice, like our memories, remains. And when it is heard, it says something vital about the deepest layers of our identity, our commitment, our intentions, and our aspirations.

Yet the voice is not always as resilient as we might hope. When it goes wrong, it becomes a mystery. It may fall victim to physical problems. It may be compromised by age or ill health. It may be affected by stress, anxiety, unhappiness, or lack of confidence, revealing information about our psychological well being that we would prefer to keep private. It announces our presence before we come into view. It can betray our moods and attitudes, allowing listeners to detect excitement or boredom, approval or disapproval, appreciation or disdain. Or it can simply get into bad habits through prolonged misuse. Even when we know these things, it is difficult to separate mind from matter, to keep the voice and the sounds it produces objective in a way that might be possible when we play a different kind of instrument.

In many ways, the voice is not so much an object as an action. Unlike other internal organs, "it has no location in the body except when it is in action, sounding" (Fitzmaurice 1997: 247). When the production process is set in motion, it manifests itself as a series of waves and pulses. We may begin, then, to describe the passage of air across the larynx and explain the properties of airwaves. But the voice cannot be reduced to the science of physics or biology alone. There is something else, something ineffable and less easy to put into words. Sounds made by the voices of others have a somatic effect on us. They can make us quiver, give us goose bumps, make the hair stand up on the back of our neck; they can make our blood surge and our hearts beat faster. Less benign voices can make our hearts sink, muscles tense, and adrenalin pump as we run for cover. The voice is clearly more than the sum of its physical parts. The vibrating bands of muscle, ligament, and mucus membrane we call the vocal cords are only half the story.

When, in the post-industrial, urbanised, Western world, we think of the singing voice, we may hear in our mind's ear the voices of opera singers, cathedral choirs, the popular singers of the day; we may hear, perhaps, the voices of children in the playgrounds of yore. But there are myriads of other voices less often heard or imagined—keening voices, chanting voices, clamouring voices, ululating voices; the voices of Mediterranean fishwives, Swiss cowherds, West African praise singers, Argentinian shamans, Bahrainian pearl divers, Taiwanese farmers, Korean *p'ansori* opera singers, Tibetan monks. Not all these voices sound "musical" or "nice" to the modern Western ear. Some may sound chaotic, primal, grating, or out-of-tune. Some make us uncomfortably aware of the bodies from which they emerge. But there are other ears that listen out for signs of the body in a certain roughness of the throat or a catching of the breath that reveals ways in which the body has lived and suffered and come to know both pain and ecstasy; these ears wait to be touched by what Roland Barthes speaks of as "the grain of the voice" or "the body in the voice as it sings" (1977: 188).

These other voices often seem to draw inspiration from the natural world, imitating or entering into dialogue with the voices of birds and insects, sheep and goats, wind and thunder, and borrowing qualities of timbre or styles of ornamentation. These other voices move through pitches and textures that resist being captured on paper and defy precise repetition; they exist only fleetingly, until the echo fades. They occupy realms far distant from the "clean", disembodied head voice cultivated in the Western classical world, which reaches its epitome in the prepubescent treble of the English cathedral choir. Prized for its purity of tone, precise intonation, clear enunciation, and ethereal quality, this is a voice that often appears disconnected from any base physicality.

Where, in all of this, is the "natural voice"? At the most literal level, the natural voice is the voice nature gave us, the voice we were born with—a voice that might be construed as primordial, naked, instinctive, and authentic; a voice that has not yet been constrained or adulterated by modern, grown-up, educated notions of what sounds "proper". For Kristin Linklater, author of *Freeing the Natural Voice*, "the exploration of one's own voice is the search for the ring of truth, something natural and real that began with vital authenticity in the first breath and the first cry" (http://www.kristinlinklater.com/, acc. June 12, 2013). Perhaps it is also a voice in tune with its surroundings and responsive to the rhythms of daily life. This innate voice—at once individual and a fundamental part of being human—is also ready to sing.

FRANKIE ARMSTRONG AND THE NATURAL VOICE PRACTITIONERS' NETWORK

In Britain and Ireland, the term "natural voice" has come to be associated above all with the Natural Voice Practitioners' Network, a loose-knit organisation of people who lead open-access singing groups, community choirs, and voice workshops and who "share a common philosophy in relation to singing and groupwork" (http://www.naturalvoice.net/, acc. June 12, 2013). The key figure behind the development of the network (as noted in chapter 1) was English folksinger Frankie Armstrong, who continues to act as the movement's most revered mentor. The NVPN had its tentative beginnings in 1995, at a reunion of "graduates" of the voice practitioner training weeks that Frankie had been running since 1988, and it is Frankie's vision that lies behind the official statements of the NVPN's aims, philosophy, and working principles as presented on the NVPN website. The story of how Frankie arrived at her approach to voice work, both her philosophy and practice, is crucial to understanding how and why the NVPN came into being and is therefore considered in some detail in chapter 3. Here, I focus on what has become the NVPN's credo.

The NVPN Philosophy and Concepts of Music in Society

The various position statements brought together in a document entitled "NVPN Philosophy and Working Principles" offer a useful starting point for understanding what "natural voice" means in the NVPN context and, particularly, how the principles of birthright and inclusivity are brought into dialogue with a vision of the world's oral traditions. (See the full document in the Appendix.) At the same time, they invite comparison with broader critiques of the gentrification, institutionalisation, and professionalisation of music making in contemporary Western societies.

Reading through the statements that constitute the NVPN philosophy, it soon becomes clear that the concept "natural voice" refers not only to the voice itself but also to an ideology, a methodology, and, to some extent, a repertory. If a natural voice practitioner had written the book *Lies My Music Teacher Told Me* (Eskelin 1994), for example, at the top of the list of myths to be toppled would have been: "Some people can sing and some people can't." Natural voice practitioners are united in the conviction that "singing is everyone's birthright" and believe without reservation the truth of the adage, "If you can walk, you can dance; if you can talk, you can sing." This belief is, of course, not exclusive to the NVPN. John Potter writes in his introduction to *The Cambridge Companion to Singing*: "You don't have to be a virtuoso to express your own emotions. Everyone can speak, and everyone can sing" (2000: 1). The central mission of the NVPN is to help people reclaim this birthright, which leads logically to their commitment to inclusivity and their development of teaching styles that accommodate differing levels of musical experience and ability.

The fundamental tenet that "singing is our birthright" (affirmed at the beginning of "Philosophy and Working Principles") leads to a statement that alludes to the historical role of singing as part of everyday life and its potential for sustaining community:

> For thousands of years all over the world people have sung—to express joy, celebration and grief, to accompany work and devotion, to aid healing—without worrying about having a "good" voice or "getting it right". Song has been a part of life, a way of binding the community together. We aim to recreate the sense that vocalising, singing and singing together is natural and open to all.

The notion of community reappears later in the text with the statement that "creating a sense of an accepting community is an essential element of our approach in working with groups".

The next point is about the individual and the way in which singing may relate to physical and emotional states:

> Each person's voice is as unique as their fingerprint and, respecting that individuality, we aim to provide people with opportunities to express themselves vocally and to develop their full vocal potential. The voice we are born with is capable of freely expressing a full range of emotions, thoughts and experience— this is what we mean by the "natural voice". However, the tensions and stresses of daily life create physical and emotional blocks to the natural voice. We therefore focus on breath and bodywork as the foundations of healthy voice use.

The triad of voice, breath, and body alluded to here puts in frequent appearances in my later analysis of teaching method, particularly with reference to the nature and function of warm-up exercises (see chapter 4).

The text then goes on to refer more explicitly to the idea that therapeutic work may be required as part of the process of realising one's vocal potential:

> In this culture many people see themselves as non-singers because of previous experiences of criticism and judgement. Many are excluded from singing groups if they do not have music reading skills. Therefore, in our work we aim to counteract these experiences and to give people confidence in their melodic voice by providing a supportive learning environment.

In practical terms, the most obvious way to create a learning environment that is open to anyone, regardless of whether or not they can read music, is to replicate "natural" modes of transmission. This is explained in a list of the ways in which the principles ascribed to by natural voice practitioners inform their practice:

> The majority of music in the world comes from the oral tradition and we aim to teach songs as far as possible by ear, recognising that this is the most accessible and effective way for the majority of people to learn and retain songs in the longer term.

The rejection of scores as a point of departure goes beyond questions of accessibility, however. Working orally can be seen as part of a broader ethos that looks beyond the elements that can be fixed in written notation by a composer or scribe—to be more or less slavishly followed by the performer—to other, more ephemeral components that engage the human body and spirit. Within an oral/aural tradition, music is brought to life as it is created anew in the very moment of performance and, in the case of multipart singing, this requires listening to and interacting with others. It is significant that this mirrors a fundamental (if oversimplified) distinction between the approach of the historical musicologist, who works primarily with manuscripts and records from the past, or with repertory that is essentially static, and that of the ethnomusicologist, who typically engages with people in present-day societies and with traditions that are alive and changing.

The notion of singing as a "natural" part of everyday life, accessible to and inclusive of all, is certainly reinforced in much of the writing about music in Africa. The authors of *Let Your Voice Be Heard*—a collection of songs from Ghana and Zimbabwe published by the World Music Press that is found on the bookshelves of many voice practitioners—owe the inspiration for their title to Francis Bebey, who writes in his book *African Music: A People's Art*:

> Any individual who has the urge to make his voice heard is given the liberty to do so; singing is not (generally) a specialized affair. Anyone can sing and, in practice, anyone does.... This is the essence of the collective aspect of African music; no one is ruled out because he is technically below par. (Bebey 1975: 115)

The authors of *Let Your Voice Be Heard* concede that experts do exist, as do complex forms of music requiring a high level of skill or specialisation, "but within the context of most African vocal music there is also ample room for participation by those with less polish but equal motivation" (Adzinyah, Maraire, and Tucker 1986: 2). The songs included in the collection lend themselves to working with groups of mixed ability or experience so that a lively, rhythmic, and harmonious sound is achieved quickly and relatively painlessly. As well as being structured in a way that facilitates participation, the songs also provide an opportunity to explore different qualities of voice. The addition of movements or simple dance steps increases enjoyment while also improving coordination. It is hardly surprising, then, to learn that songs from different parts of Africa have proved especially popular in natural voice circles.

The authors of *Let Your Voice Be Heard* also quote John Blacking's description of his observations of music making among the Venda people of South Africa:

> It is the process of music making that is valued as much as, and sometimes more than, the finished product. The value of music is, I believe, to be found in terms of the human experiences involved in its creation. (Blacking 1973: 50)

Constructing music so as to maximise participation correlates with "the most fundamental aesthetic" that (to use John Miller Chernoff's phrase) "without participation there is no meaning" (1979: 23). This is another principle that is carried over into natural voice contexts. Here, the concern for accessibility combines with a focus on "the enjoyment of singing" to inform the statement in the NVPN's "Philosophy and Working Principles" that "the main focus is on the process of coming together to sing whilst at the same time developing people's vocal skills". Performance is not ruled out—"within the context of performance [we aim] for the highest standards"—but it is not the primary goal and, as noted earlier, some natural voice groups describe themselves explicitly as "non-performing".

The question of whether music itself is a universal language may be contentious, but appreciating and making music would certainly appear to be a universal feature of human society. Many writers from outside the field of ethnomusicology have been quick to seize on John Blacking's oft-quoted (if debatable) assertion that "there is so much music in the world that it is reasonable to suppose that music, like language and possibly religion, is a species-specific trait of man" (1973: 7). Less ambitious is Blacking's claim that music "is there in the body, waiting to be brought out and developed, like the basic principles of language formation" (100). Some scholars of human evolution have suggested that singing, in fact, preceded speech. Blacking himself argues that there is evidence that singing and dancing preceded speech by "several hundred thousand years" (1987: 22), and Jean-Jacques Rousseau, in his *Essai sur l'origine des langues*, construed the earliest language as a kind of song or chant. Steven Mithen, in *The Singing Neanderthals*, sets out to explore and vindicate Blacking's proposal that there had been a "nonverbal, prelinguistic, 'musical' mode of thought and action" (2006: 5).[1] Noting (among other indicators) that the manner in which adults instinctively communicate with babies offers corroborating evidence that "music has a developmental, if not evolutionary, priority over language", he argues that the conditions of child development suggest that "the neural networks for language are built upon or replicate those for music" (69–70). If this were indeed so, then we might invert the "If you can talk, you can sing" mantra to "If you can sing, you can talk". At the bottom line, as David Reck so vividly expresses it, "every human being on earth is (potentially, at least) a walking, living, breathing machination of sound" (1997: 44).

The image of the open, egalitarian, naturalistic singing community that natural voice practitioners seek to recreate would appear to be diametrically opposed to the contemporary Western model of the highly trained professional musician performing pre-composed works, usually read from a printed score, in a dedicated arts venue for a comparatively passive audience, most of whom—whilst appreciating music—would not consider themselves to be "musicians". Even in the West, however, such a clear-cut distinction is of relatively recent origin and is not universal; nor are the two models mutually exclusive.

Frankie Armstrong has on numerous occasions elaborated the notion that many people in modern British society are actively discouraged from singing. As children, they may have been told that they were "unmusical" or a "growler", or they may have been labelled "tone-deaf". In classroom singing they may have been instructed only to mouth the words so that they would not "spoil" the "nicer" sounds made by the other children. Frankie proposes that the nineteenth-century Northern European notion that "some people could sing and some people couldn't" easily translated into "some people should sing and some people *shouldn't*"—a state of affairs that had "much more to do with acceptability and gentility and the aspirations of the educating and cultured classes" than with musical ability per se (Armstrong interview 2008). In Frankie's assessment, the critical turning point was the introduction of compulsory schooling, following Forster's Education Act of 1870 (Armstrong 1997: 44). Her vision of the way in which the naturally "raucous" singing of children did not match the ideals of refinement embraced by their teachers brings to mind Grant Olwage's discussion of the rise of the bourgeois voice in Victorian Britain. This approved voice (the domain of the white middle class) created its antithesis in what Olwage calls the "anachronistic voice"—the type of voice used by children, slum-dwellers, black Africans, and other supposedly uncivilised peoples. If the bourgeois voice signified all that was "good", "pure", "refined", and "cultured", then the anachronistic voice could be censored as "ugly", "rough", "vulgar", and in need of reform (2004: 206–207).

John Potter similarly sees the rise of what we now refer to as "classical singing" as being linked to the ascendancy of the middle class in the nineteenth century, arguing that "the increasingly powerful middle class...created the atmosphere in which a new concept of singer could flourish: the singer not just as artist, but singing as an exclusive art form, which required not just art but artifice" (1998: 63). He also believes this shift to be related—in England

and other English-speaking countries—to the establishment of Received Pronunciation, prescribing a new standard accent for English in which all traces of regional accents were eradicated. This pronunciation demanded that the larynx be lowered and the oro-pharynx widened, a position that closely resembled that required by the new singing technique (64).

Gary Tomlinson draws our attention to a parallel development whereby, in broader terms, music as an art form underwent a redefinition as instrumental music. In the eighteenth century, he writes, "a full-blown modern conception of music had not yet taken hold so that song could still pose itself as an expressive mode shared by Europe with the rest of the world". Later, however, non-European singing came to be regarded "not as equivalent...to contemporary European practices but as a survival in far-off places of practices Europe had long since outgrown". "Song" was now replaced by the concept of "music", "represented above all by the burgeoning genres, institutions, and traditions of instrumental music", which posed "a new, exclusionary category redolent of European spiritual superiority" (Tomlinson 2003: 33–34). The places where culture was now located added to its exclusive status. Simon Frith writes of how, in the nineteenth century, so-called high art was institutionalised by the bourgeoisie "as a transcendent, asocial experience (in the contemplative bank-like setting of the gallery and the concert hall, the museum and the library)" (1996a: 116).[2]

The class-based analysis that unites these perspectives is shared by John Blacking, who views the musical specialisation that took hold in modern industrialised societies as representing a backward step. If (he asks) all members of an African society were able to make music and understand and appreciate their musical system, as he had experienced at first hand when living among the Venda, why should such capacities be more restricted in a society assumed to be more advanced? These musings give rise to another of Blacking's often-quoted formulations about the invention of "unmusicality":

> Does cultural development represent a real advance in human sensitivity and technical ability, or is it chiefly a diversion for elites and a weapon of class exploitation? Must the majority be made "unmusical" so that a few may become more "musical"? (Blacking 1973: 4)

What is at stake, Blacking argues here, is not an individual's inherent musicality but the ways in which a society defines musicality and then proceeds to label as "unmusical" those who do not meet its criteria. It is also clear that, in contemporary Western societies, such as Britain, access to music does not depend solely on "talent", however that is defined. It also depends on financial status, parental encouragement, and personality type—matters on which Christopher Small has much to say in *Music, Society, Education*. Music education in British schools has usually depended on a child's family being in a position to contribute to the cost of individual weekly lessons and to hire or purchase a musical instrument. In the early stages of learning, children also stand a far greater chance of success if their parents have the time and inclination to supervise daily practice and, later, to accompany them to orchestral rehearsals at the weekend. The children themselves must have the capacity for working alone: they need to be self-motivated and tenacious. The "hard work" required as a child makes his or her way up the ladder of graded examinations on the path to "becoming" a musician might also be related to the Protestant ethic of deferred gratification that adheres to schooling as a whole.[3]

Small takes up the theme in a more revolutionary call to arms in his later book *Musicking*. If so many people in Western societies "believe themselves to be incapable of the simplest musical act", it is either (he suggests) because they were deprived of the means to develop their latent musicality while the nervous system was still forming or, more often, "because they have been actively taught to be unmusical". Agencies that Small identifies as "militating against the musicality of ordinary people" include "the system of stars and superstars that...lives on the assumption that real musical ability is as rare as diamonds and as hard to cultivate as orchids" (1998: 210). Many schoolteachers, rather than view their task as one of helping to bring out each child's inherent musicality, actively contribute to this process of "demusicalization". Small reserves his greatest wrath for the "odious" label "tone-deaf" and for the all-too-common instruction given to children who have difficulty learning to sing in tune to mime the words:

> The voice is at the center of all musical activity, but it is all too easy to silence and very hard to reactivate, since those who have been silenced in this way have been wounded in a very intimate and crucial part of their being. In my opinion any music teacher caught doing such a thing or using the epithet tone-deaf of a pupil should be sacked on the spot. (Small 1998: 212)

Adopting a critical stance towards the institutionalisation and gentrification of music as an "elite" art form does not mean that what has often passed for "proper" singing is to be rejected out of hand, as Frankie Armstrong is quick to point out: "The style of singing that grew up in the courts, churches, parlours and, later, concert and opera halls of Europe is, at its best, both sublime and dramatic and we would be spiritually and culturally impoverished without it." The problem lies in "the inappropriate dominance and imposition of this aesthetic on the majority (through the education system) [that] still filters down to children today" (1997: 44). The NVPN, alongside other community music organisations, plays a complementary role by offering a different order of experience aimed at a broader cross-section of society, only a small percentage of whom will ever aspire to a professional singing career.

In one sense, then, the natural voice movement sets out to revive the way things used to be. Frankie recalls being told by A. L. Lloyd (singer, folklorist, and leading figure in the second wave of the British folk revival in the 1950s and 1960s) that, in the seventeenth and eighteenth centuries, "we English were known on the continent as the 'singing English'". The manner in which she developed her voice workshops was informed by her understanding of how this sea change in attitudes towards the voice and the teaching of singing came about, and by an explicit desire to "encourage people to reclaim this natural and spontaneous form of expression" (Armstrong 1997: 43). Viewed from this perspective, democratising singing becomes a sociopolitical act that makes a stand for an alternative value system while simultaneously offering the possibility of a cure to individuals who, burdened with negative judgements of themselves as would-be singers, have come to hate, fear, or disown their voices. The profound personal transformations many natural voice practitioners bear witness to are proof of the importance of such work. Kirsty Martin, founder of Brighton's Hullabaloo Quire, who describes herself as a "choral activist", refers more generally to "this feeling and this look on people's faces when they finally realise that they're allowed to do it and they don't have to read it or be trained" (interview 2008).

Overcoming barriers and constraints, be they physical, psychological, or social, is crucial if the voice itself is to be freed to realise its full expressive potential. For Frankie, "it's about release":

> Most people's voices are limited by tensions and some of them are physical habits, so that you have to help them release physical tensions; some of them are to do with emotional, psychological, fears, anxieties, embarrassments—because of having been told they can't, or that they should be a certain way—but it's always, in my experience, to do with actually getting people to let go, to let go of the things that get in the way in order to release. And once you've found that *authentic* voice, you can then place it in all kinds of different ways. (Armstrong interview 2008)

The process of releasing the voice is very different from the process of training it: "It's not training in the formal sense of layering," Frankie explains, "it's actually shedding." Singers trained in the Western classical idiom can also achieve a state of vocal release, but this stands in opposition to an aesthetic that concerns itself only with the technical aspects of voice production:

> It's "nothing getting in the way" singing... nothing getting in the way between you and the audience. Not: "Am I singing correctly? Have I got a beautiful voice? Is my technique correct?" (Armstrong interview 2008)

This does not mean that there should be no attempt to shape the voice or cultivate a particular quality of sound. Frankie herself encourages the use of the open-throated singing style "found in cultures that sing in the open air, singing as naturally and spontaneously as they speak" (Armstrong 1997: 107). When an individual has established a voice that is "grounded, centred, well-supported...and open-throated", he or she "can then do all kinds of things, in terms of more subtle placements, according to which kind of cultural style [he or she is trying to emulate]" (interview 2008). As well as freeing the voice itself, then, the singer is also freeing him or herself from an ethnocentric conception of what music is and how it should sound.

THE GIVING VOICE PROJECT, THEATRICAL ROOTS, AND THE NATURAL VOICE IN PERFORMANCE

Pursuit of the "natural" voice is, of course, by no means the sole prerogative of the Natural Voice Practitioners' Network. The term has currency in other contexts, times, and places, together with related concepts such as the "authentic" or "naked" voice. Much pioneering work on the voice has also emerged from the world of contemporary theatre, particularly from the schools that subscribe to what Kristin Linklater refers to as an "inside-out" approach to actor training (see http://www.kristinlinklater.com/, acc. July 6, 2013).

A unique forum for engaging with the voice in a way that bridges artistic, scientific, and therapeutic modes is the Giving Voice Festival, an international voice and theatre initiative directed by Joan Mills which is part of a portfolio of projects curated by the Centre for Performance Research (CPR). Building on the work of its predecessor, the Cardiff Laboratory Theatre, the CPR was established in 1988 by Richard Gough and Judie Christie, and in 1995 it relocated from Cardiff to its new base at the University of Wales, Aberystwyth.[4] Although Giving Voice is not a formal membership organisation, it does, like the NVPN, have an identifiable ethos to which its core associates subscribe and to which its more casual delegates are exposed. Giving Voice is informed by a fundamental belief in the ability of voice to communicate beyond language differences; it aims "to advance the appreciation and understanding of the expressive voice and celebrate its many and varied manifestations across time and culture" (http://www.thecpr.org.uk/, acc. June 12, 2013). First staged in 1990, the festival brings together an extraordinary assortment of performers, teachers, scholars, healers, and therapists—both world famous and lesser known—for an action-packed programme of workshops, performances, presentations, and lectures taking place over a period of up to sixteen days. The event was held in Wales until Arts Council Wales withdrew its regular funding in 2008, forcing the CPR to make major changes in its operation. Since 2009, the Giving Voice festival has taken place outside the United Kingdom in collaboration with overseas partners.

Some of the questions posed by Joan Mills in the brochure for the first Giving Voice Festival would certainly strike a chord with many natural voice practitioners. Can the voice be trained by purely scientific and formal technique? What part does the psyche play in vocal development? What part may be played by body awareness techniques in the development of a performer's voice? What is the relationship between speaking and singing? What can we learn from other cultures' vocal expressions? The booking information for the inaugural festival noted that, while the workshops included in the programme were aimed particularly at those working with the voice and performance in a professional capacity and as such would be challenging and hard work, they were also open to anyone with a love of using the voice and would not normally require an ability to read music.

From the outset, Giving Voice has sought out leading practitioners from across the globe whose work resonates with its ethos and aspirations and those practitioners, in turn, have contributed to its evolution and identity. At one end of the continuum are those whose artistic practices are grounded in their own ancestral heritage. At the other are those who engage in pioneering reflexive or experimental practice, often built on a philosophy and methodology that they have developed as part of their life's work. A brief introduction to a some of those in this latter category will help to elucidate the nature of what is to some extent a shared vision, and will also allow the reader to discern points of contact with the philosophy of the NVPN as presented in the first half of this chapter.

Kristin Linklater and Michele George

A regular presence at Giving Voice festivals and a member of its international advisory board, Kristin Linklater is author of the seminal *Freeing the Natural Voice*—first published in 1976 and in 2006 appearing in a revised and expanded edition that incorporates new material developed during the intervening three decades. Kristin now occupies a central place in the history of voice training in the United States, alongside such other luminaries as Edith Skinner, Arthur Lessac, and Evangeline Machlin. Born in Scotland, Kristin trained as an actress at the London Academy of Music and Dramatic Art (LAMDA), where her voice teacher was Iris Warren. Warren, in Kristin's words, "moved the science of voice production for British actors into a new phase ... by adding psychological understanding to physiological knowledge". In her exercises for actors suffering strained voices, Warren worked by "shifting the controls from external, physical muscles to internal, psychological impulses" (Linklater 2006: 5–6). After being taken on by Warren as a teacher trainee, Kristin taught for six years at LAMDA before relocating to the United States in 1963 to set up her own private studio in New York. She later held the posts of Professor of Theatre at Emerson College in Boston and Professor of Theatre Arts at Columbia University in New York City.

Kristin's approach—sometimes referred to as "Linklater Voice" or "Linklater Method", and sometimes as "Freeing the Natural Voice"—is "designed to liberate the natural voice and thereby develop a vocal technique that serves the freedom of human expression" (2006: 7). Several aspects of the philosophy informing her method have direct parallels in the NVPN's "Philosophy and Working Principles". "The basic assumption of the work," she writes, "is that everyone possesses a voice capable of expressing, through a two- to four-octave natural pitch range, whatever gamut of emotion, complexity of mood, and subtlety of thought he or she experiences." She goes on to describe the tensions, defences, and inhibitions, which may be physical, emotional, intellectual, aural, or psychological, that "diminish the efficiency of the natural voice to the point of distorted communication". The goal of her work is not only "the development of a skillful musical instrument" but also "the removal of the blocks that inhibit the human instrument", with the ultimate objective being "to produce a voice that is in direct contact with emotional impulses, shaped by the intellect but not inhibited by it" (2006: 7–8). The description of her work included in the brochure for the 2009 Giving Voice Festival notes that "emphasis is placed on freedom and release rather than control". Bodywork also plays a central role, since "to free the voice is to free the person, and each person is indivisibly mind and body" (2006: 8).

The theme of liberation from constraints is equally central to the philosophy and life work of Toronto-based singer, actress, and self-styled "therapeutic voice specialist" Michele George, another veteran of Giving Voice.[5] In her private practice, Michele aims to help her clients "find and express the most profound levels of their being through the voice", and to "rediscover the power and beauty of the voice [they] were born with" (http://michelegeorge.com/, acc. June 12, 2013). Freedom of expression, however extreme the results may sound to the more guarded ear, lies at the heart of Michele's mission. On her website she elaborates:

> There is a general notion that a loud or fully resounding voice is a negative one.... We have lost the right to whoop for joy, to grieve through wailing, to call out loud in love or need, to sing our own true song.

Her work is therefore underpinned by a commitment to enabling participants

> to examine and acknowledge the right of each one of us to have our say in this world, to re-member the voice we were born with as a prime instrument of communication, to recognize that this voice has been denied and suppressed; and then to begin to explore the practical possibilities available to support the recognition and repair the self. (http://michelegeorge.com/)

In a personal interview, Michele explained further the relationship she perceives between liberation on the one hand and, on the other, artistic creativity and individual choice:

> It is my firm belief that we all have an absolutely unique story that is about when we were silenced and we had our voices stolen from us and, as artistic people, to get a hold of that story and to claim it is a gateway to unlimited creativity because it's a way of knowing what I'm made of, where the habits and patterns got put in place that shut me down and that limited my creativity.... If I break these patterns and habits that limit me, I have choice. (George interview 2008)

Material drawn from the vocal traditions of different cultures also plays a central part in Michele's work. She was a founding member of Peter Brook's groundbreaking International Centre for Theatre Research (established in Paris in the late 1960s), and it was through her extensive travels and world-wide performances with the company that she was able to accumulate "much of her multicultural understanding of musical and vocal possibilities" (http://michelegeorge.com/).

Alfred Wolfsohn and Roy Hart

Giving Voice and its associates also honour and build on the legacy of an earlier generation of pioneers who are no longer with us, but in whose work we find the antecedents of many of the natural voice principles. In her initial statement in 1990 about the raison d'être of the fledgling Giving Voice project, Joan Mills evoked Alfred Wolfsohn's characterisation of the voice as "the muscle of the soul"—an image that has been a constant presence throughout the life of Giving Voice. Wolfsohn (1896–1962) devoted his career to exploring the nature and possibilities of the voice, particularly "the potential of the voice as not only an instrument of artistic expression but also of human development, psychology, and therapy" (http://www.roy-hart-theatre.com/site/, acc. June 12, 2013). He is credited by his followers as being "among the first people in the West to recognize the profound value of 'unacceptable' human sound" (Kalo 1997: 185). If Wolfsohn had written *Lies My Music Teacher Told Me*, close to the top of *his* list would have been: "The normal human voice has a register of up to two-and-a-half octaves." Wolfsohn insisted that "the natural human voice, freed from all artificial restrictions...is able to go much further", and he trained his pupils to "break their vocal and personal psychological barriers" by developing a vocal range of between four and eight octaves (ibid.). His ultimate aim was to to develop an "unchained" voice, which he called "the voice of the future".

German-born and of Jewish descent, Wolfsohn was conscripted into the German army at the age of eighteen to fight in World War I. Later, in 1939, he escaped from Berlin to London. Suffering from shellshock, Wolfsohn was haunted for the remainder of his life by his experiences in the trenches. And it was his vivid memories of the norm-shattering and almost superhuman cries of injured and dying soldiers that propelled his explorations into the potential of the human voice. He learned his craft largely by giving singing lessons to people who had lost their voice or were struggling with other vocal difficulties. Wolfsohn's fundamental insight was that their problems most often lay not in a physical malfunctioning of the larynx but in the depths of the soul or psyche. Vocal improvement in such cases was predicated on the healing of psychological damage, and he therefore immersed himself in the literature of psychoanalysis and psychotherapy. Wolfsohn was particularly drawn to the work of the Swiss analytical pyshologist Carl Gustav Jung, in which he recognised many principles that were confirmed by his own observations. Wolfsohn believed that the integration of the personality could be demonstrated in the human voice and that Jung's archetypes "exist in the body of every person and can be reached…through sound" (Kalo 1997: 187). In his own writings, Wolfsohn stressed that he did not consider singing to be only "an artistic exercise" but also to create "the possibility and the means to recognize oneself and to transform this recognition into conscious life" (cited in Günther 1990: 70).

Wolfsohn's legacy is most forcibly felt in the work of the Roy Hart Theatre. Roy Hart (1926–1975) was born in South Africa, where he originally studied psychology and English before winning a scholarship to London's Royal Academy of Dramatic Art (RADA) in 1946. His life was transformed as a result of meeting Wolfsohn—a meeting that led him to abandon a promising career in the West End to become Wolfsohn's pupil. Hart was Wolfsohn's protégé for sixteen years and continued his mentor's work after his death, referring to his own work as an "eight-octave approach to life". Hart gradually resumed his performing career; it was for Hart, whose vocal range and virtuosity were admired by many contemporary composers, that Peter Maxwell Davies composed *Eight Songs for a Mad King* (1968). The group of actors Hart worked with in London began to call themselves the Roy Hart Theatre, and in 1968, they performed their first full-length production (a preverbal interpretation of Euripides' *The Bacchae*). In 1974 the group relocated to the South of France and took up residence at the twelfth-century Château de Malérargues, which remained their headquarters following Hart's untimely demise in a car accident in 1975. Using words that are by now familiar, Hart once described the voice as "at once the most intimate and naked revelation of our essential self" (http://www.roy-hart.com/, acc. June 12, 2013). Like Wolfsohn, he viewed both psychological work and physical preparation as vital prerequisites to vocal development, and this led him to observe: "It is not surprising…that the mental and physical demands of our work caused our meeting place gradually to be regarded as a combined Church/Theatre/Gymnasium/Clinic" (Hart 1967: n.p.). Today the Roy Hart Theatre maintains its centre at Malérargues, although some of its practitioners now operate from other bases across the globe.

Jerzy Grotowski and Włodzimierz Staniewski

Polish theatre director Jerzy Grotowski (1933–1999), together with contemporary companies who continue his work, also warrants a special mention as a member of the CPR's international extended family. Celebrated as the father of experimental theatre, Grotowski established his Laboratory Theatre in the city of Wrocław in 1965; in 1986 he was invited to relocate to Pontedera, Italy, where he founded the Workcenter of Jerzy Grotowski. Grotowski travelled widely, seeking in the different cultures he encountered elements of traditional practice and technique that, combined with a re-injection of ritual, would facilitate a heightened communion between actor and spectator, with the potential for both personal and social transformation. He dubbed the approach that informed his work in the 1960s "poor theatre", the guiding principles of which are outlined in his book *Towards a Poor Theatre* (1968). In the productions of the Laboratory Theatre, conventional props were more or less dispensed with, allowing the focus to shift to the physicality of the performer, who also created his or her own music using the voice alone. During the final phase of his work, referred to as "art as vehicle" or "ritual arts", Grotowski developed performances that incorporated "actions related to very ancient songs which traditionally served ritual purposes and so can have a direct impact on—so to say—the head, the heart, and the body of the doers, songs which can allow the passage from a vital energy to a more subtle one" (cited in Thibaudat 1995: 29). Like the members of the Roy Hart Theatre, Grotowski's actors were required to commit to rigorous training regimes and became, in the words of the *Britannica Online Encyclopedia*, "disciplined masters of bodily and vocal contortions" (http://www.britannica.com/, acc. June 12, 2013).

Grotowski's legacy lives on in the work of such companies as Theatre Zar and Teatr Pieśń Kozła (Song of the Goat), both based in Wrocław, as well as others outside Poland, such as the Odin Teatret in Denmark, founded by Grotowski's one-time apprentice Eugenio Barba. These companies have a strong presence at CPR events. Poland's Gardzienice Theatre, directed by Włodzimierz Staniewski (at one time a close associate of Grotowski), is also part of the jigsaw. Again, the company accords a prime place in its performances to music, which Staniewski describes as "a key which opens heart and soul" (http://www.gardzienice.art.pl/, acc. June 12, 2013), and company members undertake regular expeditions to work with indigenous communities in rural regions of Poland and elsewhere in the world (part of the culture of theatre anthropology). The relevance of the Grotowski and Staniewski strand for our present purposes lies not only in its focus on exploratory voicework but also in the incorporation of songs from living oral traditions into theatrical productions and in the intercultural encounters that lie behind such endeavours.[6]

Giving Voice as Culture and Community

Initiatives like Giving Voice, then, owe much of their impact to their ability to gather so many world-class experts and iconic figures together in one place for a concentrated period of time. In so doing, they bring these different specialists into dialogue with one another and make their work accessible to a large and varied cohort of international delegates who are thus exposed to new ways of thinking while also developing their own practice. Since many of the core associates and delegates return on a regular basis, the project has come to represent a kind of culture or community in its own right where friendships are made and professional relationships strengthened. In this respect, Giving Voice festivals are similar to the annual gatherings of the NVPN and the Unicorn Natural Voice Camp (see chapters 3 and 8, respectively). The cumulative list of practitioners and scholars who have been part of the faculty for past festivals (a list that often appears in the brochure for a new edition) further reinforces the sense that Giving Voice is a professional body and, in some ways at least, a community of practice.

The line-up at the first Giving Voice Festival and Symposium in 1990 featured Kristin Linklater, together with several other practitioners bringing influences from the above lineages. These included Zygmunt Molik, a founder member of Grotowski's Theatre Laboratory; Roberta Carreri of Odin Teatret; Kozana Lucca, an Argentinian actress, teacher, and director who played an instrumental role in the development of the Roy Hart Theatre; and Derek Gale, a drama therapist and psychotherapist whose work is based on Wolfsohn's philosophy and techniques (Gale's voice teacher, Emmanuel Klein, had been a pupil of both Wolfsohn and Hart). Also present as both speaker and workshop leader was Frankie Armstrong, who referenced Wolfsohn's now legendary designation of the voice as "the muscle of the soul" in her symposium presentation. And in the programme notes for this inaugural festival, director Joan Mills acknowledged her personal debt to many of the invited teachers in assisting her on her own vocal journey.

Subsequent festivals were constructed around themes reflected in their titles, such as A Geography of the Voice (1994 and 1995), An Archaeology of the Voice (1996 and 1997), A Divinity of the Voice (1999), and The Voice Politic (2002). The roll call of contributors shows the net being cast ever wider in terms of both geographical and disciplinary spread. Among the artists present, some already have an established reputation in world music circles; others are rare finds and have never before appeared in a public venue. Several ethnomusicologists serve as symposium presenters, often attending alongside artists from their research field for whom they act as interpreters. Notably, Helen Chadwick, who is a member of the Giving Voice advisory board, also emerges as a key player.[7]

In 2009, almost twenty years after its inception, Giving Voice left Wales for the first time and was hosted by the Grotowski Institute in Wrocław as part of the Grotowski anniversary celebrations. In tribute, the festival proposed to "take inspiration from Grotowski's profound and pioneering work on song and the voice in action" (Giving Voice programme 2009). Kristin Linklater was again on the programme; so, too, was Jonathan Hart Makwaia, stepson of Roy Hart. Among the workshops devoted to studying songs from a particular culture and their associated vocal techniques were Polyphonic Singing from the Ukraine, led by Maryana Sadovska, and The Voice of the Performer, led by Ukrainian singer and actress Natalia Polovynka. Both women specialise in teaching songs from their own country—Ukraine—but do so in a way that has been strongly influenced by the work of Grotowski and Staniewski. Maryana was part of Grotowski's Slavic Pilgrim Project, based in Pontedera, Italy, and was subsequently invited to join the Gardzienice Theatre Association, with which she remained for ten years as an actress and a musical director. It was this work that inspired her to develop "a system of exercises enabling the discovery of the bonds between singing, gesture and voice, rhythm and breath" (Giving Voice programme 2009). Natalia's experience with the Workcenter of Jerzy Grotowski in Pontedera likewise was "a key turning point in her artistic exploration" (ibid.). These histories and kinships are important to note, not least because, through attending workshops such as these, amateur participants whose primary desire is to learn new songs are at the same time introduced to methods developed in professional theatre contexts.

Traditional singers from different parts of the world who still sing as part of their everyday lives and who have not undertaken any formal training in either singing or teaching (even if some also tour in semi-professional performing groups) may also be introduced to both natural voice and experimental theatre networks through events such as Giving Voice. Featured in the 2009 workshop programme, for example, were the Corsican group Tempus Fugit, members of the Cuncordu de Orosei and Tenores Antoni Milia from Sardinia, and the Pilpani family from Svaneti (Republic of Georgia), each of which taught material from the polyphonic singing traditions of their own region. Here, cross-influences are at work in both directions; the workshop leaders are introduced—through observing the work of other artists and attending more theoretical presentations—to new ideas and methodologies that they may later incorporate into their own teaching. Other "ethnic" performers, some of whom led workshops as well as giving concerts, included

N'Faly Kouyate (Guinea), Hasmik Harutyunyan (Armenia), Mahsa and Marjan Vahdat (Iran), Svetlana Spajić (Serbia), La Kaita (Spain), Bente Kahan (Norway), and Jawaher Shofani (Palestine). Also on the bill were Meredith Monk (USA), the ensemble Kitka (USA), Bragod (Wales), Michael Ormiston (UK) and his khöömii teacher Tserendaava (Mongolia), Lalish Theater Labor (Kurdistan/Austria), and Teatro delle Albe (Italy). Finally, the performances of Theatre Zar (*Gospels of Childhood* and *Caesarean Section*) and Pieśń Kozła (*Macbeth*) included songs from Corsica, Bulgaria, Romania, Greece, Georgia, Chechnya, and Iceland. These artists showcased a staggering range of vocal qualities and colours and—even when not confining themselves to indigenous songs from their own heritage (as in the case of Theatre Zar, Pieśń Kozła, and Kitka, for example)—offered rare, first-hand insights into the functions and meanings of these expressive forms in their cultural context.[8]

A MEETING OF WORLDS: GIVING VOICE AND THE NATURAL VOICE NETWORK

On the surface, the two "cultures" examined in this chapter might appear to enjoy parallel but largely separate lives. The one manifests itself in the type of professional voicework engaged in by actors as well as singers which is showcased in international events such as the Giving Voice Festival; the other, in the comparatively localised activities associated with the NVPN, whose membership is predominantly British and whose primary focus is on amateur and emerging singers. Certainly, the prospect of working on the voice (and the psyche) at the intense, personal level demanded of acolytes of Roy Hart or Grotowski, for example, would appear daunting to the average community-choir member. For other reasons, too, Giving Voice festivals are likely to attract more theatre practitioners and singers who are committed to performance than amateur, recreational singers. There are, nonetheless, several ways in which bridges are built between the two environments.

For many NVPN practitioners, Giving Voice has been seminal in providing them with opportunities to work alongside outstanding teachers and performers from across the globe, not only to learn new musical material, vocal styles, and teaching techniques, but also to gain a window onto the worlds from which the songs come and a deeper understanding of the part played by music in lives lived elsewhere. It is through Giving Voice that many were introduced to Georgian, Corsican, Ukranian, and Mongolian vocal traditions, for example. Others who may never have attended the festival in person are aware of Giving Voice as a significant keystone in the natural voice edifice, not least for what one speaker refers to as its "cascade effect". Many more benefit—often unconsciously—as they are introduced at second or third hand to ideas, exercises, or songs first shared in workshops led by Kristin Linklater, Michele

George, Maryana Sadovska, and others. As the foregoing survey of artists and activities assembled under the Giving Voice umbrella demonstrates, the potential for cross-influence is considerable and it is through this wider web of connections and spin-offs, as well as through direct participation, that Giving Voice makes its influence felt. Of particular note is the fact that the CPR was responsible for bringing Georgian singer and ethnomusicologist Edisher Garakanidze to the United Kingdom, initially in connection with a theatre project and later as part of Giving Voice (a story I pursue in greater detail in chapter 6). Edisher's influence spread rapidly as he was invited to lead workshops across the British Isles by choir leaders who first encountered his work at these events and it was Joan Mills and other CPR colleagues who helped nurture his collection *99 Georgian Songs*, subsequently published on the CPR's Black Mountain Press label. The CPR thus paved the way for the thriving network of Georgian singing enthusiasts and dedicated Georgian choirs found in Britain today.

A regular presence at Giving Voice since its inception, Frankie Armstrong pays homage to the extraordinary teachers and performers she has met there who have contributed to the evolution of her work. Her association with the CPR, and more particularly her close friendship and professional collaboration with Joan Mills, in fact dates back to the early 1980s and the days of Cardiff Laboratory Theatre. It should therefore come as no great surprise that, looking back on this joint journey in 2006, she should describe the NVPN as having "a rich symbiotic relationship" with Giving Voice (Armstrong 2006: 35). It is also no accident that her collection *Well-Tuned Women* (Armstrong and Pearson 2000) includes chapters by Kristin Linklater, Michele George, and others who have appeared at Giving Voice, as well as Joan herself.

This perception of a common quest is shared by Joan Mills, even if (as she was keen to establish during the final plenary session of the 2009 festival) Giving Voice "really comes from performance". In engaging with different vocal forms, she explains, she and her fellow practitioners are not motivated by any desire to revive or preserve them as such but rather to use them as inspiration for their own creative work. Yet for her, there are at the same time obvious links between the community choir world and the type of work showcased at Giving Voice. As an adjunct to the festivals already described that sit at the centre of the Giving Voice project, she has also invested considerable resources in promoting community choir activity in Wales under the banner of Local Voices, Worlds of Song. This initiative has embraced a range of activities, including (in 2002 and 2003) short residential gatherings at the CPR's base in Aberystwyth, where choir members could take part in a series of half-day workshops and also join together for an evening of performance. The overlap with the interests, convictions, and methods that characterise the NVPN world is clear from the description of the workshop programme in the promotional material for the first such event:

The workshops aim to provide a range of stimulating teaching: some offer a particular singing style to which participants may not often have access; some are about working on *how* we sing, the quality of the voice, issues of confidence, better listening; some particularly focus on the co-ordination of body and voice [...]; some are to encourage a free exploration of each voice in an enjoyable, easy atmosphere. (Unpublished information sheet, 2001)

Having had a taster of the kind of workshops typically on offer at a full Giving Voice festival, many participants were inspired to return in order to attend more intensive sessions with a chosen artist or to sample a wider range of offerings. A parallel initiative was the launch of a programme of weekend workshops led by artists associated with Giving Voice which took place in different parts of Wales. This made the work accessible to a far greater number of local choir members on their home ground. The sense (for participating choirs) of being part of a wider network was further strengthened by projects such as Traveller, centred on a new work—*Travels with My Uncle*—commissioned from the composer Karl Jenkins. With a preparation period of several months that included regional workshops led by a team of tutors (including NVPN members Roxane Smith, already encountered in her role as conductor at Sing for Water, and Pauline Down, director of Bangor Community Choir), this project culminated in another mass choir performance, this time at St. Donat's Castle in South Wales.

THE NATURAL VOICE IN PERSPECTIVE

Where, then, does all of this leave us in our quest for the natural voice? Certainly there is ample evidence of multiple networks of individuals from different cultural backgrounds and walks of life who come together around a commitment to something they call the natural voice or who are attracted to the kind of activity that is labelled as such by others. But is there such a thing as a universal "natural" voice? The considered answer has to be no. Clearly, voices in different parts of the world have quite distinctive sounds (even if they can be modified). The glossary entry for "natural voice" from the booklet in the *Voix du Monde/Voices of the World* compact disc set produced by the CNRS/Musée de l'Homme begins by stating that "a 'natural' sung voice is when its timbre is closest to the spoken voice", but immediately adds: "In so far as spoken voices are themselves dependent on large cultural variations...the notion of 'natural voice' is therefore of a strictly relative value" (Léothaud, Lortat-Jacob, and Zemp 1996: 180).

In some ways, the "natural" qualifier says more about what a voice is *not* than what it is. In a Euro-American context, one might say that the natural voice is not a classically trained voice. But this is unsatisfactory too. Frankie

Armstrong makes it clear that she does not view the natural voice as a straightforward gloss for the non-professional or untrained voice: "I think Maria Callas used the natural voice. It was highly trained but it's absolutely up from the soles of the floor [sic]" (interview 2008). A "natural" voice in this sense might be better described as a voice that is "released" and "unrestrained" and that communicates a depth of feeling that listeners experience as "authentic".

"Natural voice" seems to be more useful, then, as a designator of a broader approach to working with the voice. It may be helpful here to draw an analogy with another movement using the "natural" label, the natural childbirth movement. The National Childbirth Trust (NCT) was founded in 1956 as the Natural Childbirth Association. It found its inspiration in the writings of British obstetrician Grantly Dick-Read, author of *Natural Childbirth* and the international bestseller *Childbirth Without Fear* (initially published under the title *Revelation of Childbirth*), whose mission was to help mothers to give birth naturally, with as little medical interference as possible. The organisation's fundamental aim was to challenge the medicalisation of childbirth that had accompanied what was then a relatively recent shift from home births to hospital births, to question the routine use of drugs and other interventions during labour and delivery, and to keep open the option of a more natural alternative. Tidy, technologised births, like the classical voice, might be viewed as a modern, Western, middle-class invention. No one would deny that vital progress has been made in reducing birth trauma where medical intervention is necessary; the problem, again, lies in the imposition of the new norm on those who do not require a high-tech approach and where the dividing line between assistance and constraint is more thinly drawn. Above all, the NCT is concerned with the quality of individual experience, and with the emotional and spiritual—as well as physical—wellbeing of mother and child. Interestingly, Sheila Kitzinger, who occupies a mentor position not unlike that of Frankie Armstrong (she was once referred to by *The Independent* as "the high priestess of the childbirth movement"), was also inspired initially by insights she gained as a social anthropologist by observing the way in which childbirth is managed in other parts of the world (see Kitzinger 1978).

What has become abundantly clear is that the concept of the natural voice does not refer only to one type of voice or voice production, or to the voice alone. For the professional performer, it indicates a search for authenticity in the sense of an expressive power and creative capacity that is unencumbered by artificial constraints. The voice that emerges is individual and unique, in direct contact with the emotions but not bound by them. In amateur contexts, it signifies a concern with rediscovering the joy of singing. For some individuals, it has a therapeutic dimension. In the more specific context of the NVPN, it denotes a shared philosophy and methodology that continue to be negotiated. It also serves in part as an indicator of the type of repertory one might expect from a natural voice choir or workshop (broadly speaking, songs from oral traditions rather than the classical standards favoured by more conventional amateur choirs). As David Burbidge puts it, members of the NVPN use "natural voice" as a kind of shorthand "to show that we express certain core beliefs in our way of working" (http://www.lakelandvoice.co.uk/, acc. June 12, 2013). Frankie Armstrong reflects:

> What I would hope [is that] the baseline of the natural voice is still to create a place—an accepting, non-judgmental place—where people can come and sing, as indeed they did in the past, ... at harvest suppers and singing rounds in the pub and whatever—where they can have that experience of social singing. (Armstrong interview 2008)

She sums up: "For me it's a whole thing to do with both the kind of historical, social, political, cultural development of the voice in the way that we use it and the contexts in which we choose to use it, and the actual physicality of how the voice is formed" (ibid.).

Critics will be quick to point out that the natural voice movement itself isn't free and unfettered. It has an ideology; it promotes a methodology; there are expectations that anyone using the natural voice label will adhere to a set of agreed principles and a code of practice. Practitioners might talk about the natural voice in terms of liberation from rules and norms, but they tend to undertake a particular kind of training and use particular types of exercises (see chapter 4). Again, an analogy with the natural childbirth movement may be helpful. It also promotes a specific philosophy, method, and approach; teachers are trained and certified (in this case, the training is more formal); participants in classes learn a particular set of exercises. This does not diminish in any way the underlying ethic or objective, which is to empower the individual and to offer an alternative to the industry standard. Even in societies where people supposedly "live close to nature", there is always some degree of guidance, conditioning, or training. Children learn through stories, songs, and rituals; they learn by imitation and example. They are not simply left to their own devices.

In the same way that natural childbirth principles have increasingly made inroads into the mainstream (many hospital maternity units now provide a more homelike environment and offer birthing pools, for example), so the causes embraced by the natural voice movement appear to be on the brink of achieving wider currency. Members of the NVPN would no doubt be heartened to know that, more than a decade ago, John Potter wrote on the first page of his introduction to *The Cambridge Companion to Singing*:

> If I had to predict where significant developments in singing will come from in the future, I would hazard a guess that what we now call world music is the well-spring from which new forms of vocal expression will flow.... At almost

any other time in recent history a singing Companion would probably have meant an anthology of writing about fairly narrowly defined "classical" singing. Looking backwards to the latter part of the twentieth century and forwards to the twenty-first, it is possible to see a major and continuing change in our perception of what singing is, to the extent that it is no longer possible to come up with any single meaningful definition. (Potter 2000: 1–2)

Those active in the natural voice world are contributing significantly to this shift of consciousness, whilst also putting theory into practice in a way that brings the promise of vocal liberation within the reach of an ever-widening constituency of amateur and aspiring singers.

NOTES
1. Mithen goes on to outline his vision of a "sophisticated communication system" used by Neanderthals, to which he gives the name "Hmmmmm", an acronym for Holistic, Manipulative, Multi-Modal, Musical, and Mimetic.
2. Banks in the neoclassical style—as well as concert halls, galleries, museums, libraries, and churches—were, of course, modelled architecturally on ancient Greek and Roman temples as post-Enlightenment shrines to civilisation.
3. See also Blacking's reference to the "aura of morality" that adheres to "the diligent practice of scales and arpeggios" (1973: 109).
4. Cardiff Laboratory Theatre was founded in 1974, and Richard Gough served as its director from 1981.
5. Michele holds a Diploma from the Central School of Speech and Drama in London and a Bachelor of Arts (BA) in speech and dramatic arts.
6. Space does not allow a more extensive appraisal of the many complexities, ambiguities, and controversies surrounding Grotowski's work. A wealth of material, including a substantial encyclopedia and bibliography, can be found on the website http://www.grotowski.net/en. See also the website and other outcomes of The British Grotowski Project, directed by Paul Allain: http://www.british-grotowski.co.uk/. For a critical history and evaluation of Gardzienice, see Paul Allain's *Gardzienice: Polish Theatre in Transition* (1997, reprinted 2004).
7. Documentation relating to past festivals (and to many other CPR events) can be found in the Projects section of the CPR website: see http://thecpr.org.uk, acc. April 21, 2014.
8. Erik Hillestad of KKV Records (like myself, an invited speaker at the 2009 festival) said that he was struck by the fact that all the voices presented during the week were "authentic" (pers. comm. 2009). There was a marked absence of bel canto traditions, stage divas, and the more conventional "choral" sound of Western choirs.

CHAPTER 3

Natural Voice Practitioners and Their Journeys

Histories and Connections

A GATHERING OF THE NATURAL VOICE CLAN

January 2010 is marked by the heaviest snowfall Britain has seen for many years, and South Yorkshire is no exception. Wortley Hall sits majestic and secure on its twenty-six-acre estate, surrounded by formal gardens and picturesque woodland covered in a blanket of white stretching as far as the eye can see, silently awaiting the arrival of the next party of guests. From all corners of the British Isles and beyond, we make our way towards the beacon of light and the warm welcome we know we will find at the end of our journey. Trains are delayed and cancelled; some set off but grind to a halt in a Narnia-like land we can barely see through the whirling flakes of snow that fall ever thicker and faster. Taxis lose their way and drivers lose their nerve when they find the usual route to the hall closed. The lane that eventually brings us to the gates is still just about passable.

Apart from a few brave diners who will emerge, ghostlike, from the snowy wastes to partake of the Sunday lunchtime carvery, we have the house to ourselves and soon take possession of what are now familiar haunts: the lounge, dining rooms, library, garden room, conference rooms, ballroom, the Henry Collins Room, and the Stuart Charnley Room. The opulence of the setting belies the more humble environments to which we are more accustomed. The well-appointed rooms are lavishly fitted out in neoclassical style, with fluted Corinthian columns and pilasters made of light stone or green marble, ornate cornices and architraves, and ceilings heavy with embellished plasterwork. Vast fireplaces, mirrors, and chandeliers complement oak panelling and heavy wooden doors and shutters, with their decorative mouldings and reliefs. The rooms intended for relaxation are tastefully furnished; their generously proportioned windows look onto Italianate gardens whose well-maintained lawns and beds—asleep for now beneath a crystalline quilt—are studded with fountains, statues, and topiaries.

Wortley Hall, with its multiple staircases and warren of passageways, and still unexplored nooks and crannies, would make the perfect setting for a murder mystery weekend or a live game of Cluedo. We, however, have other things on our minds: we are here for the NVPN Annual Gathering. We assemble in the ballroom for the welcome session and a preview of the programme of activities for the next three days, drawn up with the help of the "wants" and "offers" noted on members' booking forms. Options include a range of singing workshops and song-swaps, together with practical and discussion-based workshops on a variety of topics, including song-writing, improvisation, conducting, developing leadership skills, working with different target groups (e.g. children, adults with learning difficulties), and the practicalities of establishing and maintaining choirs. There are also optional early morning chant and yoga sessions, post-breakfast warm-ups, evening singing sessions for the whole group (at which songs, often new, original compositions, are taught by different teachers), and a singing walk. From time to time there are spontaneous flash-mob performances as smaller groups take their place on the main imperial staircase to entertain the listeners gathered in the hall below. On Saturday night, the ballroom is transformed for an exuberant cabaret-style party and awed silence alternates with joyful hilarity as all manner of performing talents emerge. Those who have energy to spare after an action-packed day take up residence in the bar, where they continue to construct ever more elaborate harmonies late into the night.

Given the fundamental principles embraced by many in the NVPN, it seems entirely fitting that for the past sixty years Wortley Hall—formerly the ancestral home of the Wharncliffe family, who had made their fortune from the coal mining industry—has been co-owned by the trade unions, the Labour Party, and the co-operative movement. Following extensive renovations that rescued the building from its semi-derelict state, the hall was reopened in 1951 as an educational and recreational centre, thereby restoring the fruits of their toil to the people. It is for this reason that some of the main function rooms are now named after a political figure or a specific union. We gather for breakfast beneath a plaque that reads: "This Dining-Room was endowed by the Fire Brigades Union 1952. Knowledge is Power, and Knowledge in the minds of Working Men and Women, is Power in the hands of those who will change the World." For many of us, the time we spend here is a highlight of the year—an opportunity to catch up with friends and colleagues, refresh repertoires, and seek help with specific problems encountered in our own work. Above all, the annual gathering reminds us of the power of song to change lives.

Fast forward two years: the 2012 gathering reflects some of the ways in which the network has continued to evolve. This year we are joined by special guest teacher, Kathy Bullock, who is a professor of music at Berea College in Kentucky. She is also an inspirational gospel singer and workshop leader, and over the next three days she will take us on an uplifting and informative journey through the African American singing tradition. The ease with which the singers pick up the parts and words of the songs she brings, without recourse to either scores or word sheets, is testimony to their impressive aural skills, while the ecstatic heights reached by more than eighty of us singing and improvising together are revelatory of the strong sense of community that has built up over the years and into which those new to the network are now drawn (▶ see video tracks 03.01–03.03).

Other workshops offered during the weekend are illuminating in different ways. A session focusing on "failsafe" songs is an interesting indication of the type and range of repertoire that might be found in a natural voice choir, as are the song-swap sessions where volunteers take turns teaching the parts to favourite songs that they wish to pass on to fellow choir leaders. The songs that emerge include original compositions, quick-and-easy rounds, songs from a host of foreign lands, and a healthy number of English folk songs. Other sessions on singing in hospitals and hospices and on working with people with dementia reflect the growing interest in using singing in health settings.

The tables on which attendees display items for sale and leaflets advertising future events seem fuller than ever. The delights on offer this year include books and CDs by Frankie Armstrong and songbooks and teaching CDs featuring original compositions by other NVPN members, including Alison Burns, Nick Prater, Helen Yeomans, Kirsty Martin, Polly Bolton, and Pauline Down. There are also CDs made by choirs directed by some of the practitioners attending the gathering, and these offer intriguing clues to the lives of individual choirs. Hot off the press is *Lilizela!* by Rough Diamonds, one of several choirs directed by Hilary Davies. The predominance of South African songs in this choir's repertoire is explained by the fact that this 24-strong ensemble was specially formed for a trip to South Africa in 2008. There, the ensemble worked with the Diamond Choir, established by a group of mine workers from the Cullinan Diamond Mine near Pretoria who two years previously had accepted an invitation to visit Hilary's choirs in the United Kingdom. Profits from the sale of the CD will support HIV/AIDS programmes and community projects in the township that is home to the Diamond Choir. This CD therefore points to the practical links that are increasingly being forged between British community choirs and local communities elsewhere in the world.

Possible dates for this year's diary suggested by the colourful array of flyers include "Carry It On", a training, support, and networking weekend at Kinnersley Castle led by Frankie Armstrong, Rowena Whitehead, and Pauline Down; "Leading a Community Choir—Starting Out Training", a day workshop in London led by Gitika Partington; a songwriting weekend at Oak Barn in Shropshire, led by Polly Bolton, Sue Harris, and Gitika Partington, with poet Gill McEvoy; "Sing Folk", another weekend at Oak Barn where Polly Bolton will teach her own arrangements of traditional British folk songs together with vocal ornamentation techniques; a series of weekend courses led by Maddy Prior, Rose Kemp, Abbie Lathe, and others at Stones Barn, Maddy's venue in Cumbria; a songwriting weekend with Helen Chadwick at Hawkwood College in the Cotswolds; "The Alchemy of Song", a three-day residential course in songwriting, arranging, and improvisation led by Nick Prater and his daughter Susie at Holycombe House in Warwickshire; "Rise Up Singing", a week-long summer camp on Dartmoor whose portfolio of teachers includes Helen Yeomans and Roxane Smith; a series of events led by David Burbidge under the auspices of his Lakeland Voice project, including a four-day singing walk along Hadrian's Wall, a folk carols weekend, and a harmony singing week on the Scottish island of Jura; "Sing Out on Kos", a weeklong Greek island singing holiday led by Dave and Liz Stewart; and "Singing in the Olive Lands", another singing holiday in Turkey led by Rowena Whitehead.

The presence of Kathy Bullock as this year's special guest and the recent appointment of a design team for a brand new NVPN website are two indicators of the healthy financial and organisational base the NVPN now enjoys. Fifty-five new members have joined in the past year, and a quarter of the eighty-odd practitioners lucky enough to have secured a place at this year's gathering are here for the first time. One thing that has changed little is the gender balance: our company includes only ten men. The number of younger faces, meanwhile, offers reassurance that the future of the network is secure.

The physical journey that brings us together for these few days may—as in that snowbound January of 2010—have its share of challenges and diversions. We start from different places, travelling by different means; for some, the journey may be comparatively short and direct but for others it can be protracted, unpredictable, or circuitous. What of the longer journey each has taken to get to this place in his or her life? How did these disparate individuals, with their many talents and enthusiasms, varied experiences, unusual generosity, and seemingly boundless energy, find their way to the NVPN clan?

THE ROADS THAT LEAD TO THE NATURAL VOICE

In this chapter we delve deeper into the world of the voice practitioners and choir leaders who have gathered under and around the natural voice banner in the United Kingdom. Alongside a predominance of British-born teachers who (to varying degrees) draw on songs from many different musical cultures, we meet others who have grown up elsewhere in the world and specialise in teaching songs and techniques from their native musical traditions. Almost all of those featured are members of the NVPN. Several were among its founding members. Others have a looser affiliation and are also members of other professional bodies or networks; in this case they may not use "natural voice practitioner" as their primary identification. Finally, there are representatives from a wider pool of UK-based community music practitioners who may not be formally affiliated with the NVPN but are nonetheless part of a recognisable culture that we might imagine as a series of intersecting networks with many points of contact and modes of communication. They, too, are known to many of the singers in choirs run by NVPN members who attend their workshops or come into contact with them at larger singing events.

As we travel through this landscape we will pass a series of landmarks that serve as anchors or signposts and we will pause to listen to the tales they have to tell. We will also stumble on hidden clearings where people arriving from different directions exchange insights and visions as well as songs. By the time we reach the end of our journey through this chapter, we will have a better understanding of not only the shared experiences that brought this particular band of travellers together but also the historical context of the natural voice scene in the United Kingdom and the different musical, social, and political currents that have informed its philosophy and practice. We begin, however, with the seminal journey taken by Frankie Armstrong (figure 3.1) (☉ see web figure 03.01).

Frankie's Singing Journey

By what route, then, did Frankie arrive at the convictions and insights that form the bedrock of her inimitable brand of voice work, whose influence is today felt not only across the length and breadth of the British Isles but also in parts of Australia, North America, and the European mainland? A brief survey of some of the most relevant milestones in her life will help to explain how her work has been informed in equal measure by her passion for traditional singing styles, her fascination with the way in which free use of the voice can enhance personal well being and strengthen community spirit, her understanding of pedagogical methods that are nurturing and enabling, and her broader engagement with a variety of sociopolitical movements.[1]

Frankie's musical journey began in the late 1950s with an attraction to skiffle. She first performed in public in 1957 with the Stort Valley Skiffle Group (based in Hertfordshire), which subsequently changed its name to the Ceilidh Singers as its repertoire shifted towards folk music. She became an avid listener to now-legendary blues and folk singers and was "transfixed by the rawness and directness" of their music:

> In my teens I loved classical music and singing, Elvis, Little Richard, Fats Domino and also the great Broadway musicals. But something profound happened

Figure 3.1 Frankie Armstrong at the Natural Voice Practitioners' Network annual gathering, Wortley Hall, Sheffield, January 2011.
Source: Photo courtesy of Caroline Bithell.

when I first heard the early blues singers, the chain gang songs of the Southern Penitentiaries and the mountain songs of the Carter Family, and the political songs of Woody Guthrie. (Armstrong 2004: 21)

She also listened to The Weavers, and in 1963 she was at the Royal Albert Hall when Pete Seeger's voice rang out from the stage, proclaiming: "Everyone can sing!" Soon she was working with the leading lights of the British folk revival. She talks of her "own personal voice workshop" beginning when she started to sing with Louis Killen, who encouraged her to listen to source singers, in particular singers from the Gypsy and Traveller communities. As a result, she says, "I changed my whole style of singing completely" (interview 2008). Most notably, she began to explore the chest voice that she had never used up to that point.[2] Her greatest influence from the folk world—"the person who really spoke to my heart and soul"—was A. L. ("Bert") Lloyd (interview 2008). It was his album *Folk Music of Bulgaria*, released by Topic Records in 1964, that introduced her to Bulgarian singing. "I wore it nearly thin," she recalls, listening to it over and over in her tiny bedsit and trying to reproduce "that glorious sound" with her own voice (interview 2008; 2004: 21). When she visited Bert at his home in Greenwich, he would play her extracts of field recordings he had made in different parts of Eastern Europe.

It was in 1964, too, that Frankie began performing professionally as a folk-singer and joined what became known as the Critics Group. During the group's weekly meetings at the house of Ewan MacColl and Peggy Seeger, Frankie was introduced to more recordings featuring vocal styles from different parts of the world. As a member of the Critics Group, she took part in several theatre pieces, recordings, and radio productions, often using approaches derived from the work of Russian actor and director Constantin Stanislavski (who was an important influence on Ewan MacColl). Ewan also gave his apprentices reading lists that included titles from anthropology, social history, political thought, and drama theory, as well as works on folk songs and traditional cultures, and these would inspire regular debates. Frankie considers her time with the group to have been an important part of her education, vocal and otherwise.

Among other noteworthy influences, she cites Hans Fried, who worked at Collet's record shop in Shaftesbury Avenue. She describes how she would go to the shop to buy the latest Watersons record, for example, and Hans would say, "Frankie, listen to this!" It was there that she heard a UNESCO recording of Georgian polyphony—"I just thought it was absolutely stunning," she recalls—and had her first taste of Mongolian overtone singing (interview 2008). Recognising her passion for unusual vocal styles, other friends and colleagues brought her recordings they thought might interest her. She found further treasures on her travels. When she began running workshops in Sweden in the late 1970s, for example, some of her trainees gave her recordings of Tuvan singers "and various other strange and wonderful styles from right across the Soviet Union" (interview 2008). In this way she accumulated an extensive collection that she still dips into to play to participants in her workshops.

Frankie describes the continued development of her own vocal quality at this time as "very much trial and error" (1997: 46). As she had done with Bert Lloyd's record of Bulgarian singing, she would spend hours experimenting on her own, trying to fathom out how to reproduce the voices she heard on the various recordings that fell into her hands. She attributes the intensity with which she applied herself to these vocal experiments in part to the loss of her eyesight (she would be registered blind in 1975), which gave her "a ferocious capacity to attend to the unending range of expression of which [the voice] is capable" (2000: 68). Her visual impairment also, of course, precluded the use of scores, but in many ways this is beside the point. Her attention was focused first and foremost on matters of timbre, placement, and ornamental technique—sonic dimensions that are critical to establishing vocal identities and rendering performances culturally "authentic" but that elude being captured in written form.

As she was developing her career as a folk singer, Frankie was also accumulating many other skills that would add important dimensions to her approach to voice work when she later began to lead singing groups and voice workshops for amateur and aspiring singers. The deterioration of her eyesight in her teenage years had thwarted her childhood ambition to become an artist and forced her to rethink her future, and she had trained as a social worker. In the early 1970s, she helped to set up the Co-operative Training Services and discovered a fascination with training, and more specifically with role play and simulation. Exploring with fellow social workers issues they were faced with in their work, she learnt many techniques that she would later use in her work with novice singers, including the value of constructive feedback: it was, she observes, "a constant challenge for us to find ways of being honest which were not judgemental or rejecting and collusive, and that gave useful, respectful feedback" (1992: 75). Later, she also began teaching Assertiveness Training and further honed her skills in evaluation, team development, and group training as part of becoming an Action Research worker.

A major turning point in allowing Frankie to make a direct connection between the vocal and the therapeutic was her meeting with American singer, folklorist, and collector Ethel Raim (founder of The Pennywhistlers). An initial invitation to perform at the Mariposa Folk Festival in Canada in 1972 had led to a return visit to North America the following summer. This time, Frankie combined an appearance at the Philadelphia Folk Festival with visits to drug projects around the United States, supported by a Travel Study Award from the Ford Foundation.[3] On her first evening in Philadelphia, she found herself dining out with Ethel. "My cup was overflowing," she recalls. "We adored each other from that first meeting" (1992: 81–82). Ethel had conducted research in Eastern Europe and was at the centre of the Balkan music scene in the United States, having launched her first voice classes in Philadelphia in 1967 before going on to establish her Vocal Workshop in New York in 1969. Frankie had her first taste of the way Ethel worked when she attended an all-women evening class in New York's Greenwich Village:

> I guess it was the singer in me that revelled in the sounds we made and songs we learnt, while the social worker in me observed with delight the changes that came over individuals in the group. As a group, too, we quickly developed a sense of support and collective identity. Though I had no idea at the time, this was the experience that would eventually change the direction of my life. (Armstrong 1992: 85)

She was struck by the effect of this singing on the other members of the group:

> It was very obvious to me as a social worker, group worker, that people went out bright-eyed and bushy-tailed, even if they'd come in dragged off the New York subway pretty bedraggled.... You could actually see people's *physicality* change. (interview 2008)

Another thing she found interesting was "to hear, see what happened to women when they found the bigger, peasanty voice". "So right from the beginning," she reflects, "it was...the musical, the social, and the psychological elements that intrigued me and that excited me" (interview 2008). From Ethel, then, Frankie acquired not only a repertory of Balkan songs, together with specific techniques for achieving the so-called open-throated style that is widely used in Eastern European singing, but also an insight into the way in which this choice of musical material functioned in combination with a broader teaching ethic to produce such a dramatic effect on the group's vocal attainment. Ethel's method was notable, she observes, for its "constant encouragement, rather than discouragement". At this point, with a decade's experience as a social worker behind her, Frankie was able to recognise "what a potent tool this way of working with the voice was for building individual confidence and for creating group support and cohesion" (1997: 46).

Back in London after a further summer in America, during which she had been able to attend Ethel's daily Balkan song workshops at Sweets Mill Music Camp, Frankie enthused about her experience to her friend Shirley Peters, who ran the Singers Club, and Shirley responded with the suggestion that Frankie should lead an Ethel-type session.[4] On her most recent visit, with Ethel's permission, Frankie had "recorded a goodly number of these songs and so returned to London with three or four cassettes marked 'Ethel'" (1992: 104–105). These were the songs she taught that first night (in 1975) to members of the Singers Club, complete with Ethel-style warm ups. Her fellow singers immediately wanted more, and what had been intended as a one-off experiment developed into a weekly group. Frankie gradually added more diverse material drawn from her ever-expanding collection of traditional music recordings and, as news of her work spread, she was invited to lead workshops in different parts of the country.

At the same time, her political engagement opened up a wider range of performance opportunities, and she now appeared regularly at events sponsored by the women's movement and CND (Campaign for Nuclear Disarmament). She wrote her own songs for these and other causes close to her heart, some (like those of Woody Guthrie, Pete Seeger, and the young Bob Dylan) inspired by contemporary events, such as the encirclement of the Greenham Cruise Missile Base by the Women's Peace Camp in 1982.[5] Now she was using her voice not simply to entertain but to speak out, spread a message, and uplift and inspire. It was in the context of these political happenings that some of those who would later find their way to the NVPN first encountered Frankie.

At some point, Frankie's reputation in Britain shifted (as she describes it) from "performer" to "singing person". She was receiving invitations to run workshops not only for folk festivals and theatre companies but also for women's groups, community centres, psychiatric hospitals, day centres, and disability groups. "That," she explains, "was where I cut my teeth....I started working across a much broader base in terms of doing the voice workshops than I would have done had I just stayed in the folk music scene" (interview 2008). In 1985, she made the decision to leave social work and become a full-time professional singer and voice worker, a step that coincided with her first invitation to Australia to give both concerts and workshops. There, she met her future husband and co-worker, Darien Pritchard, a massage trainer and Feldenkrais practitioner. In response to demand from a growing number of people who had been inspired by Frankie's voice workshops and wished to lead singing groups of their own using a similar approach, she and Darien established their residential Voice Training and Resources Week. The first training week took place in the United Kingdom in 1988 and, using Kinnersley Castle in Herefordshire as its base, the training became established as an annual event.[6] The seeds of the NVPN as a formal body took root at a party-cum-reunion held at Kinnersley Castle in 1995 to celebrate Frankie's birthday, where the majority of guests were active voice practitioners who had already trained with her. The unanimous feeling that "we must do this again" led to the establishment of an annual Kinnersley reunion, which later functioned as the annual gathering of the NVPN until the expansion of the network forced a move to a larger venue. The NVPN was officially constituted, and its mission statement formulated, in 2000.

Frankie and Darien's week-long residential courses for voice practitioners and workshop leaders continue to act as an important training ground for new recruits.[7] Although originally intended for people who had already taken part in one or more of Frankie's shorter voice workshops, the courses now attract participants from a range of professions, including teachers, community musicians, drama therapists, and actors. Some also come from overseas, especially from Australia, where Frankie continues to work for part of the year, and from America, where many know of her work through her involvement with the Voice and Speech Trainers Association (VASTA), of which she is an honorary member. She has also taught at the Central School of Speech and Drama and the National Theatre Studio in London, and she continues to teach on a number of theatre courses during her annual visits to Australia, including those run by the National Institute for the Dramatic Arts in Sydney and the Victorian College for the Arts in Melbourne.[8]

MEETINGS WITH VOICE PRACTITIONERS: CONTEXTS AND CONTINUITIES

Frankie's career, then, offers an instructive indication of the diverse strands that are woven together to form the complex and dynamic web of philosophies, ideologies, experiences, influences, initiatives, and actions that I set out to explore in these pages. A number of key ingredients may be extrapolated from Frankie's story as recounted above: a fascination with the unexplored potential of the human voice; an interest in English folk music leading to the discovery of folk music from other parts of the world; an insight into the effect of vocal liberation on the body and emotions; a combination of musical acumen and skills gained from experience in social work and counselling; a commitment to the principles of accessibility, inclusivity, and personal empowerment; interactions with the world of theatre; involvement in a variety of social and political movements, especially the women's and peace movements; a process of building skills and knowledge through what would be referred to in contemporary education-speak as "self-directed learning"; and finally, the part played by key mentors, life-changing encounters, and other eureka-like moments of discovery and understanding. It should at this point be clear how these various ingredients became part of Frankie's own practice and, in turn, fed into the philosophy and working principles of the NVPN outlined in chapter 2.

Perhaps not surprisingly, many of these same ingredients are to be found in the life and work stories of other practitioners, in several of which Frankie herself now features as a key mentor. When I interviewed Sarah Harman, for example, she began by enumerating four different strands that had fed into her own work with the voice—the folk tradition, the classical tradition, theatre, and political activism. In some cases, practitioners-to-be did not initially set out on a musical career, but happened, as if by chance, on experiences that held the seeds of their future calling. For others, their musical career took a different turn when they discovered an affinity with the natural voice aesthetic. Some of those drawn into the same orbit brought to it new kinds of knowledge and skills that enriched the ever-expanding field of practice now associated with natural voice work, broadly defined. In this part of the chapter, then, I propose to unpack further dimensions of certain of these ingredients—conceived from this point on as "connections"—and consider at greater length the properties that made them so well matched to the natural voice endeavour, while also illustrating their relevance as stages in the individual journeys of other voice workers and pioneers. What follows is therefore a combination of analytical commentary, historical contextualisation, and oral history. My primary source for the latter is a set of semi-structured narrative interviews carried out between 2007 and 2012, supplemented where appropriate by quotations from personal websites and other writings. The voices of many of those to whom the reader is introduced here will be heard again in the course of the descriptions, analyses, and debates that are the subject of later chapters. [9]

Musical Lives

By this point, some readers may well have detected a countercultural streak running through the natural voice world as I have depicted it. I begin, therefore, with a word of caution. It may be the case that the average NVPN member will not have the kind of focused musical background that we might associate with professional performers, conductors, or music teachers—excelling at instrumental lessons at school, singing in youth choirs or playing in orchestras, studying music at a university or conservatoire, and then perhaps gaining a diploma in performance, composition, or teaching—although, as we shall see, some have followed precisely this path. For the rest, this does not mean that they are lacking in either musicality or skill. However they have arrived there, a significant number of NVPN members now sustain busy lives as professional performers, music educators, or music therapists, alongside running community choirs or other dedicated singing groups, such as a mother and baby group or a Singing for the Brain group (the latter in association with the Alzheimer's Society). Some run their own music-related organisations; others maintain a private practice as a vocal coach. A surprising number have published original compositions and arrangements. Statements made by some practitioners themselves about their lack of formal training or advanced qualifications in "music" often mask a wealth of musical experience and competency and can therefore be misleading.

Gitika Partington's account of her musical background offers an interesting insight into the kind of rich and eventful musical journey that can exist in parallel with the conventional classical path (Partington 2001; http://gitikapartington.com/, acc. July 6, 2013). Gitika grew up in a working-class mining community in Lancashire, in a family of self-taught brass players, pianists, and choral singers. As The Partington Family Singers, she and her parents and siblings performed at community events, their repertoire ranging from American protest songs to four-part sacred music; among her memories of this time is a full-length concert that the family gave at Wigan's main concert hall when she was only ten years old. At school, however, she was not among the elite orchestral players who were considered the "real" musicians and so felt excluded from the world of "proper" music. An important formative experience came when, during her pre-university gap year, she studied meditation at an ashram in India, where the hours devoted to dancing reinforced her feeling for "the necessary link between music and dance". At university in London, she led weekly dance sessions at which she taught simple songs and dances from different parts of the world. Finding other musical activities closed to her because she had not, as she puts it, "climbed up the 'Examination Grades' ladder", she joined a rock band and began to write her own songs in a variety of styles using a four-track recording machine ("So I had no use for traditional notation," she explains). She earned a Bachelor of Arts (BA) degree in performance arts, to which she later added a Licentiate of the Guildhall School of Music (LGSM) diploma in jazz, a Postgraduate Certificate in Education (PGCE) in secondary teaching (specialising in music), and a Master of Arts (MA) degree in choral education. She also completed Estill Voice Training levels 1–3.

As well as working as a choral animateur for the British Federation of Young Choirs, she has delivered numerous long-term projects in schools, including her work for the Sing Up Vocal Force initiative, and she runs in-service training in singing for local education authorities and music services. This is all in addition to having undertaken (many years ago) one of Frankie's voice practitioner training weeks and having attended a host of workshops devoted to different genres and styles—from Georgian and Bulgarian, through gospel and shape note, to doo-wop and jazz. She has also published two volumes of her own pop arrangements (*Sing Pop A Cappella: Book 1* and *Sing Pop A Cappella: Book 2*) and is co-editor, with Ali Burns, of *Community Voiceworks* in Oxford University Press's Voiceworks series. Clearly, this is the profile of an accomplished musician whose training and experience is just as rigorous and valid as that of someone who has followed the more conventional (and quite possibly less varied) route of a strictly classical education.

The Folk Connection

Like Frankie, several practitioners have one foot in the folk world, and some played a prominent part in the English folk revival of the 1960s and 1970s. Sue Harris, who is also an accomplished hammered dulcimer player, has from the early 1970s been a familiar presence on the folk scene, performing and recording as a duo with John Kirkpatrick and playing in revival bands, such as the Albion Country Band. Touring around folk festivals in the early days gave her the opportunity to hear a lot of traditional singers—people who were "part of the unbroken tradition" rather than the revival (interview 2009). It was also through travelling to sessions in different parts of the country that Sue first crossed paths with Frankie and other folk singers who are now part of the natural voice network. Janet Russell, a later arrival on the folk circuit, made her mark in the 1980s with her work on Scottish traditional music and her own topical songs relating to women's issues. She continues to perform and record both as a solo artist and with the politically engaged *a cappella* group Sisters Unlimited and the newly formed JigJaw. The political commitment that is evident in her folk-related work carries over into her work with community choirs, in particular the East Lancs Clarion Community Choir. Other NVPN members who balance active recording and performance careers as folk musicians with directing community choirs include Yvette Staelens (founder member of the Roots Quartet, with which she performed from 1984),[10] Kate Barfield (also an accomplished fiddle player, who has performed and recorded with the Boat Band since 1989), and the late Sarah Morgan (a member of the *a cappella* trio Craig Morgan Robson, whose varied folk career spanned more than thirty years).[11]

Polly Bolton also started out as a folk singer in the early 1960s and in 1970 began performing professionally with the acoustic folk-rock band Dando Shaft (while also studying for a degree in zoology). She went on to work with a host of folk and jazz luminaries, including Bert Jansch, Ashley Hutchings, Kevin Dempsey, Alan Stivell, the Albion Band, and Show of Hands. Like Frankie, Polly cites Bulgarian music as an early discovery that came through her folk connections, recalling how John Martyn "turned us on to Bulgaria" by playing Bulgarian records when his musician friends came to visit. Attending one of Frankie's workshops turned out to be a major turning point for Polly. It was, she says, "the most wonderful day I'd ever spent in my entire life". An important dimension, she explains, was the effect of group harmony singing: as a solo performer, she'd never experienced "that fantastic feeling of singing with loads of other people". She came away thinking "I might have a bash at doing this" and then embarked on "a very, very steep learning curve of feeling that it was everyone's right to sing and wanting to help empower people to find their voices". "I'm *so* grateful to Frankie," she concludes. "She's an absolute inspiration.... I can't *imagine* what my life would be like had I not gone down that road" (interview 2009).

It is perhaps natural that working with songs from the British oral tradition should, for some at least, have led to an interest in songs from the oral traditions of other nations. The ethos of folk music as "roots" music (as opposed to the commercialised variety that has become part of the music industry) is also well matched to the natural voice philosophy that "anyone can sing". Source singers—and indeed, many revival singers—do not, as a rule, have formal music qualifications, and few have undertaken any kind of classical voice training. In the 1940s, 1950s, and 1960s, the message of Pete Seeger and other musical missionaries in the United States—promulgated in publications like the *People's Songs Bulletin* and *Sing Out!* as well as in the camps, rallies, clubs, and coffee houses where they performed and met their public face-to-face—was that anyone could pick up a guitar or banjo and sing. In this context, the voice was principally a vehicle for telling a story and spreading a message, not a carefully refined instrument to be judged on its aesthetic merits or its mastery of "technique". And when Pete Seeger got the crowds singing, he did so without having trained as a conductor. The songs themselves typically had accessible choruses that invited participation in the form of singing along, and they were meant for sharing.

Here it is worth recalling Walt Whitman's notion (expounded in the *Broadway Journal* in 1845) that if Americans were to build a morally responsible society, they would have to replace the courtly traditions of European "art-singing" with an aesthetic that subordinated style to substance in the form of "heart-singing" (Garman 2000: 81). Deliberately fashioning himself in Whitman's image, Woody Guthrie—the archetypal troubadour—saw himself not as an entertainer but as an educator, and set about redefining a place for "culture" in the lives of common working people. As Charles McGovern puts it:

> Here Guthrie's legacy to rock and roll was one with the legacy of the blues and country music: you didn't have to be a schooled musician or have a trained voice to communicate.... That aesthetic was essential for linking music and social change. (McGovern 1999: 125)

Guthrie was to echo Whitman's sentiments in a letter he penned to fellow Almanac Singers Pete Seeger, Lee Hays, and Millard Lampell in 1941:

> And it is our job if we claim the smallest distinction as American Folk Lorists [sic], to see to it that the seeds are sown which will grow up into free speech, free singing, and the free pursuit of happiness that is the first and simplest birthright of a free people. (quoted in Cohen 1999: 144)

Sentiments such as these clearly resonate with the ethics and ideology of the NVPN. The front page of Guthrie's book of songs and jokes called *On a Slow Train to California* (which he sold for twenty-five cents) famously bore the inscription: "This book has an iron-clad copyright.... Anybody caught singing one of these songs... will be a good friend of mine, because that's why I wrote 'em." Again, it is interesting to find statements in a similar spirit in some of the books of original compositions produced by NVPN members.

The Political Connection

If, in many parts of the world, collectively sung songs play an indispensable role in social life, newly composed topical songs in the folk idiom have provided a more direct link between folk revivals and contemporary sociopolitical movements, as has been well-documented with regard to the American civil rights and anti-war movements of the mid-twentieth century, for example. David Burbidge, who uses a lot of English folk material in the community choirs he runs in the Lake District, says it was partly these political associations that first attracted him to folk music in preference to rock, which he found too aggressive. The "revolutionary spirits of the time" to whom he was drawn as a teenager, he explains, were mostly folksingers (interview 2007). It is not surprising to find that many natural voice practitioners in Britain had their first powerful experience of unaccompanied, collective singing at rallies or benefit concerts connected with the Campaign for Nuclear Disarmament (CND), the anti-apartheid movement, the women's movement, or the miners' strike of 1984–1985. It is in these same contexts that some were also introduced to songs from other countries, notably South Africa. Collective singing in turn reinforced the association of singing with a sense of community and solidarity. Reflecting on her strongest formative memories of singing with others, Moira Hill, for example, cites

CND marches in the 1960s, followed by Reclaim the Night marches in the 1970s and Greenham Common in the 1980s. Years later, Moira joined the East Lancs Clarion Choir directed by Janet Russell, and then went on to launch the Bolton Clarion Choir as well as the Preston People's Choir and Kadenza women's choir. "Every song we sing," she writes, "from Georgian music to folk songs, to songs from other countries, and songs of protest and revolution, shows us and those we sing for that we are part of a bigger picture and that singing is political action too" (2007: 19). Jules Gibb identifies the tradition of the political choir that was especially strong in the North of England as part of another important pathway that would lead some people to the NVPN. These choirs (described in more detail in chapter 7) were a prominent feature at the marches and strikes that proliferated during the years Margaret Thatcher was prime minister, and they formed an informal network through which songs were exchanged. It was in this context—a decade before "community choirs" and "workshops" became fashionable, Jules comments—that she and others first cut their teeth in the song-teaching business (interview 2011).

Political engagement is also an important strand in Sarah Harman's story of finding her way to the natural voice clan. She was a member of the Cardiff-based Côr Cochion (Reds Choir), which "used music in a campaigning way", to support the miners' strike and the international anti-apartheid movement, for example.[12] She remembers "singing in supermarkets [and] getting dragged out by the police for stopping people buying South African goods". "So," she reflects, "some of my singing tradition is about being punished for singing." It was through her political involvement that she first became aware of Frankie Armstrong. "She was one of my heroines," she explains, "mostly because I used to go on CND marches and Frankie used to be on the stage singing" (interview 2008).[13]

The Theatre Connection

My discussion of the Giving Voice initiative in chapter 2 has already highlighted the influence of trends in contemporary theatre on the approach some natural voice practitioners take to voicework. Reference has also been made to Frankie's theatrical involvement. Theatre figured prominently in the career paths of several practitioners I interviewed, and was often the bridge over which they crossed into the world of voice. In particular, Dartington College of Arts, Cardiff Laboratory Theatre, and the Centre for Performance Research emerge as important training grounds for several NVPN members. Helen Chadwick attended Dartington, and it was her subsequent work in theatre that furthered her interest in singing. (Her attraction to unaccompanied harmony singing began in her early teens when she heard church music by English composers, such as Stanford and Byrd, at King's College Chapel in Cambridge, where she grew up.) In 1979, she became a founder member of Dr. Foster's Travelling Theatre Company, which soon established itself as a leading community theatre group in southwest England, and not long afterwards she joined Cardiff Laboratory Theatre. Attending a series of voice workshops around this time (including one led by Frankie Armstrong) allowed her to explore a wider range of vocal styles and techniques.

Chris Rowbury (founder of Coventry's WorldSong choir) became involved in experimental and physical theatre after initially training as a computer scientist. It was in the context of his work with Cardiff Laboratory Theatre's successor, the Centre for Performance Research, that he was introduced to intensive voice work that included regular vocal workouts with Joan Mills supplemented by specialist workshops with guest practitioners. "I'd never really sung before in my life," he recalls, "and then I found myself singing Balkan songs and weird stuff…. I just fell in love with it, really." He was working as a senior lecturer in theatre in the Performing Arts Department at Coventry University when he established his own singing group. He reflects that, while he had much to learn about "the musical side of it", his twenty years of teaching experience had prepared him well for the role of group leader (interview 2008).

Sarah Harman and David Burbidge also started out in theatre. After earning a degree in English and theatre, Sarah worked for some time as an actress before discovering the voluntary arts and becoming a drama worker in community arts organisations. It was at this point that she also encountered community music through the newly established Cardiff Community Music programme, and, soon after completing the community music teaching course, she took over managing it. Her encounter with the natural voice world in the early 1990s coincided with her shift of focus from drama to voice work. Her theatre skills stood her in good stead, and, in the early days of running singing groups, she used many of the warm-up exercises she had learned during her theatre training (interview 2008). David began his voice-work training while he was still at drama school, and subsequently worked as an actor while developing parallel careers in journalism and psychotherapy. In his present work he also draws on more than thirty years of yoga practice and incorporates elements of other body-based disciplines, such as tai chi, Feldenkrais, and the Alexander technique. In his early years as a natural voice practitioner, he was an avid workshop participant, honing his working methods at events organised by the Centre for Performance Research and other bodies, such as Folkworks.[14] In addition to Frankie Armstrong (with whom he trained), he counts Kristin Linklater, Enrique Pardo, and Augusto Boal, who all come from the theatre world, among his main influences.

The Classical Connection

In the sections that follow, we hear from a number of practitioners who had trained as classical musicians but later found greater fulfilment working in the voluntary sector and put the classical world behind them. Here I consider briefly two practitioners who remain committed to the fundamental tools and techniques with which their classical training has equipped them while applying their skills to the project of bringing a wider range of music to a more inclusive singing community.

Michael Harper, the classically trained counter-tenor, opera singer, and accomplished gospel singer introduced in chapter 1, describes how he reached his personal "fork in the road": "I was knocking at these doors in classical music and sometimes they were opening and a lot of times they weren't.... [At the same time] there were people opening doors for me in this world music area and saying, 'Come, we want you to do this'." He therefore proceeded by simultaneously pursuing work in the worlds of community music (including running his own arts organisation, the Lodge Farm Project), music education (including working as a consultant and trainer for Youth Music and Sing Up), and classical music (including acting as Associate Artistic Director and Chorus Master for Pegasus Opera Company and maintaining his own private practice with studios in England and Norway). As part of his mission "to get Britain singing again", he has been keen to break down some of the barriers between these different worlds. If he has any misgivings about the NVPN, he says, they concern "the technical side of it", and one of his contributions to the Unicorn camp has been to offer introductions to sight reading. He meets other natural voice practitioners on common ground in his commitment to "empowering people to sing but not only to sing, because I think singing goes deeper than that. For me the singing is only a tool...It's a journey, it's not just about my voice" (interview 2008).

Michael Deason-Barrow, director of the Tonalis Music Centre in Stroud, similarly seeks to bring about a more holistic engagement with diverse musical repertoires, from classical, early music, and contemporary classical to world, folk, and jazz. His voice was first brought to a national audience when as a choirboy with Salisbury Cathedral Choir he was featured as a soloist on radio and television and also made a number of recordings. He later went on to study singing at the Royal College of Music in London. In his account of his growing attraction to sounds from more distant parts of the world, it is interesting to find references to some of the same landmarks that appear in Frankie's story. He mentions, for example, the draw of Collet's record shop in the 1970s and tells of being so struck by the voices of Le Mystère des Voix Bulgares bursting out of his car radio that he had to stop driving and listen. *Mankind's Music*, a radio series by David Attenborough, was another revelation (pers. comm. April 27, 2013). When he came to pursue his fascination with world vocal styles at closer quarters, he was able to apply his expert technical knowledge to analysing how different sounds and effects were produced and, in his teaching, his intimate understanding of how the vocal mechanism works allows him to help his students explore unfamiliar vocal qualities in ways that are both effective and healthy. At the same time, his grounding in anthroposophy informs his promotion of "holistic music teaching methods that speak to the whole human being—body, mind, heart and spirit" (http://www.tonalismusic.co.uk/, acc. July 9, 2013). Michael's professional work now ranges from giving masterclasses in conservatoires to working with community choirs, children's groups, and "uncertain singers". At the Tonalis Centre (which he founded in 1991), he offers a suite of two-year vocational training courses, including Music Education, Community Music, Music as a Therapeutic Practice, and Choir Leading and Choral Conducting. The extensive list of weekend workshops that he delivers at locations across Britain include Giving Voice to Community, Renewing Music as a Community Art, and World Voice. Publicity materials for World Voice carry the taglines "Expand the Borders of Singing" and "Discover your Multi-cultural Voice". An acknowledgement and appreciation of the "multiplicity of extraordinary world singing styles and beautiful choral idioms" to which our ears have been opened since the late 1980s lies behind Michael's insistence that "what we mostly hear today is the specialised voice, not the 'whole voice'". His aim therefore is to lead singers towards "new more open-minded and holistic paradigms in singing" that bring together "voices from ancient traditions with modern research" (World Voice promotional leaflet, 2013). This and other descriptions that appear in Michael's publicity materials—we find further references in the publicity for World Voice to a "singing adventure", "celebrat[ing] the richness of singing in its broadest sense", creating "a unique singing community", and discovering the "healing power" of singing in different vocal styles—clearly chimes with the philosophy of nurturing, empowering, and broadening horizons that is a hallmark of the natural voice ethic.

The Community Music Connection

The community music world has served as an alternative training ground for some practitioners, who may be members of Sound Sense (the national professional association for community musicians) as well as the NVPN. The community music movement shares with the NVPN a cardinal commitment to extending music-making opportunities to those who are more often excluded. A statement formulated by the Community Music Activity Commission of the International Society of Music Education lists as its guiding principles decentralisation, accessibility, equal opportunity, and active participation in music making, noting that "these principles are social and political ones, and there can be no doubt that community music activity is more than a purely musical one" (Olseng 1990: 59). Community music organisations typically act as an umbrella for a wide variety of activities, including specialist work with people with physical, sensory, or learning disabilities or mental health issues or addictions, as well as people confined to institutions, vulnerable young people, refugees, and suburban communities that have been identified as suffering from economic and social deprivation; they may also offer more broadly recreational and educational courses aimed at the general public. Here we begin to appreciate the point at which some kinds of community music activity move closer to the world of therapy, as discussed in the following section. A broader contemporary definition given by Lee Higgins, however, is applicable to many natural voice practitioners and resonates clearly with the NVPN philosophy:

> Often a response to an unjust situation, community music practice has at its heart a commitment to cultural democracy, a call for both action and appropriate intervention, a system of support and respect for the many cultures and communities across the world. (Higgins 2013: viii)

Jane Wells (co-director of the Big Heart and Soul Choir in Castle Acre, Norfolk) found her feet in the community music world after first following what she refers to as "a rather standard middle-class classical music education", which included attending the junior department of the Royal College of Music before studying for a degree in Music at Durham. She also undertook postgraduate study in composition. As a freelance musician, however, Jane was incrementally drawn into the world of community arts. She worked with the Arts and Education team at Battersea Arts Centre and later moved to Norfolk, where she worked as an Arts Council funded musician-in-residence and as a project worker with Norfolk Music Works. In Norfolk, she was introduced to the work of Sian Croose—"probably the first person on this patch working in that way"—and this inspired her to establish a series of singing groups when she took up a new post as County Music Worker in Lincolnshire (interview 2008).

Based in Norwich, Sian Croose is well known in natural voice circles, not least because of her involvement with Sing for Water (as both a soloist and a conductor), but sees herself as having stronger ties with the community music world, since it was this network that nurtured and nourished her. She notes that the community music movement predates the consolidation of the natural voice network, and comments that while the remit of community music is broader, its ethos is in many respects similar: "very much about participation and about an alternative to...the straight music world—the more experimental, the multicultural, all of those things" (interview 2008). Her trajectory towards becoming a voice practitioner began in 1980 with her first work experience (as part of the Youth Opportunity Scheme) at Norwich

Arts Centre. For her, the arts centre functioned as "a kind of informal university of performing arts". She was able to take part in the arts centre's progamme of public workshops and she joined the Theatre in Education group that was based there. A weekend workshop led by Helen Chadwick was a turning point for Sian, and she has never looked back: "Probably about half an hour in, I thought, 'This is what I want to do.'... All of it was just a great experience and I think literally the next week I started a choir." The Norwich Women's Soul Choir quickly became a quirky and much-loved feature of Norwich life and later had a moment of national fame when it appeared on the popular BBC television programme *That's Life* (presented by Esther Rantzen). Sian recalls how, setting out with just a single song ready to teach, she kept a step ahead by learning a new song every week. At the same time, she enrolled in a one year apprenticeship with the newly formed Community Music East, where she was introduced to music fundamentals, learned about the mechanics of running groups, and immersed herself in a new, unconventional sound world, where "the musical boundaries were really a long way out". She augmented her material and skills by attending events such as those organised by the Magdalena Project in Cardiff,[15] where she once did a weeklong workshop with Frankie Armstrong, and by frequenting places like Laurieston Hall.

One of Sian's recent initiatives is The Voice Project, an innovative music education and performance project that "bring[s] together outstanding musicians and community choirs in events that combine the ethos of community music with cutting-edge creativity and high performance and production values" (http://voiceproject2.wordpress.com/, acc. December 23, 2011). Sian, then, is another example of someone on a quest to bridge the divide between different musical worlds by challenging assumptions and extending the boundaries of what is possible.

The Therapy Connection

The NVPN counts a number of qualified therapists in its ranks. These include registered music therapists, psychotherapists, and counsellors, alongside teachers of the Alexander technique, shiatsu, and other body-based disciplines. As we saw in Frankie's case, work in these areas, even when it is not directly concerned with music, can be a source of valuable insights that may be applied in natural voice work. Those who have worked in the field of community or co-operative development, for example, have become adept at managing group dynamics, while those who have trained in counselling or stress management are equipped with an understanding of the ways in which an individual's creative energy can become blocked and with a toolkit for helping to release these blocks.

Music therapists share with other kinds of therapists the humanistic goal of helping individuals realise their full potential. Community music therapy is now a recognised movement within contemporary music therapy, and it also embraces some of the guiding principles of community music—participation, accessibility, equal opportunity, empowerment, and enabling individual creativity. Juliette Alvin, writing in 1966, characterised music therapy as "a rational discipline which adds to music a new dimension, binding together art, science and compassion" (1991: 3). Alvin and other pioneers in the United Kingdom (among them Paul Nordoff, Clive Robbins, and Mary Priestley) worked within the broader context of the post-war promotion of health and education for all; they thus may be counted as early champions of musical democratisation. As Brunjulf Stige expresses it:

> Music therapy...has challenged restricted notions about what music is and about who could and should participate in music. In this way, music therapists have contributed to a better understanding of how music may link to human values such as dignity, respect, and quality of life. (Stige 2010a: 13).

While Alvin and others experimented with ensembles and music clubs as well as working intensively with individuals, the practices that were subsequently formalised focused largely on one-to-one work. As music therapy became increasingly professionalised in the 1980s and 1990s, clinical work within conventional therapeutic boundaries took precedence: music therapy became affiliated with medicine, special education, and psychotherapy, and much of its literature dealt with music's effect on individual pathology and symptomatology (Stige 2010a: 10).[16] In Britain, as in many other parts of Western Europe, professional music therapy is now part of a formalised process involving patient assessment procedures, goal-oriented treatment programmes, and appropriate forms of evaluation.

Community music therapy, on the other hand, is less a unified theory and practice than "a broad perspective exploring relationships between the individual, community, and society in relation to music and health" (Stige 2010a: 15–16). Community music therapy functions as a way of "giving voice to the relatively disadvantaged" within a broader agenda of promoting empowerment and participation (11). Grounded in a psychosociocultural as opposed to a biomedical model, community music projects are not usually treatment oriented; rather, they are designed to promote health and prevention, and may be offered in collaboration with other sectors such as education and social care (Stige et al. 2010b: 282). Stige's characterisation of the post-2000 international community music therapy movement as a form of practice that "goes beyond conceptions of music therapy in community settings to also embrace music therapy *as* community and music therapy *for* community development" (Stige 2010a: 10) clearly chimes with the kind of work undertaken by many natural voice practitioners who, whether or not they have had formal training in music therapy (or, indeed, any other therapy), are clearly using music in ways that are broadly therapeutic, while remaining firmly positioned in the realm of "community".

It is easy, then, to see how readily some of the principles of music therapy and community music therapy can be adapted to working with open-access choirs, and more particularly, with individuals who may feel vulnerable or challenged, where the ability to maintain a positive and nurturing environment is crucial. Working with specific client groups (e.g. the mental health or primary care services) requires one to be interested in, and good at, working with people as much as music, and in some cases to have specialist knowledge of particular health conditions. Unlike a professional choir conductor, the leader of an open-access choir is not there simply to direct the musical activity, impart musical expertise, and develop musical competence. He or she is also there to build community and to foster what Stige calls a "culture of care" in which self-care, care for others, and professional care "seem to be linked in many ways" (2010c: 269).

Teresa Verney is a natural voice practitioner who combines a solid classical music background with training as a therapist. Prior to her entrée into voice work, she had worked as a professional freelance musician, and had also spent fifteen years as a social worker before retraining in hypnotherapy and psychotherapy. She grew up in what she describes as "a very classically orientated family" and later won a place at Birmingham Conservatoire, where she studied oboe, piano, and voice. Her first job as a professional musician, however, was a profound disappointment, and—playing cor anglais in the hot, dusty orchestra pit of a theatre—she found the working environment uncongenial. A major turning point came in 2000, when a brochure from Cortijo Romero, a residential centre in Spain that offers alternative holidays, dropped through her letterbox. A course entitled "Find Your Voice", led by Frankie Armstrong and David Burbidge, caught her eye. She describes the week she spent in Spain as "life-changing":

> The impact of Frankie's approach was enormous and none of my previous training experiences had ever touched me so deeply. For the first time I was not judged and every sound I made was "good enough". I found my own very special voice and with it I was able to express many emotions that had been hitherto suppressed. (http://teresaverney.com/, acc. December 23, 2011)

This was her entrée into a world that would allow her to deploy her musical skills in a more rewarding setting. Part of her immediate reaction was to say: "Well, if this has had this effect on me, what on earth is it going to have on other people?" Informed by her training as a therapist, she now embarked on a mission "to integrate the idea of using your voice as a way of working therapeutically" (interview 2008). Alongside the regular weekly singing groups she now runs, she also offers individual sessions in which she takes people's personal stories as a starting point for helping them find their voice. This work, she says, has convinced her that "[working with] the voice as a therapeutic tool is far more affective than spending many hours talking through life experiences" (www.teresaverney.com, acc. May 1, 2009). The overriding advantage of natural voice work in general, she observes, is that "you can pitch it at any level you want or at any type of person or client group you want—anything. It's completely all-encompassing, because almost everybody loves to sing" (interview 2008).

The Circle Dance, Summer Camp, and Alternative Community Connection

The journey that led Nickomo Clarke to the NVPN took him along pathways that appear only tangentially in Frankie's story but are equally important to the overall picture. I tell Nickomo's story in a little more detail here since it also provides the background to my case study of the Unicorn Natural Voice Camp in chapter 8. Nickomo shares with most of his fellow practitioners a strong childhood attraction to music. The Beatles were his most profound influence, and he later developed a passion for the blues and African music. Bulgarian music also features in his story: he tells of how his parents took a trip to Bulgaria and brought back a record that made a deep impression on him. At secondary school, he played in a band which, he says, was "almost like a skiffle band ten years too late", and in his undergraduate years he was in a traditional folk band which played in folk clubs in South Wales. Although he first entered college to study music, he found himself uncomfortable in an environment where creativity was discouraged in favour of a strict academic approach ("it was almost stifling my love of music") and he eventually graduated with a degree in philosophy before going on to train as a primary school teacher (interview 2007).

The path that would eventually lead him to the natural voice world began when he discovered circle dancing. In the context of what would take on the attributes of a scene in the United Kingdom, "circle dance" refers to folk dances (mainly from different parts of Europe) danced in circles as opposed to couples or sets. A selection of such dances was introduced to the Findhorn community in Scotland in the mid-1970s by German dancer and choreographer Bernard Wosien (1908–1986). Wosien believed that the dances contained important cosmic and spiritual symbolism (the circle, representing unity and wholeness, offered protection against the forces of chaos) and thus had the potential to nurture and sustain community (for which Findhorn offered fertile ground).[17] Circle dance or "sacred dance", as it came to be known in Findhorn, spread throughout Britain and beyond, transmitted by a growing network of teachers via weekly dance groups, weekend workshops, and summer dance camps—a format that would later be followed in the natural voice world.[18] The circle dance scene has its parallel in the Society for International Folk Dancing (SIFD), and many of the same dances constitute the repertoire of SIFD teachers. In the SIFD world, however, the dances tend to be approached in a more athletic manner and participants generally have minimal interest in the esoteric dimensions, whereas in Findhorn and elsewhere sacred dance/circle dance continues to be viewed—in part, at least—as ritual and spiritual practice. The circle dance repertoire also includes newly choreographed dances set to classical, contemporary popular, and New Age music, whereas the SIFD repertoire consists entirely of "authentic" (if stylised) folk dances accompanied by traditional songs and melodies.[19]

From the outset, many people were drawn to circle dance as much for the music they danced to as for the dancing itself, and several musical ensembles were formed in different parts of the country to provide live music for dance sessions as an alternative to the music recorded on cassette tapes that circulated in the 1980s. The core repertory consisted of dances from Eastern Europe, and for many singers these served as their first introduction to songs from this part of the world. The dance camps established in the 1980s that had circle dance as their main focus were the direct inspiration for the dedicated voice camps that arrived later, beginning with the Unicorn Natural Voice Camp in 1998.

It was at his first-ever circle dance event, a day workshop in Bristol led by a teacher from Findhorn, that Nickomo met James Burgess, with whom he would later collaborate as part of the Unicorn Camps team. Through the weekly circle dance group that Nickomo then joined, he heard about the Glastonbury camp that he attended in 1986.[20] It was here that he met (among others) Colin Harrison and Nick Prater, who would become long-standing friends and collaborators. Colin Harrison—who would later be a key player in the launch of the NVPN—was one of the leading circle dance teachers in the United Kingdom at the time and also taught material from his one-time home of South Africa. (Nickomo and his partner, Rasullah, would subsequently join Colin and his then partner, Anne Monger, to form a four-person team teaching South African songs and dances.) Nick Prater was part of two groups, Gnawa and Prana, which were active on the festival circuit, teaching chants as well as performing. Gnawa was a drum and dance group that had formed in Stroud under the guidance of Ghanaian master-musician Ben Baddoo. Prana, taking its name from the Sanskrit word meaning "breath" or "life-force", had grown out of a self-development and healing group based in West Wales and drew its musical and spiritual influences from the "Medicine songs of the North American Indians", the "ancient teachings of India", and "the impulse of the New Age" (1991: 1). In that first Glastonbury encounter, Nick appeared as a kind of role model for Nickomo: "I remember watching Nick Prater teach this song and it was kind of like I could see myself doing that" (interview 2007). When Nickomo later drew up the programme for the first Unicorn Natural Voice Camp, Nick (by this time specialising in gospel singing) would be invited as one of the core teachers.

Inspired by their revelatory experiences at the Glastonbury camp, Nickomo and Rasullah offered to host a Tarot group that James Burgess wished to start. Nickomo wrote some chants to help explain the Major Arcana, and before long the group had become the Bristol Chant Group, singing Prana chants, Taizé chants, and songs from the circle dance and universal peace dance repertoires that would be disseminated further through the songbook and tape/CD set *Chants for Sharing*.[21] Using this same material, Nickomo also began offering song sessions at some of the new summer camps that were springing up in the late 1980s, including Dance Camp Wales. This, together with the success of the South African package he developed with Colin Harrison, expanded his audience and eventually led to the birth of the Unicorn Natural Voice Camp.

Dance Camp Wales became an important meeting ground for those working at the intersection of music and dance. It also served as a critical turning point for Jackie Roxborough in the way that the Cortijo Romero "Find Your Voice" week had for Teresa Verney. Jackie is another practitioner who began her career in the classical world, where she spent several years performing and teaching classical guitar after completing a degree in music at Huddersfield. Later, her work with contemporary music brought her into contact with extended vocal technique, which presented itself as a form of liberation. In 1992, she found herself at Dance Camp Wales and it was there that she met "this whole culture...of natural voice". The experiences at the camp were her "baptism into global music", particularly, "a baptism by fire into African music" as she was faced with the unexpected challenge of mastering the cowbell part in the percussion group directed by Ben Badoo. It was the South African singing, however, and the contrast it provided with the kind of choir experience with which she was more familiar that really got her "hooked in". "It was a real moment of, gosh, this is a real joy singing this music and also having to move your body. You can't stand still!" (interview 2007). The training she underwent with a teacher of Postural Integration in Los Angeles the following year equipped her with further skills that aided her project of "opening out" and freeing herself from the constraints of being a classical musician. Along the way, she also acquired qualifications in business applications and information technology, and holistic massage, relaxation and stress management, and these were among the many strands that came together in her own voice work. At the time of our interview in 2007, she was running a number of singing groups, including Birmingham International Voices, a group she had set up by invitation of the director of the College for International Citizenship to bring together musicians and singers from different parts of the world. She had also established the United Kingdom's first female Muslim performance group, the

Muslim Women's Collective. She went on to develop several new projects, some under the auspices of Ulfah Arts, a not-for-profit organisation devoted to using the arts to bring about social change, working in particular with Muslim communities. What is of interest here is the way in which Jackie's chance attendance at a summer camp at which she was first introduced to "global music" in company that was not, in itself, ethnically diverse led to such extensive, direct collaboration with members of Britain's resident ethnic communities.[22]

The new Unicorn camps, in their turn, provided road-to-Damascus-style moments of revelation for a younger generation of voice practitioners, as exemplified by Bruce Knight. Bruce recounts how, after enjoying his first taste of African, Bulgarian, and gospel songs at singing sessions in Cambridge led by Rowena Whitehead (his musical activities to this point not having extended beyond "a bit of karaoke" as a teenager), he picked up a leaflet for the first ever Unicorn Natural Voice Camp and booked a place "on a whim". His stay at the camp turned out to be a life-changing experience, introducing him to a world he had never before imagined:

> From the very start I was totally into it, completely blown away by the whole experience of camping around fires. The whole subculture was very new to me and for the first time in my life I experienced physical spine-tingles from songs and enjoyed spiritual, "holy" moments in the big top singing a lovely song, and getting a wonderfully sublime feeling. (Knight interview 2008)

He was especially excited by the South African songs he learned with Colin Harrison and Nickomo and the gospel songs taught by Nick Prater. The camp also alerted him to the fact that there was a countrywide network of community choirs that operated along similar lines to Rowena's group in Cambridge and that some people managed to earn their living doing this kind of work. This realisation planted the seed that would later lead him to establish his own choir in Leamington Spa, abandon his career as an environmental scientist, and go on to become part of the Unicorn teaching team.

Meanwhile, Kate O'Connell was instrumental in grafting a natural voice branch onto the sacred dance tree that had taken such firm root in Findhorn. Kate had initially trained as a drama/movement teacher at Dartington. In the late 1970s she went to live at Laurieston Hall, an intentional community near Castle Douglas in southwest Scotland, and it was there that she first encountered Frankie Armstrong.[23] She recalls the immediate impact Frankie had on her: "I went to one of her workshops and she got us all making a great loud noise and I walked out of the workshop and went: 'Oh, I can do this.' And that was it. That was how I started." Kate also makes an explicit link with the women's movement and the growth of feminist consciousness: "We'd come from being sweet singers at school [and] suddenly there was this women's movement, Frankie Armstrong, natural voice, 'yes, we can sing out!' and it all just came into focus" (interview 2008). The experience inspired Kate to start running her own workshops at Laurieston. Later, she was invited to become part of the music team at Dance Camp Wales, co-leading the choir and, as part of a small ensemble, playing live music for dancing.[24] By this time, she had moved to Findhorn and with her partner Rory had launched a resident band to provide live music for sacred dance. Kate inaugurated the Midsummer Festival of Sacred Dance, Music and Song in 1992, seeing it as a way of "bringing the dance camp energy back to Findhorn". Kate's greatest achievement there, in her own estimation, is to have staged the international singing conference and festival Songs of Heaven and Earth (1996) in partnership with fellow Findhorn resident Barbara Swetina (who also taught Taizé chant at Dance Camp Wales). Among the invited teachers were Helen Chadwick, Edisher Garakanidze (from Georgia), Ysaye Barnwell (of Sweet Honey in the Rock fame), and Noah Pikes (from the Roy Hart Theatre). A number of NVPN members were among the more than two hundred delegates drawn from across the globe. Kate also responded to Nickomo's call for teachers when he was setting up the first Unicorn Natural Voice Camp and has attended almost every year since.

Ali (Alison) Burns also lived at Laurieston in the 1980s, and it was there that she took her first steps in songwriting, initially writing songs for the annual Women's Singing Week. Thanks to the numbers of people who passed through Laurieston, Ali's work quickly became known and she began to receive invitations to lead workshops in other parts of the country. In the early 1990s, she attended one of Frankie's training weeks, where she met other emerging practitioners, and she went on to play a central role in establishing the NVPN (interview 2008). Jules Gibb emphasises the "phenomenal" nature of what she terms "the Laurieston effect", observing that it was at Laurieston that she herself "became a voice worker"; many of the other singers she met there also went on to direct community choirs (interview 2011). For Rowena Whitehead, Laurieston Women's Singing Week, at which she was invited to teach, also functioned as an important "plug-in". It allowed her to meet other teachers and to assemble a substantial body of additional material to use with her own choirs (interview 2007). Kirsty Martin refers to the first Laurieston Women's Singing Week she attended as "the epiphany" and "the home-coming I'd been looking for all my life really". In her years of travelling, she explains, she had been looking for "this sort of feeling and this sort of community" but had never found it in one place before. Now, she knew that "that musical feeling was possible" (interview 2008).[25]

The World Music Connection

The first proper stirrings of the natural voice phenomenon coincided with the rise of world music. We have already seen how the circle dance and camp scene, on the one hand, and the more specialised workshops hosted by the Centre for Performance Research and led by overseas artists, on the other, gave for those who were so inclined to the opportunity to participate directly as singers, musicians, and dancers in the musical traditions of other cultures. The burgeoning of the world music industry also played its part. When Rowena Whitehead, for example, was launching her first singing group in Cambridge, she was working with a music venue called The Junction. Her role included programming world music nights and bringing in visiting musicians, some of whom she would also accompany when they undertook residencies in schools. It was in this way that she not only encountered such artists as the British Asian singer Samia Malik, Zimbabwean singer and mbira player Chartwell Dutiro, and the group Black Umfolosi, but was also able to train with them (interview 2007).

Other future practitioners had spent time living overseas and therefore had more sustained encounters with these "other" musics. David Burbidge was exposed to a range of music in his childhood years, which were spent in a series of foreign locations because his father worked for the United Nations. He still has vivid memories of fruit sellers in the Tatra Mountains in Poland who advertised their wares in song, and of folk song and dance in the Cypriot village he once called home. Likewise, Sally Davies (director of the Cecil Sharp House Choir and Hackney's Wing-It Singers), was exposed to music from many different cultures during her upbringing in an international children's village in Switzerland, where her parents were house parents. (The village had been set up at end of the Second World War as a home for displaced children from all over Europe and then continued on as a home for orphans.) The children were encouraged to keep their traditions alive, and so national dancing and singing were much in evidence. Sally recalls "pretend[ing] to speak all the languages... making the sounds" and how she especially loved the "slightly funny intervals" and "gutsy" sound of the Hungarian songs, alongside which the English offerings seemed somewhat lacklustre (interview 2008). This fascination with other sounds and styles accompanied her into her adult life. Also graduating from Dartington, where she majored in dance, she toured for several years with a variety of fringe theatre companies, writing music as well as performing. She later spent ten years as musical director and composer for Green Candle Dance Company. Many of the company's shows centred on a particular geographic location, so she would research and listen to the music of places like Zanzibar and Brazil and then write music sparked off by her explorations. She went on to study for a master's degree in ethnomusicology and composition at Kingston University. Eventually, in 2000, she was introduced to the NVPN and two years later began to work with community choirs. While she continues to use world songs in her work, Sally now specialises in original arrangements of English folk songs that are clearly influenced by the various musical idioms she has become familiar with through her research as well as her own life experiences.

Dessi (Dessislava) Stefanova and Polina Skovoroda-Shepherd are both highly proficient musicians who had undergone extensive training in the musical traditions of their respective national cultures before establishing a new life in Britain and being drawn into the natural voice orbit. Both women balance professional performing careers with their natural voice work, which focuses on specialist choirs and workshops dedicated to their native music. Dessi Stefanova is the founder-director of the London Bulgarian Choir, the Swiss Bulgarian Choir, and a professional vocal trio, the Dessibelles.[26] The London Bulgarian Choir gained national exposure when it won first place in the Open Category of the BBC Radio 3 Choir of the Year competition in 2006, and in 2009, it performed with rock band Doves at the BBC Electric Proms. The choir can also be heard on the soundtrack of *The Virgin Queen*, Paula Milne's dramatisation of the life of Elizabeth I, and on the Microsoft video game *HALO 4*.

Originally from Thrace in central Bulgaria, Dessi began her training in Western classical music at the age of six. At the same time, she was part of the children's folk music and dance company Zagorche, which was based in her hometown of Stara Zagora. After moving to the capital to study linguistics at Sofia University, she gained a place in the Philip Koutev National Folk Music and Dance Ensemble, with which she sang professionally for three years before moving to the United Kingdom in 2000. The London Bulgarian Choir, which she established not long after her arrival, resulted from an auspicious encounter with the natural voice network. She was alerted to an NVPN fundraising weekend at the Round Chapel in Hackney, and within ten minutes of arriving, she recalls, was asked if she would like to teach a song as part of the programme for the following day. There she also met a member of the London Georgian choir (later renamed Maspindzeli), who urged her to start a Bulgarian choir. Although she intially found it difficult to believe that anyone in London would want to sing Bulgarian songs, she soon had a fledgling group up and running and before long the choir blossomed into a community that became as important to Dessi herself as to any other member.

In addition to her busy schedule of running weekend workshops around the United Kingdom and elsewhere in Europe, Dessi has taught at the Unicorn Natural Voice Camp, at summer camps organised by the Vermont-based association Village Harmony (both in the UK and overseas), at the SOAS World Music Summer School, and at Laurieston Hall's Harmony Week. She has also been engaged to run sessions at music education conferences, such as MusicLearningLive. In addition to the repertoire itself and an intimate knowledge of the cultural context of the songs she introduces, one of the most valuable things Dessi has to offer is at the level of vocal technique and timbre as she guides her students through a series of exercises designed to bring them closer to the Bulgarian sound.[27]

Polina Shepherd, who enjoys an international profile as a performer of Russian and Yiddish songs, grew up in a musical household in Siberia and later trained at Kazan State Conservatory in Tatarstan. Currently based in Brighton, she performs with several ensembles including the Eastern European–style brass band Fanfara, the Merlin Shepherd Quartet, and the Sound & Light Cinematic Duo. She also does solo work as both singer and pianist and composes her own songs. She has established several community choirs, including the Brighton and Hove Russian Choir (winner of awards at the Russian Song Competition in London in 2010 and the Maslenitsa Competition in 2013), the London Russian Choir, the London Yiddish Choir, and, at University College London (UCL), the UCL East European Choir. The latter, which was active from 2010 to 2013, was co-directed with Bulgarian singer and fellow NVPN member Eugenia Georgieva, who subsequently launched a new Bulgarian choir, Veda Slovena, also based at UCL.[28] Like Dessi, Polina also teaches at the SOAS World Music Summer School and leads weekend workshops in different parts of the country, as well as teaching internationally: Austria, Switzerland, Eastern Europe, and Brazil are among her regular ports of call. Again, her teaching includes expert instruction in vocal style and technique, with an emphasis on ornamentation and improvisation. Together with others who teach their traditions to foreigners, both Polina and Dessi offer valuable perspectives on the questions of cultural exchange to which I return in later chapters.

THE NVPN AS COMMUNITY OF PRACTICE

The fact that individual practitioners have found their way to the natural voice and community choir world by many different routes and from many different starting points should not surprise us. Unlike music therapists, for example, natural voice practitioners do not undergo a formally accredited training programme, and there is no established career progression model. Apart from Frankie's training weeks and other privately run short courses an individual practitioner might invest in, much of their learning takes place on the job, with the help of a strong but informal peer-support network. Natural voice work has, in any case, only very recently been consolidated as a body of practice, and many of the teachers, performers, and practitioners we encountered in this chapter are among the pioneers who have contributed to its development.

As their stories show, the knowledge and skills acquired in a range of other professions have been of direct relevance to the kind of musical work undertaken by NVPN members. The profile and approach of the leader of an open-access, non-auditioned, non-sight-reading choir will inevitably differ from that of the conductor of an amateur classical choir or choral society in interesting ways. These differences relate to the choice of musical material, the teaching method, and the choir's perceived purpose or function. The notion of music as action rather than object implies, a priori, a different way of working. So, too, does a greater emphasis on participatory as opposed to presentational performance. Working from scores requires a particular facility on the part of the conductor, and, if the choir's main focus is on formal staged performances, then an appropriate level of polish and refinement must also be achieved; this in turn demands a certain kind of discipline. In the case of natural-voice-style choirs, the main activity may be singing, and the choir may at some point perform for others, but there are other goals and values at stake as well. This results in a rather different emphasis in which any "objective" notion of musical quality, or the assumption of musical "perfection" as the ultimate goal, is not necessarily the prime or sole consideration; compromises may be made in respect of such musical "standards" so that other goals may be achieved and other values are *not* compromised in the process. The achievement of these other goals requires its own kind of training and sensibility.

In the survey of "ingredients" and "connections" that has formed the basis of this chapter, it is interesting to note not only the recurrence of particular themes and experiences that were to become part of the natural voice jigsaw but also the significance of multiple meetings and crossings of ways that fed into shared histories and long-standing collaborations, with different kinds of milestones serving as muster points for those not only of different backgrounds and preferences but also of different generations. With respect to common experiences and defining moments, several intriguing threads emerge. Moments of conversion, liberation, and empowerment abound, often described by the speakers as an "epiphany", "revelation", or "baptism by fire". Not surprisingly, Frankie Armstrong has been directly responsible for many such conversions; similar life-defining moments were also orchestrated (albeit unintentionally) by Helen Chadwick, Nick Prater, and Ben Badoo. Laurieston Hall has featured as a beacon for a number of individuals, as have summer camps such as the Glastonbury camps, Dance Camp Wales, and the Unicorn Natural Voice Camp, alongside Kinnersley Castle and later Wortley Hall. In addition to functioning as fertile ground for informal, collective music making and for sharing resources, these have also been a step on the way to finding community or finding one's clan, with some of those attending then seeking to recreate that community spirit in their own locality. Circle dance has also been identified as an example of parallel network, a decade or so ahead of the natural voice network, which has both provided ways in and suggested ways forward.

In the early days of the natural voice enterprise, Frankie and Darien's training weeks and the reunions held at Kinnersley Castle fulfilled a crucial function in bringing both established practitioners and practitioners-to-be into contact with one other, allowing them to see themselves, for the first time, not as lone operators but as part of a peer group of like-minded professionals. Rowena

Whitehead describes the week she spent at Kinnersley in the mid-1990s with fourteen other trainees as an "ecstatic" experience. She had already been running her own singing group for some time but only now did she discover that "other people were doing what I did and stuff that I'd evolved on my own was happening elsewhere and it was wonderful". From then on, the annual reunions offered by the Kinnersley gatherings, the Laurieston singing weeks, and the Unicorn camps provided her with the "luxury" of having "a sort of staff room—somewhere to go to talk about what you do and people who know what it's about" (interview 2007). Nickomo was not part of the close-knit group that had originally formed around Frankie, but he found his way to the infamous Kinnersley party at which the NVNP was conceived via his friend Colin Harrison. Like Rowena, he was "astonished to meet a whole bunch of people who did the same thing that I did. It was a revelation!" (2007a: 23). He recalls his now legendary pronouncement: "This is the peerest peer group I've ever been in!" (interview 2007).

A useful point of reference here is Eugenio Barba's notion of "third theatre", a term adopted to cover the growing constituency of theatre makers that existed between the two more visible poles of official, subsidised theatre and the avant-garde. Barba's description of this middle world might well be applied to the NVPN in its formative period:

> The Third Theatre lives on the fringe, often outside or on the outskirts of the centres or capitals of culture. It is a theatre created by people who define themselves as actors, directors, theatre workers, although they have seldom undergone a traditional theatrical education and are therefore not recognized as professionals. But they are not amateurs. (Barba 1985: 193)

Barba had identified, in Susan Bassnett's gloss, "a new phenomenon...that of a collective turning to theatre not as a profession but as a way of life" (1989: 18). The metaphor he chose to characterise these collectives of in-between practitioners was "floating islands". This, too, would seem an apt descriptor, not only for the scattered individuals and groupings we have been concerned with here, but also for the sanctuary-like places where they come together. The sense of collegiality that is especially evident at the network's annual gatherings at Wortley Hall has been strengthened by the steady expansion of the NVPN newsletter and website. The level of consolidation arrived at by the annual gathering of 2013 was marked by the adoption of the descriptor "community of practice", defined by Etienne Wenger as "a group of people who share a concern, a set of problems, or a passion about a topic, and who deepen their knowledge and expertise in this area by interacting on an ongoing basis" (2002: 4). Wenger identifies three characteristic dimensions of such communities: mutual engagement, joint enterprise, and shared repertoire. The latter is, of course, especially apposite in the case of the NVPN. The members' area of the website now includes a page titled Community of Practice that carries notices about resource-sharing, regional networking meetings, and opportunities for "learning visits" to observe other choirs in action. It also lists details of experienced NVPN members who now offer their own training sessions for voice leaders.

The coming of age of the organisation itself been paralleled by a significant shift from what may have seemed like the diversions of niche or alternative contingents in the 1980s towards a more mainstream, middle-class identity by the early years of the new millennium. On returning to Britain after spending ten years in New Zealand, Nick Prater noticed a change in the types of people attending his workshops and choirs. What had previously been "quite a minority thing", attracting (in his experience) mainly "the long-haired hippies", now had a far wider appeal, pulling in "just ordinary people really getting into singing" (interview 2007).

This sea change is also reflected in the numbers of practitioners who are now able to make a living from running choirs and other voice-related projects. Income may be comparatively modest, but job satisfaction is high. Many of my interviewees spoke of the deep pleasure they derive from seeing so many of their choir members and workshop participants transformed by their singing experience. Dee Jarlett (co-director of Bristol's Gasworks Choir), when asked if she has a "best memory" relating to her work in this field, responds: "There are so many! It's such a lovely job. I just love the fact that singing makes so many people happy." She describes how when Naked Voices (a smaller *a cappella* ensemble of which she was a part until its dissolution in 2008) was invited to perform, they would always run a workshop before the concert and then invite the participants up on stage during the evening show:

> It's inevitable that wherever we go, those people in the workshop come out absolutely ecstatically happy because they've *loved* the afternoon's workshop, and then they come to the gig, they *love* the gig and they *love* singing on stage and everybody's happy.... And what a great job to be in, to make people happy! What could I ask for more? (Jarlett interview 2007)

She compares this with her previous experience of teaching computing skills, where her students "might be satisfied or they might learn something but they didn't come out with huge smiles on their faces, which they do after they've been singing". Polly Bolton also compares the personal satisfaction she derives from her present work with past experiences—in this case, the pressures of a "gigging" lifestyle, and more particularly the "paranoia" associated with the performance world and the sense of desolation she would often feel returning home late at night after a solo gig. Leading a workshop, by contrast, leaves her with "a fantastic feeling": "You drive home and you think: actually, I've done something really good today. I feel good about what I've done, where I've been, and how I've earned my pennies" (interview 2009). On her webpage she has written in a similar vein:

> I have spent many years dabbling in the music business, and have worked with some of the best folk and jazz musicians in the country. I have recorded several albums and have travelled and toured on and off for three decades. Nothing has given me more musical satisfaction, however, than the voice work I do now. (http://www.naturalvoice.net/pages/polly_bolton.html, acc. May 1, 2009)

This satisfaction rests not only in passing on musical knowledge but in becoming an agent of personal emancipation or collective transformation at a more radical, existential level.

Katherine Zeserson (member of the *a cappella* vocal ensembles Mouthful and Human Music, a familiar presence at Sing for Water, and, since 2002, the director of Learning and Participation for Sage Gateshead) alludes to the extensive range of skills that voice practitioners bring to the job:

> Being a voice worker is a bit like working for a roadside rescue firm—people are so pleased to see you. You engage in psychical midwifery, alchemy, psychology, body work, musical direction, teaching, information sharing, artistry, poetry, dance, consciousness-raising, leadership, philosophical enquiry, challenging, directing, nurturing, healing, partying. (Zeserson 2005: 125)

The manner in which these various components begin to take shape in a choir rehearsal or workshop is the subject of my next chapter.

NOTES

1. The details in this section are drawn primarily from an extensive personal interview with Frankie in 2008 and from her autobiography, *As Far as the Eye Can Sing* (1992). These are supplemented with additional data from her website (www.frankiearmstrong.com), her contributions to Armstrong and Pearson 2000 and Hampton and Acker 1997, and more recent conversations.
2. Frankie notes that she finds the designation "chest voice" problematic and now prefers to refer to this voice as the "basic voice".
3. Frankie's initial motivation for this visit to the United States was her desire to observe the work of Archie Lineburger, a highly respected, blind, group therapist in Philadelphia. Once there, she received invitations to perform at folk clubs, coffee houses, and other festivals across the United States and was able to extend her stay.
4. The Singers Club began life as the Ballads and Blues Club, founded by Ewan MacColl and A. L. Lloyd.
5. The Greenham Common Women's Peace Camp was established in 1981 as a protest against the British government's decision to site American cruise missiles at the RAF base at Greenham Common near Newbury in Berkshire. At the "Embrace the Base" initiative of December 1982, 30,000 women joined hands to form a chain almost ten kilometers (six miles) long that encircled the entire

base. The following April, an estimated 70,000 people formed a human chain that covered the twenty-three-kilometer (fourteen-mile) stretch from Greenham past Aldermaston, where the Atomic Weapons Research Establishment had been built on the site of former RAF Aldermaston, to the Royal Ordnance atomic weapons factory at Burghfield, near Reading. Frankie took part in the encircling of Aldermaston and Papworth Common, as well as the Greenham base.

6. Kinnersley Castle, the family home of NVPN member Katherina Garrett-Adams, plays host to a range of residential events.

7. When I interviewed Frankie in 2008, she and Darien had just completed their twenty-third training week. They have run similar courses for voice practitioners in Australia.

8. Over the course of her career, Frankie has also worked with a number of theatre companies, including Welfare State International, Opera Circus, Compass Theatre, and the Graeae Theatre Company (with which she toured to India).

9. Short biographies of the teachers and practitioners who receive more than a passing mention in the book, together with links to their websites, can be found on the book's companion website. The NVPN website also carries profiles of all its members. For an additional account of a personal vocal journey told in the practitioner's own words, see Goodman 2000.

10. Yvette's folk-related work—in this instance pertaining to her position as an academic associated with the Centre for Archaeology, Anthropology and Heritage at Bournemouth University—also includes The Singing Landscape Project, supported by a Knowledge Transfer Fellowship from the Arts and Humanities Research Council (see http://www.bournemouth.ac.uk/caah/culturalresource-management/folkmaps.html, acc. July 6, 2013).

11. Sarah's published songbooks include arrangements of English folk songs and original compositions in three- and four-part harmony for community choirs.

12. In 2013, Côr Cochion listed on its website the following campaigns as being among those to which it lent its support: Amnesty International, Liberty, Cymru Cuba, Nicaragua Solidarity, Campaign Against Arms Trade, Campaign for Nuclear Disarmament, Voices in the Wilderness, Women for Peace, Medical Foundation for Victims of Torture, Palestine Solidarity Campaign, Greenpeace, Unite, Searchlight, and Colombia Solidarity (see http://www.corcochion.org.uk/, acc. July 6, 2013).

13. When Frankie later moved to Cardiff, she and Sarah worked together in a community music programme which Sarah ran and for which Frankie became a tutor.

14. Folkworks, now part of The Sage Gateshead, was established in 1988 by Ros Rigby and Alistair Anderson as the folk-music development agency for the North of England.

15. The Magdalena Project was launched with the International Festival of Women in Experimental Theatre held in Cardiff in 1986. Magdalena '86 (as the event came to be known) was staged in association with Cardiff Laboratory Theatre, of which Magdalena's director, Jill Greenhalgh, was then a member. Vocal work featured prominently, with workshops led by (among others) Helen Chadwick, Kozana Lucca, and Ida Kelarova, and this set the trend for future festivals, with some overlap in both workshop leaders and clientele between Magdalena and the projects curated by the Centre for Performance Research.

16. In 1958, Alvin had founded the Society of Music Therapy and Remedial Music, which in 1967 was renamed the British Society for Music Therapy (BSMT). The

Guildhall School of Music and Drama went on to establish, in 1968, the first full-time course that trained qualified musicians as therapists, initially under Alvin's direction. The Association of Professional Music Therapists (APMT) was formed in 1976; its membership was open to qualified therapists only. In 1982, the Department of Health and Social Security finally established a career and grading structure for music and art therapists, recognising them as members of a paramedical profession, similar to speech therapists, physiotherapists, and occupational therapists.

17. The Findhorn Foundation—today styling itself a spiritual community, ecovillage, and international centre for holistic education—had its beginnings in 1962, under the spiritual guidance of Eileen Caddy, one of its three co-founders. The programme of workshops and other events offered by the Findhorn Foundation community association attracts approximately 3,000 residential guests annually.
18. The circle dance network is now represented by the organisation Circle Dance Friends Company Ltd. (http://www.circledancenetwork.org.uk, acc. July 6, 2013).
19. Readers familiar with the Balkan dance scene in the United States will recognise points of contact with both the SIFD and circle dance ethos.
20. What are referred to (here and more generally) as the Glastonbury camps should not be confused with the world-famous Glastonbury Festival. They are two completely separate ventures.
21. So-called Taizé chants originated with the international ecumenical Christian community based near the village of Taizé in Burgundy, France (founded in 1940). Home to over a hundred monks of thirty or more nationalities, Taizé attracts more than 100,000 visitors a year and is widely known for its distinctive repertoire of simple, meditative songs, sung in harmony. The nature of the Taizé repertoire and its appeal in the natural voice context is explored in greater detail in chapter 5.
22. Jackie was also involved in establishing Kissing It Better, an initiative directed at improving the patient experience in hospitals and care homes that began as a pilot project in Walsall before going national (see http://www.kissingitbetter.co.uk). Her brief here was to develop activities for patients (particularly those with dementia and Alzheimer's) that would use singing to engage them through reminiscence. At the same time, she expanded her work in the corporate sector, becoming the main voice trainer for the National Association of Schoolmasters Union of Women Teachers (NASUWT), the UK's largest teachers' union. "All of this," she says, "came out of my Natural Voice approach and I'm ever grateful to the Natural Voice Practitioners' Network for enabling me to evolve such a platform for myself" (pers. comm. July 21, 2012).
23. Laurieston Hall was established as a community in 1972. Between Easter and October, it hosts a programme of residential courses and workshops managed by the co-operative Laurieston Hall People Centre.
24. Kate and I ran the choir at Dance Camp Wales together for several years, starting in 1988. I also played and sang in the ad hoc circle dance band, together with Kate, Rory, and others.
25. It is, of course, noteworthy that these references are specifically to the Women's Singing Week. In the NVPN as a whole, women significantly outnumber men.
26. Since leaving Bulgaria, Dessi has also performed with London-based Balkan groups Izvor and Dunav, the British-Bulgarian story-telling company A Spell in Time, the medieval ensemble Joglaresa, and the New York–based worldbeat

fusion outfit Balkan Beat Box, in addition to appearing as a soloist on numerous film soundtracks. She is also the music director of the choral performance project Whispering Woods.
27. Dessi also holds a master's degree in music from London's School of Oriental and African Studies and has completed Estill Voice Training to Level 3.
28. Eugenia performs with a variety of professional ensembles and is the artistic director of the Perunika Trio. Her voice can also be heard on film soundtracks, including *The Virgin Queen*.

CHAPTER 4

From Principles to Practice

The Culture of Natural Voice Choirs and Workshops

IF YOU CAN TALK, YOU CAN SING

It is a dull, damp evening in early November.[1] Sixty people form a large circle in a community hall that has been cleared of its chairs and tables. We range in age from our early twenties to late seventies, but the majority fall into the band of mid-thirties to mid-sixties, and women outnumber men by around four to one. Most of us are wearing casual, comfortable clothes, sometimes still moist from the rain. A few latecomers, visibly harassed by whatever challenges they had faced in getting here, squeeze into place as the warm up gets under way. We begin by jogging lightly and loosely on the spot. We make flicking gestures, as if shaking water from our hands, and then do the same with our feet, as if trying to kick off our shoes, before coming to rest in a spirit of relaxed alertness. Our choir leader, Jo, guides us through a short sequence of body movements. With our hips and knees, we describe circles and figure eights, imagining that we are stirring porridge. Rising to our toes, we stretch our arms upwards, reaching for a golden balloon that is just beyond our grasp. Then, puppet-like, we let ourselves flop forward, bending all the way over until our fingers touch the ground. Bouncing gently from the knees, we focus our awareness on the weight of our hands as our fingers lightly scrape the floor, and imagining a gentle tug on our "strings", we begin to uncurl, one vertebra at a time, until we are upright again. Standing at ease, with our shoulders relaxed and our knees still slightly bent, we carefully tilt our heads backwards and forwards, and then from side to side. We circle our shoulders, first both together, and then one at a time. We pull our shoulders up to ears, hold our breath, and count to three, then release the breath slowly as we let our shoulders fall back into place. We mimic the sounds and actions of noisy kissing and of chewing sticky toffee. We clean our teeth with our tongues, then laugh at one another's frowns of concentration as we try to follow the instruction to imagine that our tongue is a pen and that we are writing our name on the inside of our cheek. Feeling we have nothing to lose, we proceed to scrunch and contort our faces, then massage them lightly with our fingertips.

We follow Jo's invitation to breathe in deeply through the nose, as if we are inhaling the most intoxicating scent in the universe. As we exhale on a hum, we direct our attention to the resonance in our heads and faces. Releasing our bellies, we allow the breath to fall in again; this time, we let it go on a slow, soft hiss, prolonging the out-breath for as long as we can. We imagine that we are blowing a piece of thistledown across the room, first on a silent breath, then on a gentle "sh", and then a soothing "ah". We feel our abdominal muscles work as we make sharper, shorter exhalations; we imagine that we are blowing out the candles on a birthday cake, before giving our lungs a final flush-out as we do our best to pant like puppies.

Now we begin to play with sounds, echoing a sequence of exclamations—oh, ooh, ah, hey—that gradually become sustained calls. We are encouraged to imagine that the sounds we are making are rising from the earth, through the soles of our feet and up through our bodies, to be released through an open throat. We imagine the sound of a siren as we throw the voice up then let it swoop down to the depths and back up again. We explore different timbres and moods by repeating a note at the same pitch but with different colourations: angelic, nasal, metallic, harsh, husky, dark. Jo sets up a simple four-beat stepping pattern—side right and close, side left and close—as she moves us into a more organised call and response format. We echo playground-style motifs that gradually become more melodic and take us through a series of rhythmic variations using nonsense syllables. With no words to worry about, we give ourselves over to the spirit of the game. Smiles spread as people get into the groove, then turn to laughter as we realise that, without knowing what was happening, we have already learnt the first line of the first song—"Sin nje nje nje ngemi thandazo". The alto and tenor parts are easily added: since they move more or less in parallel with the lead voice, all that is required is to repeat the pattern at a lower pitch. The bass is fairly predictable, too, and, five minutes later, we are singing in four-part harmony. Before we move on to the second verse, Jo stops to explain that this is a traditional Zulu song from South Africa, usually known as "Babethandaza", and that the arrangement she is teaching us is by Ysaye Barnwell (of the group Sweet Honey in the Rock).[2] The words we have just been singing mean "Things are as they are because of prayer, Ngemi", and the second part will say, "our mothers [or women of old] used to pray". We resume singing with renewed vigour, repeating the two verses over and over until we no longer need to think about either the words or the melody, and the song takes flight.

The next piece is designed to shift us up a gear and will demand more focus. "Batonebo" is a three-part healing song from Guria in western Georgia that is traditionally sung for children suffering from an infectious disease such as measles. Jo explains that the sickroom would be decorated with flowers and candles and that the women would sing to appease the spirits who might otherwise carry the child away. The words are written with a marker pen on a large sheet of paper that is pinned to the wall. We begin by repeating the words, line by line, doing our best to get our tongues around unfamiliar consonants. We then turn our attention to fitting the words to the music, starting with the top voice. Jo breaks the line down into bite-sized chunks and uses hand signals to guide us, raising and lowering her arm to indicate the direction of the melody and give a rough approximation of the distance between notes. Concentrating hard, we repeat each phrase until it is secure in our mind. As the other parts are added one by one, we feel the thrill of the novel harmonies with their sudden clashes and unexpected resolutions.

After a short break, we reassemble for a brief housekeeping session to finalise the practical arrangements for our spot in a forthcoming fundraising event for the local hospice and discuss our plans to host a Bulgarian singing workshop with guest teacher Dessi Stefanova. We then return to an *a cappella* arrangement of "Something Inside So Strong" which we have been working on for the past few weeks. We spend some time on a passage that is still causing us difficulty, but everything finally clicks into place, and there is a palpable sense of elation as we arrive at the triumphant final chord. We round off the evening by running through the spiritual "All Night, All Day", a current favourite that has filtered down to us via Tony Backhouse (leading exponent of gospel singing in Australia and New Zealand).[3] As we head for home, some of us pay our customary visit to one of the local bars where, still in high spirits, we treat our fellow drinkers to a spontaneous reprise of "All Night, All Day", followed by a South African freedom song and topped off with a Russian lullaby.

WORKING WITH THE VOICE

In the second issue of the NVPN Newsletter, Frankie Armstrong noted:

> When we drew up the Statement of Philosophy and Principles and Practice we were very clear about why we called ourselves Voice Practitioners and not Singing Teachers.... It's not just what we sing but how we sing and why we sing that stirs and challenges me.... We want to get others recognising that the voice can be so much more than the singing of songs, though songs will always be a core part of our work and play. (Armstrong 2004: 22)

How, then, do these principles translate into practice? How does a natural-voice-style choir session or workshop differ from the weekly rehearsal of a choral society or a masterclass given by an expert from the classical world? How is a typical session structured? What kinds of songs are chosen, and why? How are the songs learned? In what ways do they help to maximise the potential for inclusion? My opening vignette provided some preliminary answers to these and other questions. In hinting at the range of skills the choir director brings into play, it also offered some practical insight about the relevance, utility, and application of the different kinds of professional training and experience discussed in chapter 3.

In the discussion that follows, we investigate in greater depth the ramifications and resonances of some of the themes introduced in chapter 2. Questions about the nature of music education—or more precisely, schooling—are again on the agenda as we enter into brief dialogue with Ivan Illich and his more radical thinking on deschooling and conviviality, both of which he associates with the revival of community responsibility. We also return to the ideas of Christopher Small and Thomas Turino, each of whom has made a significant contribution to what we might call the politics and poetics of participation. As part of this analysis, I probe more deeply into the theme of transcending constraints, considering the different levels at which emancipation may take place and the mechanisms that make this possible. We begin, however, with a more down-to-earth examination of the main components of a typical choir or workshop session.

PREPARING TO SING: THE FUNCTION OF WARM-UP EXERCISES

The kinds of warm-up activities featured in my opening vignette are high on the list of techniques that distinguish natural-voice-style community choirs from the types of amateur choirs or choral societies where preparatory exercises tend to have a more conventional form and a strictly musical focus, with pride of place given to the practice of scales and arpeggios and correct use of the diaphragm. Practitioners who undertake Frankie Armstrong's training are equipped with a starting kit drawn from her rich, multi-disciplinary repertory of exercises, games, and improvisations; they acquire more from visiting workshop leaders or in sharing sessions at the NVPN annual gathering. Frankie notes that she herself no longer uses the term "warm up", which for some people has negative connotations. She now refers to this work as preparation, voice development, and voice awareness—descriptors that give people a sense that they can learn from these activities, rather than thinking of them as something that has to be endured before getting on with the "real" business of singing. (I continue to use the term "warm up" in the present discussion, however, as an easy kind of shorthand.)[4]

Beyond the form of the exercises themselves, what is of interest to us here is the rationale informing the way in which the warm-up session is structured and the explication of the function and impact of the chosen exercises as part of a broader, holistic understanding of how voices and their owners "work". The practice of beginning each singing session with a warm-up routine that pays careful attention to the triangulation of voice, body, and breath is seen as fundamental to the NVPN philosophy: "Vocal and physical warm-ups are an essential element of our work. They ensure healthy vocal use by anchoring the voice in the body and breath and generally prepare the voice for action." The benefits of warm ups are related to both individual and collective goals: "They also allow opportunities for increasing creativity, practising listening to others and creating a sense of community" (see "Philosophy and Working Principles" in the Appendix).

In his blog article "Preparing to Sing: Why Bother?" choir director and NVPN member Chris Rowbury (2009) breaks down what he sees as the ten functions of warm-ups. Additional formulations and nuances that came out of a brainstorming session at the January 2008 NVPN annual gathering, entitled "Why Warm Up?", are inserted in parentheses.

(1) Transition from the everyday (arriving, letting go of the day, easing people in).
(2) Relax and release tension (warm up/calm down, grounding).
(3) Connect body, breath, voice (get physically ready, get lungs ready).
(4) Engage imagination and creativity (experimenting, exploring using the voice in a different way).
(5) Hone listening skills.
(6) Develop self-awareness (focusing).
(7) Increase confidence, lose inhibitions (establish safety/trust).
(8) Improve pitching and vocal range using a centred, healthy voice (tuning up, developing range/power/control).
(9) Develop sense of timing and rhythm.
(10) Awareness of working with others (engaging with leader, becoming receptive, opening emotional warmth, connecting group, creating focus for group identity).

Arriving and Tuning In

An effective warm up will be structured in such a way as to vary the pace and energy levels, shifting between a group focus and personal exploration, and between concentrated listening and "letting off steam". Chris elaborates on the need to begin by orchestrating a shift from the stresses and strains of the day:

> The atmosphere we are trying to create is one of relaxed informality, of focus and concentration, of silliness and imagination, of creativity and beauty, of timelessness and joy. Most of these elements are missing from our everyday lives, so we have to allow a period of transition for people to settle into a different world. (Rowbury 2009: n.p.)

For choirs or singing groups that meet on a regular basis, the warm up functions as a ritual that re-establishes the group's identity, and at the same time marks the shift (in sociocultural terms) to "time out" from normal social constraints and responsibilities. Suggestions of this passage through a liminal space can be found in Jackie Roxborough's description of how, at the completion of the systematic physical routine with which she begins her weekly sessions, she feels a palpable sense of "arrival" that signals to her that she can start to work more directly on the voice (interview 2007).

The final function in the above list—awareness of working with others—might be seen to extend to the bonding that takes place when everyone in the room has gone through the same process: specifically, one not overtly intended to reveal who is a more or less accomplished singer or a faster or slower learner. The leader's instructions and demonstrations of the different exercises provoke an almost automatic physical or vocal response on the part of group members; the individual thus enjoys safety in numbers and so does not risk having his or her weaknesses exposed. The warm up offers—to again use terms from the 2008 brainstorming session—an "immediately shared experience" that seeks to create a "level playing field" as well as to "set the mood". Part of the art of the leader lies in drawing everyone in and keeping things moving so that the individual is carried along and does not have time to become overly nervous or self-conscious. One reader commenting on Chris Rowbury's blog suggests the term "tuning the choir" as an alternative to "warming up". Whilst on the surface this might suggest a more limited "tuning up" of the vocal instrument, the concept can also be understood in terms of bringing the choir together psychologically as well as sonically, as a foundation for building both musical and social harmony. It is interesting to note in this regard that singers on the Mediterranean islands of Corsica and Sardinia often speak of the need for members of an ensemble to be "in accord" ("in harmony", but with connotations of being "on the same wavelength"): if you do not feel comfortable with your fellow singers, they say, you will not be able to find the harmonies. The bonding that happens during warming up or tuning up, then, can be seen as intrinsic to the ability to sing in tune and in harmony with others.

Voice, Body, Breath, Mind

In Chris's third function we find the voice-body-breath trinity that is at the heart of what we may be tempted to term the "new" voicework—but which, as Chris reminds us, lies at the heart of many kinds of music making that are part of everyday life and work:

> Gone are the days of the clenched buttocks, feet in second position and formally held hands of the posh recital. We need to get back to the cotton fields, the chain gangs and the weaving looms and sing with our bodies, breathe with our imagination, and dance with our mouths. (Rowbury 2009: n.p.)

Not only does working on the voice in isolation reinforce a sense of separation between the vocal apparatus and the rest of the body or person; it also neglects the fact that paying attention to breathing and posture can prove just as effective, in terms of vocal results, as working directly on the voice itself. The form that such connections might take may not be immediately obvious. Voice coach and NVPN member Alexander Massey explains that knee exercises, for example, can help wake up the abdominal muscles and the muscles of pelvic floor so as to aid deep breath support. Rocking or rotating the pelvis also keeps the abdominal muscles moving. Doing "silly walks" works in a similar way. "The beauty of it," Alexander writes, "is that when we do such exercises, the voice starts working more efficiently quite automatically, and we don't have to get so self-conscious and tense about trying to work out the 'right' way to breathe" (2005: 9).

To our three elements of voice, body, and breath we might add a fourth: mind. Frankie sees freeing the power of the imagination as the key to her method, experience having shown her that once the imagination is unlocked the voice will follow. Many of her exercises therefore involve visualisation or role play, and she includes carefully chosen imagery in her instructions for carrying them out. She emphasises the importance of choosing words especially carefully when talking about the breath, noting her preference for the term "rib accordion" or "rib concertina" over "rib cage" to suggest flexibility rather than rigidity. For similar reasons, she speaks in terms of letting the breath drop into the body rather than instructing her students to "take a deep breath"—an image that also encourages them to extend the act of breathing to all parts of the body, not just the lungs. She explains that she often models exercises on animals, not only for the sounds they make, but also for the way they move:

> I just think, particularly playing with the animals, you have a visual image, you have a kinaesthetic approach, it gives you a playful, an imaginative way in. You know, I'm not being me the schoolteacher or me the tax inspector, I'm being an elephant or a cat or a puppy, or a Maasai calling in your sacred cow.... I'm just

constantly trying to find images from nature, physicality, kinaesthetic, imaginative, social—things that just break down that idea that "to sing correctly I have to stand stiffly and hold my hands together or stiff by my side". (Armstrong interview 2008)

Frankie elaborates on the more pragmatic reasons behind her increasing focus on the connection between body and voice: "Body work was something that needed to happen but of course by this time I had very little sight so I grew my whole style of work, in a sense, predicated on the fact that I couldn't see my participants." In developing her distinctive repertory of physical exercises, she drew on yoga, tai chi, and the Alexander technique. When she later began working with Darien Pritchard, whose work was body-focused, "it meant that we could really put these things together so then, when I came across Kristin [Linklater]'s work and various other of the theatre voice teachers, it all kind of fell into place" (interview 2008). Kristin, in turn, added to the body of exercises she had inherited from Iris Warren: "I have appropriated and absorbed them from many different sources and married them with voice so that they have often undergone a sea change." She cites the example of "movements reminiscent of gym exercises" where the goal has been changed from muscle development to energy flow (2006: 3).[5] Many NVPN members similarly draw on their knowledge of body-based disciplines. The "very loose physical regime" with which David Burbidge likes to begin his sessions, for example, incorporates breathing exercises from yoga and movements from Feldenkrais, tai chi, and chi gung, all of which he has practised himself (interview 2007).

Individual exercises, then, serve multiple purposes over and above the obvious ones. This applies not only to specially devised activities but also to more conventional exercises and to seemingly casual gestures. Exercises to soften the lips, relax the jaw and throat, expand the lungs, or strengthen the abdominal muscles may include a psychological component. Laughter is an excellent tool for promoting release, relaxation, and bonding, and adds a general feel-good factor; it is also part of the bridge between the speaking and singing voice. Kristin Linklater places great emphasis on sighing and yawning as "organic animal activities" that give the body an extra charge of oxygen and as such have the power to "revitalize your body and your mind". Yawning opens the throat, limbers up the soft palate, stimulates the breathing apparatus, and releases tension. The "sigh of relief" has the added advantage of making a connection with the inner world of feeling; being "triggered by a thought-feeling impulse", it reopens "the primary neuro-physiological routes between brain and body" (Linklater 2006: 50–51).[6]

Sustained movement is integral to many of Frankie's exercises, often in association with vocal work based on call-and-response patterns that edge participants incrementally closer to melody. Her development of this kind of exercise was, again, prompted in part by pragmatism after her original weekly singing group in London had to move to a new venue—a dance studio with no chairs. "It was much less tiring," she explains, "to move as we called, chanted and sang, so simulated work movements and simple 'dances' became a hallmark for my work" (1997: 46–47). An activity she sometimes refers to as Copy Cat begins with everyday sounds and exclamations—sighs, oohs and aahs, calling to a long-lost friend across a busy street—which can be accompanied by simple movements (e.g. a throwing action or a flicking gesture). The types of motifs heard in children's playground calls (such as "na na na na na") give rise to more structured calls or hollers that also have a rhythmic element and can be classed as a form of heightened speech. Simple melodic patterns are then introduced, using heys and hos, other meaningless syllables, or a more elaborate made-up language. These are accompanied by a simple, rhythmic movement—stepping from side to side in time with the beat, or Frankie's famous "hoeing" where participants set up a swinging action in imitation of a rhythmic work movement (right foot forward, step with left foot on the spot, right foot back, step with left foot on the spot again). Other work activities that might be imagined (and that in many cultures are in fact accompanied by rhythmic chanting, often using the call-and-response format) include scything corn, pounding maize, treading grapes, hauling in fishing nets, pounding washing, or waulking the tweed. Frankie notes that these physical actions can aid the type of psychological and vocal release that natural voice work aims for: "Encouraging simple, collective rhythmic movements such as simulating work actions...can free people from the fear and anxiety that holds their bodies stiff and their capacity for self-expression in chains" (Armstrong and Pritchard 2005: 16).[7]

The distraction provided by such movements has its own further rationale. Frankie observes that even in the early part of a workshop the majority of participants can follow unpredictable melodies "if a) you keep them short and b) you give the group something else to focus on so they don't think they're Singing with a capital S" (Armstrong and Pritchard 2005: 40). A related "trick" (building on what she learned from Ethel Raim) is to make the move from speech to song as unobtrusive as possible—"to give people the experience of speech, heightened speech, chant and song, as a continuum with no mystifying disjunctures". Getting workshop participants to echo call-like phrases, including hollers and yodels, and simulated chattering or gossiping sounds "takes us into what children do naturally, the seamless switch from the spoken to the sung". She soon realised that using this approach—in which people often start singing before they realise what is happening—"often allowed people previously deemed tone deaf to sing perfectly in pitch right from the beginning of a workshop" (Armstrong 1997: 47)[8] (▶ see video tracks 04.01–04.05).

Paving the Way for Singing in Style

Individual exercises may also be designed to achieve a particular voice quality; to focus on elements of pitch, rhythm, or harmony; or to work on such skills as listening or blending. Dee Jarlett, speaking of her work with Bristol's Gasworks Choir, emphasises the importance of listening skills. Since the songs that are to follow later in the session will be taught by ear, she says, choir members need to be accustomed to listening carefully to her demonstrations so that they are able to sing the line back as accurately as possible. A substantial proportion of the choir's warm-up time is therefore devoted to imitation and call-and-response excercises, and some of these will be designed to ease the group into the spirit of the song that is to be the main focus of the session. If she and her co-director, Ali Orbaum, are planning to introduce a blues piece, for instance, they build in motifs that include semi-tones and slurs; a Bulgarian song, on the other hand, will require exercises that pay attention to tone and timbre (interview 2007). Frankie notes that call-and-response was also central to Ethel Raim's method for "encourag[ing] people out of their 'choir' voices" so that they could better find the quality required for singing Balkan songs (Armstrong 1997: 46). She recalls observing Ethel working in this way with a class of more than sixty "non-singers" at a Folk Life Festival in California (in 1975) and, in only three hours, turning them "into something that sounded like a Yugoslav village chorus" (presentation at Giving Voice Symposium, 1990).

Language also has a bearing on how one works toward achieving the desired vocal quality. Simulated "gossiping" using nonsense syllables or made-up languages allows participants to play with sounds without being distracted by the meaning of the words and any psychological "baggage" that may be attached to them. Chants and songs in foreign languages work in a similar way. Frankie explains:

> Getting outside the structure and content of our daily language and returning to something like a pre-verbal state can help us to get away from fears of the old patterns of self-criticism and negative judgement that so many of us carry.... To chant or sing in *gobbledegook* or in a foreign language... invites us to stay with a voice that comes from the earth through the soles of our feet, gathers its power and expression in the centre of our body, the abdominal muscles, the diaphragm, and the solar plexus, the seat of the emotions, and releases sound through open lungs and open throat. (Armstrong and Pritchard 2005: 18)[9]

It is interesting to note that some voice practitioners who teach songs from their own cultural heritage use similar techniques to help their Western students achieve the special vocal quality required. As we learned in chapter 2, Ukrainian singer Maryana Sadovska's professional background includes working with the Polish theatre directors Grotowski and Staniewski. This training enabled her to step outside her own tradition and adapt techniques from the world of experimental theatre—reinforced by her personal experience of learning songs from other cultures—to teach Ukrainian songs to non-natives.[10] Many of her exercises are designed to help cultivate a more nasal sound; others to anchor the voice more firmly in the body. Animal noises (cats, sheep, cows) feature prominently, as does simulated or mimicked conversation, in this case using bleating or creaking noises, or crying or laughter. Making bleating sounds is useful preparation for the type of ornamentation found in many Eastern European styles, while cat-like calls help push the voice to the front of the face and lowing draws attention to the chest resonator. It is worth noting here that in many of the world's oral traditions, singers take inspiration from the sounds of nature. In Albania, Sardinia, and Corsica, for example, the different voices in a polyphonic song are often likened to those of goats, sheep, and oxen; this relates, among other things, to the different registers, tessituras, timbres, modes of voice production, and styles of ornamentation that characterise the individual voices. Experimentation with animal calls is not, therefore, mere idle play even if it also serves as a source of lighthearted relief.

Dessi Stefanova likewise uses the technique of getting workshop participants to mimic well-known sounds, including bagpipes, daleks, and machine guns, as well as the ubiquitous bleating, as a means of approximating the timbral quality and style of ornamentation characteristic of Bulgarian singing.[11] She describes how she devised her method by "trial and error"

> because in Bulgaria traditional singing is taught by imitation, mostly of well established or older singers of your region. Nobody teaches vocal technique unless you are professional and you're looking to blend the voices of singers from different areas in a choir, for example. In Bulgaria, a traditional singer would be told not to sing in her nose or not to constrict her throat but without much guidance about how to achieve the desired effect....
>
> I found very quickly that you can't teach non-native singers just by imitation. I had to go and educate myself a bit more and really start observing myself a lot more. (Stefanova interview 2008, pers. comm. 2013)

In this way she equipped herself with the understanding and terminology that allows her to describe what she wants her students to do in a quasi-scientific manner, as an adjunct to her demonstrations.[12]

Similar techniques have been developed by Russian singer Irina Raspopova. In the slim volume entitled *Irina Raspopova's Method of Voice-training in Folk Styles of Russian Polyphony*, she describes a series of specially designed exercises—which she demonstrates on the companion cassette—to teach the techniques required for singing polyphonic songs from different parts of Russia.

Before moving to the Netherlands in 1993, Irina had undergone fifteen years of formal music education, including five years at the Moscow Institute of Culture, where she specialised in voice training in folk styles. As was the case for Dessi, however, embarking on the project of teaching her musical heritage to non-natives forced her to "fundamentally think over and put into words that which I did earlier without conscious effort" (1996: 7). This resulted in the development of "a special system which...clearly and graphically conveys to students quite complicated techniques", together with a manner of voice production that was unfamiliar to her Dutch students, who were used to singing in the head register (5). Irina shares with Frankie an insistence that voice training is not simply a matter of working directly on the voice but also of prompting people to set aside their habitual restraint. Russian singing is, as she describes it, "a volcanic outpouring of emotion". She therefore begins her work "with training in spiritual fortitude, that is, in the display of strength of character" (7). Her exercises cover a range of foci, including posture and breath control, the articulation of Russian speech sounds, vocalising in different registers (chest, head, and mixed), styles of ornamentation, improvisation, and other special techniques (such as chain breathing and word breaks). In a manner now familiar, Irina makes frequent use of imagery to help her students achieve the desired effect, and this is reflected in the graphic names she gives to her exercises—Mosquito, Nightingale, Pregnant Cow, Flat Tyre, The Siren, Mortar Bomb, Musical Saw, and Balalaika, for example.

How Times Have Changed

A cursory survey of my collection of singing manuals and handbooks for choral directors published in the early to mid-twentieth century throws into sharp relief the distance travelled, not only in respect of the types of vocal exercises recommended but also in the tone adopted by their authors, which would surely make all but the most dyed-in-the-wool contemporary choir director blanch. These volumes may be largely a sign of the times in which they were written, but since these are the times in which the older generation of current choir members grew up, this may very well have been the style of instruction they had in school or church choirs. Many of the "experts" who authored these books assume an unremittingly didactic tone, issuing instructions that permit no dispute and making no concessions to feelings or sensitivities. Some have no compunction about using excessively negative and censorial language. Examples of bad habits or poor practice are cheerfully lambasted as "wrong", "terrible", 'painful", "repellent", "an ugly habit", "a serious offence", or "a sin". Singing is all too often presented as a strenuous activity that demands strict discipline and self-control. Charles Cleall, for example, writes in *The Selection and Training of Mixed Choirs in Churches*:

Control of the breath is tiring, for it involves muscular effort of two kinds: it involves considerable muscular effort in setting the shoulders back and down, *and in keeping them there*. When you stand to sing, set the shoulders into position: do not move their position till you sit again.... Your breath will last longer, and your voice will sound richer and better focused. That is a strenuous act, for the shoulders will ache and fight for relaxation; you must gainsay them and forgo it. (1960: 34; italics in original)[13]

In *Vocal Physiology and the Teaching of Singing*, David D. Slater proffers more tempered advice for curing a "throaty or guttural tone": "Exercise *will power* to keep the tongue flat, and the surrounding parts in a loose and unconstrained condition. If necessary, hold the tongue in position with the aid of a silver spoon" (n.d.: 79–80; italics in original)[14]

The notion that singing is part of humanity's natural birthright is summarily dismissed by Richard Graves, author of *Singing for Amateurs*, despite the fact that his stated objective is "to provide assistance and entertainment to amateur singers, to justify them to themselves and to enlist the sympathy of the public, many of whom regard amateurs, especially singers, with a snobbish superiority" (1954: 1). Central to his motivation, he assures us, is the conviction that "there is a vast number of people who can take pleasure (without giving pain) in community singing, singing in church, singing at school or singing on the march in addition to those who can aspire to sing solos acceptably", leading him to conclude that, "were it not for the menace of television which looks like debauching still further the citizens of our Welfare State, I should have said that the prospects for singers were hopeful" (2). This, however, is prefaced by the observation:

> Having frequently witnessed the development of a voice "from nothing" to a pleasing and sometimes beautiful instrument by a teacher who knows his business, one is tempted to believe that all human beings have voices and are capable of becoming singers. This is not so. There are millions of people who cannot and never will sing in tune, and a good many others whose voices are unpleasing in quality and better restricted to speech, in which a disagreeable voice is considered a natural and excusable defect. (Graves 1954: 1–2)

Graves asks even accomplished and distinguished singers to heed "the general rule... that singing unaccompanied solos to one's fellow-creatures is cruelty to animals" (4–5). Meanwhile, Cleall was later to write of the new sound of the sixties: "In the home, it is deplorable; meriting tears. In the Church, it is a scandal; a stumbling block; a pollution: an intolerable blasphemy" (quoted in the blurb for Wright 2008).

The clash of sensibilities and convictions could not be starker. The ethos of the natural voice movement and its counterparts, such as the *a cappella* movement in Australasia, is in many ways diametrically opposed to that embraced by the school to which Cleall and Graves belong. This points to another level at which, for Frankie and the NVPN, the wider world is firmly inside the frame of what is deemed to be a natural—and civilised—approach to singing as they draw inspiration from cultures where music making is a source of joy and a tool for empowerment and celebration. Tony Backhouse, a key player in the Australasian *a cappella* movement, refers in a similar spirit to the wellspring of his own work as choral director:

> I'm inspired by what I've experienced in black churches: an atmosphere of encouragement, safety and joy, where you feel permission to be as big as you dare. ("We're here to have a good time", as they say.) I want to lift the group, be lifted and see the group lift each other—so I try to make it safe, collaborative and fun. (Backhouse 2010: 2)

This does not in any way equate to a lack of discipline. Rather, it subscribes to the well-established wisdom that people have the best chance of achieving their full potential in an environment that is positive and nurturing.

THE AURAL METHOD: TEACHING AND LEARNING BY EAR

Since they come from oral tradition, the majority of songs used by natural-voice style singing groups do not have a primary existence in notated form. Some may subsequently have been transcribed, either by outside enthusiasts, collectors, or researchers (including ethnomusicologists) or by professionals within the culture for educational purposes. Many of them, however, still circulate *only* in oral form, and continue to be taught and learnt by ear in any new environments to which they find their way. The absence of a score that is readily available for hire or purchase is one reason why these bodies of song do not appear in the repertoires of other types of amateur choir that adhere more closely to the classical or presentational model.

In a choir led by a member of the NVPN, even a song that was initially learnt from notation will be taught by ear in line with the statement from the Philosophy and Working Principles: "We aim to teach songs as far as possible by ear recognising that this is the most accessible and effective way for the majority of people to learn and retain songs in the longer term" (see Appendix). No matter how complex the arrangement, then, in the NVPN world all songs are taught aurally, line by line and part by part, using the pattern of listening, imitation, and repetition that has been established in the call-and-response exercises during the warm up. Unlike the conductor of a choir that relies on sight-reading, who may also have access to a piano on which to pound out problematic phrases, the leader of an open-access choir needs to be able to demonstrate each line by singing it solo in front of the choir. This, of course, means that he or she needs to have memorised all the parts to a song before being in a position to teach it. As part of this process, he or she will also have identified some points in the piece that are likely to require additional focus in order to pin down, such as an unusual interval or a tricky rhythmic motif. He or she might then include an additional exercise meant specifically to help overcome the obstacle. Another advantage of the aural method is that it enables the choir leader to demonstrate such features as timbre and voice placement or subtle nuances of timing and pitch inflection, which cannot adequately be conveyed in a musical score. Here we have an additional reason for not using a piano, which would push the songs into the European equal tempered scale.

While the process of learning by ear may be modelled on the oral tradition, it is clearly different from the scenario whereby a child grows up hearing songs repeated over a period of many years, absorbing them almost by osmosis. In the community choir context, songs have to be taught in a more conscious and deliberate fashion, supported by appropriate aids and techniques. In the case of relatively simple songs or songs with minimal text, learning the words and the music relies entirely on memory (although individual parts might be recorded on a practice CD or placed on a members-only section of the choir's website as MP3 files, alongside word sheets, to allow the choir members to review the material in the run-up to a performance). When the choir is learning longer songs, the words are often provided, usually written on a large sheet of paper pinned to a wall or board, in preference to individual copies that might take people's eyes and attention away from a common focal point, alter their posture, or become an unnecessary crutch. When teaching the parts, a choir leader will typically use hand signals to mirror melodic movement, moving the arm up and down to indicate direction and the size of the interval between two notes. Other gestures might cue changes in tempo, volume, and vocal quality or indicate individual part entries, song sections, repeats, or places where a line should be ornamented (▶ see video tracks 04.06–04.11).

One potential drawback of the aural teaching method is that while attention is focused on one voice part, the rest of the choir is kept waiting. A number of techniques can be brought into play as a way of keeping everyone actively engaged. In the case of a short and relatively simple song, the whole choir might learn all the parts together before individuals choose which part to sing. Longer, more complex songs may be broken down into small chunks, with all of the parts for one such unit being taught before the choir moves on to the next. This method has the added advantage of whetting the singers' appetite, giving them a taste, early on in the learning process, of what the harmonies will sound like.

Some choirs might sit while parts are being taught; other choirs will stand throughout the evening (with the obvious exception of individuals who need to sit for reasons of health or age). With the singers arranged in a horseshoe or open circle formation, as opposed to sitting in straight rows two or three deep, each member is able to see the word sheet, the gestures of the choir leader and, as they become less dependent on these cues, their fellow singers. They are also able to maintain an upright yet relaxed standing posture that affords the voice unrestricted passage through the throat, facilitates good breathing habits, and allows the body to move. Tony Backhouse succinctly encapsulates his own rationale for working with singers standing in a circle as opposed to sitting in rows:

> There's nobody on the end, everyone is equal and connected, and we can all hear each other. We thus create our own very welcoming, safe space in whatever physical area we happen to be. Everyone can see everyone else and this helps create intimacy and community. Standing keeps the energy up, and standing makes it easier to reshuffle positions and sections as needed. (Backhouse 2004: 11)

If, as it is in the NVPN, the learning-by-ear approach is rooted in a commitment to accessibility and demystification, it is also the case that some styles of music are not served well by Western notation. Village Harmony co-director Larry Gordon, for example, feels that notation is "just an impediment" to learning South African songs:

> We've just found that teaching the South African songs from the music is totally counterproductive because it's impossible to capture the nuances of the South African songs in a transcription...and when you do try to capture the nuances of it, it looks really, really ridiculous on the page and it's really hard to read because the rhythms are hard. On the page they're hard, but they're not *as* hard when you learn them by ear. (Gordon interview 2005)

Notation may also fix one particular arrangement as the definitive or "correct" interpretation, thereby discouraging the creative variation that is so often considered part of an authentic performance. The authors of *Let Your Voice Be Heard!* make precisely this point when they stress that the transcriptions included in the book

> present the songs as "frozen" at one point in time, in one particular configuration of parts, and with one specific melodic and rhythmic form. In actual practice, it would be unlikely to find a song...from Ghana or Zimbabwe performed in precisely the same way each time, or in such a rigid fashion that the rhythm of every note or phrase would fall precisely within regularly divided measures. (Adzinyah, Maraire, and Tucker 1986: ix)

An additional problem with using scores is that those who are proficient at reading music, and are the product of a culture where the score is assumed to represent the original, authenticated version of a work, are likely either to raise objections or to become confused when faced with even minor departures from the notation.

While singers who are used to reading music may, at times, feel frustrated at not having a score to refer to, others welcome the opportunity to refine their listening skills and strengthen their capacity for memorising both music and words. Sarah Harman, whom we met in chapter 3, identifies her attendance at a two-day workshop led by Ysaye Barnwell in the late 1980s as a critical turning point in her journey as a singer. At the time, she did not think that she was capable of learning a song unless she had the written music in front of her, and on leaving the workshop she promptly forgot everything she had learned. A week later, however, she was able to recall nearly all of the songs, complete with their three or four part harmonies. She experienced this as "a real shift...away from using written music, and trusting *my* body....There's something about...soaking it up by repetition and soaking it up by feeling where it is in your body that makes it stay with you for *years* afterwards" (interview 2008). When songs are stored in the memory and in the body in this way, they are also available for spontaneous performance at a later date in a way that music that has been read, but not learnt, is not.

REPERTOIRE: SONGS FROM THE ORAL TRADITION

Broader questions concerning the appeal of songs from diverse "other" cultures, and the rewards of singing them, will be explored in some depth in chapter 5. Here, I focus primarily on questions of function. Songs from the oral tradition suit the natural voice ethos for several reasons that merit brief review. The fact that, in their natural habitat, these songs are passed on, from individual to individual and from generation to generation, directly from mouth to ear and so do not require musical literacy is clearly critical. Songs destined to be sung by an entire community usually have relatively few words and make liberal use of call-and-response and repetition, rendering them easy to memorise. Songs that are sung as part of daily activities are often executed without instrumental accompaniment (apart from percussion, for which household utensils or naturally occurring objects such as seed-filled gourds, as opposed to specially constructed musical artifacts, may be called into service) and thus allow the voice free rein with regard to pitch, tempo, and expressivity. Many songs belong with dances or accompany activities that involve movement (e.g. pounding grain), making them well suited to the NVPN principle of rooting the voice in the body. As a general rule, the reasons and occasions for singing such songs—to invoke divine protection, to bring rain or heal the sick, to co-ordinate physical work, to celebrate births and marriages, to mark death and other rites of passage, to reinforce social norms and moral codes, to bring hope in times of trouble or to orchestrate resistance—relate to deeper social functions that assume or demand a shared commitment from all involved. At this level, they may be perceived—in terms of both structure and intention—as enabling people to pull together (whether literally or metaphorically), reinforcing group identity, bolstering a sense of solidarity, or inspiring collective action. In this sense, musical style and structure may be seen to mirror a broader worldview: the kind of worldview on which many African and African American traditions build, for example, results in a musical style founded on co-operation rather than competition, and the act of singing operates as a powerful force that unites rather than divides.[15]

The same songs lend themselves to the natural-voice worldview for reasons that should now be clear and they may be employed to fulfil at least some broadly similar functions, even when divorced from their original contexts or practical applications. In the setting of a community choir meeting or open-access workshop, different kinds of songs also serve particular purposes as a session unfolds. Some work well as warm-up songs at the start of a weekly rehearsal or in a free-standing workshop where the aim is to get large numbers of people, many of whom have not met before, singing together in harmony as quickly and painlessly as possible. Call-and-response songs, where the group either repeats a line sung by the leader or responds to each call with a standard refrain, place a minimum of responsibility on individual members of the group while serving the function of training the ear. Rounds can be taught quickly, since everyone is going to be singing the same words and melody, and at the same time they offer a relatively easy way for people to experience singing in harmony and learning to hold their part. Rounds might be lighthearted, rousing, or meditative and so can also be used to establish a particular mood. In a beginners group, a call-and-response song or a round might be followed by a short song in three- or four-part harmony—one that, again, has quite simple melody lines and few words and can be repeated until everyone is comfortable with their part.

A song like "Babethandaza" offers a good balance between reassurance and challenge. The words are few in number, but memorising them still requires some effort. Learning the syncopated rhythm also requires focus but when mastered it beckons to the singers to move to the beat. Because the piece is built on parallel harmonies and European-style triads, once the first melody line has been learnt, the other parts are quite straightforward. When the song is performed, the parts can be added one at a time. With this kind of song success is more or less guaranteed: it establishes an atmosphere of safety, gives participants a sense of achievement, and allows the group as a whole to experience the joy of singing together. This provides a firm foundation for moving on to longer, more ambitious songs that require more concentration to learn.

The collection *Singing in the African American Tradition*, in which Ysaye Barnwell's arrangement of "Babethandaza" is found, features chants, ring shouts, spirituals, gospel songs, songs of the civil rights movement, and contemporary songs of resistance and protest (including songs from South Africa with lyrics in Zulu and Xhosa).[16] A variety of different performance styles are represented: call-and-response, congregational/communal, quartet, and choral. The distinction between congregational singing and choral singing deserves clarification. As Barnwell explains it:

> Congregational/communal singing is unrehearsed, full bodied, and free. Each participant lends their voice to the whole as best they can. The wide variety of voices and natural harmonies can create a wall of sound which can fill every empty space, whether musical, physical, spiritual or emotional. (Barnwell 1989: 7)

By contrast, still following Barnwell, choral singing is rehearsed, performances are often conducted, the sound and use of the voice tends to be more European, and the arrangements tend to be more "classical", although in the case of gospel music there is still space for improvisation and movement in performance. Barnwell's description of the congregational/communal style chimes with Thomas Turino's observations regarding features common to participatory music throughout the world. These include densely overlapping textures, wide tunings, consistently loud volume, and buzzy timbres, which in combination provide what he sees as a crucial "cloaking" function that offers protection to learners and those who are less skilled (Turino 2008: 46).

Barnwell's commitment to the principles of accessibility and empowerment resonate with the NVPN ethic. She too quotes the ubiquitous maxim, "If you can talk you can sing, and if you can walk you can dance", and makes clear her conviction that music is "not art for art's sake but a functional tool for engaging in all of the activities of daily living and for coping with the full range of human emotional and spiritual responses to life" (1989: 8). Shortly before joining Sweet Honey in the Rock, she had been inspired to form the All Souls' Unitarian Church Jubilee Singers in Washington, D.C.—which she cites as a catalyst for her *Singing in the African American Tradition* workshop—"because several people, who couldn't read music and who had never really sung before, wanted to sing" (1). In her workshops, she teaches the songs orally, without printed music or words, and she urges those who use her teaching pack to resist the temptation to transcribe the songs from the recordings. The majority of those who have attended her workshops, she remarks, are not singers: "Many have been told that they should not or cannot sing and so they do not." But, having found their way to the workshop, "they find themselves singing, in harmony with others, in a matter of minutes" (1993: 272). In her own development as a singer, Barnwell has drawn on a range of influences, both within and beyond the African American community. She recalls that, as a college student in the 1960s, she taught herself—in a way reminiscent of Frankie Armstrong—"to sing 'full out,' using my whole voice, by listening to the albums of Nina Simone, Miriam Makeba, Odetta, Richie Havens, and Buffy Sainte-Marie" (258).

With their English lyrics that make liberal use of repetition and their relatively familiar harmonies based on Western-sounding chords, spirituals and gospel songs are supremely accessible for choirs in Britain and other parts of the Anglophone world. Like the freedom songs from the civil rights movement, they require minimal teaching, since they typically take a straightforward call-and-response or verse-and-refrain format. The verses are often formulaic, with only a few words being changed from one verse to the next and with some verses migrating from one song to another. For most people who have grown up in the British Isles, spirituals—"Joshua Fight the Battle of Jericho", "Didn't My Lord Deliver Daniel", "Rock My Soul in the Bosom of Abraham", "Swing Low, Sweet Chariot", and many more—will have been a regular feature of singing at school or in church. They will also have heard them on recordings made by the popular artists of the day, including folk revival singers such as Joan Baez or The Seekers. The Fisk Jubilee Singers, who toured Great Britain and what is now Northern Ireland in 1874 and 1876 to raise funds for Fisk University in Nashville, Tennessee, are credited with introducing such songs as "Swing Low, Sweet Chariot", "Steal Away", "Deep River", and "Nobody Knows the Trouble I See" into the "everyday British musical repertory" (Fryer 1984: 441).[17] In South Wales, the choir met with an especially enthusiastic reception (as would Paul Robeson later).[18] Welsh audiences, having had their own language and morals repeatedly denounced by their English neighbours, immediately identified with these young visitors who had survived the most extreme forms of humiliation and oppression. Such was their impact that in 1876 Swansea formed its own ensemble, the Swansea Jubilee Singers, which, like many other Welsh choirs, included a substantial proportion of negro spirituals in its repertoire. Many of the Fisk Jubilee Singers' songs were also adopted by singers in the Welsh chapels and included in published hymnals, and some continue to be sung in areas of Wales as part of the local heritage. Polly Bolton tells of hearing two men sing an arresting rendition of "The Lily of the Valley" in a remote pub in Pembrokeshire. Her initial search for a published source was in vain, but some time later, in a second-hand bookshop, she chanced upon a copy of *The Story of the Jubilee Singers with Their Songs* (by J. B. T Marsh, originally published in the early 1880s). Browsing through its pages, she was surprised and delighted to find "The Lily of the Valley" (interview 2009).[19]

Tony Backhouse elaborates on the benefits of repetition in the context of gospel singing: "Repetition is ecstatic. It's the easiest way to forget about the notes and get inside the music" (2004: 7). The association of repetition with an ecstatic state is noteworthy here. Barnwell herself, speaking of how "the goal in African-American culture is often to sing until the song sings itself or 'til spirit or the power of the 'Lawd descends'", suggests that the transformation that results does not only affect the singers: "the power of repetitive rhythmic patterns is that they are both transforming and trance-formative for those who produce them and for those who experience them" (1999: xii–xiii). She also evokes the transformative power of this music in connection with its rootedness in a story of triumph over adversity when she describes how the original residential workshop that led to the publication of *Singing in the African American Tradition* was founded on the belief that "African American music has been a vehicle for the survival of African Americans in a hostile universe/environment", and that "sharing the music, its values and its contexts with others can create an experience that in some way transforms the spirit of all who participate" (1989: 5). Turino also offers useful reflections on the deeper functionality of repetition:

> Repetition of the rhythmic groove and predictable musical forms are essential to getting and staying in sync with others. Social synchrony is a crucial underpinning of feelings of social comfort, belonging, and identity. In participatory performance, these aspects of being human come to the fore. (Turino 2008: 44)

If in many of the world's oral traditions greater value is placed on the process of people coming together and interacting through song than on achieving a polished end product that might be evaluated by a non-participating observer, this does not mean that all such songs are "simple". Anyone doubting the scope for variety, sophistication, complexity, and virtuosity, whether in composition or in performance, need only listen to the intricate and flamboyant polyphonic styles found in the Republic of Georgia, for example.[20] Learning these songs often requires a longer apprenticeship for native singers, and more dedicated learning when they are adopted by non-native choirs. The question of what makes these and other songs in unfamiliar languages emanating from very different musical worlds attractive to, and suitable for, Anglophone community choirs yields even more complex and intriguing answers. The case of songs that are so obviously "other" and that take Western singers ever further away from their comfort zone, introducing exotic harmonies and presenting serious linguistic challenges, is examined in greater detail in chapters 5 and 6.

Resources for Teachers

To grow up in a culture where music is preserved and disseminated solely in oral form is one thing. To master songs from a range of different oral traditions and add these to one's teaching repertoire is another. How, then, does a community choir leader build up a collection of such songs?

Choir leaders in the United Kingdom are able to source their songs from an increasingly wide range of media and interactive events. These include published songbooks, often supplemented by a CD or a DVD; workshops, festivals, and summer camps; practitioners' gatherings, training weeks, and dedicated song-swaps; overseas study tours and exchange visits with other choirs; songs collected or learnt directly from individual singers; field recordings, professional recordings, and songs heard on radio and television; and the Internet.

Workshops, as we have already seen, offer invaluable opportunities to learn songs directly from culture-bearers in a social setting. Such learning encompasses not only the songs themselves but also matters of style and cultural context, together with a model of the way in which a song might be taught. For new teachers, workshops (including those offered by established NVPN practitioners) offer a convenient starter pack of suitable songs. Many seasoned choir leaders, too, prefer to learn a song "in the flesh" and to sing it with others before passing it on to their choir.

It was once common practice for workshops participants to record the songs as they were being taught, using their own equipment (hence the vertiginous stacks of old cassette tapes owned by some practitioners). Later, it was thought that the surfeit of machines divided their owners' attention and that other participants might be reluctant to have their every utterance captured for posterity on someone else's tape. These concerns, combined with a growing awareness of intellectual property rights and the desire of some teachers to retain greater control over their material, led to the practice of offering a learning or souvenir CD, featuring either separate song parts or highlights from the day itself, to paid-up participants after the event (usually for a small additional sum to cover material and administrative costs). At the NVPN annual gathering and the Unicorn Voice Camp, the most popular songs that teachers are willing (and authorised) to share are recorded during the event and circulated later on a compilation CD. In the wireless era, audio files are also disseminated via the Internet, using programmes such as Dropbox.

Weekend workshops continue to play a crucial role in introducing new material and, since a visiting workshop leader will often teach the same songs in different parts of the country, the workshops also help to establish a common repertoire. Through the workshop network, one individual can be responsible for introducing a particular style or genre that goes on to establish itself as a new trend. A workshop attended by a substantial proportion of the local community choir provides an injection of new material that the choir might continue to work on and then include in its next concert. A more intensive experience that gives participants the opportunity to learn a broader range of material is offered by the week-long voice camps, such as the Unicorn Natural Voice Camp and Heartsong; residential singing weeks, such as those held at Laurieston Hall and Findhorn; Village Harmony summer camps; and the Giving Voice festival. Other annual events like the WOMAD (World of Music, Arts and Dance) Summer School or the SOAS World Music Summer School, which do not have any direct association with the natural voice or community choir movements but may engage some of the same tutors, provide further opportunities for practitioners to replenish their repertoire and learn new techniques from professional performers.

Just because they are not available in the form of a score, songs do not have to be learnt directly from another person, face-to-face. Many resources now exist—like Ysaye Barnwell's collection *Singing in the African American Tradition*, which consists of teaching CDs alongside a songbook—that are designed for learning by ear, and they are often compiled by a singer-teacher who is active on the workshop circuit. Typically, these resources include recordings of each of the song parts sung separately; they may or may not include notation as well. Some feature CD-Rom files with a variety of materials that can be printed out at home.

Print and mixed-media products of this kind have seen a marked increase, over the past twenty years, in both quantity and quality, and they can take many forms: collections compiled for educational purposes (such as those published by the US-based World Music Press, whose titles include *Let Your Voice Be Heard! Songs from Ghana and Zimbabwe*, or Oxford University Press's Voiceworks series); similar collections aimed at community choirs, including gospel choirs (such as Tony Backhouse's *A Cappella: Rehearsing for Heaven*); collections of traditional songs from one particular culture that, like the educational resources, include translations, contextual information, and/or performance notes (examples include Edisher Garakanidze's *99 Georgian Songs*, Mary Cay Brass's *Village Harmony* and *Balkan Bridges*, and Village Harmony's South African materials, issued as *The Folk Rhythm*); collections of rounds, simple chants, and starter songs (such as Libana's *Fire Within* and the NVPN collection *To Grace the Earth*); arrangements of choir favourites and other miscellaneous songs suitable for community choirs (e.g. Nickomo's *Uncle Zumpa's Bumper Book of A Cappella Belters*); and self-produced collections of original songs (such as those by Ali Burns, Kirsty Martin, Pauline Down, and Nickomo).[21] Many of these print resources are packaged with one or more CDs; others are matched with a CD that may be purchased separately. A small proportion may be found in the catalogues of commercial publishers but the majority are home-produced or published by small independent presses. Those produced by NVPN practitioners are listed in the resources section of the NVPN website; others can be found on the websites of organisations such as Village Harmony. Some resources may be on sale at workshops but difficult to find otherwise: this is especially the case with materials produced by visiting workshop leaders from overseas.

All of these collections are put together with the intention that the songs should be shared and sung as widely as possible; and, in the case of self-produced songbooks, they are not necessarily subject to the usual copyright restrictions. Some, such as Nick Prater's *Heaven in my Heart* and Pauline

Down's *Heartspun*, include statements that give the purchaser automatic permission to photocopy and perform the songs. Village Harmony's *Folk Rhythm* sets include a form with the instruction: "If you duplicate any of these songs, please send us a copy of this form plus a copying permission fee of $10 per song which will make any number of copies you do legal in our eyes." Since the choirs who sing these songs are learning them by ear and performing them from memory, they are in any case relieved of the need to hire or purchase multiple copies of scores, as a classical choir or choral society must do.

Recent years have seen the emergence of online song banks, to which both audio files and scores can be uploaded for sharing. The websites of some choirs and individual practitioners also feature audio files of song parts that can be listened to online and transcriptions may be available to download. Full performances of songs can easily be located on YouTube. Material is also shared more directly via the Natural Voice Dialogue, a Yahoo email group to which any interested party may subscribe. This forum is especially useful in cases where a practitioner is in search of songs from a particular part of the world or songs that are suited to working with a particular client group or in a particular environment.

EXPANDING HORIZONS

With so many rich resources at their fingertips, natural voice practitioners are able to offer their choirs a veritable feast of musical styles and forms. In gaining access to music that is differently organised, has different social origins, reflects a different worldview, and makes different demands on its performers, singers are liberated from a variety of constraints while also having their horizons expanded at multiple levels. At a practical level, they are liberated from the need to read or rely on musical notation. At a cognitive level, they are liberated from the need to worry about the meaning of words as they are uttered. At a musical level, they are liberated from ingrained notions of what is appropriate, correct, permissible or "nice", and in singing without piano accompaniment they are liberated from the constraints of the equal tempered scale. At a sociopolitical level, they are liberated from established conventions and assumptions. Vocal horizons are expanded as people learn to use the voice in new ways. Musical horizons are expanded as they explore novel ways of constructing harmonies and rhythms. Cultural horizons are expanded as they encounter songs from other places and learn something of the people whose lives they are a part of. Social horizons are expanded as they gain access to areas of activity and communities of people from which they may previously have been excluded. Each of these assertions is part of a thread that opens up significant potential for theoretical exegesis as well as more practical exploration. At this juncture, I will tease out those threads that have a particular bearing on the politics of participation; others we will revisit in later chapters.

As part of our exploration of the natural voice philosophy in chapter 2, we visited a number of critiques of the modern Western conception of music and music making, particularly, of the singing voice. Aspects of these analyses are worthy of elaboration as we consider the workings of a natural-voice-style choir at closer quarters. We saw how writers such as Blacking, Small, Olwage, Tomlinson, and Frith have argued that the tastes, values, and conventions according to which different kinds of music, and different qualities of voice, have been judged from the perspective of white European society are largely rooted in matters of class with, in some cases, a strong racial undercurrent. The distinctions that have been put into operation belong to an established (but by no means universal) hierarchy whereby education is equated with sophistication and the white Western world is equated with civilisation, and where notions of both sophistication and civilisation assume an opposite that is necessarily inferior (in terms of purported intrinsic value) or less developed (in a pseudo-evolutionary sense).

From this perspective, amateur classical choirs take their place in the sociocultural hierarchy. In modelling themselves on professional choirs, they aspire in an upwardly mobile direction. Pride of place in their repertoire is given to great works deemed worthy of performance. The performance itself becomes part of the tribute paid to these works and reinforces their place in the canon. Such works further justify their elevated position by being "difficult" and requiring more or less advanced levels of musical "skill", not least the ability to sight-read, since performers are generally not expected to master the gargantuan task of performing full-scale works from memory. At the same time, according to this line of thought, an amateur choir can only ever hope to be second best to a professional choir, recycling works that are performed in a more accomplished manner by more experienced singers.

It might be assumed that open-access choirs lie even further down the chain. The normative argument might be that, since many members of these choirs do not possess even rudimentary music-reading ability, they must content themselves with easier and, by definition, less worthy material that "anyone" could sing. Viewed from another angle, however, the story might be told quite differently. In this retelling, community choirs that are rooted in the natural-voice aesthetic appear on the scene as a breath of fresh air, offering programmes in which there is always something new that audiences have not heard before. Because they have spent more time developing their aural skills, the singers are able to perform from memory and, as a result, are able to enter into the music in a different way and to communicate more directly with the audience. What "passes" between singers and listeners is therefore of a different affective order. Far from "forgiving" them for their supposedly inferior vocal and presentational skills, the audience response is often one of surprise and pleasure: natural-voice-style choirs offer their listeners an entirely new experience with regard not only to the music they present but also to the visceral response they provoke.

The musical material that is chosen is certainly more suitable for such choirs than an oratorio or requiem mass for reasons we have already established. It is worth underlining, nonetheless, that it is not chosen simply because it is assumed to be "easier". It is chosen because it is music of a different order, designed for participation rather than contemplation. Participation goes beyond a mere "joining in". Brynjulf Stige introduces the notion of participation as (i) a style of self-presentation, (ii) the co-creation of social space, and (iii) ritual negotiation (2010b: 128). To this we might add a fourth category: social obligation. Christopher Small alludes to the story of Brahms turning down an invitation to attend a performance of Mozart's *Don Giovanni* on the grounds that he would rather stay at home and read it from the score (1998: 5). In many parts of the world, this would be viewed not merely as odd—not least for its dissociation of music from sound—but as an evasion of a social obligation. We might juxtapose this tale with Jane Sugarman's account of Prespa Albanian communities, where singing serves as the principal means of interacting at social gatherings and polyphonic singing is regarded as "a central component of an individual's social demeanor" (1989: 209). More particularly, participating in multi-part singing is viewed as part of a man's obligation to "embody and negotiate his household's honor in any public forum", his ready contribution being perceived as both a mark of respect for the host and a proper way of representing his own family (1998: 7). Admittedly, Brahms was not being asked to join in the singing of Mozart's opera but the contrast between the two types of behaviour and their underlying assumptions nonetheless alerts us to the moral imperatives of sociability in connection with music making. Perhaps the key point to extrapolate from this is that the principle of social obligation—which from a certain perspective might be seen as intrinsic to a properly functioning (non-individualistic) society—can more readily be understood in a culture where music making is truly participatory; and further, that this becomes another determining factor in the way in which much of the world's music is constructed.

In *Music as Social Life*, Turino sets out his model for conceptualising different kinds of music making as "realms or *fields* of artistic practice", as opposed to styles and status categories (2008: 25). In this model, participatory performance and presentational performance sit side by side as two distinct fields.[22] The basic distinction whereby presentational music is "prepared by musicians for others to listen to" while participatory music "is not *for listening apart from doing*" is fairly straightforward (52; italics in original). What interests Turino more is how the two types of music differ in essence. In the case of presentational music, we are dealing with music as a set item or art object. In the realm of participatory music, on the other hand, "a piece is more like a set of resources...fashioned anew during each performance" (54). Classical music, as Turino describes it, may be seen as a closed form, in which almost every detail of a performance is notated in the score. Participatory music, by contrast, may be seen as open-ended, lending itself to adaptation to the needs of a given situation. Inevitably, the intention behind each mode of music making will result in different musical forms, organisational styles, behavioural options, and value systems. Turino's statement of his overall purpose in advancing this discussion resonates with the convictions that lay at the heart of the early ethnomusicological endeavour to rescue "primitive" music from the various misapprehensions with which it was burdened:

> I want to argue that these situations of participatory music making are not just informal or amateur, that is, *lesser* versions of the "real music" made by the pros but that, in fact, they are something else—a different form of art and activity entirely—and that they should be conceptualized and valued as such. (Turino 2008: 25)

He elaborates later: "It is not that one type of music making is better or more valuable than the other; it is simply that they are different, with different social functions, responsibilities, and thus sound features that make them work" (44).

One final caveat: I am not suggesting that the community choirs I am concerned with here necessarily restrict their repertoire to the type of music that Turino qualifies as participatory, or that singers who operate in the oral tradition are incapable of learning more complex material from the written or art music tradition. A case in point is Marcel Pérès's ensemble Organum, whose membership in the 1990s included a number of Corsican singers who did not read music. This did not prevent them from learning and performing from memory the *Messe de Notre Dame* by fourteenth-century composer Guillaume de Machaut.[23] The Corsican group A Filetta has also mastered complex material by Bruno Coulais and other contemporary composers, again learning everything by ear, in this case with the help of computer software that can play the individual parts directly from an electronic version of the score. When Coulais delivered the score for his first collaborative project with A Filetta, the soundtrack for Jacques Weber's film *Don Juan*, it had not occurred to him that the singers might not be able to read the notation.[24] Even the group's leader, Jean-Claude Acquaviva, was unused to learning vocal material from notation even though, as a classical guitarist, he was a practised sight-reader. An accomplished composer in his own right, Acquaviva speaks of the different ways he approaches the task of composing. While he sometimes composes at a keyboard and then writes the music down, he at other times composes as he has always done—"in my head, even if I fix some things to some extent with the piano" (interview 2004).[25] This is how he composed *Medea*, for example, never writing anything down.[26] Observing this way of working, Coulais found Acquaviva's ability to carry the music in his head and teach it to the group phrase by phrase, each part in turn, to be quite extraordinary (speaking in Don Kent's film *A Filetta: Voix Corses*, 2002). For Acquaviva, this is a choice available to him alongside (rather than in the absence of) other possible ways of working.

Tavagna is another Corsican group whose members, despite their commitment to their own traditions and their lack of music-reading skills, have been eager to broaden their musical horizons by working with musicians and composers from outside the island. One example is their collaboration with British composer Malcolm Bothwell, who had initially worked with Corsican singers in the Organum ensemble and was subsequently invited by Tavagna to compose the music for a series of theatrical productions to be directed by group member Jean-Pierre Lanfranchi.[27] Bothwell himself sees some advantage in the position of those of his Corsican friends who have consciously resisted learning to read notation, primarily for fear that a score would constrain them (or "contaminate" them, as one singer put it) and that by intellectualising what they sing they might lose something that is fundamental to their natural relationship to music. As Bothwell observes:

> The thing that they're free of is having a vision of a keyboard or a score when they sing.... Classically trained musicians have always got a picture of something—a keyboard or a score or something—and they're free of that, which is amazing really. (interview 2004)

The process of learning Bothwell's compositions entirely by ear was at times laborious but one song, "L'Omu Seguita", was an immediate hit. Bothwell had set himself the challenge of composing the piece as a Purcell-style canon over a ground bass, and it took him four days to complete the jigsaw in a way that avoided parallel fifths. In its complexity, Bothwell remarks, the composition is far removed from anything the singers might devise themselves, yet they took to it without hesitation. "They don't even realise that it's complicated," he says. "They just love singing it.... And it's the sort of thing they'll sing mainly in bars and cafes. It's the sort of thing they'll just start after a meal." This may not be the kind of casual virtuosity to which the average community choir member aspires, but it offers irrefutable proof of what is possible.

OF LEARNING AND LIVING

As we have seen, Christopher Small has been an energetic critic of the institutionalisation of music and music education. Equally energetically, he has promoted an alternative view of music as something people do rather than a set of great works, viewing art as a whole as "essentially a *process*, by which we explore our inner and outer environments and learn to live in them" (1996: 3–4). This leads him to envision a world in which "hierarchical organisations are replaced by networks of co-operating individuals, in whose lives art becomes once more as essential an element as finding a living" (209). Here he draws inspiration from Ivan Illich, whose *Deschooling Society* rested on the thesis that "the right to learn is curtailed by the obligation to attend school" (1976a: 7). Illich insisted on this vital distinction between education and schooling. It was the latter that was the butt of his enduring critique: he viewed compulsory schooling as a type of national service into which children are drafted by the state and he viewed the school itself as a prison in which children are kept sequestered from ordinary, day-to-day life, their young lives governed by the tyranny of a graded curriculum and a monopolistic system bound by countless rules and regulations that "legally combines prejudice with discrimination" (18). Small has direct recourse to Illich in relation to his observation that, in many parts of the world, the solitary music practice of the kind usually required of a child who pursues a music education in the West would run counter to the principle of learning through social experience, quoting a passage from *After Deschooling, What?* where Illich writes:

> I believe that only actual participation constitutes socially valuable learning, a participation by the learner in every stage of the learning process, including not only a free choice of what is to be learned and how it is to be learned but also a free determination by each learner of his own reason for living and learning—the part that his knowledge is to play in his life. (Illich 1976b: 14, quoted in Small 1996: 183)

Other educational and social critics, such as John Holt (author of the influential *How Children Fail*, first published in 1964), contribute to the notion that self-regulated learning is part of a broader ethic of self-determination, underlining the need for such learning to be integrated into and directly applicable to "real" life, as opposed to existing in a category apart where disembodied "knowledge" is accumulated for its own sake.

In the case of institutionalised music education, it has to be acknowledged that—as with my collection of singing manuals from the early- to mid-twentieth century—many things have changed since the times of which Small, Illich, and Holt were writing.[28] Again, however, this acknowledgement is made with the caveat that many of those who, as adults, found their way into music making by joining community choirs were put through a state education system that many of today's educators would consider less enlightened. Recent developments in Britain certainly include significant steps in the direction of what is termed in official parlance "self-directed learning" and "widening participation". In many parts of the country, the proportion of schoolchildren learning a musical instrument has increased substantially. Sistema England is modelled on the Venezuelan El Sistema initiative; it describes itself in its mission statement as a programme that works to "transform the lives of children, young people and their communities through the power of music making" by "giv[ing] every child in England the opportunity to be part of an orchestra or choir, and strive for musical excellence, developing their full potential" (http://sistemaengland.org.uk/mission/, acc. April 8, 2014). Sing Up was a major initiative that ran from 2007 to 2011 as the Music Manifesto's National Singing Programme. "Dedicated to the proposition that all children should have access to high quality singing opportunities every day" and supported by tailor-made teacher training programmes and an online song bank, it undoubtedly led to an increase in the attention and time devoted to singing in many primary schools (http://www.singup.org/, acc. February 26, 2012). At the secondary education level, examination syllabuses are no longer restricted to the study of "great works"; some include options relating to popular music or world music, and there is scope for greater diversity in the realm of composition. At the same time, music still struggles to hold its ground in the secondary school curriculum and will find itself in an even more fragile position if music continues to be excluded from the list of core subjects in the government's controversial proposals for curriculum reform. Meanwhile, success is still measured by such indices as the higher percentage of children learning a musical instrument, and the graded examinations of the Associated Board of the Royal Schools of Music and Trinity Guildhall still influence the structure and ethos of instrumental learning across the globe. It is worth noting here that my intention in engaging critically with these trends and conventions and in giving space to the dissenting voices that have gathered around them is not to suggest that the entire edifice of state-controlled music education be summarily dismantled. But it is also quite clear that there is ample room for alternative approaches in music education—in terms of *what* is taught, *how* it is taught, *to whom* it is taught, *why* it is learnt, and what is *done with it* once it has been learnt.

I end this chapter by zooming out to the bigger picture as seen through the eyes of Ivan Illich. The different aspects of Illich's vision for a healthy and sustainable society come together in his notion of "conviviality". Since Illich uses this term in a quite specific way, it is worth quoting his definition in full:

> I choose the term "conviviality" to designate the opposite of industrial productivity. I intend it to mean autonomous and creative intercourse among persons, and the intercourse of persons with their environment; and this in contrast with the conditioned response of persons to the demands made upon them by others, and by a man-made environment. I consider conviviality to be individual freedom realized in personal interdependence and, as such, an intrinsic ethical value. (Illich 2009: 11)

We will return in later chapters to the spirit of this definition, alongside more conventional understandings of "conviviality" that are more akin to the notions of celebration, festivity, and collective joy that concern Barbara Ehrenreich. For ethnomusicologists, anthropologists, and purveyors of a liberal arts education it is axiomatic that when we talk about learning we are talking not only about acquiring skills, knowledge, or understanding. We are also—like Illich—talking about *living*, which is a far weightier concern. It is with this thought that I bring us back to the world of natural-voice choirs and world song networks, where for many (as we shall see in the chapters that follow) learning to sing with others is inextricably bound up with learning to live differently.

NOTES
1. This vignette (unlike those that opened chapters 1 and 3) is a composite of many such sessions at which I have been present, rather than a description of a single event as it actually unfolded. Some of the exercises and images mentioned can be found in Kristin Linklater's *Freeing the Natural Voice* (2006), Tony Backhouse's *Freeing the Song* (2010), articles from Chris Rowbury's *From the Front of the Choir* blog (http://blog.chrisrowbury.com), and various writings by Frankie Armstrong. The majority circulate freely in the oral tradition on which most community choir directors draw.
2. Alongside her formidable musical achievements, Barnwell also holds BSc and MSc degrees in speech pathology, an MSc in public health, and a PhD in craniofacial studies.
3. A native of New Zealand, Backhouse later moved to Australia, where in 1986 he founded the country's foremost *a cappella* gospel choir, Café of the Gate of Salvation.
4. In the case of a weekly choir meeting, where the session will last for no more than two hours, a maximum of fifteen minutes might be devoted to the initial warm up routine. For a day workshop, the amount of time given over to such exercises will vary according to the focus of the event. A workshop entitled "Finding Your Voice" is more likely to consist of exploratory activities than arrangements of songs in four-part harmony, whereas participants in a workshop entitled "Songs of the Caucasus"—especially if it is led by a visiting teacher from Georgia—might expect to move far more quickly (if not immediately) to the business of singing songs.
5. The crucial part played by imagery in Kristin's work is reflected in the subtitle of the revised and expanded edition of *Freeing the Natural Voice: Imagery and Art in the Practice of Voice and Language*. While not a singing manual as such (it is aimed principally at actors), it is packed full of exercises focusing on the body, the breath, and the way in which sound is produced, guided throughout by the overriding objective of freeing the voice and, with it, the person.
6. More familiar rationales also apply, of course, with vocal sequences used to warm the voice up slowly so as to avoid strain by over-singing or stretching too far beyond a comfortable range.
7. A selection of Frankie and Darien's exercises can be found on their practice CD *Voice Exercises & Songs*. This contains descriptions and demonstrations of a selection of physical and vocal warm-up exercises, together with simple rounds and part-songs suitable for beginners.

8. NVPN member Teresa Verney uses this technique in her one-to-one sessions with individuals who think they "can't sing", starting very simply with the speaking voice (always using imitation or call-and-response as the point of departure) before "gradually lead[ing] people into the singing voice without them realising, and then within five minutes they realise they're singing" (interview 2008).
9. The importance of the open throat in Frankie's method is reflected in two of her favourite axioms, "Your throat's job is to get out of the way" and "I voice *through* my throat not *with* my throat" (Armstrong and Pritchard 2005: 35). The notion of singing through, not with the throat echoes William Blake, who wrote, "I see through, not with my eyes". Blake's words inspired a song Frankie wrote in 1987 at a time when she was struggling with the fear of losing what little functional sight she had left.
10. During her years with the Gardzienice Theatre Association, for example, Maryana took part in expeditions to Egypt, Cuba, Brazil, Afghanistan, Lapland, and Ireland, as well as Ukraine.
11. Daleks are the fictional, extraterrestrial cyborgs that featured in the British television series *Doctor Who* from the early 1960s. Mention of them often provokes a harsh, nasal-sounding/twangy imitation of their catchphrase, "exterminate!" In 1999 an image of a Dalek appeared on a postage stamp celebrating British popular culture.
12. In the early years of her teaching career in the UK, Dessi compiled a CD entitled *Wild Wind*, conceived as "a course in authentic Bulgarian singing in easy-to-follow stages". At the time of writing, this resource is unfortunately no longer available but Dessi can be seen demonstrating a range of vocal techniques used in Bulgarian singing in a short film in the Wellcome Collection, *Singing With Two Voices*: see http://www.youtube.com/watch?feature=player_embedded&v=-o31Yg936Ac, acc. August 20, 2013.
13. Cleall, who became Professor of Solo Singing and Voice Production at Trinity College of Music at the age of only twenty-two, has enjoyed a distinguished career in the world of British choral music and church music.
14. This slim volume, which underwent multiple reprints, is presented as "A Complete Guide to Teachers, Students and Candidates for the A.R.C.M., L.R.A.M., and all Similar Examinations".
15. Ysaye Barnwell offers a useful definition of worldview as "the way in which a culture organizes its perceptions, thoughts, language and actions to order and analyze and give meaning to an essentially chaotic universe" (1989: 8).
16. *Singing in the African American Tradition* consists of an A4 size booklet and four CDs (in the original edition, six cassettes). The notes provide the user with an introduction to the historical, social, and political contexts of the different genres. In a now time-honoured format, the recordings feature each of the song's parts separately, as well as all of them sung together.
17. Founded in 1866 with support from the American Missionary Association as part of a programme to educate freed slaves, Fisk was the first American university to provide a liberal arts education for "young men and women irrespective of color" (http://www.fiskjubileesingers.org, acc. February 19, 2012).
18. Robeson, whose father was a run-away slave turned preacher, took a particularly keen interest in the plight of the Welsh coal miners.
19. This adventure inspired Polly to embark on a project on the Fisk Jubilee Singers, in the process of which she unearthed some "cracking songs" for which she then made her own arrangements, suitable for community choirs.

20. See also David Reck's observation that "much indigenous music of many of the world's peoples ('primitive' or otherwise) is technically more complex than that of Europe or America" and his proposal that the variety of harmonic systems and polyphonic styles found in oral traditions across the world "mak[es] questionable the assumption that musical notation is a prerequisite for the 'higher' and more complex technologies of musical structure" (1997: 272–273).
21. A significant new addition to these resources is the volume *Community Voiceworks*, in the Oxford University Press Voiceworks series, compiled and edited by Gitika Partington and Ali Burns. For further details of the titles listed and other similar resources, see the section Songbooks, Teaching CDs/DVDs, and Online Resources on the companion website.
22. Turino borrows these labels from James Graves (2005), who introduced them in his discussion of folk arts.
23. This is not the place to enter into the debate over Pérès/Organum's controversial interpretation of the Machaut mass, which was also released on CD (1996). For the interested reader, the reviews posted on the Amazon website offer an indication of some of the issues raised.
24. The *Don Juan* soundtrack was released by Auvidis in 1998.
25. For more detailed discussion of the Corsican examples given here, see Bithell 2007.
26. *Medea* was released on the Naïve label in 2006.
27. Bothwell's compositions can be found on the CD *Tavagna Canta Malcolm Bothwell* (2002).
28. For an insight into current trends and debates in music education in the UK, see Hallam and Creech 2010 and Philpott and Spruce 2012.

CHAPTER 5

Singing the Songs of Others

A WORLD OF SONG

On a bright Saturday in May 2009, I take a trip to the Welsh seaside town of Llandudno, where four community choirs from across North Wales—each directed by a member of the NVPN—are coming together to stage a joint concert to raise funds for Sing for Water. The short profiles in the printed programme are revealing for what they say about each choir's musical tastes and sense of identity, while the performance itself offers an instructive insight into the choirs' working repertoire. Coastal Voices, based in nearby Abergele and led by Sara Brown, sings "close harmony songs from around the world". The repertoire of Lleisiau'r Byd/World Voices from Porthmadog, co-directed by David Gunn and Christine Eastwood, ranges "from Jazz to Native American, African to Eastern European, Far Eastern to English Folk". The members of Dolgellau Choir/Côr Dolgellau, directed by Roxane Smith, "enjoy all sorts of music, from cheesy songs from the sixties to deeply spiritual songs from Eastern Europe". Bangor Community Choir, led by Pauline Down, again sings "a cappella harmony songs from all over the world".[1] Each choir performs a set of five or six songs before joining the other choirs in a grand finale of a further three songs. This composite programme features three gospel songs ("Lord, Don't Turn Your Child Away", as learnt from Northern Harmony;[2] "The Storm Is Passing Over" from Ysaye Barnwell's *Singing in the African American Tradition*; and Nick Prater's arrangement of "Love Like a River"[3]); five African songs (including two from South Africa); three songs from Eastern Europe (one Bosnian, one Croatian, one Greek); an arrangement of the Cuban classic "Guantanamera"; a shape-note song; a harmonisation of an Italian folk song by Helen Chadwick; an arrangement of an English folk song from the Copper Family repertoire; a Welsh folk song; five arrangements of contemporary popular songs (including Dee Jarlett's arrangement of Labi Siffre's "Something Inside So Strong"); and new compositions by Nickomo, Ali Burns, Ros Thomas, and David Gunn (all members of the NVPN).

CDs recorded by established choirs are a further indication of the breadth of repertoire and varied provenance of the songs that circulate in the natural voice world; at the same time, they reflect the distinctive identities of individual choirs. WorldSong, founded by Chris Rowbury in the city of Coventry (West Midlands), is an example of a choir explicitly dedicated to world music. Its ten-year anniversary CD, *WorldSong Live: A Decade in Harmony, 1997-2007*, includes songs from France, Norway, Croatia, Macedonia, Poland, Georgia, Ukraine, New Zealand, Japan, South Africa, Zimbabwe, Hawai'i, and Wales, together with a Shaker song from the United States, four spirituals, the gospel song "Lord, Don't Turn Your Child Away" in an arrangement by the Jubilee Quartet, the Rev. Robert Lowry's "How Can I Keep from Singing?" as popularised by Pete Seeger, "Unison in Harmony" by Jim Boyes, and a setting of a Latin liturgical text by Helen Chadwick.

The repertoire of Global Harmony in the Devonshire town of Totnes in southwest England combines world music with new compositions, including pieces by choir members whose song-writing endeavours have been encouraged by their director, Roz Walker. The CD *Songs for Today* (2002) features songs representing different genres and moods as well as different parts of the globe. Here, we find four African songs, a gospel song, two Georgian songs (a love song and a song of friendship), a Croatian love song ("Plovi Barko"), a Russian church song ("Tebye Pajom"), a Spanish lullaby ("A La Nanita"), and a French drinking song. These are balanced by ten contemporary compositions: "This Great Sky" by Ali Burns, a song from Nickomo's Harmonic Temple collection, one song each by members of the American ensembles Libana and Northern Harmony, and six songs written by members of Global Harmony.

Bristol's Gasworks Choir presents yet another orientation, giving pride of place to lively and sumptuous arrangements of popular songs by its directors Dee Jarlett and Ali Orbaum. *The Best of the Gasworks Choir* (2005) includes arrangements of titles by The Beatles, The Zombies, Sting, Tracy Chapman, Mike Scott, Johnny Nash, Tom Jones, Labi Siffre, and others. These are interspersed with a sprinkling of songs from further afield—a Georgian song, a South African song as popularised by Miriam Makeba, a Nigerian song, a Sephardic folk song, a gospel song and a Scottish song (the last four also arranged by either Dee or Ali).

Taken together, the foregoing examples illustrate the extent to which songs from a surprising variety of "other" cultures have entered the repertoires of individual choirs in different parts of Britain. In the previous chapter, we gained an insight into how these songs are sourced and disseminated. We also found answers to some of our questions about how "world songs" mesh with the NVPN ideology and help the movement achieve its aims. It is worth reiterating that it was the musical material—crucially, songs from outside the

British tradition—that first claimed Frankie Armstrong's attention and then led her to elaborate the principles and methodology that are now at the heart of the natural voice endeavour. A set of further questions now presents itself. How exactly do the songs work to produce the more discrete benefits to which the movement aspires? What exactly do comparatively privileged and secure Western singers identify with when they encounter a fragment of the life of a Central African forest dweller or a Bosnian shepherd? What is the appeal of singing in a language one doesn't speak or understand? What new meanings do the songs and the act of singing them acquire? In what ways might they contribute to a change in consciousness for those who enter into their deeper recesses?

In engaging in a more comprehensive and grounded examination of these matters, I seek to identify the different levels of attraction the songs might hold for choir leaders and for choir members and workshop participants. I also consider the rewards they bring, as reported by individual singers. In terms of primary sources, I draw extensively on personal interviews and questionnaire responses. As applied to quotations included in this chapter (where I do not limit myself to data from the British cohort alone), "Unicorn questionnaire" denotes responses received from a survey circulated (by email) to all attendees following the 2007 Unicorn Natural Voice Camp; most of these were UK-based. Citations referenced as "Giving Voice questionnaire" relate to delegates at the 2007 Giving Voice festival held in Aberystwyth, Wales, who took part in the three-day workshop led by members of Theatre Zar (Poland); these included participants from different parts of Europe as well as the United Kingdom. Citations referenced as "Corsica questionnaire" relate to a Village Harmony camp held in Corsica in 2004, where the majority of participants were from the United States and were active in community choirs organised along similar lines to many community choirs in the United Kingdom.

THE ATTRACTION OF SONGS FROM ELSEWHERE

Scenes from Frankie Armstrong's story, as recounted in chapter 3, revealed that her adoption of Eastern European songs was founded not simply on her aesthetic attraction to the sound but also on her recognition of the social and psychological potential of the material for British and American singers. Additional insights into the attraction of songs from elsewhere can be found in the explanations of other voice practitioners who have been drawn to songs from non-Western cultures, often independently of (or prior to) their association with the NVPN, and have discovered the value of using such songs—specifically, songs in foreign languages—in their own practice.

Sarah Harman identifies several reasons for using "a lot of material from other cultures" when she first started working with community choirs.

Accessibility and the ease of achieving pleasing results quickly and painlessly were high on the list:

> Those songs came out of traditions where *ordinary* people were singing them, they were *easy* to pick up, you got *glorious* harmony very, very quickly, which certainly in my folk tradition you didn't get.... And, for me, it was that—it was their accessibility, it was the instant beautiful harmony.

What the songs were about and what they could tell us about the lives of those who sang them in their place of origin was of almost equal importance:

> It was also that those songs were about things that either resonated with the people that I was teaching...*or* they were introducing a whole other culture and introducing ideas, they were broadening people's perspectives and making them think about what it might be like to be somebody else living in another culture—so part of the political work, if you like.

Broadening people's ideas about music by introducing a relativist perspective was also part of Sarah's mission:

> And also there was something for me...about people's rules that they've got in their head about what is a good harmony and what is a bad harmony and the whole idea that, if you lived somewhere else, what you thought was a normal, everyday, ordinary harmony would be completely different—if you lived in Bulgaria, your idea of what was a weird harmony would be very different—and I think, to give people a chance to suddenly go, "Oh, so I see, that's not weird or wrong, it's just something unusual for me." (Harman interview 2008)

Already, then, we have a series of prompts to guide our investigation, which I now pursue in the following order: first, the opportunity to explore and appreciate new sound worlds, free of one's own cultural constraints or prejudices, and to take pleasure in new experiences; second, the opportunity to enter, if only fleetingly, the lives of others, to empathise with their concerns, and to come to an understanding of shared life experiences; and third, the discovery of resources that are unavailable in one's own culture but that fulfil a present need.

Entering New Sound Worlds

Some of the less-familiar musical styles embraced by natural voice choirs and choirs of a more specialist bent, such as Eastern European choirs, and by people who attend Village Harmony camps and Giving Voice festivals, introduce a whole new layer of sound features in the form of harmonies, intervals, timbres, and other vocal effects characteristic of a particular culture. The pleasure of discovering sound worlds that are so unexpectedly and fundamentally different from their own was vividly conveyed by many of the musical explorers I surveyed in the course of my research. When asked, "What do you feel that you gain from learning repertoire and singing styles from other parts of the world?", many of my respondents spoke of the thrill they derived from these new opportunities and went on to reflect on the way in which what they learned had enriched their approach to singing in general. Charles, a nineteen-year-old American student writing after attending Village Harmony's Corsican camp, remarks:

> People... tend to use one way of singing for their entire lives... not even thinking about it because they don't need to. Actually learning music from throughout the world shows you so many drop-dead-gorgeous singing traditions, exposes you to music that moves you down to the very marrow... And it makes you exercise so many different ways of singing that you start to figure out the ways that work best, not just the ways that you've always done it. Overall, it's sort of like feeding the addiction you never knew you had for the chocolate that nobody else has discovered yet. (Charles, Corsica questionnaire 2004)

The allusion to "addiction" and the suggestion of forging a pioneering path might also catch our attention here. Anthony Johnston, a Bristol-based teacher and choir leader who attended the same camp, adds the notion of personal risk-taking to the mix:

> As a singer, I get a whole different sense of what it means to sing in terms of what timbre and what volume to use. I have to stick my neck out more in order to sound more authentic. I am required to put more of myself on the line when I sing world songs, to reveal myself more. In order to sound more Georgian, Bulgarian or Corsican, I need to explore singing in different ways, using my voice in new and different ways....

He goes on to talk about overcoming the constraints of the culture in which one has grown up:

> As a musician, my sense of what melody, harmonisation, and rhythm are is challenged too. The rules of Western music, spoken and unspoken, are questioned, broken down and seen for what they are—constraints. I gain a far more expansive idea as to what is possible in vocal music, the harmonic textures, what notes can stand next to others that you would never hear in mainstream Western music. (Anthony, Corsica questionnaire 2004)

Anthony's reference to "questioning the rules" of Western music may have an unwelcome ring for a music teacher at pains to instil the rudiments of Western music theory into his pupils. It does not take a rampant revolutionary, however, to point out the artificiality of the equal tempered scale or the absurdity of any assumption that the modern Western musical system— or what Christopher Small dubs "the logical daylit world of tonal harmony" (1996: 11)—is the only "correct" one. Since the question of "naturalness" is central to our explorations, a short diversion is in order here. In his essay "On the Musical Scales of Various Nations", British mathematician and phonetician Alexander John Ellis (best known in musicological circles for his elaboration of the cents system) observed that "the Musical Scale is not one, not 'natural'...but very diverse, very artificial, and very capricious" (1885: 526). Early scientists devoted much energy to the business of equating musical intervals with mathematical laws. Yet the scale that is achieved by dividing the octave into twelve equal semitones no longer corresponds to mathematically accurate ratios and therefore, in Anthony Storr's words, has "distanced Western tonal music still further from nature" (1992: 54). Moreover, while it may come tantalisingly close, this scale cannot be fully mapped against the harmonic series and so loses any claim to naturalness on that count: the fifth harmonic, for example, is a pure third (plus two octaves) that is flatter than the contemporary major third, while the infamous seventh harmonic falls inconveniently between A natural and B flat. Another slippage occurs with the Pythagorean comma that denotes the difference between twelve perfect fifths and seven octaves (in other words, the degree to which the note arrived at via the cycle, or circle, of fifths is sharper than that produced by the octave series). These acoustic enigmas give some indication of why the *modulatory* freedom that the equal tempered scale makes possible results in what Small refers to as "a type of mistuning...that other cultures would find intolerable" (1996: 35).

This does not mean that the "correct" solution is easily to be found elsewhere. Even a cursory tour of musical scales from different parts of the globe reveals a diversity that is clearly rooted as much in culture as in nature. While the octave, the perfect fourth, and the perfect fifth are found in most musical systems, other pitches fluctuate. Many systems employ what in Western parlance are known as as "microtones "or "expanded intervals" (intervals that are respectively smaller or larger than a semitone or 100 cents), and neutral thirds (somewhere between 300 and 400 cents) are especially common. What is in tune for one person may therefore be out of tune for another. Questions of consonant and dissonant intervals are likewise related to culture rather than nature, and even within a culture they are not necessarily stable over time. Charles Rosen notes, for example, that in Western music "thirds and sixths have been consonances since the fourteenth century; before that they were considered unequivocally dissonant" (1975: 24). Adopting an approach akin to that applied earlier to the question of presentational versus participatory music, the only legitimate conclusion to be drawn is that, from a universal perspective, no one system is more or less "correct", no one interval more or less "in tune": they are simply different.

To return to the quotations that served as our starting point for this section, Charles and Anthony's references to using the voice in new ways point not only to vocal exploration or experimentation as an end in itself but also to its centrality in the quest for a more "authentic" sound. Here again, there are useful perspectives to be gained from digging a little deeper. Songs from folk traditions, or from art music traditions in the non-Western world, are clearly not composed with the European bel canto voice in mind. This is in part for the pragmatic reason that a particular style of voice production and projection will develop to some extent in response to the environment in which the voice operates. Outdoor environments make different demands from indoor settings, and large, public spaces differ considerably from intimate, domestic ones. The inhabitants of forests develop musical structures and vocal styles that are very different from those of mountain dwellers or coastal peoples. Consider, for example, Louis Sarno's explanation of why the distinctive yodels of the Bayaka people of the Western Congo Basin are an efficient musical choice in the acoustic environment of the primary rainforest they inhabit: "Yodels . . . are the most natural and effective way to use the voice in this environment, because as the voice resonates through the trees both high and low notes hang in the air at the same time. A single voice thus creates a chord" (1995: 70). Tony Backhouse reminds us that the evolution of the Western operatic style was a necessary response to the demands placed on the singer by the increasing size of both opera houses and orchestras (2004: 6).[4] Styles that develop in this fashion then become ingrained in the identity of the music (and often, by extension, of the national or ethnic group) and established as the "right" way to do things. In this way what are seen as the music's most important defining features stay with it even when the environment changes, functioning as a marker of authenticity. This has three implications that are of relevance here. First, the preferred or approved vocal style in a modern society may no longer be quite so fit for purpose as it was at an earlier point in history. Second, assuming or insisting that a vocal style that has developed in one environment should be retained in new and sometimes radically different environments, as if it were independent of physical contingencies and functional imperatives, is less than logical. And third, working with repertoires from many different cultures of origin *requires* the use of a more varied vocal palette.

The criteria according to which a voice is evaluated also vary from one culture to another. Seemingly aesthetic preferences are often, as suggested in chapter 2, based on different underlying values. Outside the Western classical tradition, matters of intention, conviction, and communication might carry greater weight than conventional assessments of what may be considered a "beautiful" or "pleasing" voice. The pure, ethereal tone often associated with Early Music or the sound of an English cathedral choir may be admired by but, at the same time, be devoid of meaning for a listener on the other side of the globe. Similarly, as Tony Backhouse points out, some of the greatest gospel singers have "hoarse, rough voices" that appeal to listeners in their own culture for reasons that might not be immediately obvious to an ear acclimatised to cathedral choirs:

> I've heard people with lovely voices and a tonne of technique leave a congregation cold, while someone with less technical ability can light a fire under the audience through the sheer feeling and integrity of their performance. Expression, not technique is what matters here. (Backhouse 2004: 3)

Backhouse's observation correlates with my comments in chapter 4 on the positive audience reception to community choir performances that engage and provoke a visceral reaction in the listener that is independent of any objective assessment of musicianship on the basis of technique.

Not only do different cultures have their own norms and notions of what constitutes a "good" voice, but there may also be greater variety within a culture (when compared with modern Britain, for example) in terms of the range of vocal styles and techniques that may be employed. For a singer who has not undergone a formal, classical training, it is often easier to find these other voices because he or she does not have to struggle to undo set patterns, whether mental or physical, and let go of his or her notions about the "right" way of doing things. Some of the techniques found in Western popular music, jazz, and rock (e.g. belting and twang) come close to some of the sounds found in non-Western music. In this regard, Backhouse's reference to the inclusion of "moaning, growling, screaming, grunting and a whole range of effects and colours foreign to the Western model" in the "hard lead" voice in a gospel ensemble (2004: 3) points to the utility of the kinds of warm-up exercises I described in chapter 4, above and beyond simply opening up the voice.

Entering the Lives of Others

Sarah Harman's desire to use material from outside the British heritage in order to broaden people's musical experience was linked explicitly with the humanistic project of promoting greater understanding and appreciation of other cultures. This dimension also surfaces frequently in the responses of participants in choirs, workshops, and summer camps in which world songs feature prominently. In the context of his experience as a participant in Village Harmony's Corsican camp, Anthony expands on the idea of "meeting other people" through their songs:

> Each country's songs have their own unique flavour, being born out of the people's relationship to their everyday existence; their work, daily struggles, their joys, celebrations, rituals, customs, their history, their stories, and their relationship to the land. By singing songs from around the world, I feel as if I am meeting the people who sing or would have sung those songs. I meet something of who they are—their lives, their land, their soul. (Anthony, Corsica questionnaire 2004)

Rosa (part of the American contingent visiting Corsica with Village Harmony in 2004) voices similar sentiments:

> When I sing music from a certain place, I feel more connected with its people and their ancestors and more able to understand what they feel. It gives that place a certain familiarity and makes my world closer and more connected. (Rosa, Corsica questionnaire 2004)

It is interesting to note Rosa's repetition of the word "connected". This theme of connection also appears frequently in the responses to my Unicorn Camp questionnaire. Rina, for example, reports "a sense of connection to far away places and peoples that I will probably never visit". Others emphasise the idea of sharing fundamental human experiences across the geographical divide, in spite of obvious cultural-historical differences. References are made to feeling "a sense of sharing and solidarity" (Jane), gaining "a clarity about how much humankind have in common" (Gill), and "sharing hopes and dreams, knowing that we are all one, though facing different problems and similar joys!" (Angela). Clearly, this kind of realisation helps to bridge some of the gaps between cultures, beyond the realm of "the music itself".

Zarine prompts us to extrapolate further when she speaks of:

> A shared sense of humanity; a feeling that sound is healing and expressive from a heart-mind perspective rather than solely a mathematical-intellectual perspective; that voices joined in song or improvised sound and rhythm create a connection that is familiar and unselfish but is often hidden in daily (industrialised countries/urban) activities. (Zarine, Giving Voice questionnaire 2008)

Here we have the notion that engaging with songs from elsewhere can provide us with insights and resources that are not so readily available in our own society, providing us with a different kind of tool kit for approaching problems that require solving or ills that require healing. Another Unicorn respondent pursues a related theme, that of rediscovering a sense of vitality and groundedness that some no longer find in their own culture: "I think we are quite removed from our cultural heritage in this country, so often songs from other cultures seem more alive, more strongly connected to spirit, to the earth."

The notion that music serves as a bridge between cultures takes on surprisingly graphic dimensions in other accounts provided by British and American singers fresh from the experience of learning songs in their place of origin, some of which also suggest an opening-up and merging of identities. Seventeen-year-old Meiling is especially eloquent on this subject:

> I think that singing...transcends so many borders, so by learning international music you are given a common language with which to speak and connect to people you may have never considered it possible to communicate with before.... By figuring out you have so many voices within you, you figure out that we all have so many people within us; so I am no longer just an American, but I recognize that the fibre and essence of the Bulgarian, Georgian, South African and Corsican people is somewhere inside me also. (Meiling, Corsica questionnaire 2004)

This suggests that what might, on the surface, be viewed in an uncomplicated way as a singing holiday does more profound existential and moral work by prompting participants to question assumptions about their own national identities, and particularly, to reject the notion of identities as monolithic, static, or divisive. Heidi (an educational fundraiser at an American university) makes a similar comment:

> Singing the traditional songs of cultures other than our own puts us empathetically in other bodies, looking out of other eyes, singing out of other throats. It helps us to imagine ourselves in other times and places than within the narrow confines of our own life histories. (Heidi, Corsica questionnaire 2004)

By extension, songs from elsewhere offer the possibility of reinventing oneself—of imagining the self one might yet become.

Deeper Resonances: Lost Pasts and Present Yearnings

At this juncture I wish to probe more deeply into the connection between two of the threads that have emerged thus far: on the one hand, the idea that we might find in other cultures some kind of salve or solution for a problem in our own lives, and on the other, the idea that properties of the music are liberating at the level of both the intellect and the psyche. Earlier, we established the appeal of music that breaks free from the constraints of European classical harmony. At an intellectual level this applies primarily to singers schooled in the rules of composition. Singers who have not had this training will not be in a position to identify specific harmonic procedures that transcend or defy these rules. Yet they, too, experience a powerful sensory thrill—which they often characterise in strikingly visceral terms as "spine-tingling" or "making the hairs on the back of your neck stand on end"—that allows them to share the same joy of singing unfamiliar combinations of tones, such as so-called discords, parallel fifths, or tritones. This physical "buzz" is often linked with an enhanced sense of well being and an immediate feeling of being re-energised. Joan Mills makes a connection between early music and non-Western styles. In her youth, she says, she found early music "very exciting" in its use of parallel fourths and fifths:

> I think there's something about intervals—the space between certain notes meeting certain notes—that just...somehow causes something. It somehow feels like a chemical *rush* in the body.

Some years later she heard Simha Arom's recordings of Aka music, "and absolutely," she says, "my ears lit up...when I heard that." The same thing happened when she heard Marcel Cellier's *Mystère des Voix Bulgares* recordings and when she first experienced singing Balkan songs with Frankie Armstrong:

> That tingle would happen, that buzz, that extraordinary reaction....It was the *sound*, first and foremost...it was just the fact that this note touches this note and just this exciting buzz of the way they fit together. (Mills interview 2005)

Jackie Roxborough links the pull of certain harmonies with the affective experience of connectedness:

> Particularly the harmonies, I think, really sell it to people and it allows them to feel their personal vibration and their frequency of their voice—not a pitching, but a real sense of belonging. It's the community again, isn't it? (Roxborough interview 2007)

Joan Mills also makes a link between notions of musical harmony and human community when she says:

> I *loved* these songs and I *loved* the way that they required other persons to lean on and to be kind of locked into in a way that my solo culture of folk tradition— they're all solo songs and you're alone there singing those. And suddenly here was this community of other people. (Mills interview 2005)

For Nick Prater, too, "the key word is community". Singing and dancing— together with eating, drinking, and fire—lie at the heart of every culture, he observes:

> And I think the reason that we as Westerners, or as English people, are really drawn to these other kinds of music is because they represent a still cohesive

community that we've lost, so that's what they offer us.... We're left with a bit of English folk tradition and that somehow doesn't pull us together in that way. (Prater interview 2007)

Similarly, Nina Chandler, who performs Georgian songs in the United Kingdom as a member of the female *a cappella* trio Kviria, alights on the word "connection"—alongside the notion of "loss"—in trying to explain the affinity she feels with Georgian singing in particular:

I think for me, it's about a culture that I feel I'm distant from.... Somehow singing in that language gives expression to a longing for something that we don't have at the moment in our twenty-first-century technological [life], whizzing about, being busy.... It's a connection with something that I think we've lost. (Chandler interview 2009)

This nostalgia for a lost past that is imagined as more innocent, natural, and nurturing than the present fuels many revival movements. The past to which revivalists turn is usually, however, their own. Why, then, do the singers we have heard from in this chapter not join the current wave of the English or British folk resurgence? Some of the above interview extracts hint at the way in which the English folk tradition is felt to be lacking. Several of the people I interviewed share the view that the English folk tradition is not well suited to the community choir context. Both Sarah Harman and Joan Mills pinpoint one important reason: the predominance of solo songs and the comparatively thin pickings when one is looking for songs in harmony. Joan goes on to talk about the way in which songs from other parts of the world were sometimes incorporated into the theatrical productions of Cardiff Laboratory Theatre. "And why are we not singing a British song there?" she asks. "Because there isn't one." They might be looking for a song that had an aura of antiquity or ritual, she explains, and this might be suggested by the *sound* of a particular song, regardless of its original meaning or function as well as its provenance. The type of theatre they were making also needed something "to evoke community". Again, she says, this need was best met with a polyphonic song (Mills interview 2005).

Next to harmony, rhythm is a musical feature that is often cited as part of the attraction of songs from elsewhere and this, too, is sometimes presented as a feature lacking in music found closer to home. When I interviewed Margaret Walton and Lynn Yule, both members of Bangor Community Choir, they spoke about their choir's reactions to some of the British folk songs they had learnt. "I don't think they've been terribly popular, actually," Margaret ventured. "I think the choir enjoys the exotic—you know, the African and the Georgian and the Bulgarian...and the spirituals as well: they enjoy those." When choir members have the opportunity to request favourites, says Lynn, "it's nearly always the African stuff we go back to," and Margaret adds, "I think it's the big rhythmic stuff that people enjoy" (Walton and Yule interview 2007). Some choir leaders have sought to remedy the dearth of multi-part material in the British tradition by making their own arrangements of English, Scottish, and Welsh folk songs, and it is interesting to note that some of the bolder arrangements have also introduced more varied or complex rhythms. Many of the new compositions that have emerged in recent years are also more adventurous in their use of rhythm as well as harmony (see chapter 9).

There are, though, further dimensions to the kind of antipathy that is sometimes expressed in British society at large towards songs in the vernacular. For many, the English folk tradition it is a source of embarrassment that lends itself to easy parody (typically, an exaggeratedly nasal form of voice production and a finger stuck in one ear, with the singer imagined as sporting an unkempt beard and baggy homespun jumper). For others, it simply appears dull and uninteresting. Sue Harris comments that, in the early days of the community choir movement,

> there was a real resistance to English traditional song—I think maybe partly the way it had been put over when we were at school or maybe to do with very classical-type arrangements of English folk song through Vaughan Williams and people like that. (Harris interview 2009)

Even some who grew up with the English folk tradition became uncomfortable with the way it seems to revel in melancholic and ultimately tragic tales of a woman's lot; it certainly did not fit well with the rise of second-wave feminist consciousness in the 1960s and 1970s. African and Balkan songs, by comparison, were experienced as invigorating and uplifting, even if in reality their subject matter was not always so very different.

Finally, as a number of British practitioners emphasised in interviews, when people have had negative experiences of singing in the past these were usually associated with singing in English. This, then, brings us to a more detailed consideration of questions of language.

THE POLITICS OF UNINTELLIGIBILITY

"I much prefer singing songs in other languages," says Barbara. This avowal seems surprising even before she goes on to comment: "Strangely, I also find it easier to learn the words!" (Unicorn questionnaire 2007). It is one thing to be drawn to the exotic, but why would someone relatively new to singing choose the considerable challenge of learning song texts in unfamiliar languages, which often contain sounds that do not have an equivalent in English? The answer to this question is complex, but it points to a number of ways in which singing in a language one does not speak or understand can be experienced as liberating.

First and foremost, as already suggested, learning new songs in a foreign language can free the singer from inhibitions and sensitivities associated with past experiences of singing more familiar repertoire in English. In chapter 4 we encountered Frankie Armstrong's proposal that "getting outside the structure and content of our daily language...can help us to get away from fears of the old patterns of self-criticism and negative judgement that so many of us carry (Armstrong and Pritchard 2005: 18). Jackie Roxborough pursues a related theme when she describes how many of the aspiring singers who find their way to her groups have felt alienated by the more conventional teaching methods they have been exposed to in traditional choirs or choral societies and, as a result:

> They often are very self-conscious about singing songs in their own language, so as soon as you use, say, some of the African [songs] particularly—there's rhythm there, it uses the body, it uses their voice in a different way, their throat production is different, and it begins to free people up from their own language.

She elaborates on how this therapeutic or emancipatory dimension also has a profound impact on an individual's sense of identity:

> And that to me is really where the voice and identity starts to open up a little bit as people lose the restrictions in themselves and actually find the identity they've been looking for through singing and through voice. (Roxborough interview 2007)

She refers to working with people in their forties or fifties who have come to her to "find their voice" in a very literal sense. Initially, they are "incredibly nervous" but, after six to eight weeks, "suddenly we're getting completely different personalities coming through and identities". In this scenario, what began as a quest for an as yet unexplored singing voice takes on more existential proportions.

Others welcome the opportunity to be free, at a cognitive level, of the literal meaning of the words. Ann Chamberlayne, who had belonged to more conventional classical choirs before discovering her local community choir, says:

> Words, to me, get in the way a lot of the time, which is one of the reasons I really enjoy singing the world songs because I don't understand the words, so the music and the rhythm can speak to me. I think it's one of the reasons that I've loved singing.... I'd rather sing something that doesn't have words I understand. (Chamberlayne interview 2007)

Chris Rowbury similarly attests to the way in which being freed of the distraction of words allows him to shift his attention to other dimensions:

> I'm not a word person, so I like the foreign lyrics because I use the sounds of the words as a vehicle for the musical expression. But if I understand the words they get in the way, the semantics of it gets in the way. (Rowbury interview 2008)

He enjoys being left with "just the sounds of the words.... It sort of slightly takes you out of yourself". Here, then, we also have a suggestion of a transcendental quality, where the ego is momentarily set aside.

Variations of these themes appear in many of the responses to my Unicorn questionnaire (2007). Jenny, for example, speaks of "a chance to let go into my voice when I am singing sounds that are unfamiliar or words that don't carry associations for me". Sally picks up on the notion of "being taken out of yourself" when she remarks: "Sometimes it is releasing.... I notice my own language can get in the way of numinous experience." For another respondent, the emphasis is more on not liking to sing words that make her feel awkward or uncomfortable: "I get a bit hung up on the meanings of words, so unless they really jump out at me in a poetic way, I feel a bit silly singing about some things in English."

The distancing process that takes place through language choice does not negate the lexical meaning, but it filters it through a different lens and repositions the speaker in relation to the utterance. Joan Mills reflects on the different cognitive processes at work when the brain is not preoccupied with literal meanings. Thinking back again to her first experience of learning a Balkan song in one of Frankie's workshops, and why this was "kind of freeing", she muses:

> We were learning it phonetically, obviously, and she *would* tell us what the song was about...but...the fact that it wasn't in English and it wasn't recognisable I felt very strongly made a difference to how the song was *perceived* by us; and...very early on I thought: "This is going through a different bit of the brain now, this is *not* the same as when you learn the words of something that you know. I'm actually learning sounds, effectively."...And there is something different about the way...it buzzes in the body. (Mills interview 2005)

The palpable difference in the overall sound when people sang in a language that was not their mother tongue was one of the things that impressed Frankie most forcibly when she began teaching Balkan songs. In her account of the voice workshop she established in London in 1975, she recalls deciding in the second week to teach an English song. She was immediately struck by the group's "muted response":

> Quite a lot of them...dropped back into their previous habits of vocal use, which they didn't when they sang Balkan songs with words that they didn't know.... It

was so dramatic....It was much easier to get people to explore vocal qualities using songs in languages they didn't know. (Armstrong interview 2008)

Some singers are nonetheless able to carry over the new ways of experiencing sound that they discover through singing in other languages into their interpretation of English songs. David explains:

> I really enjoy the opportunity to explore the emotiveness of song and sounds through melody and breath that singing in a language I don't understand brings. When words become sounds I feel it frees the voice to explore the emotional texture of song. I then apply this to my English language singing, thinking about an expression of the sound rather than the words to convey the meaning of the song. (Giving Voice questionnaire 2008)

Sarah Harman highlights yet another dimension:

> There's something to be said for moving people away from a language that they think they're really comfortable in, into a language where they have to work much harder at the sound....It shifts the anxiety, I find, the anxiety that is in everybody when they're learning a new song....If you take it to a place where people don't *expect* to know what they're doing, they somehow *seem* to find that easier to live with. If they think it's in English, they think if they understand the words then they've got the song. (Harman interview 2008)

In this case, the anxiety attaches not to past trauma that might be reawakened but to apprehension when faced with a new challenge. Sarah also comments that working with foreign text enables people to "come into the song in a very different way."[5]

Songs from Taizé

In chapter 3, we learnt of the simple chants emanating from the ecumenical Christian community of Taizé in France that are popular in some natural voice circles.[6] The use of language in this repertoire is illuminating in the context of our present discussion. Of the sixty-four pieces included in the collection *Songs from Taizé* (Taizé 1984), forty-two are settings of Latin texts. (Favourites include "Jubilate Deo", "Dona Nobis Pacem", "Da Pacem Domine", "Confitemini Domino", and "Veni Creator Spiritus", together with several settings of the Kyrie and Alleluia.) Other pieces are presented with multiple versions of the lyrics in different languages—usually English, French, German, Spanish, Italian, and Dutch, with Welsh, Russian, Eastern European, and Asian languages also putting in occasional appearances. Thus, while the songs are all from the Christian tradition, the collection has the appeal of being a multilingual resource. It was one response to the increasing numbers of young people from all over Europe who were finding their way to Taizé in the early 1970s.[7]

Another facet of the response was to embrace Latin as a neutral and quasi-universal language. The foreword to the American edition of *Music from Taizé: Volume 1* (People's Edition) explains that songs were needed that would enable people not sharing a common language to participate directly and as easily as possible in the activities of the community. It goes on to describe how, with the help of musician Jacques Berthier, "different methods were tested, and a solution found in the use of repetitive structures—short musical phrases with singable easily memorized melodies—and some very basic Latin texts", thus obviating the need to stop and teach a song before it could be sung (Taizé 1986: 3). *Music from Taizé: Volume 1* is available in different editions. The People's Edition contains the basic melodies for the canons, acclamations, responses, and refrains. These are predominantly settings of Latin text, with English translation, supplemented by a small number of new compositions with English lyrics by Berthier. The Latin refrains "bear up under constant repetition better than any vernacular" because of "the natural 'color' of the language" (ibid.). In the introductory notes to the Vocal Edition, Brother Robert stresses that the fact that Latin is no longer spoken as a living language means that it is "a foreign element for everyone, and hence neutral"; no one is either favoured or disadvantaged (Taizé 1982: vii). Furthermore:

> Experience has clearly shown that the repetitive style quickly runs the risk of making words from one of the living languages threadbare, whereas the "neutral" nature of a word or short phrase from a traditional liturgical language (for example, the Greek *Kyrie*, the Aramaic *Maranatha* or the Latin *Gloria*) is perfectly suited to the function of a response. (Taizé 1982: x)

In the Vocal Edition, the acclamations, responses, and refrains that are presented in the People's Edition with a single melody line are scored for four voices and supplemented by verses for solo cantor, together with keyboard and guitar accompaniments. Here, a variety of living languages is used for the verses, where the words do not need to be memorised by the whole assembly and do not run the same risk of becoming "threadbare" as a result of over-repetition.

The rationale as formulated in Taizé itself about the use of Latin is, interestingly, borne out by some of the comments made by British singers in my interviews and in questionnaire responses. Speakers of English and of many other European languages often find Latin easy to sing because the phonetics are predictable, making the words easy to read and pronounce. At the same time, even if many of the words are familiar to churchgoers, whether active or lapsed, and to those who attended schools where Latin still had a place in the curriculum, they allow the singer to distance him or herself from their literal meaning. One of my respondents, for example, states quite bluntly that "some words in English hymns make me puke [but] I can sing Christian words in Latin quite happily" (Unicorn questionnaire 2007).

Text and Meaning in the Vernacular

The preference for songs in a language one does not understand or speak is, then, not as contrary as it might at first appear. Moreover, when we survey different music cultures, we find that a variety of devices are used, in polyphonic singing in particular, that obscure the semantics of the text. Even when singers use their mother tongue, they might deliberately obfuscate the lexical meaning as a means of marking the boundary between initiates and non-initiates. More broadly, the psychoacoustic experience and the quality of interaction with one's fellow singers often take precedence over the meaning of the lyric. Tullia Magrini (1995) has written about the intriguing case of the North Italian ballad tradition, where the long narrative ballads formerly sung by women were refashioned as polyphonic songs to be sung by men. In the process, the text—which in female circles had fulfilled an important educational function—was devalued in favour of the harmonic experience. Often only a few stanzas were retained and these might be repeated several times in the course of a single rendition. In performance, the songs no longer told a story. They became above all a demonstration of male stamina and social cohesion.

A similar phenomenon is found on the nearby island of Corsica. Here, male singers of polyphonic songs sometimes speak of the song text as a "pretext"; the logical development of the narrative (such as it is) is frequently disrupted as individual singers enter at different points in the line, take breaths in the middle of words, or repeat a syllable following a pause. Of far greater interest is the opportunity that multipart singing offers to engage in collective activity that has social, psychological, and spiritual dimensions and that reinforces the affective bonds between men who are obliged to live and work together—thereby linking, once again, musical harmony with social harmony. The texts themselves often consist of a single stanza (or a few at most) that might once have been part of a longer song—a lament or a lullaby, perhaps—but has been adopted into the male *paghjella* tradition for reasons that include having combinations of words that are deemed "singable" on account of their phonetic qualities.[8] As one singer explains:

> For the *paghjella* we keep those extracts...which are particularly spectacular or which in their consonances work well for singing, that is to say, those in which the configuration of the alliterations, the marriage of vowels [and] consonants make for something which is very singable. (Bevilacqua interview 1994)

In the *paghjella* tradition, there is no strict one-to-one correlation of lyrical and musical component. Texts are essentially interchangeable: any number of different stanzas can be sung to the same musical variant or *versu*, while any single text might be sung to different *versi*. In the words of another singer, "The airs were very much specific to a particular village whereas the texts could circulate. The text doesn't cause any problem" (Pasquali interview 1994). This alerts us to the danger of assigning disproportionate significance to song texts in other cultural contexts.

These examples also help to explain why the literal meaning of a song lyric can often appear to be startlingly at odds with the style or mood of the musical setting. In Georgia, too, different texts drawn from entirely different genres may be associated with the same melody. Edisher Garakanidze, for example, writes: "Most songs are constituted by their musical material; for the singers, it makes no difference which text they sing to the given melody" (quoted in Ninoshvili 2010: 82). This dispenses with any notion that the melody expresses the feelings suggested by the words and explains why an ostensibly sad song (from the perspective of the text) might be sung to a rousing melody, or vice versa. In cases like this, Chris Rowbury observes, it is not necessarily helpful for singers to be given a literal translation of the lyric before they begin to work on the song. He cites the example of a Georgian song that is "so gorgeously beautiful. It's like a church song really. It *pulls* your insides out." Yet the lyric is, on the surface, a rather banal tale of a woman going to fetch water from the well (interview 2008).

Vocables in Georgian Song

The case of Georgian polyphonic song is especially interesting for the high preponderance of vocables—that is, "nonsense" syllables, strings of non-lexical phonemes, or words-without-meaning—that are no more intelligible, in conventional terms, to a Georgian-speaker than they are to a non-Georgian. In this case, the likeness to pre-verbal babbling and the functions that may be ascribed to it applies to insiders and outsiders alike. Lauren Ninoshvili's doctoral dissertation, "Singing between the Words: The Poetics of Georgian Polyphony", is founded on the assertion that the vocable is "as common a feature of traditional Georgian song as the fully interpretable lexical item" (Ninoshvili 2010: 13). The study offers rich insights into the workings of what we might call—by analogy with Timothy Taylor's (1997) notion of strategic inauthenticity—strategic unintelligibility. Here we find some songs in which refrains built up of vocables alternate with texted verses, and others (notably trio songs from Guria) where the middle voice alone carries the text while the other voices sing sequences of vocables that correlate, in terms of their vowel preferences, with the vocal register proper to that voice-part. In other songs, again, the entire lyric might be constituted of either vocables or archaic words that are no longer understood; some linguists believe these to be the names of ancient deities to whom the songs once acted as invocations. This is the case in some of the songs still sung in the remote mountainous region of Svaneti, for example.

If vocables offer non-native singers of Georgian songs relief from the complex consonant clusters found in the spoken language, they are more singable for native singers, too, albeit for other reasons. Being comparatively rich in vowel sounds combined with alliterative consonants (as, for example, in this bass line for the Gurian song "Chven Mshvidoba": "aba delo dela va dilo andil lauo da / aba delo delo dela da adilovo dilan dila / aba delo dela ladi lan dila udovo dilandilav da"), but devoid of the complex consonant clusters found in Georgian speech (as, for example, in the word *ganbrtsqinvebuli*, meaning "radiant"), sequences of vocables provide more sonorous material than lexical utterances. Ninoshvili notes that vocables help Georgian singers to "maximize vocal sonority and 'lighten' a lexicon that is full of consonant clusters and otherwise 'heavy' syllables" (2010: 20). She also relays Malkhaz Erkvanidze's proposal that the highly sonorous vowel patterns found in vocables help singers to access the harmonic spectrum in a way not permitted by the phonetics of natural Georgian speech (95).

Ninoshvili argues for viewing the Georgian vocable as

> essentially like a shifter: culturally, socially, and politically valuable precisely on account of its multi-purposeful indexicality... or ability to mean different things to different people and accomplish different kinds of work in radically different historical and cultural contexts. (Ninoshvili 2010: 27)

She concludes that, "far from indicating an absence of sense, vocables appear as a *multiplication* of sense in an increasingly varied, crossed and re-crossed interpretive topography" (157). This way of theorising vocables may also be related to more general arguments about semiotic fluidity. First, we might assert that words have value and do important work even if they are unintelligible; and second, we might remind ourselves that meanings are not monolithic and that different layers of meaning can co-exist. It is also the case that, whether the literal meaning of the words can be discerned or not, songs also signify to listeners in other ways. Musical features, more than textual features, identify them with certain places and position them in a nexus of knowledge and imaginaries associated with those places. In this way, songs can make powerful statements that are understood by those who recognise the musical language. South African songs during apartheid are a case in point: it was not necessary to understand the words of a song in order to read its performance as an expression of resistance or a statement of solidarity.

OURS OR THEIRS? OF BOUNDARIES AND CROSSINGS

In the following chapter, we will continue our examination of music's malleable meanings in the context of local realities; we will also consider critical questions about authenticity and appropriation. Here, by way of concluding this stage of my discussion, I shift for a moment from the eclectic, multilingual repertoire of the natural voice world to the repertoires and practices that characterise parallel and sometimes overlapping fields of musical activity in twenty-first-century Britain. This brings to the table important perspectives that might usefully be borne in mind as we continue to explore the dynamics of British singers' engagement with the songs of others.

A perusal of the programmes for the 2011 end-of-year recitals by second- and third-year undergraduate students who were taking solo performance in voice as part of their music degree at the University of Manchester (my home institution) reveals noteworthy, if largely predictable, trends. Of a total of 136 pieces, fifty-nine were sung in English. Of these, approximately half were songs from musical theatre and other popular works by twentieth-century American composers, such as Bernstein, Sondheim, and Gershwin; the other half were songs in a style closer to the art music end of the spectrum, with British composers Vaughan Williams and Benjamin Britten putting in the most frequent appearances. Of the remaining seventy-seven items, twenty-seven were sung in German, twenty-six in French, twenty-two in Italian, and one each in Latin and Norwegian. Here, the most popular composers were Handel, Mozart, Schubert, Schumann, and Fauré. We might reasonably assume that these works were learnt from scores (albeit also with reference to recordings), and they were, for the most part, delivered in the classical style in which students of singing are trained in the academy. But the fact that fewer than half of the items were in English (the first language of all but one of the performers) is, if not surprising, surely worthy of comment: it is not considered at all unusual, in this context, to sing in languages that are not one's mother tongue. At the same time, the choice of the foreign language is restricted to three major Western European languages: French, German, and Italian. This, again, is significant if read as indicative of what is considered part of a shared cultural heritage that is now as much "ours" as the songs with English texts.

Above all, that these songs are included in the canons of art music, where they become naturalised as self-contained "works", would seem to legitimise them as "ours" and exempt them from the kinds of critique that might accrue to other cases of musical crossover. Singing an Italian aria does not, generally speaking, seem odd; it certainly does not attract accusations of cultural appropriation or political incorrectness in the way that singing a song in an African "tribal" language might. Even in the case of an arranged folksong, the emphasis is on the composer and not on a particular group of people from whom we might otherwise consider the song to have been "taken". For some, this state of affairs is simply normal and goes unquestioned. Speaking at a conference at Cecil Sharp House in London ("Out of This World: English Folk Song in the Community Choir Repertoire," May 15, 2011), Sally Davies, director of Cecil Sharp House Community Choir, commented that it is not customary for an English pianist to be asked why he or she plays Debussy, or for a vocal ensemble to be asked why it specialises in medieval Spanish songs. She therefore finds it strange that people constantly ask her why she is interested in Georgian music. To many, there is something puzzling and suspect about an attraction to music from a distant, supposedly mysterious corner of the globe, particularly if it is music that was once dismissed as primitive and that now falls under the shadow of cultural-imperialist scruples about plunder and profit.

Defining "our" music and "not-our" music, then, is not as straightforward as it might seem. Nicholas Cook represents a progressive voice from the ranks of British musicology in his explorations of the ways in which, as he puts it, "the 'Whose musics?' cookie crumbles" (2004: 9). In his introduction to *The Cambridge History of Twentieth-Century Music*, he describes it as

> charting a transition between two quite different conceptions of "our" music: on the one hand, the Western "art" tradition that was accorded hegemonic status within an overly...confident imperial culture centred on Europe at the turn of the twentieth century (a culture perhaps now distant enough to have become "their" music rather than "ours"), and on the other hand, a global, post-colonial culture at the turn of the twenty-first, in which "world" music from Africa, Asia, or South America is as much "our" music as Beethoven. (Cook 2004: 9)

Cook turned the tables further by titling a talk he gave at City University in 2008 "Classical Music as World Music".

The past decade has seen a dramatic increase in the number of people in Britain who have access to West African drumming and dance classes, samba, salsa, flamenco, or tango classes, steel pan, and community gamelan groups—offered as leisure-time activities by community arts programmes and often supported financially by the arts councils and local authorities. In the world of project funding, chances of success are significantly increased if an educational component is included in the form of a hands-on workshop. In this way, ordinary members of the public—and more particularly those who may be identified as under-privileged or at risk of exclusion—are able to try out many different kinds of music. At the same time, there are notable differences in the way in which popular music imports are treated. Salsa is an interesting case in point for the way in which it has been incorporated into the category of "lifestyle" that encompasses health and fitness as well as recreation. Having long featured prominently among the fitness classes offered by municipal sports centres and private gyms, it was joined more recently by the zumba craze that swept the country following its launch in the United States. While the choice of music is central to zumba's identity, the promotional branding foregrounds lifestyle elements in inviting the reader to "cut, customize and create your own look" and "party yourself into shape" via "zesty Latin music, like salsa, merengue, cumbia and reggaeton". In a triumph of the marketing strategist's equivalent of name-checking, zumba is officially defined—and trade-marked—as "an exhilarating, effective, easy-to-follow, Latin-inspired, calorie-burning dance fitness-party™ that's moving millions of people toward joy and health" (http://www.zumba.com, acc. March 12, 2012).

If we imagine those involved in a musical event as occupying a series of concentric circles spreading out from the live musicians as the nucleus, the questions that might be asked about ownership or entitlement also change according to placement. Being a passive audience member, dancing at a club night, or exercising at the gym is more neutral than being a performer on stage. It is when non-native musicians actually play the music, thereby embodying it in a more intimate way and drawing greater attention to apparent incongruities, that questions of legitimacy become more insistent. But here too, they take on a different weight and tone depending on the context in which the music is presented. If in some cases non-ethnic performers are viewed almost as imposters, in others their appearance is accepted more straightforwardly as part of a celebration of global rapprochement or some kind of historic coming-together of the "family of man". It was largely in this spirit that cultural spectacles were being prepared in the run-up to the 2012 London Olympics. The planned programming also leant heavily on London's status as one of the world's most multicultural, multilingual cities, serving as home to communities from over ninety different countries who between them speak a total of more than three hundred languages. Winning the Olympic bid offered an ideal opportunity to celebrate this cultural diversity, and London was promoted in Olympic-related advertising as "the most multicultural city in the world". Significantly for our present interests, in combination with the emphasis in contemporary cultural policy on inclusion and participation, the Olympics focus prompted the launch of a new spate of amateur choirs and might be assumed to account at least in part for the increased presence of songs from elsewhere in the working repertoires of more established choirs as well.

This new, more visible eclecticism and its attendant blurring of the boundaries between local and global, classical and popular, comfortingly familiar and exotically foreign was evident in the one-day Voices Now extravaganza held at London's Roundhouse in March 2012. Part of Music Nation, a "countdown event" for the London 2012 festival, Voices Now presented itself as a showcase for "some of the UK's best choirs" and culminated in a première of Orlando Gough's *Making Music Overture*, commissioned by Making Music (the leading national organisation for voluntary music) as part of the

Cultural Olympiad. The broad range of choirs represented included school and youth choirs, several community choirs (some directed by NVPN members), Maspindzeli (London's Georgian choir), a rhythm and blues choir, The Pink Singers (Europe's longest-running LGBT choir), a choir for homeless people, the City Shanty Band, the Finchley Chamber Choir, and the BBC Singers (a fully professional choir in the classical tradition). Songs from the world repertoire included (predictably enough) several items from different parts of Africa, such as "Senwa Dedende" (from Ghana), "Denko" (from Mali), "Iqude Wema" (from South Africa), "Dinasi Ponono" (also from South Africa), and the more widely known "Shosholoza" (a song about the train carrying miners from what is now Zimbabwe to South Africa). Also featured were a selection of Georgian songs, including "Lechkhmuri Makruli" (a wedding song), "Aghdgomasa Shensa" (a church song), and "Benia's Mravalzamier" (a feasting song); "Gole Gandom" (an Iranian harvest song); "Come Along, My Friend", arranged by Tony Backhouse; "My Peace" from the Taizé repertoire; and long-time international favourites such as "Kalinka", "La Bamba", and "Santa Lucia".

If asked, each of these choirs would, no doubt, have an intriguing story to tell about how the different songs found their way into its repertoire. As we saw in chapter 4, some world songs are freely circulated in published songbooks (albeit with their sources not always fully credited). At the other end of the spectrum, a specialist choir like Maspindzeli is far more likely to have learnt its songs directly from a native singer, quite possibly in the country of origin and as part of the kind of ethically informed transaction that in other contexts would be labelled "fair trade". A singing community of the latter kind might be seen to share something of the rationale of the Suyá people of Brazil who "perform exogenous songs [or other people's music] to reproduce the pattern of their own history" (Neuman 1993: 272). The particular history of the singing journey of a choir such as Maspindzeli serves further to illustrate the way in which, to adopt Mark Slobin's terms, a choice to follow up an affinity might lead to belonging (1993: 56). Before we pursue that path, however, the time has come to plunge once more into the bottomless—but hopefully now less muddied—ocean of world song, this time to follow the trail of particular bodies of song that are among the most popular, and most firmly embedded, in natural voice circles.

NOTES
1. Quotations are taken from the Sing for Water Llandudno Souvenir Programme. The event was organised and hosted by Sara Brown and her choir, Coastal Voices.
2. Northern Harmony is a touring performance ensemble that is under the umbrella of the association Village Harmony. A new formation, made up of approximately sixteen young singers (most from the United States), is put together for each European tour, which features a combination of concerts and workshops. A typical programme will combine material from the Balkans,

Georgia, Corsica, South Africa, the gospel and shape-note traditions, and early music.
3. The arrangement can be found in Nick Prater's songbook *Heaven in my Heart*, where Nick notes that the song was originally recorded by the Fairfield Four and appears in Tony Backhouse's book *A Cappella: Rehearsing for Heaven*. Nick's arrangement includes further additions.
4. Interestingly, Sarno goes on to say that (in his estimation) the well-honed voices of the Bayaka, with their "astonishing power and purity" and lack of tension, "rival and surpass the voice of any opera singer" (1995: 70).
5. It is interesting in this context to note composer Karl Jenkins's explanation of his use of nonsense words or invented languages for the compositions in his Adiemus series. "The human voice," he observes, "is the oldest instrument and by removing the distraction of lyrics, [I] hope to create a sound that is universal and timeless" (quoted in Taylor 2000: 18).
6. Several features of Taizé chants make them suitable for natural-voice-style groups. Rounds feature prominently in the repertoire, as do short, repetitive songs scored for soprano, alto, tenor, and bass. Some practitioners run weekly or monthly groups devoted exclusively to the Taizé repertoire. Early morning Taizé sessions are often to be found on the programme of camps and residential gatherings. Barbara Swetina's book and CD compilation *Cantiones Sacrae: Sacred Songs, Rounds and Chants for Singing in Community* (1993) includes several Taizé songs together with a selection of chants from the Gregorian tradition and from the fourteenth-century Llibre Vermell from the monastery of Monteserrat in Catalonia.
7. The Council of Youth, held in 1974, attracted around 40,000 young people from 120 countries.
8. The *paghjella* is the most common form of three-part polyphonic song that is still found in Corsica.

CHAPTER 6

Performing the Other

Appropriations and Transformations

FRAMING INTERCULTURAL ENCOUNTERS

The picture painted thus far of the song world inhabited by natural voice practitioners and choir members seems to offer clear confirmation that, as Huib Schippers puts it, "many musics travel remarkably well" (2010: 54). In some respects, music might seem to travel of its own accord. Yet it does not follow a straight, obvious, and uneventful path. It does not simply arrive. As with any journey, there are prompts and callings, preparations and diversions. Things happen along the way. How exactly, then, does a particular music make its journey? By what means and by which route does it travel? What happens to it in the course of the journey? Where does the path lead, and why? Who takes it in? How does it adapt to its new location? How does its use and function there relate to its use and function in its place of origin?

In this chapter I focus on some of the musical genres and styles from other places that have called most strongly to singers in Britain: songs from the African continent, the Balkans, and the Republic of Georgia. I also pursue further strands relating to the journeys of gospel music. All the song traditions considered here are deeply rooted in contemporary cultures, where they continue to thrive as part of a living oral tradition and to occupy a meaningful place in the life of the local community, even if in some instances their practice has declined in recent times. Each is therefore rich in potential for direct encounters between culture-bearers and non-native students. There is, quite obviously, a world of difference in the sounds and structures of these different musics, and also in the cultural and historical contexts in which they evolved; yet each has, in its own way, proved well suited to being absorbed into the community choir repertoire. In considering some of the mechanisms involved in these musical journeys and transactions, certain points of commonality will emerge at the deeper level of functions and affinities. Individual cases will also offer revealing and sometimes unexpected answers to some of the questions raised earlier and in the previous chapter. Alongside my own case studies, I bring into the discussion analyses of individual musical genres that have taken on a new life in places other than the United Kingdom, such as gospel singing in Australia and Balkan music and dance in the United States. While providing insightful critiques and useful points of comparison, these also serve as windows through which we catch a few more glimpses of a wider field of activity that exists beyond the boundaries of the British scene that has been our main focus thus far.

It is worth noting that polyphonic singing traditions from Georgia, Bulgaria, and the Central African Republic have, in recent years, been recognised by UNESCO as Masterpieces of the Oral and Intangible Heritage of Humanity.[1] "Georgian Polyphonic Singing" achieved this status in 2001; "The Oral Traditions of the Aka Pygmies of Central Africa", in 2003; and "The Bistritsa Babi—Archaic Polyphony, Dances and Ritual Practices from the Shoplouk Region", in 2005. Also worthy of comment is UNESCO's description of Intangible Cultural Heritage as "traditional and living at the same time", something that is "constantly recreated". Its dependence on living human beings for its transmission is emphasised: "The depository of this heritage is the human mind, the human body being the main instrument for its enactment, or—literally—embodiment" (UNESCO 2011: n.p.). In becoming a party to the 2003 Convention for the Safeguarding of the Intangible Cultural Heritage, the nominating state commits itself "to take the necessary measures to ensure the safeguarding of the intangible cultural heritage present in its territory" by compiling inventories and documentation, and by "endeavour[ing] to ensure the widest possible participation of those that create, maintain and transmit the heritage, and to involve them actively in its management". As part of an action plan for revitalisation, the state also undertakes to promote and disseminate the material to the wider global community. Bulgarian singing became popular in the United Kingdom long before the UNESCO proclamation, of course. The introduction of Georgian singing likewise preceded its recognition by UNESCO, but in this case the intensification and diversification of activity that followed the proclamation fed into the continuing expansion of the non-native Georgian singing diaspora.[2] The duty to ensure transmission to future generations within the home culture has, as elsewhere, led to the establishment of specialised teaching programmes, supported by new educational resources, and only a small step has been needed for some of these materials to be made available to interested parties further afield. Thus, while the project of global promotion of once local traditions that has taken root more broadly in recent years has focused principally on creating markets for cultural exports and developing cultural tourism (both of which have economic as well as cultural goals), it has also paved the way for initiatives that allow direct contact on a more intimate scale between cultural insiders and outside enthusiasts.

As we consider the different orders of attraction—aesthetic, affective, pragmatic, ideational, and ideological—that come into play when musical styles find new audiences, Turino's model for explicating the success of worldbeat artists in the global marketplace offers itself as a useful point of reference. In seeking to explain the appeal of reggae legend Bob Marley and of Thomas Mapfumo, star of Zimbabwe's *chimurenga* music, by looking at how their musical products and personal images were promoted, Turino identifies three main criteria or "streams". Coming under the umbrella of what he refers to (adapting a statement made by Chris Blackwell, founder of Island Records) as "the sociological side of the Bob Marley worldbeat legacy", these are: liberatory politics (especially as pertaining to the African diaspora), "exotic" spiritualism, and "a distinctive 'roots,' yet familiar, musical style indexing a unique [foreign] locality or community" (2000: 338). Even if the audiences for some of the song types that concern us here are far more circumscribed than the audiences for reggae or *chimurenga* (and here Turino is talking about those who listen and dance to commercially produced world music as opposed to performing the music themselves), similar lines of attraction can be discerned.

Many of the musics embraced by aficionados of world music, from festival goers to amateur singers, have, of course, already called out to others. Ethnomusicologists are prime examples of people whose professional and personal lives have come to revolve around musical styles and practices from elsewhere that have, for whatever reason, captured their attention. Several cases spring to mind of ethnomusicologists who have devoted their academic carers to the "foreign" music cultures they first encountered, and fell in love with, when they joined college-based music and dance groups in their student days. Timothy Rice and Jane Sugarman, for example, became interested in Bulgarian and Macedonian music, respectively, via their involvement in the international folk dance movement that flourished in the United States from the late 1950s (Rice 1994: 4–5; Sugarman 1997: 34–35). Many of these scholars went on to supervise the types of student ensemble discussed in Ted Solís's *Performing Ethnomusicology: Teaching and Representation in World Music Ensembles* (2004), which have their roots in the "study groups" pioneered by Mantle Hood at the University of California, Los Angeles (UCLA). Hood's initiative was based on his conviction that practical musical experience—involving bodily as well as intellectual understanding—should be a requirement for students of ethnomusicology. As Charles Seeger expressed it in his introduction to Hood's *The Ethnomusicologist*, "We have realized that to the speech knowledge of music…there must be added the music knowledge of music" (Hood 1971: vii). While by no means remaining free of pedagogical or ethical dilemmas (a point to which I return at the end of this chapter), student-based world music ensembles have become increasingly integrated in educational institutions alongside the principles of participant observation, bi-musicality, and learning to perform as part of research methodology.

At a broader level, the 1960s saw a move towards a deeper understanding of other cultures that was aligned in part with the search for alternative lifestyles. Victor Turner's *The Ritual Process*, based on a series of lectures delivered at the University of Rochester in 1966, became (to quote Roger Abrahams's assessment in the foreword to the 1995 edition of Turner's book) a way "to teach about cultures radically different from the West in terms relevant to the present American situation". "This approach to the intense experience of other cultures," Abrahams goes on, "fed that generation's drift toward education through experiencing different ways of life" (Turner 1995: viii). Turner's work, together with that of his close collaborator Richard Schechner, was fundamental to the development of the academic field that would become known as "performance studies". Of particular relevance to my later discussion are two concepts now in general circulation that were popularised by Turner and his followers: liminality and *communitas*. Turner's work on liminality built on that of Arnold van Gennep, with whom the term originated. Both used it to designate a transitional state—corresponding in anthropological terms to the middle phase of a rite of passage—between two different existential positions in which the usual conventions are suspended. The state of *communitas*, characterised by a heightened feeling of togetherness and common humanity, can be achieved at this point of liminality as the differences that normally separate individuals from one another are temporarily dissolved.

Another useful concept for us to have in mind is that of interculturality. In chapter 1, we encountered Mark Slobin's use of the term "affinity interculture" to denote "like-minded music-makers drawn magnetically to a certain genre that creates strong expressive bonding" (1993: 98). In other contexts, "intercultural" is employed as an alternative to "multicultural" to distinguish different kinds of cultural plurality and co-habitation. While multiculturalism suggests the co-existence of diverse but separate cultures, interculturalism indicates interaction and collaboration, resulting in a marriage of cultures. While the musical material with which I am concerned here is not in itself a cultural hybrid, it will nonetheless be helpful to view the stories that follow in terms of intercultural encounters and negotiations in which each party plays an active and conscious role. In the natural voice and community choir networks, we find an ever-increasing number of individuals involved in first-hand, long-term associations with musical practitioners from other cultures, whether through attending (or organising) workshops led by singers from overseas who regularly visit the United Kingdom or through coming into personal contact with communities in the music's home country. The immediacy and sustained nature of this contact underpins the histories to which I now turn.

As will become ever more apparent, these tales of musical journeys and re-inscriptions of musical meaning also complicate matters of appropriation and authenticity. The notion of ownership lies at the heart of sensitivities about adopting other people's songs. But what if those other people want to share or gift their songs? How does the picture change when the motives, aspirations, and rationalisations of culture-bearers who choose to teach their songs to foreigners are brought into the frame? What should we make of Edisher Garakanidze's assertion in his introduction to *99 Georgian Songs* that "workshop participants become the co-owners of a culture that stems from the depth of centuries and millennia"? (2004a: ix). What responsibilities might come with such a privilege? What do "they" want of "us"? Scenes from the stories that will better equip us to answer this last set of questions are spread through the remainder of the book. The trail, however, starts here.

THE AFRICAN AMERICAN CONTINUUM AND GOSPEL'S GLOBAL JOURNEYS

I begin by picking up the threads of my discussion of songs from the African American heritage, viewed from the perspective of Turino's three-pronged explanation of the appeal of successful worldbeat artists as described earlier. In chapter 4, I considered the characteristics that made gospel songs accessible and attractive to non–African American community choirs. (From here on, I use "gospel" mainly in the generic sense that encompasses the spiritual, jubilee, and quartet traditions as well as contemporary gospel.) Predominant among those features that make the songs seem so close to home for other anglophone communities are English-language lyrics, familiar subject matter including stories from the Old Testament and themes of Christian salvation, and vernacular-sounding harmonies based on Western-style chords. The fact that some of these songs may also have been part of our musical diet in our schooldays further qualifies them as in some sense "ours".

African American musical styles are comfortably familiar at a more general level because of the way in which they have underpinned most genres of Anglo-American popular music since the 1950s—genres that in an even more prominent way form part of the collective memory of entire generations. As Nick Prater reasons:

> Most people grew up with the African American tradition because that was the basis of all the pop music we grew up with.... So you can do stuff like "Amazing Grace, How Sweet the Sound" and everybody else understands this sort of thing. And the harmonies people understand because they're what we all grew up with in pop music. (Prater interview 2007)

This sense of affinity lies behind Nick's description of his first time attending a gospel-singing workshop led by Tony Backhouse in New Zealand. He immediately felt "like a duck back in the water" (2005: 14). He goes on to speak of how he recognised the potential for using gospel songs in his own work but was at first diffident about doing so. When he later attended a series of talks and workshops given by Bernice Johnson Reagon in Auckland, however, she reassured him with the idea that

> although this music came out of the trials and sufferings of a whole people, in some way it also belongs to all of us, and if we can approach the songs with respect and an understanding of where they come from, then we can receive the deep healing that is the basis of this musical tradition. (Prater 2005: 14)[3]

In my discussion of Ysaye Barnwell's *Singing in the African American Tradition*, we saw that her beliefs about the function of the songs and about matters of accessibility and empowerment are a remarkably close match with the philosophy and methodology of the NVPN. We also encountered her own conviction that "sharing the music, its values and its contexts with others can create an experience that in some way transforms the spirit of all who participate" (1989: 5). Sue Harris identifies her attendance at a day workshop led by Barnwell in Birmingham as a key point on her journey as a voice practitioner: "That completely opened my eyes and mind to masses of available material that was very accessible for people who had no musical background at all and could learn by ear." *Singing in the African American Tradition*, she says, provided her with her first real "wodge" of repertoire, and in those early days she used a lot of material from the spiritual, gospel, and African traditions because of what it represented as well as its accessibility: "It struck a note with people who wanted to really sing together, didn't read music, and needed to feel some sort of solidarity and sharing" (interview 2009).

The allusion here to "what [the music] represented" and the need to feel a sense of solidarity points us towards the second of Turino's "streams": liberatory politics. I pursue this lead with reference to E. Patrick Johnson's case study (in his book *Appropriating Blackness: Performance and the Politics of Authenticity*) of gospel music in Australia and, more particularly, of Tony Backhouse's Sydney choir, Café of the Gate of Salvation. His New Zealand origins notwithstanding, Backhouse—considered to be at the centre of the broader *a cappella* revival in Australia and New Zealand—has considerable authority and experience as a teacher and performer of gospel music. In 1990, with a Bachelor of Music (BMus) degree in composition from Victoria University of Wellington and a career as a rock singer behind him, he received an Australia Council International Study Grant to research black gospel traditions in the United States. While there, he studied blues and gospel history at Memphis State University and worked intensively with gospel choirs and quartets in the southern Baptist churches. He has since led several gospel tours to the United States taking singers from Australia and elsewhere to immerse themselves in the black church culture of New Orleans, Memphis, Birmingham, Chicago, and New York. The Café of the Gate of Salvation, which Tony directed for twenty-one years (1986–2007), is generally acknowledged as Australia's foremost gospel choir; its debut CD won three awards at the 1993 Contemporary A Cappella Recording Awards (USA). In focusing here on Johnson's critique of certain aspects of the choir, I do not mean to imply that his assessment is wholly negative. Part of the interest of Johnson's study lies in the way in which he charts his own changing reactions and understanding over the six years he was closely associated with the choir—a period in which the choir itself also evolved in interesting ways.

At a purely musical level, Johnson—writing from his vantage point as an African American and a professional performer—identifies some features of the gospel aesthetic that are "lost in translation", noting that "clapping, rocking, discipline in rehearsals and dress...are not the Café's strongest suits" (2003: 167). He adds, however, that the singers do not necessarily try to "sound 'black'" and concedes that on his first visit to a rehearsal he was "impressed" by the degree to which the choir did, in fact, approximate a "black" sound and recreate the ethos of a black devotional service (162). It is in connection with the theme of liberation that Johnson's reservations about the appropriation of gospel music by white Australians come most strongly to the fore. He writes, for example, of how some choir members—as part of the broader tendency "to generalize [the black American] experience to struggles over other forms of oppression" (180)—link their history of descent from convicts exiled from Britain and deported to Botany Bay to that of black Americans' descent from their African ancestors who were sold into slavery. At this level, the Australian singers had embraced gospel music for its cathartic potential to heal psychological wounds and as a tool for reconciliation with the past. For Johnson, however, there was a puzzling mismatch between a romanticised empathy with the suffering of an oppressed people thousands of miles away and an apparent downplaying of the ways in which this might be complicated by the plight of the Aboriginal population of their home country and their own privileged position in contemporary Australian society.[4]

At a more technical level, Johnson remarks on the way in which features of the music itself—rhythm, syncopation, repetition, and call-and-response— "all coalesce as a generative force that facilitates psychological release". In the case of the Australian singers, he suggests, part of this cathartic effect derives from "the shedding of the residual traces of British propriety", allowing them to break free of the decorum and restraint that normally holds them in check (187). What they are really connecting with, in his view, is not the oppression of black Americans but "a part of themselves that had been underdeveloped or lying dormant", and it is the sharing of these previously unexpressed parts of themselves with one another that creates such a strong sense of community (188).

Another case of mismatch has to do with the inescapably religious nature of gospel music. Johnson comments on the way in which members of the Australian choir, many of whom are agnostic or atheist, rationalise the fact that they are singing explicitly Christian words by replacing religion with a more universal spirituality—Backhouse uses the term "non-specific spirituality", referring to the need to reserve a place for "spirituality that doesn't necessarily attach itself to a label or a messiah" (166). At the same time, some singers—especially those who have visited black churches in the United States—are drawn to the transcendental quality of the style of religious expression with which gospel music is associated. Here another order of release occurs, this time from the constraints of Anglican-style Protestantism.

Johnson's critique has other, less predictable dimensions. Central to his interest in the cross-cultural appropriation of gospel is the nature of the relationship between music and power. The way in which he phrases his initial question, however, alerts us to the suggestion that the stakes are not one-sided: "How does performance reproduce, enable, sustain, challenge, subvert, critique, and naturalize ideology?" (161). Taking issue with what he terms "the authenticity bug", he goes on to develop a muscular, if sympathetic, critique of the notions of authenticity to which many of his Australian interviewees gave expression, viewing them not as a welcome sensitivity but as restrictive and misguided insofar as they "fail to articulate the discursivity of music" (198). Here, Johnson has recourse to the work of Paul Gilroy in turning normative assumptions about authenticity on their heads and suggesting that to ascribe authenticity to black Americans alone and to cast supposed appropriations by others—including oneself—as inauthentic is to perpetuate and collude with the essentialised racial discourse of authenticity that has furnished the unchanging basis for the mass marketing of black folk-cultural forms to white audiences (190; see Gilroy 1994). At the same time, he is critical of his own complicity, admitting that in interviews for Australian radio and television he has sometimes found himself reinforcing these same stereotypes by playing into the hands of interviewers who position him as an "authentic" black gospel singer. From this perspective, then, an over-emphasis on authenticity, and an overly fundamentalist interpretation of what authenticity means and what its markers are, may be viewed as a type of continued segregation or ghettoisation.

While the nature of the UK gospel scene is rather different, not least because of the greater numbers of gospel choirs that are led by, and draw significant proportions of their membership from, British citizens of African or Afro-Caribbean descent, Johnson's analysis provides us with some useful perspectives from which to view the issues surrounding appropriation and intercultural performance more generally. Once the authenticity question is put to one side, Johnson concludes, "another set of possibilities emerges". He joins Barnwell and Reagon in arguing that gospel music is "too rich a cultural form to be confined to a simplistic essentialist/antiessentialist binary" if we accept that performance has "the potential to alter one's epistemological frame of reference" (197–198). It is here that the opportunity for personal transformation lies. Referencing Victor Turner, Johnson elaborates:

> Because [white Australians'] gospel performances are in striking contrast to the socially and culturally sanctioned Australian cultural performances, they hold the potential of transgressing the strictures of white hegemonic systems that sanction behaviors, beliefs, and attitudes. It is specifically the liminal space of performance that provides this occasion for cultural reflection and critique. (Johnson 2003: 207)

BACK TO AFRICA

It is in part because of their African roots that spirituals, gospel, and other songs from the African American tradition serve as an auspicious point of entry for working with songs from different parts of the African continent. The language of the lyrics may change but there is obvious continuity, broadly speaking, at the level of song structure, approaches to rhythm and syncopation, harmonic foundation, and use of the body. Here, however, the winning combination of foreign yet familiar is at work in even more complex ways, reflecting a history of mutual cross-influence with musical idioms and sensibilities moving in both directions—some elements being taken from Africa to the Americas via the slave trade and then later finding their way back to Africa in forms that were already hybrid, and other elements arriving in Africa from Europe during the colonial period and becoming integrated into vernacular styles that would later find new audiences in the West.

The fusion of African, American, and European elements is perhaps most audible in the case of South African vocal genres. These have absorbed influences from multiple incursions and visitations, from colonial administrators and missionaries, on the one hand, to performing troupes and entertainers, on the other. The four-part hymn singing style introduced by European and, later, by American missionaries was able to take root relatively easily due to the predominance of vocal music in the indigenous musical heritage, including choral as well as polyphonic forms. The cross-fertilisation that resulted provided the foundation for many of the styles of southern Bantu vocal music that developed in the twentieth century, including popular genres such as *marabi*, *mbaqanga*, *mbube*, *isikhwela jo*, *cothoza mfana*, and *isicathamiya*. This explains further the sense of familiarity that many Western European and North American listeners experience when confronted with South African singing. At the same time, the songs retain an aura of exoticism at the level of timbre, texture, vocal technique, and styles of ornamentation.

American minstrel groups and vaudeville artistes toured widely in South Africa in the late nineteenth century. Veit Erlmann identifies the "seminal" tours of a group of African American performers under the banner of Orpheus McAdoo and his Minstrel, Vaudeville, and Concert Company, in 1890 and 1898, as having made the deepest and most lasting impression on black audiences, to whom they introduced jubilee songs and songs from the black minstrel repertoire (1996a: 47). South African mission school graduates were soon inspired to form their own minstrel troupes. Spirituals introduced by the Philadelphia-based African Methodist Episcopal Church provided further inspiration to local composers. Ragtime was also popular with both white audiences and the urbanised black elite around the turn of the twentieth century. Later, black South Africans took a keen interest in the development of the civil rights movement in the United States and noted the way in which collective singing functioned in the context of a struggle that in many ways mirrored their own resistance to the apartheid regime. Religious music in gospel style enjoys great popularity in contemporary South Africa, drawing on models of African American gospel heard on radio and television in more recent times but Africanised through the use of local languages and voices (Muller 2004: 2).

The adoption of African material by singers in the West has also been eased by the kinds of declarations made by Barnwell and Reagon about the universal dimensions of gospel music. A similar statement can be found in the introduction to the collection *Let Your Voice Be Heard! Songs from Ghana and Zimbabwe*: "African music is not for those of African extraction only. It is, rather, music to share with the world, with all who would experience the fellowship of cooperative music making" (Adzinyah, Maraire, and Tucker 1986: 3). Innumerable songs from across the African continent have become perennial favourites with community choirs and voice camp veterans in the United Kingdom. In my interviews, choir leaders often identified these as the songs that called to them most strongly when they first set out on the natural voice path, as well as being among the most effective songs for working with relatively inexperienced singers. Nick Prater, for example, remarks that "the easiest songs and the most common songs that are sung around the campfire are African songs". He attributes this in large part to the familiarity that derives from the kind of cross-fertilisation with Western idioms, including African American genres, summarised earlier:

> We've got the parts, the chords are simple, the rhythms can often be quite straightforward, and we really understand them and we love them. . . . It's just a very interesting thing that it brings something out for us. (Prater interview 2007)

Nickomo observes, in similar vein, that his attraction to African music was prepared by his prior love of African American music and black-influenced popular music:

> I felt I *knew* it, I felt I could *sing* it.... It was like I could feel a part of me that could do that.... Other people feel that, so in a way it's a very liberating thing to teach because people kind of feel that they know how to do it and it's a nice way in, often, to singing. (Clarke interview 2007)

Bruce Knight recalls learning some simple African songs when he attended Rowena Whitehead's singing group in Cambridge:

> I think that's the moment I found my voice and thought, "I can sing, I can do this", and I sang without any inhibitions. And I think it was singing songs in another language, in a kind of tribal language, I accessed my, you know, "tribal person" [laughs], and it was when I was singing and dancing at the same time, shuffling free from side to side, I got into a kind of a trancy state, when you're singing something over and over and it just feels really, really natural. (Knight interview 2008)

When Rowena taught English songs, he didn't experience the same sense of connection, whereas "with the African songs, and some of the Maori songs also, I'd put my heart and soul into it". Of particular interest here is not only the role of African songs in the "finding my voice" narrative but also the reference to "accessing my tribal person" and entering "a kind of trancy state", formulations that clearly point, once again, to the transformative potential of performance and the liminal state to which it allows access.

Jackie Roxborough also finds value in the bringing together of voice and body that African idioms facilitate and, in her experience, this in turn can help to prepare singers for less familiar, more demanding repertoire:

> I think the African is a big way in for most people. I think there's freedom in the African, which has to engage your body. You cannot stand still, you cannot just stand and deliver a voice.... Once they've done that and they've freed that up and they've realised that they can sing anything they want...the one that really does seem to draw people incredibly—which is then bringing them back into formation—is Georgian. (Roxborough interview 2007)

Similar sentiments lie behind Una May Olomolaiye's use of African material, and these combine with other now familiar themes in her explanation of her voice-work philosophy:

> I absolutely believe that people are less inhibited when they sing, especially African music. They let go and don't have to worry about understanding the

words. They are just conveying the spirit of the song. I love watching people realise their own potential.... You know, there is no mystery to singing. You just give yourself, let go, be free. When people realise there is no mystery, when they see me give myself, they just do it. They think, "*This is something I can do!*" (http://www.yamanu.co.uk/about.php, acc. June 18, 2013)

The fit between African American and vernacular African styles becomes abundantly clear in Una May's workshops, which typically feature a combination of African songs (mainly South and West African, including her own arrangements of some of the songs she has collected on her travels in Africa) and African American songs (including her arrangements of popular Motown songs with which many workshop participants are, of course, already conversant).

Alongside that of Una May, the work of Anita Daulne is of particular interest as another example of inter- or cross-cultural encounters being facilitated by a professional performer well versed in both European and African culture. Together with her sister Marie, Anita is best known in international circles as part of the female *a cappella* group Zap Mama. While Marie has concentrated on pursuing her performing career, Anita has been more active on the teaching circuit. Based for several years in the United Kingdom, she directed her Afropean Choir in Oxford and also maintained a busy schedule as a workshop leader in Europe and Africa.[5]

Of mixed parentage (a Belgian father and a Zairian mother), the sisters grew up in Belgium after their mother fled the Belgian Congo following the death of her husband in 1965 at the hands of revolutionaries carrying out a purge of mixed-race couples and children. Marie went on to study at the Antwerp School of Jazz and to pursue her interests in composition and ethnomusicology. After hearing Didier Demolin's recordings of pygmy music from the Congo, the sisters were inspired to return to the region to explore their African heritage and more specifically "pygmy" vocal techniques, which have been an important influence on Zap Mama's distinctive style. Anita has travelled extensively throughout Africa and now teaches songs from the different ethnic groups she has encountered along the way; these include songs of the Maasai, Tuareg, Peul (Fulani), and Zulu peoples, as well as the Mangbetu and pygmy peoples of her mother's homeland.[6]

Anita describes how neither she nor Marie played a musical instrument well but they wanted to make music and so they decided to use their voices: "We tried to imitate instruments and at the same time using some songs and the way of singing that our mother taught us when we were young" (interview 2009). Their mother was surprised that her daughters should show such a keen interest in these traditional songs because in the Congo, during the period of Belgian colonial rule, indigenous songs were viewed as uncivilised, and only church songs or the French songs children learned at school were approved of. It came as a further shock for her mother to realise that there were many Europeans who, after all, liked these songs—as witnessed by Zap Mama's meteoric rise to fame following the release of their first album in 1991 and more particularly its US re-release, in 1993, on David Byrne's Luaka Bop label.[7]

The idea of running workshops came from Anita's desire to share the experience of singing the songs. She explains that she has always loved the rehearsal process "because it's such a good interaction and feeling that circulates between us, so I wanted to give more than what we give on stage: the experience of that way of singing". It was evident that Zap Mama's audiences derived great enjoyment from seeing them perform on stage, "but they didn't *experience* that way of singing and I was convinced that way of singing is accessible for everybody and I didn't want that way of singing [to be] just for *them*, far away" (interview 2009). Through the workshops she also wanted to offer people an experience of cultural mixing. What she refers to as "the mix of culture" was at the very foundation of Zap Mama, since the group's members were themselves "mixed" in terms of their parental origins. In using this notion of mixing, Anita makes a distinction between culture and race. Some people, she observes, are mixed race but they don't really mix the cultures. In Zap Mama's case, it was a mixed *cultural* background that had influenced both their way of singing and their way of working, and this included reinterpreting and rearranging the material to make it more accessible for a Western audience so that their music might then act as "a bridge or a door to make people understand...ethnic music [better]". The same philosophy formed the foundation of her Afropean Choir, launched in 2007, whose repertoire was based on "ethnic" songs that Anita had rearranged, drawing on both African and European influences. She stresses that she teaches all her material by ear and she works a lot "with rhythm and harmony and overlapping". "So really," she explains, "I try to revalue the ethnic way of singing that was...crushed by colonisation" (interview 2009).

Anita also has interesting things to say about cultural stereotypes. At the time of our 2009 interview, she had just returned from leading a ten-day residential workshop in Burkina Faso, which brought together participants from Belgium, France, Italy, the Czech Republic, and Burkina itself. Because they were in Africa, the Europeans, she explained, had expected the Africans to sing the songs better than they. In Burkina, however, the dominant vocal genre is that of the griots—essentially a solo tradition of praise singing with instrumental accompaniment. There is not a strong tradition of multipart singing such as one finds in South Africa or the Congo region, for example. For the local participants, therefore, singing songs in two or more parts was a new experience, whereas for the European members of the group these kinds of songs, together with Anita's way of working, were more familiar. Rather than the Africans having a head start, then, they were all starting from a similar position. "It was very, very interesting," Anita reflects, "because every stereotype fell down and we had to readjust everything" (interview 2009).

Songs and Dances from South Africa

For the remainder of this section I focus on the contrasting cases of two very distinct kinds of repertoire that have arrived in the United Kingdom in different waves and via different channels: songs from South Africa and songs from the pygmy peoples, or forest peoples, of central Africa. South African songs are among those that have circulated longest among amateur choirs in the United Kingdom. "Nkosi Sikelel' iAfrika"—composed (in *makwaya* style) by Enoch Sontonga in 1897 and adopted as the anthem of the African National Congress in 1925—was widely sung as an expression of solidarity for victims of apartheid during the years of Nelson Mandela's imprisonment and the South African boycott.[8] Certain other South African songs have been especially popular with political choirs. Several of these can be found in the collection *Freedom is Coming: Songs of Protest and Praise from South Africa*, complied by Anders Nyberg and first published in 1980; favourites here include "Singabahambayo", "Siyahamba", and "Azikhatali". Online customer reviews indicate that this volume was widely used in the United States and Australia, as well as becoming an integral part of choral life in Sweden, Nyberg's home country. Another readily available resource, intended for use by amateur singers and sympathisers outside South Africa, was Pete Seeger's collection, *Choral Folk Songs from South Africa*, first published by G. Schirmer in 1960. This followed the earlier release, in 1955, of the Folkways album *Bantu Choral Folk Songs*, which featured ten of the songs performed by Seeger with the group The Song Swappers. *Singing in the African American Tradition* also includes six songs from South Africa, some of which became favourites with British singers who attended Barnwell's workshops or purchased the teaching pack: "Babethandaza", the traditional Zulu song encountered in chapter 4; "Somagwaza", a version of the boys' initiation song also included in Seeger's book; the lament-like "Senzenina", whose lyric translates as "What have we done? What has Mandela done? Our crime is that we are black"; "Iza Kunyathel'i Africa", a more spirited anti-Botha song; "Woyaya" ("We are going"), with mostly English lyrics; and "The Freedom Tide is Rising", again in English, foretelling the fall of Botha and the apartheid regime.

A more singular and local story lies behind the collection of material assembled by Colin Harrison that was to serve as another source of South African songs used in fledgling natural voice circles in the United Kingdom from the late 1980s. This is now available as a series of three workdiscs, *Songs from South Africa* volumes 1, 2, and 3, which feature the songs broken down into individual parts, with *Songs from South Africa: The Book* including most of the songs from the first two workdiscs. The material originated in a series of visits that Colin made to South Africa together with his then partner, Anne Monger. The motive for their first trip in 1988 was to lead circle dance workshops. While there, they were invited to teach at St. Peter's Catholic Seminary at Hammanskraal. Two of the young trainee priests attending their workshop sang and danced "Thanda" (the lyrics for which are a Xhosa version of "Love your neighbour as yourself"). On returning to England, Colin began to teach "Thanda" to his circle dance groups. Meanwhile, as he recounts, "the seminarians were getting together with the Pretoria circle dance group, creating more dances and even entering them successfully in competitions!" (Harrison n.d.: 2). When he and Anne returned to St. Peter's the following year, the group had many new songs and dances ready to show them.

It was later that same year that Colin and Anne first met Nickomo and Rasullah Clarke. Colin describes how Nickomo, when presented with the tapes, "was able to decipher layers of harmony that I had barely been aware of" (ibid.). That summer, as a foursome, they taught the songs and dances at a series of camps. Nickomo reflects that, initially, the songs were taught at dance workshops and dance camps due to the fact that they had originated in a dance setting. Voice work in the camps at that time "was kind of on the back of dance". What they offered, then, was "a kind of package where we'd teach all the parts to an African song and then we'd dance it" (interview 2007).

Back in South Africa a year later, Colin made contact with the Catholic-run Lumko Institute that published similar material in manuscript and on tape and he returned to England "with just about everything they had". The repertoire brought together in *Songs from South Africa* includes the songs and dances from St. Peter's, several Lumko items (including a version of "Nkosi Sikelel' iAfrika"), and additional songs from various other sources (including, once again, "Azikhatali"). In his introductory notes, Colin is keen to emphasise that neither the vocal arrangements nor the dance steps should be regarded as fixed in stone: "This booklet is no more than a rough description of how one group of people once danced to these songs." In Africa, he explains (echoing other writings on African music), everyone sings what he or she feels like: "The only mistake one can make is not to participate, rather than not to get it right." Describing the difficulty of notating the dance steps while also joining in (declining to join in not being an option), Colin again refers to the way in which "everyone seemed to be doing his own version. Moreover, each time I went back, they all seemed to be doing the dances somewhat differently anyway!" Hence his exhortation to the reader to "proceed with a healthy irreverence for what is written down here" (Harrison n.d.: 2).

Similar advice is found in the "Musical Instructions" that preface Nyberg's *Freedom is Coming*:

> These are freedom songs, both in form and function!... In South Africa there are no two choirs that sing one and the same song alike, nor is there any choir that sings the same song alike twice in succession!... With the African way of telling a tale, it is impossible to "sing wrong."... The essential thing is not how you sing, but that you mean what you sing and sing what you mean.... Do not let the

notes become an inhibiting factor in the creation of the music, but a point of departure! (Nyberg 1990: 6)

Authenticity, or being faithful to the spirit of the source, in this case involves spontaneity and innovation rather than a slavish adherence to a past interpretation that is, is any case, not viewed as sacrosanct by its creator.

A more recent resource is the two-volume *The Folk Rhythm: South African Folk, Church and Protest Songs*, the result of a collaboration between Patty Cuyler, co-director of Village Harmony, and Matlakala Bopape, director of the Polokwane Choral Society in South Africa's Limpopo province. Patty and Matlakala first met in 1999 at a music festival in St. John's, Newfoundland, when Village Harmony and Polokwane Choral (a community choir that is part of the umbrella organisation, Polokwane Choral Society) performed together. The books contain Matlakala's four-part arrangements of a selection of folk, church, and protest songs. The music is presented in staff and tonic sol-fa notation; the latter—originally introduced by missionaries in the 1850s as a means of enabling ordinary people to achieve musical literacy—remains popular with choirs across South Africa. Both audio (CD) and audio-visual (DVD) recordings accompany each volume, designed to convey an idea of the authentic sound and to demonstrate the steps for the dances that accompany the songs.

In her introductory notes, Matlakala explains that her motivation derives in part from the fact that music that relies on oral transmission runs the risk of disappearing as younger generations transfer their allegiance to other genres: "My documentation of this is therefore specifically to preserve this rich culture, and to share this with other nations of the world" (Bopape and Cuyler 2004: iii). Part of the mission of Polokwane Choral Society is to work "to bridge ethnic gaps in South Africa by fostering mutual understanding between people of different cultures and viewpoints" (xiii). It is a relatively small step to extend this approach to people outside the country. Several British singers have joined the Village Harmony groups that travel to South Africa to work with Matlakala there; others have learnt some of the songs at Village Harmony camps elsewhere in the world or at the workshops led by Village Harmony's directors during their UK tours.

Matlakala makes a useful distinction between "folk music" and "traditional indigenous music" in South Africa. Folk music, according to her definition, is dynamic and offers greater scope for creativity through improvisation and ornamentation. Folk songs—usually songs in four-part harmony—have a wide currency: they are known and sung by people of all ages across the country. Traditional music, by contrast, is both more ancient and more static and is usually tied to particular rituals and occasions (for example, circumcision or rain-making ceremonies) and confined to individual cultural and language groups. A third category is the "chorus" tradition cultivated in the churches that takes the form of Africanised Western hymnody, incorporating indigenous influences such as the characteristic leading-voice and the call-and-response format. Many songs that began their lives as church choruses were later adopted as part of the anti-apartheid project and became recast as "struggle songs" ("Senzenina" being a well-known example). Matlakala stresses two further points that should by now be familiar: indigenous, folk, and struggle music—including that sung in the churches—is always accompanied by dance and movement, and in the folk tradition there are no spectators or audience since the singing is communal and participatory (v–vii).

Finally, another injection of new material was provided by the documentary *We Are Together*, which tells the story of the Agape Children's Choir, based at the Agape Orphanage in KwaZulu-Natal that provides for children whose parents have died of AIDS. The theme song, "Thina Simunye/We Are Together", was taken up by a number of choirs following the film's broadcast on British television's Channel 4 and its commercial release in 2008, and the Rise Foundation, which produced it, went on to compile a songbook that includes choral transcriptions for fifteen of the songs featured, with translations and a pronunciation guide. Again, this resource is addressed to choirs anywhere who wish to use the songs, and again we find the now familiar explanation that "the same song is never performed in the same way", followed by this injunction to the reader: "When you teach, learn and perform these songs, you should do so with freedom as the people of South Africa do and make them your own" (Rise Foundation 2009: 1).

Songs of the Aka and Baka

The polyphonic songs of the equatorial forest peoples of central Africa with their characteristic use of hocketing and yodelling techniques offer a striking contrast to South African styles, even if they share a similar scope for seemingly limitless variation and reinvention in performance. In this case, part of their appeal rests on the way in which their life is imagined and represented in the West. Traditional "pygmy" society has lent itself to easy romanticisation with a succession of writers extolling the peaceable ways of these "primeval" forest dwellers that allow them to live in harmony with one another and with the natural environment—even if the present reality of communities ravaged by exploitation, inter-ethnic violence, alcoholism, and high rates of child mortality paints a far from idyllic picture. In the world of popular music, exoticised "pygmy" sounds—their value enhanced by whatever environmental, political, or spiritual associations their user chooses to attach to them—have been freely appropriated as one more gem with which to decorate the postmodern pastiche. As Steven Feld comments, "there's a pygmy for any and all consumer positions and tastes", but only at the cost of "a complex humanity" being "fixed as a tape loop in the machine of both postcolonial devastation and primitivist fantasy" (2000b: 273).

This does not mean that every appropriation of "pygmy" music is a case of insensitive or ill-informed exploitation. It is clear, however, that when the music does cross over it is not the sound alone that is being consumed or more actively embodied; it is also the values that are seen to accrue to it. The structure of multipart songs, together with the manner of their performance, has been described by a roll call of anthropologists and ethnomusicologists as a musical manifestation of the democratic values that govern social organisation. In contrast to many other African styles, there is no division between leader and chorus, and no hierarchy of voice parts. Any member of the group may start a song and it is common for individual singers to cross from one vocal line to another as all possible permutations of a song's raw material are explored. This fundamental flexibility is also highlighted in the UNESCO proclamation relating to the oral traditions of the Aka: "Unlike polyphonic systems that are written down in notation, the vocal tradition of the Aka Pygmies allows for spontaneous expression and improvisation.... During performances, each singer can change his or her voice to produce a multitude of variations, creating the impression that the music is continuously evolving" (http://www.unesco.org/culture/ich/index.php?RL=00082, acc. June 18, 2013). This freedom and spontaneity in music making is, once again, an aspect that recommends the songs to singers who adhere to the philosophy of liberation and empowerment espoused in natural voice circles.

The Aka and Baka are among the groups that have been most extensively studied by ethnomusicologists and it is their music that most often finds its way to singers in the United Kingdom. One British singer who has served as a conduit for this material is Su Hart, who with Martin Cradick formed the group Baka Beyond (styling itself an "original Afro-Celtic danceband") in the early 1990s.[9] The adventure began when they saw Phil Agland's documentary film, *Baka: People of the Rainforest* (1987).[10] The film made such a strong impression on them that they were inspired to travel to the Cameroonian rainforest, in 1992, to spend three months living and making music with a group of Baka near the border with the Congo. Martin and Su's first recording venture as Baka Beyond produced a pair of CDs: *Spirit of the Forest*, a fusion-style album featuring Martin's guitar and mandolin playing dubbed over Baka percussion and digital samples, and *Heart of the Forest*, which presents the original recordings made among the Baka. Via the charity Global Music Exchange, royalties from these and later recordings have been directed back to Cameroon to be invested in development projects.

Unlike many others who have passed through the forest, Su and Martin have maintained their relationship with their Baka friends for more than twenty years, regularly returning to offer help as well as to make music. When I asked Su whether she saw herself as a kind of bridge between the Baka and the singers to whom she now teaches the songs in the West, she replied: "I want to be a two-way bridge because I do want them to get something back." In addition to helping build a music house, Global Music Exchange has also been involved in setting up education and health projects. Since royalties have declined as a result of the way in which the record business has been hit by Internet downloads, they now have to find other ways of raising funds; a recent charity ball had raised £10,000, enough to keep a medical project running for the next two years.

On one of Su's most recent visits, the Baka women told her that she should go out and teach the songs to more people. As well as taking her singing workshops further afield, she runs occasional teacher training days and workshops for primary schools that fit with the "rainforest" theme in the curriculum; these include background information about different aspects of Baka society, illustrated by slides and stories from her own first-hand experience of life in the forest. Since 2009, she and Martin, in partnership with anthropologists Jerome and Ingrid Lewis, have also organised three-day Baka Culture Camps in the United Kingdom as a means of sharing other aspects of Baka life.

Su sees the songs themselves as a vehicle for helping the singers she works with to re-learn the arts of listening and awareness and to re-engage with the humanity that the Baka still have but that many in the West have lost touch with. She also alludes to the way in which the repetitive cyclic patterns facilitate a kind of therapeutic transcendence, not unlike that described earlier in relation to gospel music:

> You can sing for ages; you get into this other space where you don't know how long you've been doing it, and you're together. And that's the place, I think, that we want to be. We all want to be in this warm, cooperative, snug thing. That's what humans want.... It is like a healing. (Hart interview 2011)

The perceived healing potential of the songs is also fundamental to the work of John Bowker, which in this case comes with more prominent New Age resonances. Based in Ireland, John is a regular teacher at the Unicorn Natural Voice Camp and also runs his own Earthsong Camps. Having built his repertoire of songs from the Baka and Mbuti peoples of central Africa primarily by working with ethnomusicological field recordings (as opposed to traveling to their place of origin), he makes no claim to cultural authenticity. He is motivated rather by the desire to share what he sees as "amazing cultural gifts" whose wisdom and values can benefit society at large. He often draws on his own creativity:

> It might not be the authentic original African chant that I have recorded or [had] taught to me that I'm teaching but, what I notice is, the chant might have more power if I bring my creativity to it. So do I inhibit that creative process? And

where is it coming from? Is it coming from me, or am I bringing in something from elsewhere? (Bowker interview 2007)

Some people might criticise his work, he says, "because if I'm teaching a Baka chant it's not strictly original. And I'll often say: well, I've tweaked this, this is a bit of my stuff." Viewed in a different light, however, this approach could be seen as compatible, in principle, with how the songs would be treated in their original context as described earlier.

John explains his initial attraction to Baka music:

When I was getting into this sort of powerful tribal music that was really calling to me, what *really* seemed to hit the spot was *their* music, their chants. And they seemed to have a use of music as a tool for community that is very profound. (Bowker interview 2007)

He mentions a chant that is sung to a child whose mother is expecting a new baby to reassure the child that the community will always be there for him or her and there is no need to worry. This is something that doesn't occur in our culture, John comments—the notion of being held and looked after by everyone in your community. In the West, much of our ancient culture has been lost without trace, he continues, "so to go to other areas seemed to be the only choice". He refers to the kind of "powerful magical music" that is still to be found in places like Native America, Africa, and India. "So we can draw from that well for humanity," he concludes. "We can say: they held the drum, and here it is" (interview 2007).

BALKAN BRIDGES

If African songs enjoy the most widespread popularity overall, songs from different regions of the Balkans are also well established as part of the staple diet of many community choirs in the United Kingdom. Songs from Eastern Europe—most notably Bulgaria, the countries of former Yugoslavia, and, to a lesser extent, Greece—were especially popular in the 1980s and 1990s. The Balkan trend in the United Kingdom may have drawn inspiration in part from the more established Balkan music and dance scene in the United States, but many people in Britain first became aware of Balkan folk music via the circle dance groups that spread across Britain in the 1980s. This initial encounter led some to seek out ways of immersing themselves more fully in the culture of origin by, for example, joining tours organised by the British-Bulgarian Friendship Society to the Koprivstica National Festival of Bulgarian Folklore that takes place in the village of Koprivstica every five years.[11] In addition to attending the festival, such tours often included the option of enrolling on weeklong workshops in folk dancing, singing, and playing traditional Bulgarian instruments such as the *gaida, gadulka*, and *kaval*. Koprivstica offers clear evidence of the extent to which Bulgarian music has cast its spell ever wider since the festival's inauguration in 1965: the ninth festival in 2005, for instance, included twenty-three folklore groups who had travelled from Sweden, Switzerland, Denmark, France, the United States, Israel, and Japan to take part in competitions and demonstrations of Bulgarian traditional music and dance.[12]

The flourishing Balkan dance scene coincided with the "discovery" of the so-called "mystery of the Bulgarian voices" via a series of records featuring the Bulgarian State Radio and Television Choir, the Filip Kutev Choir, the Pirin Ensemble, and other Bulgarian artists. The three volumes that were released under the title *Le Mystère des Voix Bulgares* in the late 1980s featured all-female vocal ensembles performing "arranged folklore" in the form of elaborate choral arrangements and new compositions inspired by traditional idioms by approved state composers such as Filip Kutev, Nikolai Kaufman, Krassimir Kyurkchiysk, Ivan Spassov, and Kiril Stefanov. The year 1988 also saw the release of *The Forest is Crying* by the Trio Bulgarka, who came to the attention of mainstream popular music audiences when they appeared on two of Kate Bush's albums, *The Sensual World* (1989) and *The Red Shoes* (1993). Some of the songs from these Bulgarian recordings have also been adopted by community choirs.

As we have seen, Frankie Armstrong served as an early channel for the deliberate introduction of Balkan songs to what was to become the natural voice network, using as her starter pack the village-style songs she had acquired from Ethel Raim. Since the 1980s, there have also been ample opportunities to work directly with Bulgarian singers in the United Kingdom. Another professional female trio, the Bisserov Sisters, strengthened their British presence when Lyubimka Bisserova established a home in Manchester and began to lead workshops there as well as perform. Judy Greenwell and Vivien Ellis (who both attended Frankie and Darien's first UK training for voice practitioners) also offered Bulgarian workshops after spending time studying with the Bisserov Sisters in their home village in the Pirin mountains. Kalinka Vulcheva, who appears as a soloist on the *Mystère* recordings, was likewise active in the British voice network during her extended residence in the country. Members of the Bistritsa Babi (Bistritsa Grandmothers), who toured widely long before their music was given masterpiece status by UNESCO, were also invited to Britain to give song and dance workshops, bringing with them copies of their book *Ancient Magic in Bulgarian Folklore: Perls (sic) of Syncretic Folk Art, Village of Bistritsa, Bulgaria* (Aleksieva and Ancheva 1991).[13]

Balkan songs continue to form part of the standard offering in workshops led by Northern Harmony on their European tours. Thirteen songs (from Bulgaria, Macedonia, Serbia, and Croatia) are included in the Balkan section of the 2007 edition of the Workshop Book, for example. A series of Village Harmony summer camps have also been held in Bulgaria, Bosnia, and the Republic of Macedonia, giving participants the opportunity to learn from a range of native teachers in situ. Some of these tours have been co-ordinated by Mary Cay Brass, who has also edited two songbooks, *Village Harmony: Traditional Songs of the Balkans* and *Balkan Bridges: Traditional Music of the Former Yugoslavia and Bulgaria* (each linked with a companion CD). Both include songs that Mary Cay collected while living in former Yugoslavia in the 1970s, supplemented by pieces transcribed from commercial recordings. Significantly, the theme of giving back to the communities from which the music came, as well as of music as a vehicle for intercultural understanding, recurs in the introduction to *Balkan Bridges*, in which Mary Cay notes that the songs in the volume have been performed all over Europe and the United States in concerts, festivals, and benefits for victims of the wars in Bosnia and Kosovo. "We have hoped through our singing of these beautiful songs to 'humanize' the peoples of the former Yugoslavia; to give a picture of their lives," she writes, and at the same time to make them accessible to a wider public, and, by sharing them, to "help to build some new bridges between peoples" (1991: 1).

The Balkan case may escape the more obvious sensitivities surrounding issues of race and empire that attach to the appropriation of music from certain other parts of the world. It nonetheless raises similar questions about representation and the ways in which musical meanings are imagined and constructed. Why should British singers be so powerfully drawn to the Bulgarian sound and how does this relate to their own sense of identity? What makes the songs appear accessible, relevant, and rewarding to sing?

The distinctive timbre and voice placement are the first features to strike the listener exposed to this music for the first time, together with the impressive volume that the open-throated and "bellowing" techniques are capable of producing. Songs in this open-throated style, which requires singing in the chest register, favour musical structures featuring narrow-range melodies often punctuated by sustained notes, since it is not practically possible to sing wide-ranging, fast-moving melodies with this type of voice production. This in turn means that the melody lines—in their skeletal, unornamented form, at least—are not too difficult to learn. The melodies of many songs in the older, village style move mostly by step and rarely extend beyond the ambitus of a fifth, while the other voices in two- or three-part songs are often drone-based, making them supremely accessible to even the most tentative singer.

Loud singing is also necessary to create the desired ringing that is part of the Bulgarian aesthetic. The frequent use of what would in Western terms be deemed dissonances contributes to this ringing phenomenon, with intervals of a second being especially prized and with thirds and fourths often sung slightly flat of the Western norm. For Western singers, the resulting harmonies offer a welcome sense of liberation from the constraints of Western harmony. They are also exciting to sing because of the surprisingly visceral quality of the bodily sensations they induce. For the listener, too, the singing can have a "hair-raising" effect, particularly at points in three-part songs where the voices create a three-tone cluster consisting of two intervals of a major second within the ambitus of a major third. The different vocal techniques and effects used to ornament a song add to the arresting quality of the singing, with trills, wide vibrato, dramatic glottal stops, and high-pitched yips or yodel-like sounds calculated to further enhance the ringing quality. Again, these ornaments add an extra layer of thrill, often providing a therapeutic release for the performer as well as adding an aura of exoticism.[14]

Another novel feature of Bulgarian music is its apparent rhythmic complexity, with asymmetrical metres that might be notated as 5/8, 7/8, 9/8, 11/8, 13/8, and 21/8 being characteristic of many song types. Again, this is something that sets Bulgarian and some other Balkan styles apart from the Western norm in a way that can be experienced as liberating. Many Croatian songs, by comparison, are more familiar because they use symmetrical rhythms and harmonies based on parallel thirds that reflect the country's Western orientation. These songs are therefore more immediately accessible for those who struggle with unfamiliar rhythms and harmonies.

Sue Parlby (co-director, at the time of our interview, of Cambridge's Good Vibrations Community Choir) describes how she spent years singing in traditional choirs as "a very sweet little soprano", until the day she went to a Bulgarian singing workshop led by Frankie Armstrong. There she discovered, as she describes it, "this huge voice, which was terribly exciting. I didn't realise there was one of *those* lurking inside me.... That voice had always been inside me somewhere, probably, but it hadn't been brought out" (interview 2007).[15] Part of her excitement was related to her experience as a woman: "For me to discover that I do have a powerful voice that will be listened to I think is working on other levels as well. It felt like I had found a strong part of me as well." She describes how her newfound passion took her to Bulgaria, where in addition to attending the Koprivstica festival she spent a week as part of a group taking singing lessons with a member of the Kutev choir. One of the most powerful experiences of the trip occurred during an evening shared with a local band. The band's singer discovered that Sue and another workshop participant knew the song "Što mi e Milo" and suggested they sing it together. Sue's description of the experience of singing at the side of the Bulgarian girl captures the intensity of the visceral dimensions of the Bulgarian sound referred to earlier:

> I thought I had quite a loud voice when I get into Bulgarian mode and I just felt like a nuclear bomb had gone off in my face.... She was so powerful—her voice—that we got to the end of it and I was literally shaking from the vibrations and I had to go outside for about half an hour in total quiet because my body

wouldn't stop shaking. And it was to do with the actual frequencies...and the hitting and the dissonances. And her actual voice—the power of her volume was extraordinary. I was trembling right through my body. It was like someone had put an electric current through it. (Parlby interview 2007)

Dessi Stefanova offered the following thoughts when I asked for her explanation as to why Bulgarian singing should affect listeners so deeply:

I think it's mostly that Bulgarian singers sing with a lot of conviction. You don't get anybody just half-singing or quarter-singing. It's just all full on, and I think that accounts for a lot of it, just the experience of hearing somebody putting their heart and soul into a song....And I think for a lot of people the harmonies are very exciting, the fact that it's never what you expect it to do. And the loudness: being loud is a big plus. Those are the three main things that people have said to me. Also the fact that it is kind of exotic and people are attracted to that romantic idea. (Stefanova interview 2008)

Dessi says of her own way of working with the London Bulgarian Choir:

I always encourage people to try and express what they are singing in *every* way—not just to say the right words or the right rhythm but, really, through their voice and through their body and their eyes and their face...and that's very empowering for people....And it gives you a different level of communicating with an audience as well, which gives people a real buzz, to see that connection. (Stefanova interview 2008)

Perhaps not surprisingly, similar themes occur in Mirjana Laušević's discussion of the attraction of Balkan music for American participants. In *Balkan Fascination*, she describes how the repertory is seen to "foster group experience and social enjoyment...in the ways many other musical styles do not". Important contributing factors here are the "singability" of the melodies, "sitting comfortably in the average person's register, allowing for easy harmonization and responding well to being sung full voice in a noisy room" (2007: 55). Balkan music seems to offer a democratic approach to music making where, in contrast to the world of Western classical music, music and dance are not reserved for "the talented few", and "this accessibility of music making to all members of a community is very appealing to many Americans who do not want to be 'perfect,' but to make music in a communal and friendly atmosphere" (32–33). Added to this are "important musical and extra-musical associations with the ancient, the natural, and the spiritual". For example:

The presence of a drone or steady tonal center in much of Balkan music can suggest a sense of being "grounded" and connected to the rest of the world's music and people; a sense of the universal, transcending time and place. Combined with its "meditative" quality, a nexus of physical experience and cultural expectation, drone enhances the Balkanites' feelings of being one with the sound, with the earth, and with each other. (Laušević 2007: 59–60)

Among Laušević's respondents, the use of unusual modes was also associated with an experience of the communal, earthy, otherworldly, ancient, or exotic. The fact that those who became "hooked" initially responded to the music on a primal or "gut level" meant that the response "transcends the individual, cultural, and historical and is experienced as metaphysical, magical, or cosmic", leading some to interpret this in terms of reincarnation theory (66).

Laušević also comments on the more particular appeal of Balkan women's songs to those involved in the women's liberation movement of the 1970s: "Recognizing the vocal power, musical tightness, and female bonding evidenced in these songs, many women welcomed the contrast to the aesthetic values dominant in the American mainstream" (211). As she stresses, however, in the home culture of the Balkans loud and vibrant singing is not linked with any notion of "women being powerful or speaking their mind" but rather is "part of demonstrating strength, endurance and a capacity for hard labor demanded by patriarchal village life". As the songs were recontextualised, so was their meaning re-inscribed as the American women's movement used Balkan female vocal polyphony creatively to communicate its own values, employing the songs as "a means of resisting patriarchy and expressing women's liberation" (212). Laušević expands on the notion of female solidarity by explaining how "the realization of Balkan songs in two- or three-part harmony, especially in unmetered songs, demands great interpersonal concentration and silent communication between singers". Many American women, she reports, have identified the bonding that took place as "one of the best outcomes of their involvement with Balkan music" (213). This way of engaging with the material on one's own terms was in part prompted by Ethel Raim, who Laušević describes as having encouraged her students "to look internally for the very qualities they recognized in the music, and to use their study of Balkan vocal styles as an opportunity to learn about themselves, their own voices and cultural bias as well" (211). This points, once again, to the therapeutic and transformative dynamics involved in "performing the other".

GIFTS FROM GEORGIA

As we turn our attention from the Balkans to the Caucasus we will find a degree of continuity with regard both to specific features of the music that appeal to Western singers and to the meanings and values that they ascribe to it. The Georgian story is especially interesting for what it reveals about the way in which affiliations and networks develop. It also allows me to examine at closer quarters different kinds of teaching methodologies and to pursue in greater detail the theme of performance as a path to self-knowledge.

Su Parlby's description of her close encounter with Bulgarian singing as quoted above offered a striking example of the intensely visceral level at which sound can be experienced. Similarly visceral imagery occurs repeatedly in interviewees' narratives about their attraction to Georgian music, which often begins with a road-to-Damascus-style conversion or an experience akin to love at first sight. Helen Chadwick casts her mind back to her first encounter with Georgian singers in 1982, when she had travelled with Cardiff Laboratory Theatre to perform at a festival in France. Among the other performers was a Georgian choir. One evening, a feast was laid on for all the artists and in the middle of the meal the Georgians burst into song. Helen's memory of the effect this had on her remains vivid:

> The image that I have always had was that it was like sort of lightning going down and cutting my body up.... And it was so powerful.... So the falling in love happened actually then. (Chadwick interview 2008)

For Nina Chandler, too, after hearing Georgian singing for the first time there was no going back:

> It was like reaching into my heart and just grabbing me.... [It] just spoke to me really.... I love doing the other traditions. It's just something about *this* one that became important to *me*. (Chandler interview 2009)

The notion of instant recognition also appears in Roz Walker's account of her response to her first Georgian workshop experience: "This is really it...the music I've wanted to do for so long." She elaborates on what it was that held her spellbound: "You've got these ages of kind of waiting for the magic to happen and then suddenly it kicks in and you're like, whoa, you're really home, and it was very strong" (interview 2007). Images of homecoming feature more explicitly in Katherina Garratt-Adams's explanation of what Georgian music means to her:

> It's just so grounding. To me it's like home. It's hard to describe but it's like I've known it all my life and yet I haven't, but it's so familiar. It just feels very, very much a sort of primeval sound, if you like. (Garratt-Adams interview 2011)

Nina also talks about the "magic" of the harmonies. The individual parts, she muses, can sound deceptively straightforward when they're taught in isolation: "It's the alchemy of putting those three parts together and suddenly: spine-tingling" (Chandler interview 2009).

Zaka Aman has been smitten by the Georgian bug ever since he attended a workshop at the Giving Voice festival in Aberystwyth. When I asked what it was about the Georgian songs that particularly "grabbed" him, he answered without hesitation:

> The harmonies. Definitely the harmonies. I mean, definitely, definitely the harmonies.... It grinds, it rattles, it shakes me. It's like the music gets into my bones and my body and whizzes me around in a way that I *really* love and enjoy.... The sound takes me and there's nothing else.... It is like a hundred percent sound and it takes me and massages me and it brings me to the here and now and the whole rest of the world disappears and I just feel bathed in sound and absorbed in or by sound and it's really *good* sound, it's *nice*. (Aman interview 2009)

Zaka's choice of words, together with the rhythmic pattern of his speech, is especially suggestive, pointing to a state that has obvious transcendental and ecstatic qualities and may be understood in psychological terms as a euphoric peak experience (see Maslow 1964). The fact that Zaka was able to speak at some length in such an animated and intensely engaged manner while sitting, late at night, outside a pub on a busy London side street with motorbikes roaring past would seem to indicate that the sense of euphoria experienced when singing the songs can also be evoked by the memory of singing.

As in the case of Bulgarian multipart singing, some of these effects can be attributed to the way in which the music, as a structural and acoustic phenomenon, is experienced as novel, exotic, and liberating when compared with more familiar Western idioms. Especially appealing is the fact that many of Georgia's regions preserve seemingly archaic modal styles, with scales built around the fifth or fourth rather than the octave. For the listener, the music further derives its distinctive character from its finely-tuned but untempered intervals, unexpected harmonic sequences that bear no relation to those found in Western functional harmony, and a clear preference in some regional styles for chords that in the Western system would be termed discordant, such as the ubiquitous 1–4–5 chord (e.g. C–F–G, often referred to in early twentieth-century Georgian writings as a trichord or "Georgian triad"). Further thrills are derived from the penchant for parallel fifths, tritones, and other harmonic procedures that have long been proscribed in Western classical music. Like Bulgarian songs, Georgian songs may also appear to be vestiges of an archaic culture imagined as more organic, authentic, and infused with the supernatural, in this case not only on account of the sound but also because of the preservation in some song texts of a lexicon believed to be derived from pre-Christian, esoteric cults related to the sun or to ancient deities associated with fertility or healing.

The vibrancy of the Georgian singing scene in the United Kingdom is largely a legacy of the work of Georgian singer and ethnomusicologist Edisher

Garakanidze prior to his untimely death in 1998. As a student and later a teacher in the Department of Georgian Traditional Music at Tbilisi State Conservatoire, Edisher undertook regular fieldwork expeditions to remote parts of the country, thereby acquiring expertise in the different regional singing styles as well as an intimate knowledge of village life and folklore. Together with his friend and colleague Joseph Jordania, Edisher first visited Britain in 1994 at the invitation of the Centre for Performance Research. The event in question was a week-long conference on the theme of performance, food, and cookery. As Edisher recalls, "The invitation was unexpected as I had never been good at cooking" (2004a: viii). It soon became clear, however, that he was being invited to teach Georgian singing in preparation for the closing event on the final evening, which (in typical CPR fashion) was to be a Georgian-style feast that would be incomplete without Georgian-style toasts and songs. The CPR assembled an ad hoc choir of around twenty-five singers and Edisher and Joseph spent the week teaching them a set of eighteen songs. Such was the success of the enterprise that one of the guests at the feast was heard to wonder how the organisation had been able to finance bringing a whole choir over from the Caucasus.

Edisher made several return visits to the United Kingdom in the years that followed; Helen Chadwick was instrumental in strengthening this connection, initially travelling with him as a translator on workshop tours she coordinated. In addition to leading more workshops for the CPR and other organisations (figure 6.1), Edisher was soon working with community choirs across the country, many of which were directed by singers who had taken part in the original

Figure 6.1 Edisher Garakanidze leading a Georgian singing workshop at the International Workshop Festival, Glasgow, 1997.
Source: Photo courtesy of Simon Richardson (with thanks also to the International Workshop Festival).

sessions.[16] In this way, he helped establish a common repertoire that would be consolidated with the appearance of the book *99 Georgian Songs: A Collection of Traditional Folk, Church and Urban Songs from Georgia*, completed and published after his death. It was the enthusiasm, competence, and commitment of the expanding British Georgian-singing community that inspired Edisher to start work on the collection. Joan Mills, in her preface to the book, alludes to the speed with which the seeds planted by Edisher and Joseph propagated:

> That such a songbook is needed is a matter of much credit to both Edisher and his friend, close collaborator and colleague, Joseph Jordania.... Only a few years ago it would have seemed unimaginable that a book containing nothing but songs, from a country that most people in the UK would have found hard to locate on the world map, should be not only viable, but awaited with impatience. (Mills 2004: vi)

As Joan goes on to indicate, Edisher's approach was in many ways compatible with the natural voice ethos, as in his conviction that "everybody without exception has the ability to sing, just the same as to laugh, cry, and run. It is from God." She also recalls how Edisher had once spoken of workshop participants taking a "step towards working at internal obstacles and complexes and one step to an internal freedom" and had coined the term "medicine for musical difficulties" to describe what he viewed as one of the book's defining qualities. He insisted that the volume should be primarily a workbook for singers and not a technical or academic work: "It is for singers in the west who want to learn these songs, but want to know about the meaning, where the songs come from, singing style and so on" (2004a: vi). In his introduction to the collection, Edisher writes:

> From experience I have learnt that a practical workshop is still the best way to come into contact with folk music and to go deep into it. This is because it allows participants to obtain ethnomusicological, historical, geographic and ethnographic information at the same time as communicating directly with the music. This kind of empirical knowledge cannot be replaced by lectures or seminars: workshop participants become the co-owners of a culture that stems from the depth of centuries and millennia! (Garakanidze 2004a: ix)

Edisher's style of teaching offers interesting insights into the process of adapting material in a foreign musical language in a way that makes it accessible for non-native apprentices and also better suited to the choir format. The majority of Georgia's polyphonic songs are in three parts, with a smaller number in two or four parts. In most cases, the authentic performance of a three-part song requires that each of the two upper parts be sung by a single voice. Furthermore, as Edisher writes in *The Performance of Georgian Folk Song*:

> A performer who was educated in a traditional society does not have once-and-forever established single versions of songs. As a rule, a performer varies the different melodic and rhythmic features each time s/he sings a song. (Garakanidze 2007: 153)[17]

Anzor Erkomaishvili, long-time director of the Rustavi Choir and now president of the International Centre for Georgian Folk Song, underlines the same principle: "In general, there are as many variants of a song as good performers. Don't take this as boasting, but each time I sing the same song differently" (2005: 30). This is one area in which compromises clearly have to be made in adapting a song for use by a larger ensemble with more than one voice to a part. A degree of standardisation—fixing melodic and rhythmic motifs that might otherwise vary from one rendition to the next and simplifying ornamental flourishes—has to take place to enable all of the voices on a given part to sing in unison. In the early days, therefore, Edisher and Joseph selected their material carefully, giving preference to songs from western Georgia that lent themselves more readily to being performed by large groups than the less measured and more highly ornamented table songs from eastern Georgia, for example.

The pronunciation of the Georgian language, with its complex consonant clusters and inclusion of several consonants that have no counterpart in most European languages, presents a considerable challenge to non-native singers. Edisher described his twofold solution to this problem: "I usually select songs with as little text as possible for foreigners. In workshops I usually deliberately decrease the number of consonants in the text" (2004b: xv). Making such compromises was in keeping with his categorisation of the authentic, rural performance style as "a higher level of learning which is by no means compulsory for all of those interested in Georgian music". Achieving this higher level is not ruled out, he explained, but "it needs special training, which involves listening to authentic recordings, travelling to Georgian villages in different regions, and establishing personal contact with traditional singers" (xvi). Such training has, since Edisher wrote these words, been pursued by a growing number of his former protégés as well as more recent recruits, as we shall see in chapter 8. Initially, however, he did not want undue agonising over matters of authenticity to overshadow an endeavour that for him was informed by other, equally important objectives.

The process of adapting the material for choirs (as in Bulgaria, although not with quite the same aesthetic) began in Georgia with the fashion of formal ensembles offering staged performances. These can be dated back to the establishment of the Kartuli Khoro in 1885, but they were to proliferate in the Soviet years. Edisher's use of the term "secondary folklore" to characterise these ensembles referred not only to the fact that the songs had been removed from their primary habitat but also to the way in which non-traditional aspects of musical organisation and performance practice were adopted under the influence of modern European music. One European influence identified by Edisher was the deliberate teaching of individual parts and the permanent assignment of a singer to a particular part; this was in contradistinction to the natural method of learning by hearing the song in its entirety throughout one's childhood and later not only coming to distinguish the separate vocal lines but also becoming adept at singing each of them (see Garakanidze 2007: 160–161). Town- and city-based ensembles were typically made up of singers from different regions, and their repertoire featured songs from all over Georgia; this was in contrast to village ensembles that specialised in songs from their own local heritage. This in itself often resulted in a degree of normalisation as the finer nuances of local tuning systems and timbres were lost. In the case of choirs like Anzor Erkomaishvili's multi-award-winning Rustavi Choir, which undertook extensive overseas tours in the Soviet period, supposedly rough edges would be smoothed over and an extra layer of polish added in deference to the supposed expectations and tastes of Western audiences, as well as the practicalities of singing on stage in large concert halls. These processes of standardisation and adaptation, together with the narrowing of the gap between Caucasian and Western European practices, might be seen to have paved the way for the later transfer of the material to non-native choirs.

Joseph Jordania, meanwhile, has further perspectives to contribute to debates about authenticity:

> I think that when foreigners are learning Georgian songs there is this kind of fear sometimes that [because] they are singing some kind of a foreign culture, they have to stay as close as possible to be respectful to the tradition, and because of that sometimes they might restrain their creativity, restrain their feelings [about] how they would like to change there and to think the way that they would like to. (Jordania interview 2007)

For his part, he would like to hear people in the different places in which the songs settle singing them in their own way. A Mozart sonata, he says, is always the same Mozart sonata. A pianist of any nationality should play exactly the same notes, otherwise "it's wrong". It is equally wrong, on the other hand, to treat traditional songs as if they were written traditions. "It should be still a live tradition, because life for tradition is changing itself." It is important to him to teach people to understand this principle. "When you're learning," he says, "the first few songs—you're kind of more respectful…you don't know. You can't start improvising." As you become freer, however, you can start to improvise and do different things with the material.

Another fundamental component of Edisher's work was to offer a window onto the sociocultural world from which the songs came as a way of allowing people to get closer to the spirit of the music. Helen Chadwick was especially struck by Edisher's skill in presenting information about the social and historical context of the songs in such a way as to shape the sound made by the singers he was working with at any given moment. She describes how, having taught the parts to a song, he would stop and contextualise it by, for example, getting the group to imagine that they were in a tiny fifth-century church on top of a hill; or he might tell a story about the war in Chechnya. When they returned to the singing:

> The song would fly in a different way and that was wonderful.... I guess it's making a connection between the people who are in the room and the material, as opposed to it just being some nice harmonies and a few words; giving a *reason* to sing—not just it's a healing song but imagine there's a sick child or whatever. (Chadwick interview 2008)

Edisher's more general evocation of the function of songs in his home culture directly informed the affective as well as the intellectual response of many of his British students. Frank Rozelaar-Green, for example, citing Edisher's edict that "singing is about meeting and about meeting people, and that is the community of song", goes on:

> It's a physical thing; it's a visceral thing. You don't just stand and sing. In Georgia...every human activity has a song attached to it.... Every song has a specific relation to life. So in that sense I find that far easier to connect to because it's *about* something, it isn't just *a song*. The song itself has a history and has a root.... They always talk about heart, singing from the heart. (Frank Rozelaar-Green interview 2008)

Speaking of how Edisher's way of working influenced her own work, Helen also pays homage to his selfless and uncomplicated desire to share the songs: "I was very, very influenced... by the way he *taught*, because... he had this phenomenal generosity.... He just loved people to do it and he was just giving his stuff to everyone" (interview 2008). The fact that he gave permission for his transcriptions to be copied and freely circulated, and encouraged everyone to sing the songs in their own way and to the best of their ability, was fundamental to the joy, as well as the speed, with which the songs took root in British soil.

Frank Kane's methods for teaching Georgian songs to non-Georgian singers offer a fascinating complement to Edisher's methods.[18] Frank originally encountered Georgian music as a member of the Yale Russian Chorus. Following his first visit to Georgia in 1984, when the chorus performed in joint concerts with the Rustavi Choir and the Georgian State Ensemble, he co-founded the US-based Kartuli Ensemble. In 1988, he relocated to France to study Georgian language and culture at the Institute of Oriental Languages and later launched the ensembles Marani and Irinola in Paris. Combining his intimate knowledge of Georgia's regional singing dialects with an understanding of the starting point and pedagogical needs of singers from a Western background, he has become a key player in the dissemination of Georgian material outside Georgia; he now leads workshops in Germany, Austria, Switzerland, the United States, and Canada, as well as in Britain and Ireland. In 1995, he was awarded a silver medal from the Georgian Ministry of Culture for his achievements in promoting Georgian culture abroad.

Frank has developed a range of techniques that are surprisingly effective in helping non-Georgians achieve a more authentic sound. His initial experiments were prompted by his conviction that, because what the Western apprentice hears is "put through the filter of their own prior experience and frame of reference", simply listening and repeating was not sufficient (Kane 2003: 558). He therefore set out to devise exercises that would help his French students locate the untempered intervals used in Georgian singing and improve their perception of harmonics (an important component of timbre). Working with a French singer and voice trainer inspired by Tibetan and Tuvan throat singing helped his choir members develop the ability "to hear and identify those harmonics most audible in Georgian singing and also the points at which these harmonics converge when Georgian chorus sing in polyphony" (559). He then began to pay greater attention to what he terms the "physical disposition and intention" of the singers, in this case drawing on his study of tai chi and Alexander technique. Close observation of Georgian singers—how they stand, open their mouths, move their jaws, and use the breath—brought a series of further insights. These included, for example, the realisation that Georgian village singers deployed the larynx and its muscles differently from Western singers, and also that they rely more on the throat area behind the tongue for vowel formation, which then has an affect on the way in which harmonics are produced. He explains:

> By gaining a better understanding of how Georgian singers *produce* their sound, non-Georgian singers are no longer simply imitating a sound, they are imitating the physical gestures and intentions which form this sound. (Kane 2003: 561)

Of central importance in Frank's work today is the idea of vibrations. In his own attempts to get closer to "the Georgian sound", he says, he felt that there was "a big piece missing...until I worked on the notion of vibration" (interview 2012). Georgian village singers, he realised, produce a lot of vibration on the surface of the skin, especially in the face, and he now devotes a lot of time to exercises that help his students to locate, control, and amplify these vibrations.

In his workshops, then, Frank does not simply teach Georgian songs; rather, his goal is "to lead people to an experience of that sound". This goal is underpinned by the fact that he does not see a one-to-one correlation between *sounding* Georgian and *being* Georgian:

> For me, the Georgians have that kind of sound because they have implemented certain technical building blocks that get them there. In other words, they have a certain form of vocal production, a certain way of welcoming the voice in their own bodies, of harnessing vibration and using it, which produces that sound. Is it possible for a non-Georgian to learn to do that? Absolutely. (Kane interview 2012)

This in turn relates to his conviction that

> Georgian singing, as a point of entry to gain a knowledge of the voice, vibration and harmony singing, has a pan-human dimension and, like hatha yoga or tai chi, is a practice that can and should be shared with and available to all humanity. (Kane, pers. comm. 2012)

In this sense, Georgian music is not only a cultural phenomenon but also "a useful school of voice technique" that transcends national and ethnic borders (interview 2012).

David Tugwell (founder of the Edinburgh-based Georgian choir Torola, now reconstituted as Skotebi) explains that his first encounter with Frank's work represented a major breakthrough in his engagement with Georgian singing:

> I met Frank and that really changed everything about Georgian music for me. I completely saw it in a different way, what it was about, how to sing it—everything. It was really a life-changing event. (Tugwell interview 2011)

Pressed to elaborate on the nature of his new understanding, he goes on to speak of

> getting into the *connection*—this idea that you're not just singing the parts and it being a pretty kind of thing to do. It's a way of really connecting, a way of changing yourself too; a way of working, feeling all kinds of parts of your body, and opening up in all kinds of ways.... I don't think before I really realised why I was interested in it. If someone asked me "why are you interested in these songs?" I'd just say, "well, they're nice songs... I don't really know why." Frank made me realise why I liked the songs, or what I was looking for and why they were appealing. (Tugwell interview 2011)

David's subsequent reference to it being "almost an out-of-body experience when you're really in the groove of singing with people you know" suggests that the kind of deeper understanding of what he describes as "the connection" then contributes directly to the transcendental state of *communitas* that is achieved in the act of singing.

As we enter the second decade of the twenty-first century, the Georgian singing scene in Britain and Ireland is more vibrant than ever. The largest and longest standing of the dedicated Georgian choirs is the London choir Maspindzeli. Originally named Songs of the Caucasus, it was set up by Helen Chadwick the year after Edisher's death to raise money to help support his son, Gigi (Giorgi), who had survived the road accident that claimed the lives of the rest of the family. After several changes of leadership Maspindzeli is, at the time of writing, directed by native Georgian Tamta Turmanidze, who also leads a smaller female ensemble, Tabuni. Georgian choirs and ensembles can be found in a number of other towns and cities; they include Chela in Cambridge, Borjghali in Bristol, Samzeo in Leeds, Zurmukhti in Dublin, Alilo in Findhorn, and Thornlie Primary Georgian Choir in Wishaw (Scotland). Visits by Georgian singers continue to multiply; their workshop and concert tours are publicised via bodies such as the Georgian Harmony Association (formed in 1998 to serve as a forum for continuing Edisher's work), the more recently established Northern Georgian Society, and the NVPN. The singers are typically hosted by community choir members, and this further strengthens personal as well as professional connections. In addition to attending workshops in their own locality, Georgian singing enthusiasts often meet at weekend or weeklong residential events. New singing groups continue to form on the back of such workshops, which also provide new converts with a starter-pack of songs. Members of the more established choirs regularly travel to Georgia to learn directly from songmasters in the villages (see chapter 8). They might also be invited to perform on stage at a festival or at the biennial International Symposium on Traditional Polyphony hosted by the State Conservatoire in Tbilisi, where they then encounter "foreign" Georgian choirs from other parts of the world as well (▶ see video tracks 06.01–06.06).

The many gifts that Georgia has bestowed—from Edisher's initial generosity in sharing his songs to a more general perception of the therapeutic power of Georgian harmonies—have induced a strong sense of responsibility and an urge to give something in return. On learning of Edisher's death, choirs with whom he had worked all over the country set about raising funds for his son Gigi's hospital care.[19] When Russian forces invaded Georgia in the summer of 2008, a worldwide action was promptly launched under the banner "Let's Sing for Peace in Georgia", both to express solidarity and to draw public attention to Georgia's plight. Support has also been extended to broader charitable and humanitarian causes and to cultural development projects, either through such organisations as SOS Children's Villages or via direct personal connections of the kind we will learn more about in chapter 8.

AUTHENTICITY, ALTERITY, AND POSSESSION

Viewed together, the cases surveyed in this chapter point to some interesting new themes and perspectives as well as reinforcing those introduced more generally in the previous chapter. Both the personal attraction to world songs and their suitability for natural-voice-style choirs, workshops, and summer camps clearly have many dimensions over and above the appeal of the songs as purely musical entities. While many singers do experience an intensely pleasurable and irresistible response to the sound itself—especially "the harmonies"—and delight in the richness of vocal and creative possibilities that different musical styles expose them to, the songs are also valued on account of the meaningfulness that is attributed to them. This may be with regard to their role in traditional societies associated with an "ancient", "natural", or more "wholesome" way of life, or in the sense of an explicit message that is carried by the lyrics. The songs are also seen to have educational and mediatory functions, being valued for the window they offer onto other people's lives and worldviews and the potential this has to contribute to greater empathy and global understanding. At the same time, singing songs from the world's oral traditions offers a means to enter into community with others closer to home. In providing an alternative to more familiar repertoire that may be tainted by unwelcome associations or constrained by convention, these songs-from-elsewhere can also be part of a process of empowerment. This in turn relates to the way in which at an individual level the trope of "finding one's voice" takes on figurative as well as literal dimensions.

Perhaps most importantly, these case studies underline arguments for the need to rethink dominant assumptions about authenticity, appropriation, and ownership. It has become customary to present musical appropriation as an ambivalent act in which, to borrow Steven Feld's terms, "a melody of admiration, even homage and respect, a fundamental source of connectedness, creativity, and innovation…is harmonized by a counter-melody of power, even control and domination, a fundamental asymmetry in ownership and commodification" (1994b: 238)—with the latter, more negative voice usually gaining the higher ground. Feld may be referring here to blatantly problematic cases involving popular music artists like Paul Simon, where (as was the case with Simon's *Graceland* project) the line between exploration and exploitation is thinly drawn; yet similar anxieties nag at the heels of those who, like the contributors to Solís's *Performing Ethnomusicology*, promote participatory world music ensembles in educational settings. As Solís writes in the introduction to the collection, "whether we adhere fiercely to what we perceive as orthodoxy, or shed all pretexts to 'accurate' reproduction, we know we may be charged with either neocolonialism or irresponsible cultural squandering" (2004: 17). One of the objectives of the contributors to the volume is to work though these challenges and dilemmas and to present the case for the defence, arguing that, as David Locke puts it, "good information about the non-West helps open a contact zone. We need not be trapped in an inevitable world of exploitation" (2004: 188). In a chapter aptly titled "Bilateral Negotiations in Bimusicality", Anne Rasmussen points not to the imbalance of power but to the imbalance of anxiety when she describes how her "hang-up about playing the music of a people 'whose blood doesn't flow in my veins'" was dissipated by her two-year residence in Indonesia, where, in Jakarta, she witnessed professional Indonesian musicians playing all manner of "foreign" music, including rock and roll, reggae, *nuevo flamenco*, jazz, Western art music, disco, Christian hymns, and Arab religious and pop music (2004: 217).

The examples I have presented here certainly do not correspond to the image of a magpie-like stockpiling of gems and curiosities; nor, as a general rule, are songs simply plucked out of thin air, as if on a passing whim. In each case, the music's path has been paved by a series of personal connections and initiatives. Culture-bearers have been willing and proactive parties to the exchange, either assuming the role of teacher or endorsing the efforts of non-native go-betweens like Frank Kane or Su Hart, whose practice is based on intimate insider knowledge of the songs' place of origin and long-standing relations with communities in that culture. In *Borrowed Power: Essays on Cultural Appropriation*, Bruce Ziff and Pratima Rao introduce the notion of cultural appropriation as "just one form of cultural transmission" (1997: 5). As a more neutral term but one that also acknowledges the agency of the transmitter and the processes of dedicated teaching and learning that take place, transmission seems to offer a better fit for the kinds of crossovers and direct exchanges I have described here.

It is especially significant that many of the voices we have encountered speaking about cultural heritage as a human resource that should not be constrained by geographical, genetic, or political boundaries have been those of culture-bearers themselves. Here, we might again ponder Edisher Garakanidze's statement that workshop participants become co-owners of a culture. A teacher like Edisher is a kind of channel who momentarily pushes aside the veil between worlds so that the wisdom and truth of one may pass over to the other. The "learner as initiate" might also be seen as possessed—with a different voice, a different spirit, a different understanding; seeing (to invoke again Heidi's formulation, quoted in chapter 5) out of other eyes, singing out of other throats. Certainly Edisher would have his students enchanted and transported to the Georgia he conjured up for them. Here, the notion of "possessing" a song is cast in a different light. Perhaps this is a clue to what Edisher meant when he used the term "co-owners".

The position adopted by those who share their culture in this way resonates with the more positive framing of transculturalism by theorists such as Ulf Hannerz. Observing how "cultural diversity within the global ecumene can be used as a kind of reserve of improvements and alternatives to what is at any one time immediately available in one's own culture, and of solutions to its problems", Hannerz goes on to point out:

> One curious thing about the economics of culture, of course, is that this reserve, this particular kind of transnational common, does not risk becoming depleted merely because people borrow heavily from it, as people can keep giving meanings and their expressions away to others without losing them for themselves. (Hannerz 1996: 62)

Javanese musician Hardja Susilo expresses similar sentiments in a more down-to-earth way. Asked whether he ever has any qualms about appropriation (in this case, of gamelan music by American students) as an act of colonisation, Susilo replies:

> To me that is political talk. I am frankly honored that you guys are studying the gamelan, that you think it is a worthy subject. A lot of Indonesians don't think so, you know. So, appropriate all you want. You see, it isn't like "if you take it then I don't have it anymore." This is a case where if you take it then we have two, you see. If other people take it, too, then we have three of whatever it is you are supposed to take. So, it isn't like a flute; if you take it, then I don't have it. If this music culture is lost, that is not because you take it, but because they, the Javanese, are neglecting it. (Susilo 2004: 66)

One might even go so far as to argue that, faced with the invitation to join the party, keeping one's hands off "other people's music" might be tantamount to a form of cultural boycott.

Another strong thread running through these case studies is the notion of a song as a fluid entity that is never performed the same way twice. This, too, complicates notions of authenticity if authenticity is defined as "faithfulness to the source". In the case of African music, Georgian music, or almost any other music from a living oral tradition, what is to be learnt—by insiders and outsiders alike—is not so much a fixed repertoire as a way of improvising in the style, and this may be seen as part of a broader project of fulfilling one's creative potential. Michelle Kisliuk and Kelly Gross's reflections on Michelle's teaching of BaAka music and dance to a student group at the University of Virginia are pertinent here. They suggest that the goal should be seen not as *imitation* but as *interpretation*:

> Since BaAka never sing the "same" song the "same" way, how do we even know when we have learned what constitutes a particular song? Were we to become objectivist thinkers and be solely bent on imitating the sound of recorded examples, we would not learn to improvise in the style. How, then, could we judge if the sound is a BaAka sound without having come to an embodied understanding

that sound is actually fused with social process? This performing and learning context allows us to ask fundamental questions about what it means to create expressive identities through performance. (Kisliuk and Gross 2004: 253)

The transformative potential of performance as a site for reconfiguring one's subjectivity as well as one's relationship to the rest of the world has been another recurring theme. David Locke's answer to the question "why are people interested in music from other cultures?" is "because it enables them to encounter subjectivity quite different from their own" (2004: 180). In fact, performance is dialogic in a twofold sense: the performer enters into dialogue with external others but also with different aspects of the self. Once we accept that participants are not simply finding a singing voice but are rediscovering, at a far more existential level, hidden, suppressed, or unfulfilled parts of themselves, and that this is made possible precisely by engaging with "the Other"—in a way that liberates them from precisely those things that prevent such self-discovery within their own cultural norms—then this is surely too important a phenomenon to be dismissed as fake posturing or casual pilfering. If we cling to rooted historical cultural experience as the sole source of authenticity, then we miss many points about music itself: where its power lies and how it "works" in the interstices of the technical and the affective. And if the transformation offered by performance is seen (in psychoanalytical terms) as part of the process of self-realisation, then shying away from the challenge and possible trauma of this encounter becomes an expression of cowardice or what Dwight Conquergood has dubbed "the Skeptic's Cop-out" (1985: 8). The notion of performance as a route to liberation and transcendence may also be related to Patrick Johnson's insistence on the need to challenge racial stereotypes and look beyond what Stuart Hall has termed the "obsessive fascination with the bodies of the performers" that all too often precludes a more fruitful discussion "of music and its attendant dramaturgy, performance, ritual and gesture" (cited in Johnson 2003: 197). In challenging monolithic, essentialising notions of identity, then, performance does important political work. As Johnson puts it, "the mutual border crossing of identities may be a productive cultural and social process that furthers a progressive politics of difference" (197) with music providing "an opportunity to engage in a conversation with the Other and the self so that both may be better understood" (206).

NOTES

1. Nineteen masterpieces were recognised in the first proclamation (May 2001), twenty-eight in the second (November 2003), and forty-three in the third and final proclamation (November 2005). The proclamation format has since been replaced by the Representative List of the Intangible Cultural Heritage of Humanity, launched with the ninety "elements" from the three original proclamations, and the List of Intangible Cultural Heritage in Need of Urgent Safeguarding. The first inscriptions to these lists were made in 2009.

2. For further discussion of the impact of the UNESCO declaration on cultural developments in Georgia, see Bithell 2014.
3. Gospel figured prominently in Nick's work from that point on, and his songbooks (including *Heaven in my Heart* and *Everytime I Feel the Spirit*) feature a number of arrangements of traditional gospel songs, together with his own compositions in gospel style.
4. Johnson adds that this tendency to universalise gospel music that emerged in early interviews with choir members did change following a trip that the choir undertook to the United States to visit a series of black churches where they could experience what they saw as "authentic" gospel.
5. Following Anita's return to Belgium, the Afropean Choir continued to operate under its new name, Mizike.
6. The English term "pygmy"—which technically applies to any ethnic group in which the height of the average adult male is under 150 cm—is now generally considered a pejorative. It is difficult, however, to find a satisfactory alternative that embraces the many different groups covered by this term. The Ba-Benzélé (a subdivision of the Aka) use the designation Bayaka to refer to all "pygmy" peoples in central Africa, themselves included, but this usage is by no means universal. In many sources, including those I am drawing on here, pygmy (or the French *pygmée*) continues to be used without further qualification and without scare quotes.
7. The Luaka Bop release remained at number one on *Billboard*'s World Music Album charts for a period of four months.
8. By the 1990s, "Nkosi Sikelel' iAfrika" had been adopted as the national anthem of several other African countries, including Zambia, Zimbabwe, Tanzania, and Namibia.
9. See http://www.bakabeyond.net/, acc. March 21, 2012.
10. *Baka: People of the Rainforest* was screened again on BBC2 in February 2012, in tandem with a new film, *Baka: A Cry from the Rainforest*, made during a follow-up visit to the same Baka family twenty-five years later.
11. The British-Bulgarian Friendship Society was founded in 1952 as a non-political organisation aiming to promote friendship, understanding, and cultural relations between the people of Britain and Bulgaria. See www.bbfs.org.uk, acc. March 22, 2012.
12. Data from http://www.bnr.bg/RadioBulgaria/Emission_English/Theme_Music/Material/ koprivshitsa_festival.htm, acc. July 20, 2009.
13. This slim volume contains transcriptions, lyrics, and translations for several songs, together with vivid descriptions of local rituals.
14. For a more detailed explication of the kinds of effects referred to here, see Rice 1988.
15. Sue's account is reminiscent of Ethel Raim's description of how, after hearing a fellow American woman producing an authentic Balkan sound and thus realising that singing in this way "was within my *physiological grasp*", she "got on the parking lot and... started letting loose and to my amazement there was this whole recourse of sound that I never knew was there" (quoted in Laušević 2007: 210).
16. Helen also hosted Edisher in London, where she arranged for him to work at the National Theatre Studio. It was the singers from the National Theatre Studio Choir who would later form the core of the choir for the first Sing for Water.

17. From "Conclusions", English translation by Joseph Jordania. The book was written by Edisher in 1992–1993 and published posthumously, with the addition of Joseph's translation of the concluding summary.
18. My present exposition of Frank Kane's teaching methods is a variation on an earlier discussion where I developed at greater length the theme of non-native teacher as transmitter and intermediary between culture-bearers and Western apprentices (see Bithell 2012).
19. Gigi Garakanidze went on to assume leadership of Mtiebi, one of the groups founded by his father, and also taught regularly in the UK. When Gigi passed away unexpectedly at the age of only thirty, contributions were made to help his wife and small child.

CHAPTER 7

Singing Communities

The World of Community Choirs

SINGING IN THE STREETS

It is July 2012 and I am in the small market town of Bury, in the heart of England's North West region, where choirs from as far afield as Aberystwyth, Brighton, and Edinburgh have come together for the annual spectacle that is the National Street Choirs Festival. The singers have spent the morning in the cavernous sports hall of the local leisure centre, running through the songs for the 600-strong mass sing that is to be staged in the town centre at midday. I quickly set up my camera as the singers now take their places in the middle of the pedestrianised shopping area and, without pomp or ceremony, launch into action. The bright harmonies and light-footed rhythms of "Jikelele" call to passers-by to join the crowd that begins to form. "All people everywhere, we understand each other; we are all alike," the Zulu words ring out. "I Want Rosa to Stay", a new song penned by Alun Parry, has a more urgent message. In the tradition of topical songwriting, it tells of a friend who is threatened with deportation and points to the scaremongering surrounding "illegal immigrants" that, fuelled by the popular press, takes attention away from the failure of the system to address more fundamental social and political malaise. Half an hour later, the "Internationale", sung with English lyrics by Billy Bragg, brings the set to a close on a more strident note as the singers raise their fists in the air for the final chorus[1] (see web figures 07.01–07.04).

The super-sized pop-up choir dissolves as quickly as it formed as individual choirs set off to take up their busking positions in different locations around the town centre: in front of Barclays Bank, the Royal Bank of Scotland, and the Post Office; in the Market Square; by the Peel Statue; in the Lion Gardens, Kay Gardens, and Gallipoli Gardens; and in the Art Gallery and Mosses Centre.

Each group offers enthusiastic renditions of three or four songs, sometimes with simple dance steps thrown in, before another takes its place. While some of the singers are in everyday clothes, others have adopted a distinctive colour scheme. Choirs like the Liverpool Socialist Singers, East Lancs Clarion Community Choir, and Red Leicester Choir not surprisingly account for a predominance of red. Some have a brightly coloured banner bearing their name or a slogan: "What we sing is what we are", declares the banner of East Lancs Clarion Choir, somewhat incongruously positioned in front of branches of Cash Converters and Mr. Simms Olde Sweet Shoppe (figure 7.1). One of their numbers has the refrain "Here we stand, we shall not be moved" and verses appealing to justice, peace, and freedom; from where the singers are standing, the verse about the greed of city bankers might well be aimed at the ill-fated Royal Bank of Scotland just across the street (which is once more teetering on the brink of collapse despite a £45 billion government bail-out in 2008). Further down the main thoroughfare, Red Leicester are belting out one of their anti-capitalist favourites, with verses criticising the unscrupulous dealings of city bankers and calling for the abolition of the controversial university tuition fees that have tripled under the new Coalition government. This is followed by "Brother, Can You Spare a Dime", an anthem of the Great Depression in America whose line "Why should I be standing in line just waiting for

Figure 7.1 Members of East Lancs Clarion Community Choir performing in the town centre during the Street Choirs Festival. Bury, July 2012.
Source: Courtesy of Chloe Grant.

bread" has a topical ring in the context of the food banks to which more of the British people are having to turn as unemployment continues to rise and benefits are cut. Members of Côr Gobaith (Choir of Hope), a self-designated peace choir from Aberystwyth, are clad in dark T-shirts imprinted with the image of a white dove. They, too, are suggestively positioned in front of a large McDonald's billboard announcing: "Limited time only. Just like the British summer." ("Just like the British economy," many of those gathered here would no doubt like to add as their eye catches the store front of the Yorkshire Building Society just to the left.)

Passers-by look on quizzically, unsure about what exactly is going on. Some hang back on the periphery; others come close and enter into the spirit of the more animated performances, such as that offered by Manchester-based Open Voice, whose members dance their way through "Iqude Wema" in front of Barclays Bank. Exaltation of Larks is another group from Manchester, made up of three choirs and singing groups (usually non-performing) led by Faith Watson. Informally dressed in everyday garb, the singers could just as well be ordinary Saturday shoppers, until they take their positions and burst into song in the more intimate setting of the enclosed Market Square. Their set includes the spiritual "I Stood on the River of Jordan" and the haunting Bengali lullaby "Ami Tomake". Inside Bury Art Gallery members of Manchester Community Choir, resplendent in shades of green, are arranged on the first-floor gallery around a circular stone balustrade which looks down into the generously proportioned ground-floor foyer. Viewed from below, they are framed—more fittingly this time—by the gallery's motto, which is emblazoned in bright blue neon around the inner rim of the balustrade: "Different Languages Same Places—Different Places Same Cultures—Different Cultures Same Horizons". The resonant space is filled with the harmonies of "Kothbiro" by Kenyan singer-songwriter Ayub Ogada, the Croatian song "Plovi Barko", and Nickomo Clarke's "I Am a River" as onlookers catch glimpses and echoes of the singers from different parts of the building (● see web figures 07.05–07.08).

We reconvene in the leisure centre for a more formal evening concert that features twenty-eight choirs in succession. First, we welcome the WAST Nightingales, a small choir associated with the group Women Asylum Seekers Together and made up, as its name suggests, of asylum seekers from different parts of the world who have found a new home in and around Manchester. The eight women on stage tonight have arrived without their musical director, who has just been detained and taken to Yarl's Wood Immigration Removal Centre on the other side of the country. "We Are Here Today", they sing, to palpable encouragement from the packed hall. The feast that follows includes songs from countries as diverse as Palestine, Brazil, New Zealand, and South Africa alongside songs from closer to home: several Chartist and anti-royalist songs, arrangements of regional English folk songs and popular hits, original compositions by choir leaders, and newly penned political songs—one, "The Ballad of

Nick and Dave", memorably accompanied by cardboard mask-like images of the faces of Coalition leaders David Cameron (prime minister) and Nick Clegg (deputy prime minister) waved aloft on sticks (▶ see video tracks 07.01–07.06).

The workshops on offer the following morning include a songwriting workshop with Alun Parry. Two new songs emerge as collective compositions commemorating experiences of the previous day. One tells the story of a group of singers that was, in fact, moved on from their position in front of Barclays Bank. The other draws inspiration from another choir, which, by chance, had launched into a Zimbabwean marriage song just as a Zimbabwean couple were walking past: after recovering from their initial surprise, the couple had joined in the singing along with the choir.

CHOIRS, CHOIRS EVERYWHERE

We will return to several of the themes suggested by my opening vignette as this chapter unfolds. In particular, we will examine in greater depth the kinds of performances in which community choirs typically engage and the rewards that such activity brings. First, though, we take another journey. This time we travel through the varied geographical and historical landscape of choral activity, alighting at different points along the way to visit festivals, competitions, and other singing extravaganzas. We linger just long enough to acquaint ourselves with the repertoire of the moment and to understand something of the motivations and concerns that distinguish each of the communities we encounter. In the process, we learn more about the different networks of people who are brought together through a shared belief in the power of song.

Choirs in the British Media

The now well-aired pronouncement that Britain today boasts more choirs than fish and chip shops certainly seems to be borne out by the greatly increased visibility of choir activity and the unflagging promotion of the choir image by the British media. In November 2011, the BBC screened *Military Wives*, the fourth series of *The Choir* featuring choirmaster Gareth Malone. Malone's project on this occasion was to form a choir made up of women living on two British army bases in Devon while their husbands and partners were deployed on a six-month tour of duty in Afghanistan. The project culminated in a high-profile appearance at the 2011 Festival of Remembrance at London's Royal Albert Hall, where the choir performed the Paul Maelor commission "Wherever You Are". Released on CD, the song subsequently claimed the coveted place of "Christmas number one" in the UK Singles Chart. Jonathan Freedland, writing in *The Guardian*, praised the series for marking a move away from what he calls "malice TV": "There are no withering one-liners, no pantomime villain judges, no losers.... The only prize is a sense of camaraderie and communal connectedness, a prize everybody wins" (2011: n.p.). Freedman was especially cheered by the impression that the women had quite genuinely been transformed from "a collection of individuals, each going through her own private hell" to feeling "like sisters". All of this helped consolidate Malone's status as a household name—for some of his most enthusiastic advocates, a "singing saviour" and for others, the music world's equivalent of celebrity chef Jamie Oliver.

Malone's first steps on the path to becoming national choir guru were less assured. The plot for the series debut (*The Choir*, 2006) saw a surprisingly youthful Malone being given nine months to form a choir in Northolt High School, a comprehensive school in Middlesex, entirely from scratch and to secure a performance at the World Choir Games in China. Here, competition and harsh medicine took precedence over camaraderie and empathy; 160 pupils with no previous singing experience (a few exceptions aside) were put through sometimes painful auditions for only thirty places. Audience responses to the show posted on the television company's website made interesting reading. While some viewers claimed to find the programme "inspiring", "motivational", and "touching", others were dismayed by Malone's evident lack of experience. One critic, a professional musician and teacher, lambasted him for his "lack of sensitivity to the children as individuals and his inexperience in pastoral and psychological matters". Another, who described himself as an experienced choral animateur, was likewise disturbed by the "constant criticism and negativity", concluding, "All in all, this programme has set back the cause of choral singing, animateur work, and indeed classical music education by about 50 years" (viewer posts, December 2006, http://www.unrealitytv.co.uk/reality-tv/the-choir-bb2/, acc. January 28, 2008). Such criticisms notwithstanding, the series went on to win an award at the 2007 British Academy Televisions Awards (BAFTAs) for Best Feature. Several further awards were won by the second series *The Choir 2: Boys Don't Sing* (2008), in which Malone was dispatched to the Lancaster School, an all-boys school in Leicester, with the challenge of forming a 100-strong choir to perform in the Schools Prom at the Royal Albert Hall. In *The Choir 3: Unsung Town* (2009), Malone took on the residents of South Oxhey, Watford, where he was tasked with creating a community choir and staging a choral festival at South Oxhey playing fields.

The Choir was not the first series of its kind; it had, in fact, been beaten to the post in 2006 by Channel Five's *The Singing Estate*, which followed conductor Ivor Setterfield as he set about forming an auditioned choir on Oxford's Blackbird Leys estate, and prepared them to perform in a Classic FM Live concert at the Royal Albert Hall. Alongside the basic formula, what these early enterprises shared was their apparently unquestioning reinforcement of hand-me-down teaching methods and musical values. As NVPN member

Chris Rowbury reflected in an interview with Kevin Stephens for an article that appeared in the community music magazine *Sounding Board*:

> Both [Gareth] Malone and Ivor Setterfield got to a point in their TV series where they seemed to stress the importance of now doing some *proper* music with the choirs so that they could get a sense of pride that they were a *real* choir. This led to teaching classical songs using written scores, the implication being that all the other stuff didn't count! (Stephens 2009: 9)

This anachronistic view of both music and choirs was all too clearly underscored by the BBC's *How a Choir Works* (2009), again featuring Gareth Malone together with the BBC's in-house professional chamber choir, the BBC Singers.[2] This exploration of "the styles and techniques that create a choir" was extraordinary for its evolutionary conception of musical style and its unqualified assumptions about the Western art tradition serving as the foundation for all music. Ralph Allwood (former Precentor and Director of Music at Eton College) appeared on screen to explain that "many years ago, we started with chant, in monasteries usually, and usually not written down. Then gradually people started singing in harmony." Harmony, the viewer was then informed, is based on a very simple principle: "which notes go most closely with this [a note played on the piano]". The result was a (tempered) major triad, which, we learned, "is the basis of all harmony". Malone stepped in at this point to continue the lesson: "Hundreds of years ago we just had those simple chords. Now we have much more advanced harmony available to us." Sevenths and ninths, among other things, make contemporary music "much more colourful". "What I really love about choral harmony," he confided, "is how its influence has spread far beyond classical music." And so we arrived at a Beach Boys hit that the BBC Singers performed from the score, before moving on to a similarly "professional" rendition of Queen's "Bohemian Rhapsody". So much for how music works, and the explication of how a choir works was hardly more encouraging. From the perspective of an ethnomusicologist or a community musician, this seemed like an alien world and in educational terms it was surely a retrograde step. It certainly did nothing for the cause of making choirs sexy.

This was one charge, at least, that could not be laid at the door of *Last Choir Standing*, another much-feted choir extravaganza that aired on BBC1 over nine weeks in the summer of 2008. Competition was still the organising principle, however, even if the contest was open to all comers. The format was that of the amateur talent show; members of the public could apply to audition before a panel of celebrity judges and if accepted, would go on to compete in a series of knock-out rounds.[3] Styled as "the ultimate sing-off" (and following on the heels of NBC's *Clash of the Choirs*, screened in the United States in December 2007), the series was originally advertised as *Choirs Wars*.[4]

The change of title notwithstanding, the war imagery remained in place with the presenters launching the first instalment by announcing that "all styles of choirs, from all four corners of the country, are about to go into battle... and they're going to fight to the end... because ultimately only one can be—the last choir standing".

The series did nonetheless go a long way towards updating the traditional choir image and, in the process, touched on some of the themes that are the concern of this chapter. Judge Suzi Digby said of the show:

> We're on a cusp of launching into a new era of choral music. Whereas before it's always been associated with churches and cathedrals, now what's happening is that we're getting that same quality coming from this 500 year old tradition of people being able to do anything musically with their voice, but being directed at a mass audience. It's a new era; we couldn't have done this ten years ago. (http://www.bbc.co.uk/lastchoirstanding/about/suzi_biog.shtml, acc. July 1, 2013)

Fellow judge Sharon D. Clarke emphasised:

> Sometimes it's not just about the singing, it's about the community—about... a team of people coming together, committing to each other, supporting each other and helping to get the best out of each other and enjoying singing as well. (http://www.bbc.co.uk/lastchoirstanding/about/sharon_biog.shtml, acc. July 1, 2013)

Yet the show was (as viewers were regularly reminded) all about "power, passion, and performance". Much of this power was invested in the judges, who were by no means supportive of the efforts of all the choirs who appeared before them: they reserved some of their most caustic and unkind comments for the highly polished and youthful Amabile Girls Choir, winners of the BBC Radio 3 Youth Choir of the Year award in 2006, who on this occasion did not make it past the first audition.

The variety of choirs on the show was certainly refreshing. Those who made it through to the final fifteen included a range of contemporary *a cappella* choirs (among them Sense of Sound from Liverpool and Alleycats from the University of St Andrews in Scotland), gospel choirs (Revelation from East London, the ACM Gospel Choir from Guildford, and Dreemz from Birmingham), male voice choirs (Bath Male Choir, Hereford Police Male Choir, the slick and youthful Only Men Aloud! from Cardiff, and the Brighton Gay Men's Chorus), and the Open Arts Community Choir from Belfast. As some of these names suggest, the focus was not on show choirs. Some of the smaller ensembles had been formed by a group of friends who enjoyed singing together; others had originated as work-related choirs. Dreemz had been started to keep vulnerable young people away from the dangers of the city streets, and Open Arts

Community Choir was made up largely of people with different kinds of disability. The final spread included a preponderance of energetic younger singers who clapped, danced, and beamed their way into the viewer's heart. All the choirs performed their songs from memory. Their repertoires consisted almost entirely of well-known pop songs with English lyrics: of the 112 songs in the full track listing for the televised heats, there were only four exceptions (the Welsh hymn "Cwm Rhondda", Franz Biebl's "Ave Maria", Karl Jenkins's "Adiemus", and "O Fortuna" from Carl Orff's *Carmina Burana*). Revealingly, the runners-up—Ysgol Glanaethwy choir from the Welsh-speaking part of North Wales—explained that one of the biggest challenges of the competition for them had been learning to sing in English (it was their set that included "Adiemus" and "O Fortuna").[5]

Last Choir Standing does appear to have been directly responsible for a surge of new members for many choirs, natural voice choirs included. The programme's website, like that of *The Choir*, includes prominent links (in keeping with the "how-do-I-get-involved?" ethos) to choir-related organisations, including the NVPN. Choirs run by NVPN members also feature on other sites, such as that of British Choirs on the Net, which carries listings for almost three thousand British choirs.[6] The upsurge of interest was both remarked upon and fuelled by articles in the press bearing such titles as "Choirs Are Becoming Cool" (Sally Kinnes, *The Sunday Times*, June 22, 2008) and "On Music: Falling for the Human Voice in 2008" (Jude Rogers, *The Guardian*, December 12, 2008). Many of these articles recycled statistics from TONSIL (The Ongoing Singing Liaison Group), an informal association representing fourteen organisations concerned with the promotion of choral singing—ranging from the Royal School of Church Music to the British Association of Barbershop Singers—which, according to the TONSIL website, together support over 25,000 choirs.

The trend continued with BBC Radio 4's mini-series, *Joan Armatrading's Favourite Choirs*, broadcast in May 2009. In this case, two of the five featured choirs were directed by NVPN members: WorldSong in Coventry, whose leadership had recently passed from Chris Rowbury to Una May Olomolaiye, and the London Bulgarian Choir, led by Dessi Stefanova. (The latter already had among its credits the first-place award in the Open Choir category of the BBC Radio 3 Choir of the Year awards in 2006.) Later that same year Robert Wyatt, guest editor of BBC Radio 4's *Today* programme, invited amateur choirs in the United Kingdom to send in recordings, a selection of which he would then play on his programme for New Year's Day 2010. Inundated with submissions, the BBC made the 117 audio clips it had received by mid-January available on its website, where they were linked with an annotated map; these recordings were still available as of this writing.[7] Meanwhile, the Radio 3 programme *The Choir*, launched in 2006, continues to occupy its ninety-minute slot on Sunday evenings.

Amateur Choirs in Britain: Social and Political Legacies

This contemporary fashion for choirs builds, however indirectly, on earlier waves of activity which energetically promoted amateur choral singing in Britain, often as part of broader educational, philanthropic, or reformist endeavours. The scale of this activity is indicated in Dave Russell's description of how the "formalised versions of pre-industrial clubs" characteristic of the North of England and larger choirs, such as the Birmingham Festival Choral Society and the Bradford Festival Choral Society—created (in 1845 and 1856, respectively) specifically for local choral festivals—were joined by the end of the nineteenth century by "choirs...from every conceivable organisational background", including those linked to chapels, banks, mills, Pleasant Sunday Afternoon organisations, and political parties (1997: 249). Today's jargon may be novel, but recent government initiatives aimed at social inclusion through the arts are by no means a new invention. Henry Raynor refers to the growth of amateur choirs in nineteenth-century England—outside the main centres of London, Manchester, and Liverpool, at least—as "carefully designed 'social engineering'" (1976: 93). The large choral societies that developed in the industrial towns were linked with the spread of religious nonconformity, particularly, the Methodist enthusiasm for education, and it was the Congregational minister and educationalist John Curwen who promoted the system of Tonic Sol-fa as an accessible alternative to conventional notation. Championing choral singing in part as a distraction from vice, the Tonic Sol-fa movement also had links with the temperance movement, and the annual mass temperance meetings held at the Crystal Palace from the 1860s featured choral contests for temperance choirs (see McGuire 2006). Wales, meanwhile, became renowned for its strong tradition of male voice choirs associated with the coal and slate mines as well as the chapels; many of these are still active today.

Among those of most interest to us here are the Clarion choirs that were linked with the trade union movement. The Clarion movement took its name from the newspaper established in 1891 by Robert Blatchford to advocate socialism in Britain. It soon gave rise to the Clarion Cycling Club, and the cover of an 1895 issue of *The Clarion* bore the slogan "Socialism can only arrive by bicycle" (a reference to the fact that the paper itself was delivered by bicycle). Local cycling clubs multiplied rapidly and were soon joined by ramblers' clubs (known as field clubs), handicraft guilds, dramatic societies, and choirs, or "vocal unions". These recreational activities offered respite from the toil and dreariness of everyday life and sought to embody the William Morris–inspired vision of a better life under socialism. Singsongs were often held in the open air as part of Sunday outings (a report of one such gathering refers to a "forest chat" by Morris himself), and from 1899 until the early 1930s Manchester's Free Trade Hall was host to the Clarion Vocal Union United Concert, at which choirs from across the country competed for the Challenge Baton[8] (🌐 see web figures 07.09–07.10).

With the exception of the cycling clubs, the Clarion movement began to lose momentum after the First World War, and its choirs would remain more or less dormant after the Second World War. The Thatcher years, however, spawned a new generation of socialist choirs, some of which took the Clarion name. While in many respects these choirs have a different lineage to that of the natural voice movement, several are, in fact, directed by members of the NVPN (figure 7.2) (🌐 see web figure 07.11). They now come together at festivals such as Raise Your Banners and the National Street Choirs Festival. Raise Your Banners, the national festival of political song, was inaugurated in 1995, and from its present base in Bradford continues to uphold the political traditions most often associated with the North of England.[9] The 2011 festival sported the tagline: "Celebrating the power of political music and campaigning arts; giving voice to struggles for liberation, equality and justice, in defence of the environment, and for a better world." Here we may note—alongside the direct political references to campaigning, struggle, justice, and defence— the interweaving of the key concepts of celebration, liberation, equality, the

Figure 7.2 Bolton Clarion Choir with East Lancs Clarion Choir performing during an exhibition about the Clarion movement, with NVPN member Moira Hill conducting. Working Class Movement Library, Salford, March 2012.
Source: Courtesy of Chloe Grant.

power of music, and giving voice, some of which will continue to resonate throughout this chapter.

The 2011 event included two three-hour concerts in Bradford Cathedral featuring a total of twenty-nine choirs. The political orientation of the majority was clear from their names: East Lancs Clarion Community Choir, Bolton Clarion Choir, Nottingham Clarion Choir, Liverpool Socialist Singers, Strawberry Thieves Socialist Choir (named after William Morris's Strawberry Thief design), Red Leicester, Côr Cochion Caerdydd (Cardiff Reds Choir), and Protest in Harmony, for example. The short biographies provided by participating choirs referred to a range of activities, including singing at union rallies and protests against the recent government cuts; performing at fundraising events in support of the Palestine Solidarity Campaign, Holocaust Memorial Day, Campaign Against the Arms Trade, and Amnesty International; singing at Green Fairs and Fair Trade events; and initiating work with asylum seekers and refugees. Like natural voice choirs, these are open-access choirs, but for most members, the primary motivation is political; they use their singing in the service of activism. They also differ in their choice of repertoire. While some include world songs, most give pride of place to newly penned lyrics in English sung to well-known tunes. The practice of setting verses on topical issues to popular melodies—ranging in this case from Beatles songs, Christmas carols, and children's rhymes to the "Ode to Joy" from Beethoven's Ninth Symphony—is central to the political choir tradition because it means that new songs can be sung instantly without the need to learn the music. As in the long history of protest song, the focus on the message as a tool for raising awareness also means that words are more important than either harmonies or original melodies. Revolutionary standards such as "The Internationale", "Bandiera Rossa", and "Bella Ciao", alongside a few South African favourites, put in frequent appearances as well, again often acquiring new verses in English.[10] In the contemporary British scene, prominent players like Frankie Armstrong and Janet Russell provide a direct bridge between the folk-inspired world of political song, on the one hand, and that of the more eclectic community choirs and the natural voice ethos, on the other.

Many of the choirs that frequent Raise Your Banners can also be found at the National Street Choirs Festival (the event featured in my opening vignette). This festival had its origins in the National Street Band Festival, first held in Sheffield in 1983. It has existed as a separate event since 1997, staged in a different host town or city each year. Initially created "to promote the development—through song—of a society free from all forms of oppression, exploitation, exclusion and violence", the festival's ongoing aim is "to create a connection and sense of community between choirs nationwide" (http://streetchoirwhitby2011.wordpress.com/about/, acc. November 21, 2011). Over the years, the festival has grown to embrace not only choirs with a political agenda but also "those community choirs who sing a wide repertoire, for the love of singing (itself a political act!)", and this is reflected in a varied musical palette that now encompasses world music, folk, pop, soul, and rap as well as protest song. In addition to performances by individual choirs, as we saw earlier, the programme includes a mass sing featuring a selection of songs that all participants have learnt in advance (MP3 files of the vocal parts, plus scores, are made available via the festival website). The selection for the 2012 festival, hosted by the Bury AcaPeelers choir, offers an interesting insight into the marriage between political song and world song that has taken place: a traditional South African song (arranged by Mandla Sibanda) and a Korean song (arranged by Bury AcaPeelers's director, NVPN member Eleanor Hill) are complemented by Alun Parry's "I Want Rosa to Stay" (a contemporary song about the case of an asylum seeker, again arranged by Eleanor), Eleanor's own song "We Join Together", Ali Burns's song "Always the Singing", and "Billy Bragg's Internationale" (featuring English lyrics by Billy Bragg set to the original melody by Pierre De Geyter).

Meanwhile, other British cathedrals have (occasionally, at least) resonated with diverse voices singing different kinds of songs. England's Three Choirs Festival was first held in 1715 and continues to be staged annually, alternating between the cathedrals of Hereford, Gloucester, and Worcester. The 2007 festival included a performance in Gloucester Cathedral of "Song of the Earth", a programme of "sacred choral music from all around the world" conceived and directed by Michael Deason-Barrow. This included traditional songs from Japan, India, Georgia, Israel, and Ireland; a Native American "Song to the Four Directions" (attributed to the Alabama-Coushatta tribe); a piece entitled simply "Baka Chant"; and the "Sanctus" from the Congolese Missa Luba, together with John Tavener's "O Do Not Move" and Deason-Barrow's "Come Holy Spirit". These works were performed by the Three Choirs Plus Community Choir, put together specially for the occasion and featuring 246 singers from community, gospel, and male voice choirs; barbershop groups; choral societies; and folk groups. With the singers clad in bright rainbow colours and accompanied for some of the pieces on a range of non-Western instruments, including African drums and Indonesian gamelan, the performance was both visually and acoustically arresting. Events such as this—occupying prominent public spaces that are normally reserved for more conventional programmes—challenge the primacy of the Western art music canon and the trained bel canto voice and make another important contribution to the democratisation of singing.[11]

International Perspectives: Building Bridges through Song

The Second World War may have marked the end of an era for the Clarion Vocal Unions, but it provided the impetus for fresh initiatives with the vision of building a new world in which communities would be united by choral singing. The Llangollen International Musical Eisteddfod—a gem of the summer festival season that brings thousands of visitors to the small town of Llangollen in North Wales—was established in 1947 to help counteract the trauma of the war by bringing together people from all over the world in a spirit of peace and harmony.[12] The "international language" of music and dance was seen as the ideal vehicle for promoting co-operation and the Eisteddfod took as its motto "Byd gwyn fydd byd a gano; gwaraidd fydd ei gerddi fo" (Blessed is a world that sings; gentle are its songs). The first event attracted forty choirs from fourteen countries, and the prizewinners included the Hungarian workers' choir, whose members had hitchhiked across France when their onward trains from Basel were cancelled due to a rail strike. Today, the event draws over 4,000 performers and 50,000 spectators to partake in a colourful weeklong programme that culminates in the Choir of the World final. In this case, the competition framework may provide the motivation, but the event is above all a joyful celebration of cultural diversity and common humanity in which the battlefield imagery found in *Last Choir Standing* certainly has no place.[13]

Llangollen sits within a far larger international network of choral activity and, as we entered the new millennium, this world, too, was undergoing interesting transformations. In 2011, the two leading associations for the promotion of choral singing in Europe, Europa Cantat and the Arbeitsgemeinschaft Europäischer Chorverbände, merged to form the European Choral Association—Europa Cantat.[14] Like the Llangollen Eisteddfod, both organisations had their origins in the impulse to promote peace and solidarity between nations in the wake of the Second World War, using music as a tool to bring people together across political, cultural, and linguistic divides. Early initiatives included international youth camps and festivals at which participants shared their repertoire as well as their company. In recent decades, the choir image has been refreshed by an injection of new compositions designed to appeal to younger singers, and social inclusion has now joined cultural inclusion as a priority area for development. These trends were highlighted in the January 2011 issue of the new organisation's *European Choral Magazine*, which took as its overall theme "transformation". Among the new projects instigated by Europa Cantat prior to the merger were Hearts in Harmony, which brought together young people with physical and mental disabilities, and Singing the Bridge, which used music to bridge divides within societies. The success of Hearts in Harmony inspired another new annual event, the Inclusion and Choral Singing Conference, the first of which took place in 2010. With the goal of exploring "the potential of choral practice to transform individuals and society; an inclusive society...where everyone will have secured the right to sing" (*European Choral Magazine*, January 2011: 16), the meeting typically includes workshops and concerts alongside lecture presentations and round tables. Each year, it focuses on a different theme, the themes for 2010 to 2014 being physical disabilities, immigrants, older people, mental disabilities, and prison inmates.

The kinds of new choral works and newly choreographed arrangements of national folk songs that have become popular with youth choirs in particular were very much in evidence at the 2011 Festival 500: Sharing the Voices. This biennial festival of choral music has, since 1997, been hosted by the small town of St. John's in Newfoundland, in tandem with the Phenomenon of Singing International Symposium. Conceived around the ethos of "singing as community", the festival prides itself on being non-competitive, although participation is by invitation and choirs have to audition.[15] A more recent arrival on the international scene—and a return to the competition format—is the biennial World Choir Games. The first Games took place in Austria in 2000. (The fourth, held in China in 2006, was the destination of Gareth Malone's fledging choir from Northolt High School.) Operating under the auspices of Interkultur (established in 1988 by Günter Titsch as a means of "building bridges between people") and inspired by "the Olympic ideals", the Games aim to "peacefully unify singing people and nations connected by song in a fair competition" (http://www.interkultur.com/world-choir-games/, acc. July 1, 2013). The Sixth World Choir Games, held in China in 2010, featured 472 choirs from 83 nations, totalling over 20,000 active participants, in addition to more than 220,000 spectators. Here again, the popularity of the event, together with its predominantly youthful contestants, is presented as evidence of the fact that "choral song, one of the world's oldest musical traditions, is enjoying a modern-day renaissance" (http://www.interkultur.com/, acc. January 11, 2010).

Locating the Community Choir: Worlds within Worlds

Natural-voice-style choirs and singing groups take their place within this kaleidoscope of choir-related activity. The foregoing tour of choral worlds also offers ample evidence of a wealth of non-competitive amateur singing that takes place beyond the confines of the natural voice network while sharing at least some of the same values. The notion that singing is everyone's birthright and a belief in the power of music to change the world for the better underpin many of these endeavours. The themes of social harmony, community building, and intercultural cooperation are prominent and move beyond a broad humanitarian rhetoric to more local concerns for justice and equality. Some of the choirs we have encountered use their voices to convey an explicitly political and sometimes revolutionary message. For others, singing is in itself a political act because it enables ordinary citizens to lay claim to public spaces and to have their personal voice witnessed. The recent focus on music and health and wellbeing (itself not unique to the UK) has further shifted the emphasis away from the correlation of "music" with the classical, professional world, and from the expectation that assumptions about "talent", "quality", and "high standards" that belong to the classical world should carry over into the amateur world as the sole concern of any respectable musical undertaking. More people are now alert to the many other dimensions of voluntary music making and its impact on the social worlds of which it is a part.

One thing that stands out from our survey is the extent to which different networks are characterised by different bodies of repertoire. Viewers of *Last Choir Standing* were treated to a whirlwind tour of the back catalogue of chart-toppers such as Elton John, Celine Dion, Beyonce, Take That, George Michael, Michael Jackson, Stevie Wonder, and Queen, interspersed with songs from musicals like *Chicago* and *The Lion King*.[16] At the Raise Your Banners concerts in Bradford Cathedral, by contrast, the tone was set by numbers like "Ode to Privatisation", "Rosa's Lovely Daughters", "Avanti Popolo", and "In Gaza Tonight", while favourites from the contemporary (published) choral repertoire on display at Festival 500 included "Butterfly" by Mia Makaroff and "Can You Hear Me?" by composer-in-residence Bob Chilcott. This throws into sharp relief the distinctiveness of the kinds of community choirs that are my main concern in this book—especially, but not only, those that identify themselves as world music choirs or natural voice choirs—with regard to repertoire. The dividing line is, of course, by no means clear-cut. *A cappella* arrangements of popular songs find a place in the programmes of many community choirs, and NVPN-listed choirs singing predominantly pop arrangements or gospel music are, on the surface, similar to some of those featured in *Last Choir Standing*. In this case, they are distinguished less by their chosen repertoire and more by the ideology they embrace and the contexts in which they perform, although here, too, there is some crossover. Choirs whose repertoire includes songs from the oral traditions in many different parts of the world remain the most distinctive and, often, the most elusive as far as public awareness is concerned; the songs are little known outside the network, in large part because they are not available as published scores. This points to another fundamental difference, namely the ubiquity in the NVPN world of weekend workshops that give choir members easy access to primary culture bearers from whom they learn the songs directly and, in the process, build up a repertoire that they share with other like-minded choirs. Finally, like the choirs represented by Europa Cantat, natural voice choirs have their own new repertoire in the form of songs by NVPN members and associates. Usually composed specifically with open-access choirs in mind, these new songs range from the quick-and-easy songs brought together in the collection *To Grace the Earth: Short and Easy Warm Up Songs by the Natural Voice Practitioners' Network* to more complex but popular compositions by Helen Chadwick, Ali Burns, Kirsty Martin, and others that are also disseminated through the workshop and camp scenes.

Very few of the choirs we have just encountered on our tour of choral worlds, past and present, match the cliched image of the amateur classical choir with its uniform appearance and reserved body language, its singers arranged in orderly rows and partly shielded by their music folders. Everywhere we went, we found colour, movement, passion, more varied voices, and many very different kinds of songs. A brief foray into the world described by Ruth Finnegan in *The Hidden Musicians* throws into sharp relief just how much things have changed. Finnegan describes the choirs she encountered in Milton Keynes in the early 1980s as being very much part of the classical world, "a natural outgrowth of the strong choral tradition in the area" (2007: 38). She estimates that around one hundred choirs were active in the town at that time. These included a plethora of church and school choirs, together with a number of independent choirs equipped with a musical director or conductor (usually with formal classical training) and a piano accompanist. An essential requirement was that members should possess "long-practised skills in sight-reading from written music" (39). Standard choral repertoire by Handel, Haydn, Mendelssohn, Brahms, Bach, Vivaldi, and Fauré was supplemented by modern works by English composers, such as Vaughan Williams and Britten, and "light classics" by Bizet or Sullivan. For their public performances, the larger and more established choirs, such as the Milton Keynes Chorale, Danesborough Chorus, and Sherwood Choral Society, would often secure orchestral accompaniment and visiting soloists. Smaller choirs also sang at churches, fetes, or clubs to raise money for local charitable causes and provided entertainment at hospitals and old people's homes. While these smaller choirs placed less emphasis on classical training, they still put a premium on maintaining "high standards". Choral singing provided a striking contrast with many of the other forms of music making that Finnegan documents—folk, country and western, jazz, rock, and pop bands, for example—where "full participation" was possible without musical literacy and it was far more common for those involved to be self-taught, often learning on the job, from recordings, or via direct apprenticeship to peers (139).

Finnegan's account would seem to offer a fair reflection of the fact that choirs have taken somewhat longer to move away from the classical mould, in part because, unlike aspiring teenage rock bands, they lack alternative role models. It is interesting to note that none of the choirs and singing groups listed by Finnegan includes "community" in its name. While the larger choirs designated themselves as choruses or choral societies, "singers" was the preferred stylisation for smaller choirs, as in the Orphean Singers, Guild Singers, Canzonetta Singers, and St. Martin's Singers. The names adopted by contemporary community choirs provide the first indication of the major sea change in the choir world. Variations on "The X Singers" still exist but they are overshadowed by more inviting upbeat or light-hearted appellations, such as Sing for Joy, Sounds Lively, Sing Owt!, People of Note, Hullabaloo Quire, Global

Harmony, Kaleidoscope Community Choir, Patchwork Choir, VocalAntics Community Choir, The Morning Glories, and Purple Cats Community Choir. Behind these and other names we find many different kinds of choir, and these now offer a wide choice of role model. Each opens a door for someone—and more often than before, it is likely to be someone who would not have been able to audition successfully for one of the older-style classical choirs.

While I do not wish to detain us at this point by making an exhaustive attempt to establish a definition for a "community choir", some comment is nonetheless called for. The American Choral Directors' Association offers what is perhaps the broadest, and therefore least satisfactory, definition:

> A community choir is a choir that draws its membership from a community at large, not restricted to a single institution. This means that community children's choirs, symphony choruses, professional, semi-professional and amateur choirs, can all fall under the genre of community choir. All of these choirs are unique yet all are the same for they share the goals of advancing the choral art through rehearsal and performance and the production of beautiful vocal music. (http://acda.org/repertoire/community_choir, acc. April 16, 2012)

This is one of the definitions that lies behind Cindy Bell's assessment of the state of community choir activity in the United States and her conclusion (in a short paper entitled "Toward a Definition of a Community Choir") that many have now evolved into "semi-elite performance machines that are no longer characteristic of the community", thanks in large part to their auditioning practices (2008: 229). Usage differs in the United Kingdom, where it is more common to view community choirs as a parallel tradition to amateur (and certainly professional) choral societies, with sight-reading requirements serving as the critical dividing line, together with repertoire. In crude terms, choral societies generally expect sight-reading skills, are more likely to hold auditions, and draw their material mainly from the Western classical canon, while community choirs do not audition or require sight-reading but are open to all, including those with no previous musical experience, and gravitate more towards popular music, gospel, and world music.[17] Alongside the more imaginative choir names listed earlier, many community choirs in the United Kingdom (NVPN-related or otherwise) simply refer to themselves as, for example, Winchester Community Choir, Salisbury Community Choir, and so on, "community choir" in this case indicating "open-access choir". Other choirs that, according to the above distinction, fall under the community choir umbrella but are targeted at specific groups of people (e.g. the lesbian and gay community) or promote a quite specific repertoire (e.g. barbershop) often reflect this orientation in their choice of name.

There does, then, appear to be a genuine renaissance in the world of singing, reflected in a new generation of choirs of all shapes, sizes, colours, and tastes.

Having established that natural-voice-style choirs do not have a monopoly on the term community choir, that choirs that explicitly identify themselves as world music choirs are not the only ones who sing "world" repertoire, and that some choirs led by NVPN members are by no means averse to singing rousing renditions of popular hits, I wish to return now to my central focus as I take a closer look at the activities of a selection of NVPN-related community choirs and probe more deeply into the nature of the rewards that individual singers derive from belonging to choirs of this kind.

THE CHOIR IN THE COMMUNITY AND THE COMMUNITY IN THE CHOIR

Choirs have long been associated with local communities, and promoters and participants alike have intuitively recognised the way in which communal singing enriches both communities and individuals. Questions about the role of music in society have been central to ethnomusicology for much of its history; more recently, the nature of the individual's experience has become a productive focus for investigation as well. These themes relate to broader processes or phenomena that have also been the subject of extensive theorisation in other disciplines, and in some cases this has had a clear impact not only on public awareness but also on government policy.

Social capital has been embraced as a key concept in sociology and political science and has extended its reach outside the academy to exert a significant influence at governmental level, in the United States and Britain in particular. Now associated principally with Harvard political scientist Robert Putnam, "social capital" refers to the preconditions for social life as distinct from "physical capital" (tangible assets, or the material conditions of social existence) and "human capital" (skills, knowledge, and competencies, or the attributes of individual social actors). Joseph Lewandowski offers a generic definition of social capital as "consist[ing] of those networks of trust and social norms that facilitate human actions of various kinds" and proposes that "social capital is best understood as the harnessing or 'capitalizing' of a distinct form of social interaction or human association that Georg Simmel called 'sociability' (*Geselligkeit*)" (2007: 14–15). Putnam's slant builds on Alexis de Tocqueville's vision in that he argues for "a *causal* link between networks of trust and social norms and the practical realisation of the political ideals of democracy" (17). According to this logic, a climate of generalised trust, mutual obligation, and cooperative action ensures that communities remain vital and healthy and allows democracy to flourish. Most significantly for our present purposes, networks are viewed as fundamental to the nurturing of social capital, and successful networks not only benefit their immediate members but also have a positive trickle-down effect in the communities and neighbourhoods in which they operate. Based on their accumulated evidence, Robert Putnam and Lewis Feldstein state confidently in their conclusion to *Better Together*:

> A child born in a state whose residents volunteer, vote, and spend time with friends is less likely to be born underweight, less likely to drop out of school, and less likely to kill or be killed than the same child—no richer or poorer—born in another state whose residents do not. (Putnam and Feldstein 2003: 269)

It is for this reason that governments in recent times have been persuaded to increase their investment in community arts and other recreational activities, alongside concrete regeneration projects focused on the built environment.

Clearly, the more inclusive a choir is in bringing in members, the more people will reap the full panoply of rewards associated with singing on the one hand and group belonging on the other. At the same time, if we follow the logic of the social capital thesis, those to whom the choir reaches out via its performances will also benefit. By extension, the nature of a choir's performing activities and the manner in which it engages its audience—including the places and contexts in which it performs—are another indicator of its inclusivity and the degree to which it may be seen as truly representative of the local community.

A choir is, of course, a community in its own right, often imagined as an extended family, or what Gregory Barz, in his study of a Tanzanian *kwaya*, terms "a microcosm of an idealized social system" (2006: 21). Choir leaders and members regularly speak of the way in which their choir comes to represent a kind of family, one where members can experience a strong sense of togetherness and find friendship and support without needing to know a great deal about one another. As Kate O'Connell (co-director, with Bill Henderson, of the Forres Big Choir in Scotland) puts it:

> I think when you sing with people you get to know them at a very deep level without necessarily ever talking to them, because we open up some part of ourselves and there's a very deep connection. (O'Connell interview 2008)

Choir members often share important life moments when they sing at one another's weddings and funerals, and their bonds are further strengthened when they travel together to workshops, festivals, or singing retreats. Kate goes on to speak of how members of the Forres choir, for example, spend a week together each year on the island of Iona and during the rest of the year, hold monthly singing suppers. Many now count the people they have met though the choir as their closest friends and refer to the choir sessions as the highlight of their week. Dessi Stefanova speaks in a similar vein of her London Bulgarian Choir:

> We're each other's best friends and whenever we get together there's singing, there's going to the pub and so on, parties. You could have a very full schedule [even] if you didn't know anybody else! (Stefanova interview 2008)

Anna, filling out a version of my questionnaire for choir members, responds to the question "In what ways do you find your participation in the choir rewarding?":

> The feeling of community—no, I can put that more strongly—they are "family"—the first people after blood relations I would take any problems or joys to. We have built up an incredibly strong bond over the years and are not afraid to voice any differences of opinion. I think a huge amount of trust in each other builds up over years of close harmony singing. (Anna, Unicorn questionnaire 2007)

Being in sympathy with a choir's underlying ethos and being drawn to particular types of repertoire are also crucial factors in explaining why many singers feel so much "at home" with their community choir. Gill, another of my questionnaire respondents, writes:

> My local community choir has proved to be an emotional/spiritual and friendship lifeline. Access to Nick Prater workshops and Nickomo and Rasullah's Harmonic Temple have led to some of the most profound spiritual experiences I have ever had. Singing in a choir of what are broadly like-minded people regarding values/philosophy has been a wonderful experience, creating a place of safety to release emotion and to feel connected to a community as well as something larger. (Gill, Unicorn questionnaire 2007)

At a deeper level, then, these comments would seem to reinforce the association between musical harmony and social and spiritual harmony (recalling the notion of being "in accord" encountered in chapter 4).

Others refer to the way in which each individual becomes part of a greater whole. Sue Harris, who runs three community choirs in the Welsh Borders region, reflects:

> One of the things that has always struck me about choirs... is that everybody is a cog in this big machine. In a choir, everybody plays a vital part and when they come together and work together it's the most beautifully honed machine you can imagine, and I think that is just an amazing reflection on life, really—well, the perfect ideal life. I suppose that's an important part of what choirs hold for me. (Harris interview 2009)

Pursuing a similar line of thought, Kirsty Martin, the director of Brighton's Hullabaloo Quire, comments on how much she cherishes the "ego-less state" that can be achieved through singing with others:

> The best *a cappella* experience is totally ego-less because of the whole being greater than the sum of the parts. So you've got all these kind of broken down

parts but the magic that is interwoven into all the parts is just something far bigger than you could anticipate. (Martin interview 2008)

This resonates with Brian Eno's more public pronouncement on America's National Public Radio, inspired by his newfound passion for communal singing. Here, he also makes explicit reference to the notion of empathy:

A cappella singing is all about the immersion of the self into the community. That's one of the great feelings—to stop being me for a little while, and to become us. That way lies empathy, the great social virtue. (Eno 2008)

Ann Chamberlayne, who sings with Bangor Community Choir in North Wales, draws on similar imagery in describing at greater length what the choir means to her:

It's connecting, for me, on a very deep elemental level, a thread which draws us all in. You can forget about the individualities.... It's a deep connectedness... so that sense of community.... Everything else goes out of the window. We are all human together and we all share very deep, essential feelings and connectedness with the earth and with each other. Sometimes you go out to work and it just isn't there. There's a lot of things that get in the way and, for me, it's nice to get back to that.... It's like individual droplets of water: you join them all together, they start to merge and then they become a deep ocean, and then suddenly the individual drops have dissipated and all become one and merged. So that really has been the most important thing about singing and expressing myself, that connection. (Chamberlayne interview 2007)

Ann's use of "connection", "connecting", and "connectedness" (a concept already encountered in some of the earlier interviews) is especially striking. The link between "becoming one" and self-expression also seems to point to the sense that one's own identity is strengthened rather than diluted by the "merging" that takes place.

Some of these benefits, of course, may in principle be derived from any choir. What, then, is different about a natural-voice-style community choir? Ann, who at the time of our interview had been a member of Bangor Community Choir for four years, offered detailed and vivid answers to this question as well. She began by explaining how for many years she had sung with an operatic society and other choral groups that allowed her to hone her singing skills while exposing her to a variety of performance contexts. This was followed, however, by a fallow period when she no longer belonged to a choir. Her immediate response on discovering the community choir, as she relates it, was: "Yeah, this is me!" She goes on to talk about the sense she had had at that time of an "enormous gap" in her life:

> It wasn't just a gap of singing—it was an emotional and spiritual gap, not being able to sing with other people.... It filled me with a lot of hope again and a sense of joy, which I think had been missing for a while. So it was very, very important for me when I first joined it.

Asked if she can identify which aspects of that particular choir made her feel so immediately at home, Ann reflects:

> Particularly the fact that we were singing in a circle...felt very special. It felt far more connected than standing in rows and holding your music. It was non-judgemental....The pressure was off. It really was just a sense of: "This is for joy, this isn't about competition and getting somewhere—it's just being in the moment."

She also refers to "the freedom to actually move with the music—with the choral groups that was lacking". It was because of the movement, combined with a sense of "the deep connectedness with the earth", that she was especially drawn to African songs. The opportunity to explore different aspects of her voice through improvisation also opened up new realms of experience. She talks about how she has always enjoyed free expression—listening to something, getting into the swing of it, and then starting to harmonise in her own way (singing along to the radio, for example). This had always been something she did just on her own, however, until, together with fellow members of her choir, she attended a residential singing weekend co-led by the choir's leader, Pauline Down. One of the other tutors on that occasion was Zimbabwean singer and mbira player, Chartwell Dutiro. Ann describes how Chartwell began one session by teaching "a very, very simple song":

> And he spent about twenty minutes keeping us on this very simple song and then he was saying, "and now let yourselves go off wherever you want to". And that was a wonderful experience. Suddenly I was going wherever I wanted to go and I was doing it *with* other people, but I was doing it with other people going where *they* wanted to go, which wasn't necessarily where *I* was, and it was all *working*. It was like a waterfall which you were standing a distance from and you could see it as a whole and then suddenly you'd draw near and you'd see little bits of it and other bits were coming down to join it and then you'd kind of draw back and just have the whole again. And for me I think that was a kind of breakthrough from: this isn't just about community singing, this is about finding *my voice*, and using it and feeling confident about using it with other people around, where *I* want to go not where other people want me to go. What do *I* want to express, what does this song bring up in *me*? (Chamberlayne interview 2007)

Here, then, we have a more nuanced image of the interplay between the individual and the collective, together with obvious suggestions of personal empowerment and self-realisation in connection with the "finding my voice" trope. We are also offered a fascinating window onto the ways in which being part of a choir of this kind is about far more than simply learning repertoire.

My interview with Ann was among a series of interviews I carried out in the summer of 2007 with members of Bangor Community Choir (figure 7.3) (🌐 see web figure 07.12). It was especially interesting for me to journey back into the history of a choir that I had initially launched, back in 2000, in partnership with Pauline Down, under whose leadership it continued to grow and diversify after I had left in 2005. A joint interview with Margaret Walton and Lynn Yule highlighted a number of additional dimensions that I now wish to pursue. Lynn related how she had come to join the choir in the early days, when I was still co-directing it, following our initial meeting at an Irish session:

> I was just looking for *somewhere* to sing.... And I just thought: "Ooh, yes! Just to be able to go and sing in a relaxed atmosphere, that's definitely for me." And it didn't bother me whether it was going to be British songs or Welsh or anything, that didn't bother me in the slightest. And then when I started I remember thinking, coming from there, "Ooh, I really like the way that's structured"—because of how relaxed it was and the fact that, at that time, it was songs like "O Signore" [a three-part setting of words from the prayer of St. Francis of Assisi]

Figure 7.3 Members of Bangor Community Choir singing in front of Bangor Cathedral on carnival day, June 2010. Choir member Colin Douglas leads a song. Choir director Pauline Down is fifth from left (wearing white trousers).
Source: Courtesy of Caroline Bithell.

and "Ja Helo" [a Czech barley-reaping holler], which were quite quick to learn. And I thought, "Gosh! Here I am, I've sort of just arrived and by the end of the evening I'm singing a song, you know, and it sounds fantastic." Because it is a fantastic sound, isn't it? And that's what I liked about it. I didn't sort of set out thinking "I want to find a choir that sings world music". (Yule interview 2007)

Margaret, one of the original members of the choir, who had previously attended a series of evening classes I had run as part of the university's Continuing Education programme, had a similar reaction:

> I think you sort of expect the first time you go to something like that, that you're going to be struggling for a bit and it's all going to be awful and you're going to have to sort of make a big effort—and it wasn't like that at all. (Walton interview 2007)

Lynn went on to reflect on her experiences with another choir that she still sang with when she first joined the community choir. This was a more formal ladies choir where she struggled to learn classical repertoire from the score. The director was excellent, she says, and she learned a lot from him, but:

> People used to come to watch me in that choir and watch me in the community choir and they used to say that ours sounded so much better because with his choir we were all so wound up about the music and we weren't really listening to each other.... And I don't think we sang well at all.

The audience members in question had attended the different concerts primarily to support their friend, without being predisposed to prefer one kind of singing over the other. What they appear to have picked up on is the greater sense of ease and security among the community choir singers during the performance, and this in turn prompted a positive evaluation from the perspective of the listener.

Lynn and Margaret also talked about other new interests to which they had been introduced through the choir. Lynn confessed:

> Until I joined the community choir I knew nothing—seriously nothing—about world music... and it's got me into a whole new scene—you know, the WOMAD thing—and I've got loads and loads of world music CDs now because of different things we've done in community choir that I've thought: I *really* like that.[18]

Margaret added:

> The only thing I knew about this—and I didn't think of it as world music—was just Paul Simon and the Black Mambazo backing, and I thought they were great.... But no, I knew nothing about these songs at all. It was quite a revelation.

Lynn also learned about circle dance through the choir, and she became an enthusiastic member of a local salsa club, which, she said, had "the same sort of ethos as the community choir because it's run by people who are not professional dance teachers or anything like that, just people who love dancing salsa and are willing to teach it to other people".

When I asked about their best memories of being in the choir, Margaret immediately alighted on a concert and workshop with *a cappella* ensemble Black Voices that we had organised at Bangor University:

> I was really, really impressed by those five women, the Black Voices. I was amazed by them. They did the workshop in the afternoon and...I was just sort of fascinated by them.

She and Lynn also spoke with great enthusiasm (as did every other member of the choir I interviewed) about a "magical" weekend in Machynlleth, where they had stayed in a youth hostel with other community choirs and they had all taken part in a concert together. Continuing the theme of memorable moments, Lynn reflected:

> There are some nights when we'll be singing a song and somebody will say, "when I hear this song I think of somebody or something", and there's something particularly personal. And we're all together in that—everybody is behind everybody and there's this great sense of community.... You can go into all that with the community choir. There's enough room for improvisation. You wouldn't ever get that with barbershop. It's the freedom of just being able to all sing together in whatever way you want and it all comes together in a particular way, but you'd never get that in barbershop, no.

The comparison with barbershop relates to the fact that she and Margaret joined a local barbershop group—which they love singing with for different reasons—following an encounter at a Christmas event, at which the community choir and the barbershop singers had both performed. Interestingly, Lynn concluded her comparison with a formulation that has become one of the catchphrases of this book: "It's not better or worse. It's just different."

Some members of Bangor Community Choir also attended a drop-in-style choir, Côr Ysbyty Gwynedd (Gwynedd Hospital Choir), run by Pauline Down for patients and staff at the local hospital. Pauline described this venture as "tak[ing] the choir to the patients". Her approach was to hold the sessions for several weeks at a time in different long-stay units, such as the Psychiatric Unit and the Cancer Unit. Sometimes the choir might practise in one of the main hospital reception areas, where people waited for blood tests. "This is great fun," Pauline commented, "as often a small crowd gathers and sometimes hospital staff passing through stop to find out who we are or if they can join." The core members of the group (including those who came in from the local community) did occasional participatory performances in other settings as well, including the Dementia Care Unit, Medium Secure Unit, Learning Disability Unit, a day hospice, and residential nursing and care homes. Pauline noted that the choir also had

> the wonderful opportunity of singing in the cathedral—once at a special service for nursing staff and once at an incredibly moving service for parents whose children had died. I shall never forget that experience; the choir sang so beautifully and many people in the congregation came up to share how much they'd appreciated the singing afterwards. (Down, pers. comm. 2012)

Here, then, is a clear example of the ways in which a choir can be of service to different sectors of the community. (Further examples will be considered later in this chapter.)

Interviews with members of the London Georgian choir Maspindzeli revealed further variations on the choir-as-community theme. Maspindzeli differs from the average community choir in several respects. First and foremost, it specialises in the music of a single culture and so attracts members with a clearly defined musical taste. The fact that, instead of holding a weekly evening rehearsal, it meets on one Saturday afternoon a month for a four-hour session means that it can include members from a much wider catchment area (one member travels from as far away as Leeds, for example). Geoff Burton, one of the choir's former directors, echoed the sentiments of some of my other interviewees as quoted earlier:

> I definitely see this choir as a community, this group of people as a community first and a choir second. If you look at what people think of as a choir, it's a group of people who meet up regularly, rehearse and perform. And on one level we appear to do that but actually—for me, at least—it's not the rehearsing and the performance that makes it what it is. There's a very strong sense of a family. (Burton interview 2009)

The Georgian word *maspindzeli* translates as "host", Geoff explained, "and I think we've grown into it". They have frequent visits from teachers and choirs from Georgia "and suddenly there we are in this hosting position, which is a very Georgian place to be". It is perhaps pertinent to note here that "hospitality" is identified by Lee Higgins, in his foreword to *Community Music Today*, as a core value that is deeply embedded in community music practice (2013: viii). Geoff continued: "There's a lot of things that we take from Georgian culture into how we do things together that gives it all a lot more meaning." He explained, for example, that the choir's performances often involve shared meals in the style of a traditional Georgian feast (*supra*), complete with toasting rituals.

Bernard Burns, who was also present at the interview, commented on the significance of eating together outside a formal *supra* as well:

> Because our rehearsals are on a Saturday afternoon, often after the rehearsal a group of people will go out for a meal, and eating a meal together with people that you've just sung with is a very community building type of thing. (Burns interview 2009)

Because members of the choir often travel together to different parts of the country, and to Georgia itself, to take part in residential workshops and to perform, they also feel very much part of a wider national and transnational community (figure 7.4) (◉ see web figures 07.13–07.14).

In choirs made up of people belonging to minority groups or those who share the same health challenges, the choir's function as a safe haven and supportive community is especially prominent. The notion of the choir as a surrogate family takes on a particular poignancy for refugees and asylum seekers. Woven Gold is a London-based choir made up of refugees from Algeria, Burma, Chechnya, Congo, Guinea, Iran, Kenya, Kurdistan, Nigeria, Pakistan, Russia,

Figure 7.4 Proposing a toast at a *supra* hosted by Michael Bloom and Eliso Tsiklauri, with members of Maspindzeli. Tirdznisi, Georgia, October 2010.
Source: Courtesy of Caroline Bithell.

and Uganda. Part of the Creative Arts Programme run by the Helen Bamber Foundation, a charity that supports victims of human rights violations, the choir meets each Saturday at the foundation's headquarters to work with a volunteer team of professional musicians. As well as sharing songs from their home cultures, some members also write songs. Helen Bamber emphasises that those who have suffered deep trauma and are unable to talk about their experiences can be helped by music in a way that traditional therapies cannot replicate. Individual members say that the choir represents happiness, stability, safety, and support, and that it gives them the freedom to express themselves, helping to rebuild their confidence. Through their public performances, they can also make a positive contribution to British cultural life and can interact in contexts where they are not—as they are so much of the time in the British asylum system—required to give an account of who they are, why they are here, and what happened to them in the place they were forced to flee.[19] A young woman from Pakistan, speaking on Radio 4's *Woman's Hour*, encapsulates what the choir means to her:

> It just completely changed my life. I've got something to look forward to. I feel much more integrated in the society. I feel I'm not just a refugee; I'm not just a number any more.... We look forward to every Saturday to come and just be happy. (*Woman's Hour*, BBC Radio 4, December 13, 2011)

SINGING, HEALTH, AND HAPPINESS

The trope of the choir as a life-changing experience, as well as a source of everyday happiness, figures prominently in the accounts of many individual choir members. There are also initiatives to promote singing or joining a choir as a way to improve overall health and fitness or, in some cases, to ameliorate specific chronic medical conditions. Some of these potential beneficial effects might be derived from any choral experience, whereas others apply particularly to open-access community choirs and natural-voice-style singing groups. At this juncture, then, I propose a short detour to examine, from a variety of historical and disciplinary perspectives, the ways in which music and its affordances have been construed in relation to health and wellbeing.[20]

Over the past decade, the health benefits of singing have come under increasing scrutiny by researchers in the fields of psychology and public health. At the time of writing, large-scale research projects are being carried out in the United Kingdom by research teams associated with the Sidney De Haan Research Centre for Arts and Health, based at Canterbury Christ Church University, which bring together researchers from the areas of health, social care, music, and psychology. "Enhancement of health and well-being through singing" is one of three research themes of AIRS: Advancing Interdisciplinary

Research in Singing, a project funded by the Social Sciences and Humanities Research Council of Canada which includes more than seventy scholars from a range of disciplinary backgrounds, working in sixteen countries.[21] Recently published surveys include *Choral Singing, Wellbeing and Health: Findings from a Cross-National Survey*, and *Singing and Health: A Systematic Mapping and Review of Non-Clinical Research*, both by the Sidney De Haan team (Clift et al. 2008a and 2008b); *The Chorus Impact Study: How Children, Adults, and Communities Benefit from Choruses* (Chorus America 2009); and *Benefits of Group Singing for Community Mental Health and Wellbeing: Survey and Literature Review*, a report produced by a research team at Victoria University in Australia on behalf of the Victorian Health Promotion Foundation (Gridley et al. 2011). A wealth of further information, including reports, literature reviews, and bibliographies, can be found on the websites of these research centres and organisations.

This renewed interest in the health benefits of singing, like the more established and formalised practice of music therapy, grows out of a long tradition that recognises music's efficacy on the social and psychological planes. A detailed treatment of scientific research on music and the brain or on music and medicine is beyond the scope of the present discussion. My primary purpose, rather, is to survey some of the key principles and proposals that have become part of a popular or lay understanding of music's effect on the mind and body. These same principles inform uses of music that are related to, but go beyond, concerns with "the music itself" and underpin the promotion of music-related activity for non-musical ends.

In many accounts of music's therapeutic qualities, the figure of Pythagoras looms large—a seminal figure in the history of the Western world for his discovery not only of the Pythagorean theorem but also of the arithmetic ratios of the consonant harmonic intervals. Clustered around this early philosopher-scientist, the astronomers and mathematicians of the Ancient Greek world mapped out complex relationships between the relative positions and movements of the celestial bodies and musical intervals and harmonics, believing each to be governed by the same mathematical laws. Each known planet in the solar system was thought to emit a sound, and the intervals between the different pitches were believed to correspond to the distances between the paths traced by the planets in orbit. Music was at the heart of cosmology, not merely as part of the natural order of things but as a primordial force in the creation of the physical universe.

Music was believed to exert no less an influence on human affairs in the temporal, sublunary world. Pythagoras' *musica mundana*, from which the notion of the music of the spheres derives, sat alongside *musica instrumentalis* and *musica humana* to form the trio of classes into which he divided music as a whole. *Musica humana* was conceived as the music made by the human organism, including the resonance between the body and soul. Being in harmony indicated a healthy organism, whereas being out of tune indicated disease or imbalance. Music, then, also had the power to heal the individual, and musical harmony held the key to social harmony by bringing people to a state of accord.

As well as getting even more deeply (and, ultimately, inconclusively) embroiled in the supposed workings of the planetary scale, Plato took up the notion of *musica humana* with a vengeance. The different musical modes, he believed, stirred different emotions and impulses and so induced people to act in certain ways. Particular modes were necessary to keep the cogs of a peaceful and democratic society well oiled, while others must be banished. Used judiciously, music could help build and sustain the ideal republic. Conversely, exposing people to the wrong kind of music would lead to anarchy. Here, then, we have an additional lens through which to view my earlier exploration of the choir as a "microcosm of an idealized social system".

Music can also oil the cogs of the brain. Due in part to its positive effect on mental alertness but more importantly to the way in which it modifies neural pathways and processes in the brain, listening to or making music can lead to improved cognitive functioning that carries over into other activities. The so-called Mozart effect has become part of popular belief in the benefits of exposure to classical music, thanks to its commercialisation and promotion by sound healer Don Campbell, who trademarked the term. The claims made by Campbell and others for the almost magical powers of Mozart's music had rather more modest roots in a study by Frances Rauscher and colleagues at the University of California, Irvine. The study results seemed to show a short-term enhancement of abstract spatial reasoning in subjects who had listened to a Mozart piano sonata for ten minutes, when compared with a second group who had listened to taped self-hypnosis instructions and a third that had remained in silence (Rauscher et al. 1993). While this work remains controversial, more recent research has suggested that singing in the classroom can improve memory and strengthen literacy and numeracy skills, as well as build self-confidence and enhance a sense of community (see Sing Up 2011). Music's impact on both cognitive and motor skills is most startlingly revealed, however, in studies of individuals with impaired brain function. For one of Oliver Sacks's patients, famously dubbed "the man who mistook his wife for a hat" (and immortalised as such in the title of one of Sacks's books), singing literally kick-started his world. Only when he was singing was he able to eat, take a bath, and dress himself. Sacks's "prescription" for this patient was "a life that consisted entirely of music and singing" (2008: 379). Elsewhere, Sacks elaborates on the power of music to awaken post-encephalitic patients "to alertness when they were lethargic, to normal movements when they were frozen, and, most uncannily, to vivid emotions and memories, fantasies, whole identities which were, for the most part, unavailable for them". Here, as Sacks explains it, music re-joins the neural circuits and acts like "a 'prothesis' for the damaged basal ganglia" (283).[22]

Dramatic demonstrations of people being animated in similar ways through music can be seen in the documentary film *Alive Inside: A Story of Music and Memory*. Film-maker Michael Rossato-Bennet followed social worker Dan Cohen as he awakened dementia-afflicted residents of nursing homes by playing highlights from the music that had been the soundtrack to their youth. Cohen created a personalised playlist for each patient using an iPod. After distributing 200 iPods to patients in four facilities in New York, he received a flood of stories about the increased sociability in the patients who had used them. A preview of the film shows an elderly man, Henry, slumped over in his chair; he is unresponsive, virtually inarticulate, and apparently unable to recognise his daughter. Headphones are placed on his head and he hears a much-loved song from his younger days. Immediately, he becomes animated: he sits up straighter and his eyes become brighter, and he begins to sing along with and move to the music. When the headphones are removed, he is able to answer questions, talk coherently about his musical preferences, and sing extracts of old favourites. When asked, "What does music do to you?" Henry replies, without a moment's hesitation: "It gives me the feeling of love and romance. I feel right now the world needs to come into music, singing. You've got beautiful music here—beautiful, oh lovely. And I feel a band of love and dreams" (http://www.musicandmemory.org/, acc. July 1, 2013). Here, music's direct effect on the human organism is to induce a sense of wellbeing that is as much existential as it is physical.

The association of music and medicine or healing also has a long history, albeit one that is often more philosophical or intuitive than scientific. The Greek god Apollo was revered as the god of both music and medicine, and Pythagoras is said to have spoken of "musical medicine" with regard to using music in the treatment of mental conditions (Alvin 1991: 39). In the medieval period, music was one ingredient in recipes designed to prevent melancholia and avoid disease: here, music was conceived as a means of maintaining the resistance of the physical organism primarily by keeping the spirits high. It is in this context that we find a host of writers confidently prescribing wine, women, and song to cure afflictions of the mind (prescriptions made, of course, by men for men; see Horden 2000). Closer to our own time, the eighteenth-century English writer Richard Browne recommended regular doses of singing and dancing to combat melancholy. Dancing, Browne advised, should be undertaken for "an Hour or more at a convenient time after every Meal" (1729: 65). And on singing, he had this to say:

> Thus we may see what a vast Influence Singing has over the Mind of Man, and with Pleasure reflect on its joyful Consequences, and at the same time be amaz'd that it should be a Diversion or Exercise so little practis'd, since the Advantages that may be reap'd from it are so very numerous. (Browne 1729: 16)

Meanwhile, the eighteenth-century German Romantic writer Novalis contributed the much-quoted dictum: "Every disease is a musical problem—every cure a musical solution."[23]

The broader contemporary interest in music and health is reflected in volumes such as *Music, Health, and Wellbeing* (MacDonald, Kreutz, and Mitchell 2012). A growing body of research has explored specific applications of music in medical contexts.[24] In considering the health benefits of singing for the general public we are, of course, in a very different non-clinical realm. Some of the same principles apply nonetheless as we consider how music works on the body as well as the mind. As numerous studies have shown, indicators of the state of physiological arousal caused by music may include a rise in blood pressure and heart rate, an increase in muscle tone, a decrease in the electrical resistance of the skin, and changes in the respiratory rate (all functions controlled by the involuntary, autonomic nervous system). Biological research has also identified links between music and hormone release.[25] Of particular interest to us here is the fact that a number of the studies reviewed by Clift et al. (2008b) found an increase in oxytocin, a hormone generally associated with feelings of wellbeing and the processes of interpersonal intimacy and bonding: in the context of choirs, this would suggest a direct link with the feelings of "connectedness" described by many singers. Altenmüller and Schlaug (2012) report on music's effect on the release of the neurotransmitters serotonin and dopamine—associated with feelings of satisfaction and pleasure—and how this may also lead to transfer effects that result in improved cognitive function. At the same time, some kinds of music may reduce testosterone levels, which are linked with aggressive and competitive tendencies, with the result of further enhancing group cohesion (Clarke et al. 2010: 104–105). Studies of singing in particular have indicated an increase in the singer's secretion of immunoglobulin A, a substance released by the immune system that is associated with positive or relaxing experiences, and a decrease in cortisol, a hormone linked with emotional stress (see e.g. Beck et al. 2000; and Kreutz et al. 2004). Alzheimer's patients undergoing music therapy have also exhibited increased levels of melatonin, which helps regulate other hormones and maintains the body's circadian rhythm.

For these and other reasons, singing in a choir may be presented as a form of workout, not far removed from a visit to the gym: it exercises the lungs and heart, tones the abdominal and intercostal muscles, increases oxygenation of the blood which in turn increases mental alertness, improves stamina and posture, and produces the much sought after feel-good factor, popularly related to the release of endorphins. These benefits, again, may be derived from any kind of singing. But there is an added twist, as Ruth Rosselon writes in an article in *The Mirror*, in that "even if you hit the wrong notes, you'll still get all the physical benefits" (2000: n.p.). Combined with the social benefits indicated earlier, this perspective helps explain the existence of choirs where the criteria for selection have nothing to do with musical competence. Mercédès Pavlicevic, for example, describes a children's choir in South Africa for which children are auditioned not to determine their singing ability but to identify those who might benefit the most from the choir experience—"those who seem most alone, most lonely, and in need of friendship" (2010: 233–234). A study of choirs in Sweden by Dorota Lindström (2006) includes choirs referred to specifically as "health choirs" or "rehabilitation choirs". New initiatives in the United Kingdom have also been launched under the banner of the health benefits of singing. In 2010, for example, Arts Council England, in partnership with Choir of the Year and the British Association of Barbershop Singers, offered funding for seven choirs to run free six-week courses to teach people to sing. Participants were promised that they would "not only learn to sing with confidence and discover the joy of group singing, but also secure the huge health benefits that singing provides and meet new people" (http://makingmusic.org.uk/html/703.shtml, accessed January 16, 2010).[26]

A survey of choirs and singing groups run by NVNP members reveals several with health references in their names, including Parkinsongs (led by Janet Stansfeld in Oxford for people with Parkinson's disease and their friends, family, and carers, in partnership with the Oxfordshire branch of Parkinson's UK), aMaSing (led by Pauline Down in Bangor for people living with multiple sclerosis), Sing for your Lungs (led by Phoene Cave at Whittington Hospital, North London, for people with lung conditions), and Singing for Breathing (led by Maya Waldman, Jo Frost, Judith Silver, and Angela Reith at the Royal Brampton and Harefield hospitals). Several other practitioners run Singing for the Brain groups in association with the Alzheimer's Society. Some NVPN members are also engaged in research. Alise Ojay, for example, is the creator of Singing for Snorers, a singing-based throat exercise programme that has also been shown to benefit people with sleep apnoea and has been the subject of a clinical trial at the Royal Devon and Exeter Hospital (see Milton et al. 2013 and http://www.singingforsnorers.com/, acc. July 19, 2013). Andrea Small (another founder-member of the NVPN) was, at the time of writing, completing a master of science degree in Dementia Studies with a focus on singing, alongside running seven Singing for the Brain groups. The Sidney De Haan Centre has also, to date, produced a series of four guides: *Singing and Mental Health* (Morrison and Clift 2012a), *Singing and People with COPD* (Morrison and Clift 2012b), *Singing and People with Dementia* (Vella-Burrows 2012), and *Singing and People with Parkinson's* (Vella-Burrows and Hancox 2012). These guides (to which several NVPN members have contributed) include summaries of research evidence, case studies, practical guidance for setting up and running singing groups, and links to further resources.

Adherents of the arts-in-health movement have long been aware of the way in which social benefits may themselves contribute to health benefits. As described by Mike White, the field of arts-in-health (which, in the United

Kingdom, has gained significant ground since the mid-1990s) encompasses work in hospital acute services, primary care, respite care and rehabilitation, community health and public health, and social services (2009: 2). It builds on the fundamental premise that creative self-expression can enhance social relationships, and that a rewarding social life can have a direct impact on physical as well as emotional health. It also is based on the belief that many of the complaints that are presented in the general practitioner's surgery have their roots, at least in part, in social or emotional factors as opposed to being purely medical issues with a strictly physical basis (21). Referring to research cited by Putnam that shows that "the extent of a person's civil connections rival marriage and affluence as predictors of life happiness", White notes that the degree of integration with the local community also correlates inversely with the incidence of colds, heart attacks, strokes, cancer, depression, and premature death (58). It follows, then, that a prescription of community arts activity may be just as, if not more, efficacious when compared with a course of drug treatment, while also being free of potentially harmful side affects. In the longer term, it may also prove more cost-effective—hence the growing number of Primary Care Trusts across England offering Arts on Prescription schemes. Community arts projects can also lead to positive material changes in the lives of their beneficiaries, thereby further reducing the burden on social services. In their study of a choir for homeless men in Montreal, Canada, for example, Betty Bailey and Jane Davidson (2002) reported quite dramatic changes in the lives of its members. Not only did the men who took part in the study show increased self-esteem, improved concentration, and the ability to structure thought processes and to cooperate with others more effectively; during their time with the choir, all moved to permanent housing and some found part-time work.[27]

One of the most moving things about Henry and other dementia sufferers portrayed in *Alive Inside* is the way in which music evokes in each such visible pleasure, joy, and happiness. To further aid our reflection on music's power to induce a deep sense of contentment, transcendence, and personal transformation, we turn to the work of psychologist Mihaly Csikszentmihalyi and his concept of "flow". Csikszentmihalyi uses "flow" to designate a peak or optimal experience that is akin to a state of bliss, euphoria, or ecstasy and involves both deep absorption and expanded consciousness. The terms Csikszentmihalyi uses in writing about flow are frequently evocative of the kind of imagery used by my interviewees and questionnaire respondents, and throw more light on the case of Henry and others like him.

Csikszentmihalyi speaks of how negative emotions such as sadness, fear, anxiety, or boredom produce psychic entropy—"a state in which we cannot use attention effectively to deal with external tasks, because we need it to restore an inner subjective order". By contrast, positive emotions like happiness, strength, or alertness represent a state of psychic negentropy in which "psychic energy can flow freely into whatever thought or task we choose to invest it in" (1997: 22). "A typical day is full of anxiety and boredom," Csikszentmihalyi says later. "Flow experiences provide the flashes of intense living against this dull background" (30–31). He harnesses Durkheim's notion of collective effervescence and Turner's notion of *communitas* when he writes of the "oceanic feeling" of infancy persisting in adulthood "as the 'collective effervescence' that takes over in ritualized social situations, or as the sense of 'communitas' that is so enjoyable when social roles are temporarily suspended". The activity that prompts this oceanic feeling may assume an addictive quality since "to replicate such negentropic experiences, the self may direct consciousness to seek out conditions of this type again and again" (1988: 27).

When a person is in flow, feelings of self-consciousness and external distractions are both held at bay. Flow, then, also relates to the kind of intimations of elemental oneness and loss of ego reported earlier. The experience of flow can also have a lasting effect once the flow episode itself is over. When all the necessary elements are present, Csikszentmihalyi explains, "consciousness is in harmony, and the self—invisible during the flow episode—emerges strengthened" (1988: 33). He points to the empowering nature of flow when he makes a distinction between the happiness we might derive from "the passive pleasure of a rested body, warm sunshine, the contentment of a serene relationship"—a kind of happiness that is fundamentally vulnerable because of its dependence on favourable external circumstances—and the happiness that follows flow, which, by contrast, is "of our own making, and...leads to increasing complexity and growth in consciousness" (1997: 32).

The idea that happiness is contagious as well as addictive may be a popular truism, but it is borne out by scientific research. A report published in a 2009 issue of the *British Medical Journal* entitled "Dynamic Spread of Happiness in a Large Social Network: Longitudinal Analysis of the Framingham Heart Study Social Network" concludes:

> People who are surrounded by many happy people and those who are central in the network are more likely to become happy in the future. Longitudinal statistical models suggest that clusters of happiness result from the spread of happiness and not just a tendency for people to associate with similar individuals.... People's happiness depends on the happiness of others with whom they are connected. This provides further justification for seeing happiness, like health, as a collective phenomenon. (Fowler and Christakis 2009: 23)

In an editorial piece in the same issue, "Happiness, Health, and Social Networks", Andrew Steptoe and Ana Diez Roux remark that "if... happiness is transmitted through social connections, it could indirectly contribute to the social transmission of health" (2009: 1). If we think of happiness as occupying a series of concentric circles, then at the centre is individual happiness.

This both contributes to, and is fed by, the collective happiness of those with whom the individual engages in happiness-generating activity, represented by a second circle. Beyond this again, we may surely posit a third circle representing the wider community to which the happiness produced by the second circle also spreads by a further process of trickle-down, akin to that described by Putnam as part of his social capital thesis. Such a model would certainly seem to be supported by the responses of audience members and onlookers who witness something like the Sing for Water performance which opened chapter 1.

THE PLACE OF PERFORMANCE

To round off our foray into the world of community choirs, I wish to delve further into the nature of the performances such a choir might give and the kinds of community events in which it might take part. As we have already established, formal performances are not the main goal of natural-voice-style or open-access choirs and weekly rehearsals are not, in general, construed simply as rehearsals for a forthcoming concert. In keeping with the underlying ethos of the NVPN, some members are uncomfortable with, if not opposed to, the model whereby a comparatively small group occupying an (often literally) elevated position on stage is exposed to the judgement of a much larger group of mostly impersonal observers, especially when a choir includes less confident singers who may have been negatively affected by previous experience of criticism. A formal concert in front of a seated, paying audience in a conventional concert venue is not the only possible performance format, however. We might make a distinction here between Performance with a capital *P* and performance with a small *p*. There are many ways of conceiving of and structuring the latter. A choir might present a selection of its repertoire in the spirit of a sharing or showing, intended primarily for family and friends and perhaps construed as an end-of-term party or celebration. It might take part in charity fundraising events that the audience attends for reasons other than expecting to witness a first-class performance, often appearing alongside other community music groups (another kind of sharing). It might present its set not as a polished end product but as a demonstration of a working process into which members of the audience are drawn as active participants. It might provide animation at a community event where other activities or diversions are on offer, and attention is not solely on the choir. It might sing for a particular group of people—the residents of a care home or a detention centre, for example—where the focus is again on aspects other than a virtuoso musical performance and where interaction of some kind may be part of the goal. Finally, it might sing at the birthday parties, weddings, and funerals of its own members. In many of these contexts, the choir's performance functions as—and is usually appreciated as—a voluntary contribution as opposed to a saleable product.

The sheer range of opportunities to perform in these kinds of settings means that many choirs have busy diaries. Such opportunities readily present themselves, often via a connection with a choir member—a notable feature of many community choirs is that they tend to attract people who are also involved with local charities or other community organisations. Awareness of the potential of a choir to serve or interact with its local community (as opposed to serving the performers themselves) is especially strong among natural voice and community music practitioners and many are keen to give their choirs a variety of performing experiences in different environments. As suggested earlier, the choice of places in which the choir encounters its public becomes another dimension of its inclusivity. By helping to animate community events it opens up new spaces of conviviality in which the usual barriers between artists and audience are broken down and singers who appear as ordinary members of the public can be seen in action away from the media spotlight. In this respect, community choirs are replicating what is in most parts of the world a natural state of affairs, where music making has a far more visible presence in the day-to-day life of the local community and fulfils many functions other than pure entertainment. Choirs that operate in this way resemble folk ensembles in oral cultures more than choral societies, and when they learn songs from, for example, a visiting Georgian group, it is this kind of ensemble that serves as their role model. Many of the songs they sing are, of course, far more "at home" in these settings than on a stage, and listeners might be imagined as an outer circle gathered around the periphery of a traditional village dancing ground more than a modern concert hall audience.

Chris Rowbury brings several of these threads together in his explanation of his approach to performance. He writes of his fundamental belief that "we are not here to serve the music, but to use it as a vehicle for human expression.... Enjoyment and fun come first." This will be communicated to the audience, who will respond with "lots of happy and (naturally) smiling faces". He continues:

> My thinking... is that we're a community of human beings often singing songs from folk traditions where people are not "singers" in any formal sense.... I like to hear the humanity of a choir shine through, with all its human imperfections and mistakes. I'd rather hear guts and passion than note perfection. (Rowbury 2004: 9)

Chris Hoskins, writing about the Singing for the Terrified groups that she runs in the English Midlands, likewise emphasises the combination of humanity and community spirit at the heart of the enterprise, in this case with reference to forging cross-cultural connections as well:

> The joy of running a community group for me is about acting as a facilitator to enable others to make a journey of self-discovery.... We support one another on a weekly basis through the trials and tribulations of life, and we also reach out to the wider community, making links with people from countries whose songs we sing, as we did earlier this year during the Kenya crisis to raise funds for projects in that country. Our Solstice celebration this year will raise funds for the Homeless Centre here in Coventry and for the soup kitchens in Nuneaton to provide meals for the homeless on Christmas Day. That's the kind of spirit that's developed in our groups. (Hoskins 2008: 11)

For Rowena Whitehead, too, the question of whom or what the choir is there to serve, over and above the music, is of fundamental importance. When, in December 2007, I paid a visit to Cambridge's Good Vibrations Community Choir (at that time under the joint leadership of Rowena and Sue Parlby), I browsed through the posters for the recent events in which the choir had been involved. Themes of peace, solidarity, and change were prominent. One poster was for a concert entitled Peace in Our Time, featuring Good Vibrations with the Helen Chadwick Group. Described as "a concert of songs inspired by those who work for peace", the event was sponsored by the Baha'i Community of Cambridge and the community music charity Talking in Tune (founded by Rowena), and profits were being donated to the Mines Advisory Group. A poster for another event, Singing for Change, supporting the Pakistan Earthquake Appeal, invited the public to "Join Good Vibrations and Friends for an inspiring and uplifting evening singing songs that changed the world (or should have done!)". A third poster advertised an event called Stand With Me, supported by Cambridge City Council as part of the commemoration of National Holocaust Remembrance Day, which it described as:

> An evening of songs and stories of resistance, life, hope and solidarity from different cultures. Moving, stirring and uplifting, these songs and the people who created and sang them have amazing stories to tell. The stories we will share give voice to the inspiring bravery and courage of ordinary people who have been prepared to stand up for others against tyranny and genocide.

In an interview I conducted as part of this visit, Rowena explained that for the past two years, the choir had also made termly visits to Oakington Immigration Reception Centre, where asylum-seekers and illegal immigrants were held in prison-like conditions while awaiting their fate (which, in most cases, was deportation).[28] Taking up to half an hour to get through security, the singers would then gather in the cafe, where they would sing two or three simple songs before asking the (all male) inmates if anyone would like to share a song from his own culture—the response being such that, once the ice was broken, there was barely enough time to hear all the songs that people wanted to offer.[29] Rowena reflects: "I'm very humbled by the fact that these people are prepared to share their songs and dances.... They really go for it." By using music in this way, she says, "you can connect with people at quite a heart level. We greet them in their own languages and we say things like, 'we're really sorry about what's happening to you,' and you think, 'well, at least when they go they've got some memory of people being friendly'." She recalls the choir's very first visit, when the centre still housed entire families:

> You could just feel this energy swirling up. We had a fantastic party!...There were kids as well and everybody danced.... For me, that is the heart of what I do. I spent eight years working in community development and I think this is the best community work I've ever done. (Whitehead interview 2007)

Later in the interview, Rowena elaborated on the connection she sees between people using their voice in the service of causes they believe in and finding personal fulfilment. Reflecting on the kinds of happenings she has nurtured in Cambridge, she says:

> One of the things I feel proudest about is that there is now a sense of people feeling that they've got a voice, and that they will go and sing together, with confidence and passion, in different situations.... There's a real groundswell now of folk who are happy to get together to share their voices at social events and for good causes.... It's a Zeitgeist, a real hunger that people have, to be part of a creative community.... It's a hunger to belong, to connect with people, in a way that goes deeper than words and I know it feeds the soul. (Whitehead interview 2007)

One dimension of "feeding the soul", then, is the sense of fulfilment derived from playing an activist role or, in more modest terms, feeling that one is doing something that makes a difference and so contributes in some small way to making the world a better place. The more politically engaged community choirs are ideally placed to provide their members with this kind of opportunity.

For those who prefer to maintain an apolitical stance, there is ample opportunity to perform at neutral events such as craft fairs, summer fetes, National Trust open days, barn dances and ceilidhs, or simply to busk. The biography for Newcastle-based Heaton Voices included in the programme for the 2012 National Street Choirs Festival captures the apparently limitless possibilities:

> We've sung at a range of venues, from shopping centres to churches, Christmas markets, to concerts at the Sage at Gateshead. We've sung at train stations, Metro stations and on buses. We've sung in heat waves, monsoons (usually at street choir festivals!) and blizzards. We've startled small children, bemused

teenagers and had pensioners sing along with us at various "busks" throughout the North East.... Most of all, we've made true friendships through singing and (generally!) raised a smile wherever we go. (National Street Choirs Festival programme, 2012)

Semi-spontaneous performances (with a very small *p*) also have their place. In this case, there may be no public announcement that the singing is going to take place: as in a flash mob event, any audience will be made up of people who happen to be in the vicinity at the time. Also on offer are weekend workshops and singing weeks that bring singers together to share and learn new songs and to experience singing in different environments, and these may sometimes include or culminate in relatively informal concerts. David Burbidge specialises in organising events of this kind under the auspices of his Lakeland Voice initiative, which, as he describes it, "grew out of a purely selfish need to combine the best of what is natural in the environment with the best of what is natural in the voice" (2004: 7). David's events range from singing walks and cycle rides "when we take our songs out into the landscape, singing by waterfalls and rivers, in caves, woods and fellside chapels and round the open fires of country inns" to longer singing holidays (http://www.lakelandvoice.co.uk/, acc. April 24, 2012). One of his more ambitious undertakings was a month-long Singing Cyclists Land's End to John O'Groats fundraising tour, punctuated by joint concerts with local choirs along the way. Tours for which David was taking bookings at the time of this writing included Hadrian's Harmony, structured around a walk along the section of Hadrian's Wall between Brampton and Hexham and featuring meetings with local singers and pub singing and concerts along the way. Singing Settle Carlisle, another of David's regular programmes, offers singing on trains, in stations, and on walks through the Pennine fells, as well as a visit to the Ingleton festival. On this trip, participants are also given an insight into local history, learning songs about the men who built the railway line and visiting the remote chapel that, for many, became their final resting place. Other trips have included concerts on the passenger boats that ply the waters of the area's many lakes. (Participants on tours that include concerts are provided with recordings in advance so that they may make a start on learning their parts.)

David also hosts an annual International Choirs Meet where singers from British choirs are able to sing with visiting choirs from different parts of Europe. Regional choir gatherings held in other parts of the United Kingdom have become a regular feature of the annual cycle of activity for many choirs. These include the Community Choirs Festival in Stratford-on-Avon ("A Fabulous Day of Mass Choir Singing, Socialising, Performing and Fun"), which provides a platform for choirs to perform for one another as well as offering the opportunity to "learn and sing new songs together as a 600 strong mass choir" (http://www.communitychoirsfestival.co.uk/, acc. April 24, 2012).

Unplanned, spontaneous performances are made possible by the fact that songs that have been learnt by ear are totally portable: in principle, a choir that has learnt and retained its repertoire in this way can sing anywhere. Jane Wells, an experienced community musician with a classical background whom we met in chapter 3, speaks of her immediate attraction to this way of working:

> Though it was quite contrary to my training and reading dots and so on, what I really like is that you can go somewhere and you've got a song... and you can all do it and you don't need any bits of paper.... That really appealed to me, and the fact it was accessible to everyone... And also it sounds better—the song's just in your head and you sing it and that's it! (Wells interview 2008)

Even in the case of planned performances, it will have become clear that many of the more conventional choirs would not be able to perform in some of the settings I have described here because of their need for a piano. Performing outdoors in inclement weather or in a place with limited light would also be difficult because of their need to sing from scores. Further, in the case of songs learnt by ear the repertoire is cumulative: this is another major difference between a community choir and a choral society that, having performed

Figure 7.5 Tony Backhouse leading a gospel-singing workshop in Toddington, October 2011.
Source: Courtesy of Caroline Bithell.

a work, may never sing it again, not least because the hired scores have been returned and most singers will not be able to perform without them.

I end this section with a snapshot from a trip I took in October 2011 to attend a weekend workshop led by Tony Backhouse that drew voice practitioners and community choir leaders from across the country to Cheltenham, where the annual literature festival was also in full swing (figure 7.5) (● see web figure 07.15). At the end of the first day, around half of us adjourned to a local Italian restaurant where we occupied a long table at the end of the room. Inevitably, we broke into song and, encouraged by the positive response from the staff and other diners, we ran through some of the new items we had learnt that day. As we got up to leave, people at other tables stopped us, saying: "Are you one of the choirs performing at the festival?" They were incredulous to learn that, not only were we not a choir: some of us had met for the first time only that morning (and we didn't have any "music").

OPENING DOORS

Participation in a community choir, then, brings rewards of many different orders and can be transformative at many levels—physical, psychological, emotional, social, and moral, as well as musical. While many of these benefits might be obtained from a more conventional choir, they would normally be available only to those who already possessed sight-reading skills and had prior singing experience.[30] A large majority of those catered for by open-access choirs would clearly not have made it into the more hallowed ranks of an auditioned choir, and, for many of them, that type of choir in any case holds little appeal. Further, some orders of transformation derive specifically from the kinds of activities that take place outside the concert hall and would probably not be sought by many of those who identify with the conventional performance model. Finally, often the greatest transformation occurs in those who have furthest to travel or have been most traumatised by past experiences.

The generally buoyant state of the choir world, combined with the popularity of talent shows and karaoke, might suggest that such trauma is overstated. In almost every choir I visited for the purposes of this research, however, people voluntarily related stories of having not sung for thirty years or more after being told by a schoolteacher that they "couldn't sing". Some had been excluded from the school choir; others had been required to stand at the back of the choir and mouth the words. This phenomenon is by no means confined to Britain. Susan Knight, in drawing up what she refers to as a non-singer experiential profile based on an investigation carried out in Newfoundland, Canada, also encountered people with very clear memories of being prevented from singing or told they couldn't sing (2011a; see also Knight 2011b).[31] Amanda Lohrey, writing about the rise of the *a cappella* movement in Australia, says that she has heard variants of this tale so many times that she now thinks of it "almost as a kind of urban myth" (1998: 185). In the context of a discussion of psychoanalyst Alice Miller's notion of the true self and the false self, Lohrey goes on to reflect: "For the stifled, the voice of the true self has to find a way of speaking out and being heard, and it occurs to me that singing might be one of those ways" (197). Thoughts such as this underline the profound significance of the kind of work that is done by open-access choirs and singing groups, not only in opening musical doors that may have seemed closed forever but in offering individual participants a way of better integrating the psyche.

Once the door to musical participation through singing has been reopened, progress can be remarkable. I have also been told stories by several choir leaders and those who run Singing for the Terrified groups of individuals who, when they first found their way to a session, had been unable to make a sound but had turned out to have "fantastic" voices and in some cases had gone on to sing solos, write songs, start a choir, or even earn a university music degree. Some groups, of course, remain resolutely non-performing, often eschewing the "choir" label in favour of "singing group" or "song circle" and holding a weekly drop-in session, rather than require members to commit to a whole term. Yet, once they find their feet and gain confidence, even the most tentative singers may be eager to share what they have learnt with a supportive audience of friends and family. A group may therefore progress from being a non-performing beginners group, meeting simply to explore the voice, to performing (with a small *p*) at the kinds of events I have described here.

Widening our perspective again for a moment, we might see any choir as an ideal candidate for the type of community for which Etienne Wenger proposed the descriptor "community of practice". But if we then focus on the choir's choice of repertoire and the manner in which it goes about its business (including characteristic performing contexts and locations) as a central part of its "practice", again it immediately becomes clear that community choirs and choral societies represent two very different kinds of community. And if, as Simon Frith puts it, music is "especially important for our sense of ourselves because of its unique emotional intensity" as "we absorb songs into our own lives and rhythm into our own bodies" (1996b: 273), then again the sense of self that is constituted through membership of a community choir is quite different from the sense of self derived from being part of a choral society. The lines of inheritance or ancestry—who creates and transmits the songs, and who establishes the stylistic conventions—are also different. Here, we might recall the legendary Bantu greeting which functions as a way of asking "Where do you come from? To which village or tribe do you belong?" but is phrased as "What do you dance?" The answers given by amateur choir members to the question "What do you sing?" will reveal something of the very different paths along which their singing journeys have led them and the very different kinds of tribes to which they now belong.

The extent to which a choir might serve as a point of entry to other new experiences, as opposed to presenting itself primarily as an opportunity for participants to hone existing skills, also warrants greater emphasis. At the very least, the "openness" that lies at the heart of the kind of community choir described in this chapter—openness to all members of the community, to exploring the voice in new ways, to other cultures and their music, to performing in a range of less conventional settings and for a variety of causes, and to responding to calls for help—becomes a positive force and places such choirs beyond the reach of the kinds of charitable sentiments that often attach to "amateur" activity or to projects designed to make particular aspects of life more "accessible" to those considered less able or less privileged. Beyond that, the new social and cultural worlds to which the choir acts as a doorway may themselves prove to be life-changing in quite profound ways.

Perhaps one of the most striking trends to have emerged in this chapter is the way in which choir membership has not only introduced people to cultures elsewhere in the world but also brought them face-to-face with representatives of those cultures. Also noteworthy is the way in which such contact often involved a mutual exchange. "We" have done far more than acquire some nice new songs to spice up our collection. The stories I have related here are just a few examples of the way choirs and their members feel a sense of responsibility towards those whose lives have touched theirs and seek out ways to use their singing to help improve aspects of those lives. In the process, they contribute to raising public awareness not only of victims of disaster, injustice, and oppression in distant parts of the globe but also of cases of material hardship, suffering, and discrimination closer to home. Meanwhile, the personal connections that are forged point to other realms beyond the local community. In the next chapter, then, we follow some choir members as they step through a further set of doors, this time opening onto worlds far removed from their own locality and their normal day-to-day lives.

NOTES

1. On this occasion, for the wordier songs the singers have recourse to the specially produced songbooks included in their festival packs.
2. Available online at http://www.bbc.co.uk/sing/learning/howachoirworks.shtml, acc. July 1, 2013.
3. The judges on this occasion were Russell Watson (the so-called people's tenor), Sharon D. Clarke (best known for her part in the television soap *Holby City*, alongside her West End stage roles), and Suzi Digby, OBE (choral director, conductor, and founder of the Voices Foundation).
4. When the NVPN committee was asked by the BBC to advertise the project to its membership, it initially declined but subsequently agreed (with some reluctance) to include the basic call in its newsletter. In her reply to the BBC, the chair noted: "The term 'wars', especially as this country is currently engaged in wars, is extremely distasteful and not likely to increase community harmony and cohesion" (Hill 2008: 4). One choir led by NVPN member Helen Yeomans was

shortlisted for the programme but withdrew when they were told they would not be permitted to perform any of their own (original) material.
5. At the time of writing, a full track list for all the shows was still available at http://www.bbc.co.uk/lastchoirstanding/news/songs/track_list.shtml, acc. July 1, 2013.
6. See http://www.choirs.org.uk/, acc. April 12, 2012.
7. See "The United Kingdom in Song," http://news.bbc.co.uk/today/hi/today/newsid_8436000/8436192.stm, acc. April 12, 2012.
8. This paragraph draws on materials held in the Working Class Education Library in Salford and information carried on the library's website, which in turn draws on the work of Denis Pye (see http://www.wcml.org.uk/, acc. April 14, 2012). I am also grateful to Denis Pye for providing me with a copy of the script for his informative and entertaining talk given at the library on March 17, 2012.
9. See http://raiseyourbanners.org/, acc. July 1, 2013
10. A large collection of songsheets and lyrics for temporary political songs is available from the website of the Liverpool Socialist Singers: http://liverpoolsocialistsingers.net/, acc. July 1, 2013.
11. In this case, Michael Deason-Barrow had been approached by the festival with the specific aim of achieving a greater sense of community participation by including aural learners in an event that normally focuses on learning through conventional music notation.
12. Llangollen models itself on Wales's annual National Eisteddfod, which in its present form dates back to 1880 but is part of a tradition stretching back to medieval times. The first eisteddfod is believed to have taken place in Cardigan in 1176.
13. For further details, see http://www.international-eisteddfod.co.uk/, acc. April 13, 2012.
14. See http://www.europeanchoralassociation.org/, acc. April 15, 2012.
15. For further information, see http://www.festival500.com/, acc. April 15, 2012.
16. It should be noted, of course, that this choice of repertoire was a dictate of the programme makers and that many of the participating choirs have other kinds of music in their normal working repertoire.
17. The distinction is still not entirely clear-cut, however. Preston Community Choir, for instance, promotes itself as being "for anyone and everyone who wants to sing but has never found anywhere to do it before!" It goes on to describe its repertoire as encompassing "some of the most current classical composers like Bob Chilcott and Eric Whitacre" and "some of the choral greats of the past", alongside "everything from Musical Theatre to Pop and Rock" (http://www.prestoncommunitychoir.com/, acc. July 8, 2013).
18. WOMAD is the now legendary world music festival founded in the early 1980s by Peter Gabriel, Thomas Brooman, and Bob Hooton. See http://womad.org/, acc. July 1, 2013.
19. Comments made in a profile of the choir made for SOAS Radio: "Refugee Week Radio 2011—Woven Gold—Finding Happiness in a Refugee Choir". http://soas-radio.org/content/refugee-week-radio-2011-woven-gold-finding-happiness-refugee-choir, acc. April 19, 2012.
20. The definition of "health" most widely adopted comes from the World Health Organization, as formulated in 1948: "a state of complete physical, mental, and social well-being and not merely the absence of disease or infirmity" (World Health Organization 1948).

21. See https://www.canterbury.ac.uk/Research/Centres/SDHR/ and http://www.airsplace.ca/, acc. July 4, 2013.
22. In illuminating case studies in *Musicophilia* and other books, Sacks provides moving and often dramatic evidence of the therapeutic effect of music and its ability to elicit powerful responses in patients with a variety of neurological conditions—those afflicted by strokes, Alzheimer's disease or other forms of dementia, by autism or by parkinsonism and other movement disorders. For further research into the therapeutic effects of singing on stuttering, Parkinson's, aphasia, and autism, see the extensive bibliography in Wan et al. 2010
23. The original is in *Das allgemeine Brouillon*, 36 (1798/99).
24. For overviews of recent research into the positive application of music in clinical settings to alleviate pain and anxiety, speed up recovery time, and reduce drug dosages, including specific applications before, during, and after surgery, see e.g. Bernatzky et al. 2012; and Spintge 2012.
25. For a survey of a range of biomarkers included in the studies reviewed by Clift et al.—oxytoin, cortisol, TNF-alpha, prolactin, heart rate, blood pressure, elecromyographic tension, peripheral finger temperature, and skin conductance—see table 17 in Clift et al. 2008b: 72. The report includes further tables summarising research findings in the areas of physical health and mental health. Kreutz et al. (2012) survey work in the new branch of psychoneuroendocrinology, concerned with the interactions between psychological and behavioural process, on the one hand, and neurohumoral and somatic processes in the brain and body, on the other. This study also refers to research relating specifically to cortisol, oxytocin, testosterone, ß-endorphin, secretory innumoglobulin A, and other neuroendocrine and immunological markers such as prolactin, serotonin, and norepinephrine, with a useful summary of empirical studies published between 1993 and 2009 presented in table form.
26. At the time of writing, the scheme was inviting a new round of applications.
27. Of the choir's twenty-seven active members at the time, seven participated directly in the study.
28. In all but name a Home Office detention centre and rated the second-worst in the country, the Oakington facility has since been closed down.
29. I was interested to find the following comment in one of my questionnaire returns: "Talking to choir leaders, I've been impressed by how many songs from other countries are collected in places like immigration and detention centres" (Susanne, Unicorn questionnaire 2007).
30. For an account of the rewards of participation in an auditioned, sight-reading choir specialising in classical choral repertoire, see Horn 2013.
31. Knight uses the term "non-singer" to designate a person who believes they cannot sing rather than someone who is incapable of singing.

CHAPTER 8

Scenes from the Global Village

Singing Camps and Travels

THE SINGING VILLAGE

A steady stream of cars turns into the narrow lane that leads to the Dorset farm where, each summer, a colourful canvas village springs up to house the Unicorn Natural Voice Camp. The brightly striped, circular marquees, topped with pennants that flutter in the breeze, give the scene a quaint and vaguely medieval appearance. Smoke rises from the wood fires around which circles of smaller tents are beginning to form and steaming kettles greet new arrivals. Children run off to find friends from last year while their parents establish their temporary home. The old hands have already set to work constructing makeshift wooden trestle-tables and dresser-like contraptions where washing up can be done and pots and pans stored. By nightfall the camp has settled down. Children, warm and drowsy after stories and cocoa, snuggle contentedly into their sleeping bags. From the main marquee come strains of "Bele Mama, Bele Mama". More voices join in this simple verse from West Africa and soon an eight-part round is in full flight. Swinging paraffin lamps cast shadows on the canvas walls as three hundred people, now arranged in two huge circles facing one another, enact a simple greeting dance. Smiles spread as old friends are recognised and new faces welcomed.

The next day, under a hot sun, the camp is buzzing with a different kind of energy. In the Creativity Area, a wooden climbing frame is taking shape, while some of the younger children, boys as well as girls, are learning to knit. A group of teenagers is engrossed in a game of volleyball; later they will go canoeing on the nearby river. From several different marquees comes the sound of singing: the straining discords of a Balkan song; a spirited Zulu chorus; an exuberant arrangement of a Motown hit; the solid, earthy tones of an

American shape note song; and the novel harmonies of a new composition by Ali Burns. In the café tent, the lunchtime team is busy preparing organic soups and salads. A member of the site crew is chopping wood for the stove that will heat the water for the showers. Already a small boy is asking his mother: "Will we be coming to this camp again next year?"

As the week progresses, each circle will give itself a name. Some will construct an entrance arch out of willow, hung with decorations made by the children; others will make flags or banners. At night, the communal spaces around the campfires will be lit with lanterns and visitors from other circles may join the groups that gather to sing, tell stories, or simply talk. Plots are hatched for surprise performances at the Cabaret Night in the café and more serious rehearsals become the focus for offerings for Performance Night in the main marquee. Relations with the nearby village—a tranquil rural retreat with a population of little more than a thousand—are carefully nurtured and on Tuesday evening the village church will be bursting at the seams for the traditional concert and sing-along offered annually by the campers.[1]

Half a world away, in the Caucasus mountains, two white minibuses that have seen better days wend their precarious way along the narrow, bone-shaking, unpaved road hacked out of the rock face that leads into Upper Svaneti. Their occupants, hot and weary after the overnight train ride from Tbilisi to Zugdidi but exhilarated now as they draw near to their destination, catch their breath when a sudden bend offers a glimpse of the towering mountains that lie ahead, still glistening with snow in the bright summer sun. We are on our way to the tiny village of Lakhushdi, where we have been invited to play a part in the Feast of Limkheri. This village is a permanent home to several families, even if these days many of the younger folk move away to the city in search of paid work, further education, or a more lively social life. For the winter months, these mountain villages lie deep in snow, cut off from the outside world. The medieval towers attached to many of the houses would, in the past, have provided refuge not only from marauding invaders from across the border but also from the frequent risk of avalanche (figure 8.1).

The previous summer, travelling with different companions, I had continued on the rapidly deteriorating road for a further three hours or more to Ushguli, which, at an altitude of 2,200 meters, has the distinction of being the highest continuously inhabited settlement in Europe. In this world there are no shops, post offices, or doctor's surgeries. Few people have paid work. Electricity is a novelty. Food comes straight from the garden or the farm and kitchens are a constant hive of activity. Cows wander freely and often bed down on the stony, muddy pathways along which we grope our way back to our temporary homes in the pitch-black night. The only sounds are those of the natural and human world: rushing mountain streams provide a backdrop for the calls of birds, the humming of insects, the lowing of cattle, the chopping of wood, and the voices of children at play (figure 8.2) (🌐 see web figures 08.01–08.07).

Figure 8.1 Cluster of houses with towers, with neighbouring hamlet in the distance. Ushguli, Georgia, July 2010.
Source: Courtesy of Caroline Bithell.

Figure 8.2 Village houses and gardens. Ushguli, Georgia, July 2010.
Source: Courtesy of Caroline Bithell.

Figure 8.3 Songmasters Gigo Chamgeliani and Murad and Givi Pirtskhelani. Lakhushdi, Georgia, July 2011.
Source: Courtesy of Caroline Bithell.

We spend most of our first few days in Lakhushdi working with the three elderly songmasters, trying to pin down the ancient pre-Christian chants with their untempered intervals and ever-shifting contours (figure 8.3). When the feast day arrives, we set off early to climb the wooded hill to the tiny church. A ram has been ritually sacrificed and is now being prepared for the celebratory meal; a hefty metal cooking pot swings above a wood fire tended by the younger men. Inside the tiny stone sanctuary lit only by candlelight, we can just make out the faded frescos and ornate icons. Our teachers have now assumed a priest-like role. Standing before the altar, they raise their voices in clashing harmonies and chant invocations as they pour libations of home-distilled *chacha* on the earthen floor. The sacred rituals complete, we reassemble on the grassy clearing next to the church and join hands for a series of round dances. A simple meal of bread, mutton, and cheese, to be washed down with a seemingly inexhaustible supply of wine and *chacha*, is then laid out on the ground beneath the trees and we pass the rest of the afternoon in a convivial mood filled with traditional games, toasts, and ever-more animated singing (figure 8.4). The intensity of these shared moments of heightened empathy and carefree festivity will bind us together for the years to come (see web figures 08.08–08.11).

Figure 8.4 Givi Pirtskhelani distributes the roasted organs of a sacrificial ram. Feast of Limkheri, Lakhushdi, Georgia, July 2011.
Source: Courtesy of Caroline Bithell.

RECLAIMING PARADISE: OF FIELDS, FESTIVALS, AND FOREIGN SHORES

In previous chapters we have seen how songs from beyond one's normal, day-to-day habitat can become a very real and tangible part of one's own community, one's own horizons, one's own sense of identity; how singing and embodying these songs can lead to an appreciation of the cultures they represent and an empathy for those who sing them in their original settings; and how, with the songs acting as introduction and lynchpin, people may be brought into face-to-face contact with "others" with whom they would not otherwise have crossed paths. Increasing numbers of choir members are now choosing to devote their leisure time and material resources to pursuing these directions beyond the confines of their local community. Some set off on new adventures with fellow choir members; others strike out independently, perhaps finding a niche for themselves in the more fluid translocal or transnational formations where different networks intersect. New life experiences accumulate rapidly. For some of those attracted to the Unicorn camp, camping itself is a novel activity. Relatively independent overseas travel (as opposed to package tours) may also be a new and daunting prospect.

In this chapter, we follow some of these singers as they embark on another set of journeys. We explore the dynamics of the communities they find at their destination and the ways in which they, too, become temporary members of those communities. Some communities may, like the Unicorn camp, be entirely transient, reformed year by year by those drawn together from diverse starting points to recreate the imagined village. Others, like Ushguli and Lakhushdi, are permanently inhabited working villages that, for a designated part of the year, welcome into their midst small groups of guests, who for a few short weeks become part of local life in a way both sides deem mutually beneficial. In these journeys and sojourns, song may be the driving force and primary source of satisfaction; but beyond this, the very fact of living differently, away from one's habitual anchors, and of sharing most aspects of the daily routine with unrelated others conspires to create a particular set of conditions that can lead to powerful transformative experiences.

This phenomenon is part of a broader trend of seeking out new ways to spend leisure time and to take holidays. It can also be viewed in the context of a more widespread hunger for a lost sense of community, of nostalgia for a past envisioned as simpler, freer, and more attuned to the rhythms of nature. At the same time it is clearly evocative of the metaphorical "global village" (as conceived by Marshall McLuhan in the 1960s) in which, aided by advances in travel and technology, different cultures are brought together in one place. And finally, it is also part of the postmodern story (as told by Arjun Appadurai) of the flows and scapes from which we construct our imagined or ideal worlds.

Tapping into the Festival Current

The festival format is well-suited to aspirations to recreate the global village. The multiplication of festivals across Europe in recent decades is testimony to the fact that the urge to step out of one's ordinary life and experiment with different ways of being is no longer confined to the hippy fringe. The festivals that sprang up in Britain in the 1970s were very much part of a countercultural desire to reclaim the land and create an alternative world in which the conventions and constraints of everyday life could be left behind or conspicuously flouted. Yet, while an event like the Glastonbury Festival may have begun as "a serious attempt to stake out and remake Utopia in an English field" (Young 2010: 477), such events soon grew to gargantuan proportions. First held in 1970 with 1,500 attendees (whose £1 entrance fee also entitled them to free milk from the farm), today Glastonbury caters to around 180,000 people a year and is estimated to contribute £100 million annually to the British economy (Eavis 2011: 3). The British summer is now awash with hundreds of music festivals and alternative gatherings of all shapes and sizes, the most popular of which sell out within hours of tickets going on sale. As Philippa Bradley, writing for the BBC Money Programme, puts it, "what started as flower power is now big business" (2012: n.p.).

Given the prevalence in festival-related literature of references to Utopia, Arcadia, and the Garden of Eden, and the festival movement's bid in an earlier phase to reclaim what was once common land for the enjoyment of all, it is noteworthy that many festivals are held in the grounds of stately homes. For a few frenetic days, anyone able to afford a ticket (or find a gap in the fence) has access to gardens, lakes, and woodland where they may stumble on hidden corners transformed into enchanted dreamlands or surreal stage-sets. Those who take advantage of the opportunity to splash out on unusual items of clothing and perhaps have their hair braided or their skin decorated with henna tattoos become a visible part of the "scene", even if, for many, this particular scene does not extend beyond the festival itself.

All of this is certainly part of the attraction of the WOMAD festival that, each July, draws a crowd of around 35,000 to Charlton Park in Wiltshire. Celebrating its thirtieth anniversary in 2012, WOMAD has become a Mecca for world music aficionados. If any festival has a claim to the title "Global Village", then this is surely it. Not only are artists flown in from all corners of the globe but food, clothing, musical instruments, mirrors, rugs, wall-hangings, hand-crafted wooden furniture, and other artefacts from different parts of the world are on sale in a giant outdoor marketplace. From the outset, participation as a key to appreciation and understanding was a central feature of the WOMAD vision, together with a desire "to break open the distance between performer and audience" (Gabriel 2007: 17). As founder Peter Gabriel puts it in the short promotional trailer carried on the festival's website, "people who get their hands dirty can feel it for themselves" (http://womad.co.uk/about, acc. June 16, 2013). The result—now a feature of many festivals but a new departure at the early WOMAD events—is a full programme of participatory workshops, led by the artists themselves, scheduled to run alongside the staged performances. Serendipitously—as if to underline the kinship with the natural voice creed—one of the workshop leaders featured in the trailer affirms the familiar maxim: "If you can walk, you can dance. If you can talk, you can sing. It is true."[2]

While the Unicorn camp may in many ways be part of the same impulse that fuelled contemporary festival culture, it lies at the opposite end of the scale from many of the larger festivals that have become lucrative commercial enterprises, attracting clients who at times seem more bent on staging a global stag night than recreating Eden. At Unicorn there are no professional performers; no stages, banks of amplifiers, or lighting rigs; no beer tents, cash machines, or mobile phone masts; no thudding bass or pounding drums to keep you awake at night; no marauding teenagers tripping over your guy-ropes; no petty thieves ransacking your tent while you are off dancing; no professional promoters, corporate sponsorship, or media coverage. In this sense, the camp and others like it may be seen as a revival of the original vision of a back-to-basics, do-it-yourself, safe and peaceful gathering of like-minded folk in an English field.

Theorising Travel and Tourism

A similar difference of ethos separates the overseas tours undertaken by the singers we are following here from other types of tourism, even if they share in part the same root impulse and may be called upon to account for themselves in response to the kinds of critique to which the tourist enterprise as a whole has been subjected. It will be useful here to set out briefly some of the critical issues, conceptual tropes, and theoretical frameworks that will serve as useful points of reference for my closer analysis of the Village Harmony phenomenon and other musical journeys and encounters that will concern us later in this chapter.

The tourist experience has been extensively theorised following Dean MacCannell's seminal study *The Tourist: A New Theory of the Leisure Class* (1976). MacCannell saw the modern tourist as "one of the best models available for modern-man-in-general", driven by an unending quest for authenticity that is thought to lie "elsewhere: in other historical periods and other cultures, in purer, simpler lifestyles" (1976: 1, 3). This yearning for other times and places is inevitably overshadowed by what Renato Rosaldo (1989) has termed "imperialist nostalgia", whereby the civilised world (or the modern age) mourns the disappearance of what it has helped to destroy. In similar vein, tourism has been heavily critiqued as "a replaying of the colonial encounter" (Abram 1997: 32), as the privileged inhabitants of the developed world seek pleasure and enrichment in exotic but less developed regions, in a largely one-way traffic rooted in unequal power relations in which the dividing line between exploration and exploitation is negligible. In this way, the cycle of loss and degradation continues. Mass tourism in particular is tainted (to borrow Simone Abram and Jacqueline Waldren's words) "with the imagery of a totalising modernity that tarnishes all it touches, destroying 'authentic cultures' and polluting 'earthly paradises', so that it has become a truism to state that tourism destroys the very object of its desire" (1997: 1).

In less loaded terms, tourism (not unlike festival culture) may be seen as a form of escape, whether from the superficiality and alienation of the modern world, domestic responsibilities and the grind of the working week, or merely the British weather.[3] It is this trope that lies behind Nelson Graburn's (1978) conception of the touristic undertaking as a "sacred journey", or what Jeremy Boissevain glosses as "a ludic interlude that revitalizes the traveller, enabling him to cope again with the strictures and structures of everyday life" (1996: 2). Of particular interest to us here is the notion that travel offers an escape from the humdrum, day-to-day self, the journey holding the promise of discovering one's "true" identity in the context of novel experiences of heightened intensity. The tourist's journey, not unlike performance, becomes another liminal, potentially transformative space in which the traveller adopts "a new, temporary identity that necessarily incorporates some elements that are the opposite of the habitual personality and behaviour" (Boissevain 1996: 4). The notion of an authentic experience may, then, rest in a sense of coming into contact both with a "real" world and with one's "real" self (Wang 2000). Meanwhile, notions of the sacred recur in connection with Max Weber's thesis that rational thought drives out the sacred and the symbolic, the magical and the mystical, only to leave the world disenchanted. Travel in this context becomes a quest for re-enchantment.

Another classic of tourism literature is John Urry's *The Tourist Gaze* (1990), whose central theme is the way in which the tourist's attention is directed away from the ordinary, routine aspects of real people's lives to specially designated sights and landmarks, such as symbolic buildings and features of the landscape. Urry's protagonist, encountered again in his later work *Consuming Places*, is a "post-tourist" who "finds pleasure in the multitude of games that can be played and knows that there is no authentic tourist experience" (1995: 140). The post-tourist is happy to consume signs and simulations in destinations that increasingly resemble theme parks more than real places (there are clear echoes here of the notions of hyperreality and simulacra, associated respectively with Umberto Eco and Jean Baudrillard).

It was partly in response to the twin processes of Disneyfication and homogenisation that various forms of alternative tourism began in appear from the 1980s onward, with labels that included cultural tourism, ethnic tourism (usually focused on "exotic" peoples), ecotourism, green tourism, sustainable tourism, intelligent tourism, ethical tourism, and, more recently, extreme tourism, shock tourism, and dark tourism (respectively, engaging in dangerous activities akin to "extreme sport", travelling to places known to be dangerous and violent, or visiting sites of tragedy and disaster). Compared with the package tourist in search of little more than sun, sea, and sand, and unlikely to stray too far from the safety of the resort, the new brand of tourist was more independent, more adventurous, open to new experiences, usually more environmentally conscious, and often eager to make genuine contact with local people and cultures. Those undertaking this kind of journey often preferred the appellation "traveller" as a way of distinguishing themselves from the more common charter tourist. Just as Peter Gabriel, in his vision for WOMAD, sought to close the gap between the artists and the audience, so too do many alternative tourism enterprises aspire to close the gap between residents and visitors, in part by placing the visitor in a position of active participation rather than passive consumption. This kind of low-level, off-the-beaten-track tourism is also more beneficial to local economies since visitors are more likely to stay in private rooms or family-owned apartments, eat at family-run restaurants, drink at local bars, and support local environmental causes.

The dynamics that come into play between hosts and guests and the strategies that hosts employ to keep tourists in their place and protect at least some aspects of their lives from commoditisation have been another significant focus of attention for anthropologists of tourism. MacCannell (1973) introduced the notion of "staged authenticity" in the sense of a performance of supposedly authentic village life laid on specially for tourists in the "front" regions while local residents lived out their private lives in the "back" regions to which tourists were not normally granted access.[4] Numerous case studies have gone on to show that, far from being helpless victims of postcolonial exploitation, hosts have found ways of turning tourism to their own advantage; and even in the absence of such proactive, strategic planning, arguments have been made for the potential of the tourist encounter to lead to the cultural enrichment, rather than degradation, of the host community. Part of the objective of the contributors to the volume *Tourists and Tourism: Identifying with People and Places*, for example, was to show how tourism "can provide the setting for people [in the host community] to reconsider how they identify themselves, and how they relate to the rest of the world" (Abram and Waldren 1997: 10). Here, Simone Abram argues that the way in which symbols of the past are "sold" to tourists may, in fact, be "an opportunity for the expression of identity", enabling people "to define and express a continuity that they wish to maintain between the past and the future". Tourists may also "enhance local social activity by providing the audience required to frame a performance, and a background against which local identity can be reflected upon" (Abram 1997: 46). In another of the volume's case studies, Niels Sampath suggests that: "In the end, it may be the foreign or tourist market that preserves the art of steel pan production and tuning [...], and which injects the cash for steel pan competitions in Trinidad" (1997: 161).

In his introduction to *Coping with Tourists: European Reactions to Mass Tourism*, Jeremy Boissevain expounds in a similar spirit on tourism's potential to promote "self-awareness, pride, self-confidence and solidarity among those being visited", especially in cases where the host community is remote or otherwise peripheral (1996: 6). In many places, he argues, tourist interest and the self-reflection that this has prompted have led to the revitalisation of traditional crafts and local festivities. Museums and heritage parks established for tourists have also become popular with local residents, who have thereby learnt more about their own traditions. In some cases, too, "the importance of tourist attention and revenue has given marginal host communities the confidence and leverage to bargain for more rights from superior authorities" (7). Perhaps giving most pause for thought are indications that the development of tourism has reduced if not halted depopulation in some regions, such as the Greek island of Skyros. In all these examples, there are both losses and gains.

It is, perhaps, no coincidence that much of this theoretical groundwork lent itself to such extensive application and elaboration in the 1990s—just as the seeds of the initiatives that concern us here were beginning to bear fruit. In the new millennium, anthropologists and others have continued to pursue research into the politics and economics of cultural tourism in emerging as well as established destinations, with particular reference to the challenge of balancing local and global forces in an increasingly globalised (or globalising) world (see e.g. Smith and Robinson 2006; Smith 2009; Timothy 2011). The rapid international proliferation of festivals, with their celebratory dimension and their multiple functions of reviving or enshrining heritage, empowering local communities, and creating a space for meaningful cross-cultural encounter in the present, has been one of the most significant developments of more recent times, and this, too, has given rise to a growing body of new literature (see e.g. Picard and Robinson 2006; Gibson and Connell 2011). Meanwhile, the central tropes formulated in the early tourism classics continue to have currency. MacCannell's notion of "staged authenticity", for example, resonates behind the new paths beaten in works such as *Tourism Mobilities* (Sheller and Urry 2004), where tourist destinations are treated as not only "places to play" but also "places in play" which "'move' as they are put into play in relation to other places" and are themselves always changing (back cover). Questions of authenticity, performativity, and tourism as pilgrimage resurface in Chris Gibson and John Connell's *Music and Tourism: On the Road Again* (2005). Alain de Botton, appealing to a more popular audience, takes up the tropes of travel as healing and transformation when he writes of travel playing a vital role in "cementing important inner transitions" and, more specifically, of "places which by virtue of their remoteness, solitude, beauty or cultural richness retain an ability to salve the wounded parts of us" (2012: 273).

Travel, then, offers yet another means of experimenting with alternative ways of being-in-the-world and finding *communitas*. How far this particular dimension of the tourist experience might be seen to rest on utopian or imagined foundations is in many ways beside the point since, as Ning Wang points out, "If tourists think that they have achieved a sense of personal, interpersonal, and human-nature authenticity, then their feelings are ontologically real to themselves" (2000: 65). This does not, of course, mean that their impact on the places they visit lies outside the frame. We have also established, however, that the host community may play a far a more decisive part in the exchange than it is often credited with. The motivations, experiences, responses, and transformations that occur on both sides will therefore be part of my purview as I probe more deeply into the types of encounters that take place between singing travellers and their hosts. First, though, we return to the singing holidays that can be taken closer to home.

A VILLAGE IN A FIELD: THE UNICORN NATURAL VOICE CAMP

The Unicorn Natural Voice Camp is, at the time of writing, one of three Unicorn camps that run consecutively on the same site in August. The venture was launched in 1987 by James Burgess, who describes himself as a Sufi leader, healer, and professional astrologer; he was also a co-founder of the Peace Through the Arts International Camp and the Oak Dragon Camps. James writes of how the camps that began to appear in the early 1980s as an offshoot of the latest wave of festivals and green gatherings had a different kind of identity: "They...were fundamentally different in their purpose, which was education and personal development, and in their approach, which required that people took an active part in what went on" (http://www.unicorncamps.com/spotlight_unicorn.php, acc. June 16, 2013). His vision was of a focused, sensitive, spiritual, creative, and family-friendly environment free of alcohol, drugs, dogs, amplified music, and sleepless nights. The Unicorn project began as a small annual camp centred on Dances of Universal Peace. The Natural Voice Camp, essentially the brainchild of Nickomo Clarke, was added in 1998. Nickomo relates how he and his family were already veteran campers when they discovered the first music camps in the mid-1980s. Their attendance at the second Glastonbury music camp in 1986, where for the first time they found themselves camping not on a commercial campsite but in "a field of friendly people sharing a joy in music and dance and camping around real wood fires", had the force of "an epiphany" (2007a: 21). As he began to teach at similar camps himself, and inspired in particular by the success of the South African song-and-dance package that he helped to develop with Colin Harrison, his vision of a camp devoted primarily to singing—as opposed to the voice work happening "on the back of dance" (interview 2007)—gradually took shape. When James Burgess invited him to become part of a new core group to re-envision the Unicorn venture, the dream finally became a reality and the first voice camp—a pilot four-day event—was held in 1998. This coincided with a time when the community choir scene was burgeoning and the voice camp rapidly grew to become an important annual meeting point for NVPN practitioners and choir members, while also welcoming those new to the natural voice world attracted by the promise of a different kind of holiday. (Of those who responded to the questionnaire I circulated following the 2007 camp, approximately three-quarters belonged to, or led, a community choir, and most had heard about the camp either through their choir or from a friend who had already attended. Although more than two-thirds of my respondents had attended with family or friends, a significant number had come alone.) The Unicorn Camp has inspired the establishment of other camps with a similar ethos, including the Earthsong Camp in Ireland (co-founded by John Bowker) and the German Unicorn Natural Voice Camp (founded by Raaja Fischer, a regular teacher at the British camps).

The Unicorn Experience

A prominent tagline on the Unicorn Camps homepage reads "Alternative Family Camping Holidays—for Singers, Dancers and Magical Beings"; this is perhaps indicative of the extent to which these and similar camps, while retaining the "alternative" label, have moved out of what might once have been seen as a counter-cultural, "hippy" niche and closer to the mainstream (though in a different way to many of the festivals as described earlier). At the same time, the language used in the mission-statement-style description of the voice camp itself makes its connection with the natural voice movement abundantly clear:

> We are dedicated to finding the natural, authentic expressive voice in all of us. By really listening to ourselves and each other and by exploring our vocal potential we can experience empowerment, healing, devotion, meditation, affirmation, expression and fun. (http://www.unicorncamps.com/, acc. June 16, 2013)

"Community" is also emphasised here as "an essential part of the Unicorn Camps experience".

The fact that the voice camp has maintained a stable base over several years—occupying the same site and employing the same teachers, for example—helps create the illusion of an established village.[5] While substantial numbers of new converts find their way to the event each summer, there is also a solid core of followers who have rarely missed a year and who might be regarded as the tribal elders. Regular attendees develop a relationship with the landscape and material layout of the camp, and with its conventions, norms, and etiquette. The structure of the week's activities also contains ritual elements that both mimic the patterns of activity in an imagined village and reinforce the desired sense of community. Each morning there is an hour-long gathering in the main marquee that everyone is encouraged to attend to find out more about the programme for the day and be party to any important announcements. For the rest of the day, individuals follow their own path though a choice of activities, interspersed with domestic tasks, with the culture of cooking and sharing meals in smaller groups helping to nurture a sense of family. The whole camp comes together again for the main evening events, which often have a celebratory dimension. Wednesday is traditionally market day, when the largest marquee is overflowing with all manner of items that attendees have brought to sell: hand-knitted jumpers, felt hats, sheepskins, musical instruments, pottery, woodwork, essential oils, candles, songbooks, and CDs. Towards the end of the week, there is an evening of exuberant drumming and dancing around a large central fire, and on the last night of camp, those who have attended the main workshops that have run throughout the week have the opportunity to perform their songs for the rest of the camp.

Care is taken to cultivate a climate of respect—for one fellow's campers, for the environment, and for the residents of the nearby village. All attendees are required to sign up to the camp rules that are reproduced on their ticket and must agree to abide by those rules for the duration of their stay. These include not bringing alcohol or illegal drugs onto the site, not playing amplified music or using noisy electronic devices, using mobile phones only (if at all) away from the camping area, and not making noise that might disturb others between the hours of 11 p.m. and 8 a.m. Each person is allocated a few hours of "karma yoga", joining the site crew or area teams to help with the day-to-day maintenance and smooth running of the camp (e.g., food preparation, toilet cleaning, or lantern lighting). Attending the camp, then, involves a commitment to more than just the singing and may require individual freedoms to be sacrificed in the interests of the greater good. At the same time, personal development is encouraged and, in the view of the camp organisers, is facilitated by the clarity that results from interacting with others in a more mindful way.

The camp may have its utopian side but it is also firmly grounded in practicalities and a sense of moral accountability. Subscribing to the ethos of treading lightly on the earth and living simply on the land, it is organised in such a way that campers can be as self-sufficient as possible and will not have to leave the site once the camp is established. Lift-sharing is encouraged and all waste is recycled. In recognition of the energy use and carbon emission that is nonetheless entailed in setting up the camp as well as travelling to and from the site, substantial donations are made to a tree-planting project at the Timbaktu Collective in India. Raising funds for WaterAid—framed as a way to help improve the lives of at least some of the people whose songs are sung and celebrated at the camp—has also become a tradition; through a lively auction and other activities that take place during the week, a sum in excess of £5,000 is raised each year purely from the pockets of those attending the camp.

The Unicorn Repertoire

The material encountered at the camp ranges from short and relatively simple songs suited to early morning warm-ups or the kind of communal evening session depicted in my opening vignette to far more elaborate arrangements that require dedicated teaching and are built up progressively through the week. The editions of the *Unicorn Natural Voice Camp Songbook* that have been produced from time to time feature favourites taught at each year's camp. Volumes 1 to 3, which cover the years 1998 to 2006, reveal some interesting trends (with the caveat that the songs presented will vary to some extent according to the combination of teachers featured on the programme in any given year). Volume 1 is notable for including a predominance of African songs—a total of eighteen, including several from South Africa—together with four gospel songs (in arrangements by Tony Backhouse and Nick Prater), three Native American chants, a Prana chant, a Maori song, a song from the Pacific Islands, a song from the Caribbean, a peace song from Korea, an old French song, a Russian church song, two arrangements of popular songs by Nickomo, and seven original compositions by NVPN members. Volume 2 features African songs and original compositions in equal number—nine of each—plus two spirituals, five gospel-style songs, a barbershop song, a Bulgarian song, a Macedonian song, two Irish songs, a Hawaiian *hula* song, and four rounds. A similar spread appears in volume 3, with ten African songs, nine new compositions, four gospel songs, two Georgian songs, a Taizé-style chant in Latin, and one song each from the Georgia Sea Islands, the Cook Islands, the Torres Strait Islands, Taiwan, Israel, Romania, and Croatia.

The repertoire represented here includes a substantial number of quick-and-easy songs that are heard year after year around the evening campfires. These songs will not necessarily find their way into a more formal performance or onto a choir's CD, but they have nonetheless become part of a common, nationwide repertoire. Workshops provide the opportunity to concentrate on more complex pieces, with some taking the form of half-day sessions spread over three or four consecutive days alongside one-off "drop-ins". Here the influence of individual workshop leaders may be more obvious, especially in cases where they are teaching their own compositions or arrangements. A number of practitioners and choir directors already encountered in this book feature in the roll call of the camp's established teachers: these include John Bowker, Ali Burns, Pauline Down, Jules Gibb, Dee Jarlett, Bruce Knight, Kirsty Martin, Kate O'Connell, Una May Olomolaiye, Nick Prater, Roxane Smith, and Rowena Whitehead.

It in interesting to consider how the chosen songs might chime with the camp's ethos and contribute, at a deeper level, to the Unicorn experience. In their musical style and structure, the songs from the world's oral traditions that typically feature on the programme lend themselves to the establishment of a cohesive singing community in ways that have already been established. In the case of popular songs and chants in the English language, the sentiments embodied in the lyrics often speak to themes of togetherness, solidarity, peace, and harmony. Songs that are explicitly religious (such as gospel or shape note songs) or that have associations with sociopolitical movements (such as civil rights or anti-apartheid songs) have also evolved as songs made for binding communities together and may therefore hold some meaning on this count even for those who do not necessarily feel a personal affinity with their subject matter. Particular features of songs may also function at more than one level. For mass collective singing, preference will understandably be given to songs with relatively few words and repetitive musical structures for the pragmatic reason that what is required in this situation is songs that can be learnt quickly and effectively by a group of singers of mixed experience, sometimes working in semi-darkness. At another level, sustained repetition, together with the phenomenon of switching onto automatic pilot that verbal minimalism allows, helps create a numinous or transcendent experience which, in turn, increases the sense of bonding and what is referred to in some kinds of holistic therapies or spiritual practices as "opening the heart".

Among the more focused workshops, those offered by Dee Jarlett and Ali Orbaum (co-directors of Bristol's Gasworks Choir) emerge as perennial favourites. These typically feature Dee and Ali's lively arrangements of British and American popular songs from the 1960s onwards. Here, the community connection resides above all in the fact that these songs may be seen as part of a shared heritage that, to a greater extent than classical music, cuts across barriers of class and education. In addition, many have anthemic qualities that evoke a sense of solidarity and score high on the feel-good factor. Some embody sentiments that may also resonate with the personal experience of individual singers. The enduring popularity of Dee's arrangement of Labi Siffre's anti-apartheid anthem "Something Inside So Strong", for instance, must owe something to the fortuitous inclusion of the line "The more you refuse to hear my voice the louder I will sing". Some contemporary songs in the folk idiom appeal for similar reasons, among the most popular being "Unison in Harmony" by close harmony group Coope Boyes & Simpson—another triumphantly anthemic song that includes the resonant line "What we sing is what we are", together with the hopeful anticipation: "Nations shall sing unto nations/Until nations cease to be".

The camps have also served as a launch pad for new bodies of work by NVPN members, including Ali Burns, Kirsty Martin, and Helen Yeomans. Of particular interest to us here is Nickomo's Harmonic Temple, an ever-expanding collection of chants consisting of short, mantra-like texts from different spiritual traditions set to music and arranged in four-part harmony. As described in chapter 3, in the late 1980s and early 1990s Nickomo and his partner, Rasullah, had hosted the weekly sessions of the Bristol Chanting Group, in whose repertoire Prana and Taizé chants featured prominently. Nickomo talks of how, when he started leading workshops at Dance Camp Wales, he quickly realised that "there was a need for stuff that was *like* Taizé" but without being tied to the Christian faith (interview 2007). This prompted him to start creating simple four-part chants that used texts from different religious and spiritual paths. Sources for the material from the two original tapes, *Harmonic Temple* (1995) and *Harmonic Temple Volume 2* (1996), later brought together in the *Ateh Malkuth* CD compilation, are listed as Christian, Jewish, Qabbalist, Sufi/Islamic, Hindu, Buddhist, Inuit, Druid, Pagan, and the *Carmina Gadelica* (a collection of prayers, charms, incantations, and blessings from Scotland's Gaelic-speaking highlands and islands).[6] An hour-long Harmonic Temple session scheduled before the morning gathering has long been a feature of the camp and is one component on which many regulars will declare themselves to be "hooked": when I asked participants in the 2007 voice camp what the highpoints had been for them, the daily Harmonic Temple sessions featured prominently.

Nickomo's elaboration of the rationale behind the Harmonic Temple initiative is instructive in relation to my broader analysis of the camp ethos. In the preface to *Deep Peace* he writes:

> The Harmonic Temple shows a lot of respect for the truths and insights to be found in religious traditions, but not a lot for organized religion as such! I believe that if we view the collective spiritual wisdom of the planet as exactly that—our collective inheritance, we can work with whatever wisdom resonates with the deepest level of our being without having to buy into any particular package deal. (Clarke 2007b: n.p.)

He goes on to describe himself as "a bit of a mantra junkie", always on the lookout for new mantras that "hit the spot". Like the creators of the Taizé chants (see chapter 5), he speaks of how "using languages [such as Sanskrit and Latin] that are different from the ones in which we conduct our daily business sets them apart as special and magical". Nickomo's choice of language here is revealing, with his use of terms like "package deal" and the notion of the songs marking a "special" and "magical" place set apart from "our daily business" resonating in obvious ways with the tropes of tourism reviewed earlier in this chapter. The juxtaposition of "collective inheritance" and "buying into a deal" also chimes with the ethos of the natural voice movement as a whole and is suggestive of further oppositions such as autonomy versus subservience to institutional authority, and self-sufficiency versus consumerism. The appeal to "respect" for the "truths and insights" to be found beyond our own cultural horizons is clearly indicative of a cosmopolitan positioning, while the quest for mantras that "hit the spot" reflects an acute awareness of the power of words, as well as music, to embody shared sentiment and meaning and act as a route to attaining "flow".

For participants, the repetition of short segments of material becomes part of a process akin to spiritual practice, with the deepening relationship that an individual thereby experiences to both the music and his or her fellow singers also facilitating a sense of *communitas*. In Nickomo's own words:

> It's all based around actually entering the sound physically and being able to explore it.... You know, you learn lots of songs but sometimes you just don't have that freedom to get in the middle of a chord and just really feel what it is, and the magic of it. And Harmonic Temple is very much about that. It's not about end product; it's about experience... and you're not singing it *to* anybody, you're singing it to the whole group and you're exploring it, and I continue to find that a very rewarding thing to do. (Clarke interview 2007)

Mantra-based songs, Nickomo observes elsewhere, also travel well: "As they don't usually have many words they are not any more difficult to teach to a group for whom English is not the native tongue" (Clarke 2007b: n.p.). This adds further to the inclusivity of the experience.

Nickomo's reference to "entering the sound physically" invites us to consider Harmonic Temple as acoustic architecture as well as spiritual endeavour. As he explains in the preface to *Ateh Malkuth*, "The phrase 'Harmonic Temple' is an attempt to describe the phenomenon which occurs when these chants are sung, of a sacred space created by the sound of vocal harmony" (Clarke 2002: 1).[7] Interestingly, several of my questionnaire respondents commented (without any prompting) on their experience of singing broadly "spiritual" songs with reference to (or in opposition to) the idea of a church. One, for example, responded as follows to my question "Do you find yourself attracted to the songs of a particular culture?"

> I like African best and also simple spiritual songs—Taizé and the like that take me to a blissful place. Singing for me is a way to be in Spirit, in Joy, to be blissed out. It is about experiencing the oneness with others, with everything. I am not into the highly technical or musically challenging. It is more like "going to church" for me. (Anon., Unicorn questionnaire 2007)

In many ways, the daily Harmonic Temple sessions function as Unicorn's church, and the profound and often "magical" atmosphere they create is a fundamental aspect of the Unicorn experience for those who attend them. In it interesting in this regard to relate the Unicorn endeavour to ideas presented by Alain de Botton in his entertaining and edifying book *Religion for Atheists* (which on its publication in 2012 rapidly attained best-seller status). Here, de Botton argues for the need to separate the more life-enriching ideals and rituals from the religious institutions to which we may no longer subscribe, reclaiming them for our own use. Foremost among these are notions of community and education (under which he includes "spiritual exercises"). He also writes of his vision for a new generation of secular temples, taking many different forms, which would "function as reminders of our hopes" and "educate and rebalance our souls" (2012: 275).[8]

Each new set of Harmonic Temple chants is made available in a songbook (with musical scores, explanations of the song texts, teaching tips, and ideas for simple accompanying movements), a performance CD (with the songs performed by a massed choir), and a workdisc (with the parts demonstrated separately). All these items are available for purchase on market day, as are other songbooks and teaching CDs compiled by different workshop leaders. Combined with the CD of camp highlights that is produced (for campers only) shortly after the event, this allows attendees to take a more concrete piece of the camp experience home with them and aids the further dissemination of the material.[9] Between camps, the experience is also kept alive through the quarterly podcasts (produced by Nickomo) that offer a compilation of recordings made at the camp, interspersed with short interviews with workshop leaders.[10]

The Unicorn Community

It is, presumably, the prevalence of gospel and other religious-sounding songs and the commitment to the annual church concert, combined with the casual and at times unorthodox style of dress adopted by the campers (not unreasonably, given that they are in holiday mode), which led to Unicorn once being described in the local parish newsletter as "a Christian organisation that provides holidays for deprived adults and children". In reality, practising Christians are very much in the minority (and quite possibly outnumbered by converts to Sufism or Buddhism and those who identify with a broadly Celtic neo-pagan orientation); and while a proportion of those who frequent the camps may indeed have rejected the nine-to-five (not to mention 24/7), competitive urban rat-race, many more have one foot firmly in the middle-class professional world, albeit with an above-average proportion of charity workers and therapists. Occupations given by those who responded to my 2007 questionnaire included college lecturer, English for Speakers of Other Languages (ESOL) tutor, teacher, artist, fine arts student, performing arts practitioner, actress, writer, journalist, nurse, hospital Information Technology (IT) training manager, therapist, psychotherapist, yoga teacher, shiatsu practitioner, charity manager, and support worker. Among their declared interests and pastimes (apart from singing) were peace demonstrations, cycling campaigns, environmental group, sustainability group, community allotment, Local Exchange Trading Systems (LETS) group, charity volunteer, local gay network, personal development group, yoga, tai chi, meditation, Quakers, community theatre group, circle dance, drumming, ice hockey, University of the Third Age, Amnesty International, Greenpeace, the National Trust, and the Royal Horticultural Society. From these lists interesting lifestyle choices begin to emerge. There is a strong tendency for attendees to be involved in the caring professions, education, or the arts, and to devote leisure time to charitable, political, or community causes, on the one hand, and personal development and wellbeing, on the other.

Replies to my question about other camps the respondent and his or her family may have attended were also revealing. A high proportion of respondents reported regular attendance at camps such as Dance Camp Wales and Peace Through the Arts (the first and second highest number of mentions), Dance Camp East and Oak Dragon Camps (with several mentions each), Sacred Arts, Whitsun Voice Camp, Glastonbury Dance Camp, Dancing Circles Camp, Rainbow Circle, One World Camp, Tribe of Doris, African Arts Village, Drum Camp, Heartsound, Singing Spirit, Spirit Horse, Voices Coming Together, and residential singing breaks at Cae Mabon (North Wales) and Holycombe (Warwickshire). Again, this investment of both leisure time and financial resources is indicative of significant lifestyle choices, while the incidence of designations relating to peace, spirit, heart, and the sacred, alongside more straightforward references to dancing, drumming, singing, and the arts, is noteworthy. Some respondents also listed other camps or festivals that they had attended but not enjoyed for reasons including alcohol and drug abuse, litter, and noise.

The question "What do you (and other members of your family) most like about the camp?" yielded more discursive answers that mapped in interesting ways onto the overall ethos and inspiration behind the Unicorn venture as described earlier. Almost all responses included the word "community", with the pleasures of communal cooking and being outdoors also receiving several mentions alongside references to relaxation, friendship, and, of course, singing. Representative responses included the following:

- The Community. The beautiful harmonic singing. The camping circles and making new friends. The communal eating and singing round the campfire. The summer outdoors in England. Sitting lightly on the land.

- Re-gathering of the tribe: sense of community and shared endeavour, being outdoors, living at a more simple level than usual, the invigoration of singing each day, the incredible highs of harmony and improvisation when it clicks.

- I think the whole camp scene is spreading out of a need in each of us, to return to our connection with the land, our community with each other, need for co-habitation, co-cooking, being outside, respectful relationships and our innate need for music—particularly singing and dancing.

- I love the sense of community, camping on the land and cooking and eating together, the simplicity of life, the wonderful regard for nature and the camping environment and of course, the range of singing on offer. The fact that things happen spontaneously: a jamming session here, and a bit of a sing there, crazy stuff in the cabaret, performance night: the way that people dream up little shows and collaborate with each other to make them happen.

- The *sharing* of *all* aspects of camp life; being outdoors 24 hours a day; Harmonic Temple; time to relate to likeminded people; all of it!!!

One respondent focused on the "easy-going, accepting, open-hearted element" and the "chance to relax and let go of city stresses". Others referred to the way in which the camp was "good at bringing out the best in people", revealing a "wealth of talent in ordinary people" and offering the "opportunity to express self in many different ways". One said quite simply "belonging". Parents also emphasised "children's autonomy" and their appreciation of the way in which the camp provided a "safe space to be 'free range children'", with one adding: "I can say that as soon as Voice Camp is over, my two sons start counting the days till the next one comes round!"

The sense of bonding to which shared activities of different orders give rise may be related more specifically to theories about the power of music—understood here as a social activity and communal experience—to induce a phenomenon that Oliver Sacks envisions as "an actual binding or 'marriage' of nervous systems, a 'neurogamy'" (2008: 266). We might also reflect further on the associations made by many of my respondents and interviewees between collective singing and spiritual enrichment or a quasi-religious experience. Sacks goes on to suggest that "there is evidence that religious practices began with communal chanting and dancing, often of an ecstatic kind and, not infrequently, culminating in states of trance" (267). The use of singing and dancing as a path to ecstasy, as well as a natural means of maintaining individual and societal health, is also central to Barbara Ehrenreich's treatise on collective joy. Ehrenreich draws on Émile Durkheim's concept of "collective effervescence", a term he coined to denote "the ritually induced passion or ecstasy that cements social bonds" which he believed formed the basis of religion (Ehrenreich 2007: 2–3). She brings this into dialogue with Victor Turner's concept of *communitas*, defined by Turner as "a possible collective state achieved through rituals where all personal differences of class, status, age, gender, and other personal distinctions are stripped away allowing people to temporarily merge through their basic humanity" (Turner 1995: 18). Ehrenreich sees the notions of collective effervescence and *communitas* as each, in its own way, reaching towards "some conception of love that serves to knit people together in groups larger than two" (qualified by the observation that "there is no word for the love—or force or need—that leads individuals to seek ecstatic merger with the group"; Ehrenreich 2007: 14).

The Unicorn camp, then, offers a classic embodiment of festivity as a state or space that allows us to step (as Ehrenreich puts it) into "a brief utopia defined by egalitarianism, creativity, and mutual love" (253) and reclaim "our distinctively human heritage as creatures who can generate their own ecstatic pleasures out of music, color, feasting, and dance" (260). The "thrill of the group deliberately united in joy and exaltation" (16) may have been relegated to the margins in the modern age, but at Unicorn and camps of a similar ilk it appears to have risen, Phoenix-like, from the ashes. That the camp is able to function in this way relates not only to the kinds of activities on offer and the carefully nurtured climate of mutual respect and empowerment, but also to its relatively small size, which is another factor that sets it apart it from the majority of festivals. Ehrenreich notes specifically that "ecstatic rituals and festivities seem to have evolved to bind people in groups of a few hundred at a time—a group size at which it is possible for each participant to hear the same (unamplified) music and see all the other participants at once" (250). The fact that, at Unicorn, everyone on site can fit into the main marquee at the same time and can see and hear one another is crucial to the sense of intimacy or "belonging" felt by participants.

Sociologist Randall Collins also draws on Durkheim's notion of collective effervescence in developing his model of what he terms "interaction ritual chains".[11] Collins places particular emphasis on the importance of the emotional energy that is generated by ritual, identifying this as "the social emotion par excellence" (2004: xii). Collective (physical) movements focus the attention, which in turn enhances the expression of shared emotion, leading to a state of heightened intersubjectivity (35). He explains the chain process as follows:

> Where mutual focus and entrainment become intense, self-reinforcing feedback processes generate moments of compelling emotional experience. These in turn become motivational magnets and moments of cultural significance, experiences where culture is created, denigrated, or reinforced. (Collins 2004: xii)

This helps elucidate both the affective attachment to the camp as a whole (or rather, to the community that it represents) and also the nature of the profound emotional responses to discrete components such as the Harmonic Temple sessions.

CHOIRS ON THE MOVE

More and more often, whole choirs (or substantial proportions of them) are taking to the road. Sometimes they travel to join forces with other choirs at UK-based events like Sing for Water, Raise Your Banners, the National Street Choir Festival, or one of the many regional "big sings" or community choir conventions that grow in size and popularity each year. At other times they may head for a private retreat, which offers an opportunity for choir members to get to know one another better as well as polish and augment their repertoire away from day-to-day distractions. As mentioned in chapter 7, members of the Forres Big Choir in Scotland have made several trips of this kind to the island of Iona. Islands are also a location of choice for singing holidays led by NVPN practitioners which are advertised more widely via the natural voice network. The Forres choir's co-leaders Kate O'Connell and Bill Henderson, for example, lead an additional singing week each year on the island of Eigg in the Hebrides; David Burbidge organises annual singing holidays to Jura, another Hebridean island; and Jane Read takes groups to Bardsey Island (Ynys Enlli) off the coast of North Wales. Set apart from the mainland-cum-mainstream with the journey having an aura of adventure, islands offer the archetypal opportunity to "get away from it all" to a place where life often seems to move at a slower pace and the spirit of the past may still be tangible in the form of prehistoric remains and ancient monuments. Jura, for instance, boasts Iron Age forts, burial grounds, and standing stones. Iona and Bardsey were both important centres of the ancient Celtic church and continue to be sites of pilgrimage.[12] Very small islands with limited accommodation offer the possibility of almost exclusive occupation, while return visits allow for more than a passing acquaintance with the few permanent residents.

NVPN member Candy Verney has also taken groups to Bardsey, as well as Orkney and Skye, following on from earlier singing journeys to the Himalayas that began when she and some of her choir members accompanied a group of A level students studying Buddhism and Hinduism on a trip organised by their teacher (and choir member), Sue Glanville. Reflecting on this first trip, Candy described how, after a long day of trekking, the group would sit around the fire and sing together. On the very last night, perched on a promontory at 10,000 feet, they persuaded the sherpas to join them. As they sang their songs to one other, "there wasn't a dry eye...it was so special because we were exchanging our cultures in their landscape" (Verney interview 2008). This experience inspired the idea of "journeying", which became the name of the company that Candy and Sue subsequently set up and through which they organised a series of singing holidays. The vision, as Candy explains it, was of "trips where through the outward journey you go inward—so there is a personal development side to what we do and the whole point is to connect more deeply to the landscape...and more with our fellow travellers and with ourselves". She also uses the image of the pilgrimage, referring to an insight that had come to her on the most recent trip:

> I realised that we were on a pilgrimage because the process of walking, and getting to know each other and deepening our connection and opening out to each other—and then singing facilitates all those things...You can't stay still if you go on a walk and I think that's what pilgrimage is probably about. It shifts you, it changes you, and you go on an inner and an outer journey both at the same time, so that's what I found really interesting and exciting. (Verney interview 2008)

The journey itself, then, becomes a vehicle for transformation, and the experience of being changed in this way is all the more powerful for being shared with others. The songs that are learnt along the way become part of the process by which the journey is embodied and archived and, when they are later re-sung, serve to reinforce this reconfigured subjectivity as well as keeping the memory alive at a more mundane level.[13]

Direct one-to-one exchanges between British choirs and choirs overseas are also increasing. These initiatives may be seen to conform to the friendship model, where mutual support, appreciation, and cooperation, rather than competition, are the guiding principles, and where the sharing of musical repertoires is a natural part of the undertaking. Informal social singing, as well as shared concerts and the exchange of songs, is an important feature of such journeys. Present space allows me to make only brief mention of two examples. The association between David Burbidge's choirs in the Lake District and singers from Zreče in northeast Slovenia came about through a town-twinning scheme after the Cumbrian town of Sedbergh was the subject of a BBC2 television series, *The Town that Wants a Twin* (2005), and chose (following visits by four contenders) the town of Zreče. Regular visits are made back and forth between the two towns, and the visitors join in singing the songs of their hosts as they take part in local traditions, such as carolling at Christmas time. David's new Slovenian friends, far from cringing as some of his choir members had feared, were moved to tears when they heard their songs being sung in England. From the Slovene point of view, as David explains it, it is above all their folk songs that have held them together and defined them as a nation through centuries of subjugation in which they have always been "part of somewhere else", "and so when we sing them it's like an enormous sense of respect to them" (interview 2007). Interestingly, David also writes:

> People often say there is not just one, but several Sedberghs—referring to the different cultures who live alongside each other in our town. My experience is that as we find bridges between the differences with our Slovene friends, we also find bridges between the differences within our own society. (http://sedberghinternational.blogspot.co.uk/2005/05/slovenian-singing-group-visits-sedbergh.html, acc. June 16, 2013)[14]

In the case of the relationship that has developed between Hilary Davies's choirs in the Worcester area and the Diamond Choir from the township of Refilwe in South Africa (mentioned in chapter 3's opening vignette), initial contact was made by a choir member who was visiting relatives in South Africa. Hilary and Barbara Curry, writing in the NVPN newsletter, describe the first visit made by a group of twenty-three British singers to South Africa in 2007 as "not so much a holiday, more an experience of a lifetime". Their first day set the pace for what was to be an action-packed and heart-warming time: "The first 24 hours saw us visiting the local radio station, singing informally with a wonderfully energetic church youth choir, and ending up at a township party." They also visited the Cullinan mine, local schools, and a hospice for HIV/AIDS sufferers, as well as other projects to which money raised in the United Kingdom by the British choirs and by the Diamond Choir on their earlier visit had already been donated. Again, any qualms about singing other people's songs back to them were soon laid to rest. While audiences seemed uncertain as to how to respond to the European songs, especially when there was no movement involved, the South African songs were given a rapturous

Figure 8.5 Members of the Diamond Choir (South Africa) and Rough Diamonds (United Kingdom) give an impromptu concert before bidding farewell at the airport. Johannesburg, April 2008.
Source: Courtesy of Steve Rigby.

reception: "We were greeted with dancing in the aisles, ululating and whooping." Dee Jarlett's arrangement of "Something Inside So Strong" also "brought the house down" every time they sang it. Concerts would typically end with the entire audience coming to the front and joining in, "finishing with what became our favourite farewell song, 'Think of me, forget me not, remember me where ever you go', complete with hugs and genuine affection between strangers" (figure 8.5) (see web figure 08.12). Returning home "changed forever", the British singers redoubled their efforts to raise funds for HIV/AIDS care and other community projects in Refilwe (Curry and Davies 2008: 13).[15]

THE VILLAGE ON THE MOVE: VILLAGE HARMONY'S OVERSEAS CAMPS

As we learned in chapter 6, South Africa is also one of the destinations offered by the American organisation Village Harmony in its annual programme of overseas singing camps (sometimes designated "study-performance camps"). Other locations have included Ghana, Georgia, Ukraine, Russia, Bulgaria, Bosnia, the Republic of Macedonia, Corsica, Italy, Germany, Denmark, and Sweden, as well as the United Kingdom. Village Harmony describes itself as "an umbrella organization for a diverse range of choral, world music and harmony singing activities" (http://www.villageharmony.org/, acc. June 16,

2013). Founded in 1988 by Larry Gordon, it began as an initiative that offered extracurricular singing activities for high school students in central Vermont. In 1995, Patty Cuyler joined as co-director and was instrumental in helping expand the organisation's overseas activities. Now constituted as a non-profit corporation, Village Harmony supports—in addition to the summer camp series that interests us here—a programme of community performing and touring ensembles that runs during the school year (including Boston Harmony World Music Chorus and the Onion River Chorus, both non-auditioned choirs), the semi-professional international touring ensemble Northern Harmony (whose concert programmes typically include songs taught at previous summer camps), and a range of other musical offerings, such as performances and residencies by foreign teachers and touring groups, including those with whom Village Harmony collaborates on its overseas camps (▶ see web figure 08.12).

Despite their designation, the summer camps—which normally last between two and three weeks—do not literally take place under canvas. They begin with an intensive rehearsal week during which the twenty-five or so participants live communally in a gîte, hostel, or retreat centre and devote most of each day to learning the set of twenty or more songs that they will later offer in concert. While the main teachers will be from the country in which the camp is held, teachers of songs from other traditions may also be included in the team, together with Larry, Patty, or occasionally another member of the Village Harmony core team (● see web figure 08.12). The group will thus build up a repertoire featuring sets of songs from three or more musical cultures, some of which their audiences will be hearing for the first time, with gospel, shape note, or other songs from American folk traditions representing the home culture of the majority of those who form the Village Harmony ensemble. The group then travels around the country in minibuses, meeting with indigenous musicians, performing concerts (often with local choirs or dance groups), and staying with host families (● see web figure 08.17). The organisers also allow time to visit places of interest so that camp particpants may learn about the history and culture of the country. Campers often speak of how much they cherish the opportunity to be privy to a way of life in which singing and dancing seem to play a more prominent part than they do at home. They are often struck by new understandings about the way in which music defines and strengthens communities or can play a crucial part in post-traumatic healing and reconciliation. They also value the insights they gain into other people's lives when they stay in the homes of local choir members. As one of my co-campers wrote of the Bosnian camp we were part of in 2008:

> Singing the music was wonderful and the reason for being there, but I think served sort of as the entrance into that world. That purpose provided us [with] a lot of opportunities that we would not have otherwise had. (Tom, Bosnia questionnaire 2008)

While the majority of campers typically come from North America, most tours include at least a few singers from the United Kingdom and other parts of Western Europe. Often, some of the participants will already know one another: they may sing in the same choir or have attended the same workshops at home, or they may have met on previous overseas tours. Many of the younger singers grew up with Village Harmony's youth camps and feel very much a part of the Village Harmony family, often viewing Patty and Larry as surrogate parent figures. There are, then, already several layers of community at work even before contact with the host community is made. As in the case of the Unicorn camps, references to "community" feature prominently in participants' statements about what Village Harmony represents to them. Catherine, for example, writes:

> It's all about community: the instantaneous and ad hoc community that develops when we come together as a small group to learn songs and languages together and in some cases travel together, *and* the global community that develops as a result of connecting different cultures through a common musical thread. (Catherine, Georgia questionnaire 2010)

As with the Unicorn camps, the familiarity of the overall structure and the shared ethos of each trip reinforce the campers' sense that they are taking part in an annual gathering of the tribe, albeit in this case a nomadic one. At the same time, each new tour will have its own unique flavour. This derives most obviously from the choice of repertoire and teachers, on the one hand, and the local culture and landscape, on the other. In the case of the tours that I have been part of, it was also interesting to see different themes coming to the forefront, especially in the more detailed experiential and phenomenological accounts that participants included in questionnaire responses and interviews. Equally interesting was the symbolic meaning attached to the different visits by our hosts. It is around these themes and interpretations, which in turn resonate in instructive ways with my earlier summary of key issues and tropes in the critical literature on tourism, that my present analysis is structured.

Village Harmony in Corsica

A central theme running through the feedback I gleaned from the Corsican camps with which I had some involvement in 2004 and 2008 was the challenge and excitement of coming to understand a profoundly different musical culture—different not simply in terms of musical style but, more fundamentally, in its conception of what constitutes a song and what it means to sing with others.[16] This required a radical reassessment of participants' relationship to and assumptions about "music" as both entity and action. Many attendees were seasoned campers with a healthy repertory of songs from different parts of the world already under their belts. The Corsican songs, however, were an entirely new proposition. With their elastic rhythms and complex melismatic embellishment, Corsican songs do not exist in one fixed and definitive form. A performance always entails some degree of improvisation, while remaining within the bounds of an established musical grammar. Each interpretation is, moreover, expected to be subtly different as each new group of singers makes the song its own, rather than merely reproducing someone else's rendition. As the camp participants soon realised, what was required of them here was not simply to learn a set of songs but rather to learn a way of singing (including the related arts of ornamentation and improvisation) and of interacting with one's fellow singers; and this in turn cast a new light on the notion of authenticity, which in this case could not be equated with the accurate reproduction of an identifiable "original".

Working intensively in small groups with one voice to a part led to many eureka moments. Caitlin, for example, described how in one rehearsal with her trio:

> We were all making adjustments and trying to find the right sound and then it just suddenly happened. We locked in to each other and you could just tell it was all fitting just right. I almost stopped singing because I was so excited by the sound we were creating. (Caitlin, Corsica questionnaire 2004)

Reflecting more broadly on the process of "getting to know how the song actually fits together... and in general how all three parts move to resolve the phrase", Anthony commented: "This for me was a bodily thing, after a while it just 'felt right'; it became something automatic... beyond intellect" (Corsica questionnaire 2004). Confirmation of the extent to which at least some of the singers succeeded in their quest to embody this new musical language and achieve a convincingly authentic performance came when a young male trio from the camp entered a *paghjella* singing competition at the wine festival in the village of Luri. Dan describes their initial reception when they turned up to register: "After many confused looks, hairy eyeballs, and active attempts to pretend we weren't there, we were approached warily: 'You're not singing in French, are you? This is a Corsican singing competition.'" The trio went on to win third prize and later they were summoned to join more seasoned singers at the bar. "All in all," Dan continues, "we felt we had done well for ourselves, and were giddy and proud.... It validated our work immensely to be able to throw ourselves into the fire and come out cooked, but not burnt" (Corsica questionnaire 2004).

A highlight for the group was a concert they gave in the village church in Talasani, where they were joined for their Corsican set by their hosts, the ensemble Tavagna. Dan notes that "we would sing our version of the song, then they would perform the same song. Eventually the pace quickened and they would just come join us in mid-song." When the concert finally ended, they all moved outside where they carried on singing into the night. Dan continues:

> Tavagna closed with a breathtaking *lamentu*, [sung as] monody with all of us accompanying on a moving drone. I realized then that I couldn't ever adequately articulate how special the whole experience was—who ever goes to a country to sing its traditional music in rural hamlets at midnight? We do, I guess. (Dan, Corsica questionnaire 2004)

Caitlin recalled the same moment as one of her highlights:

> I was sitting there just completely overwhelmed by how amazing it sounded and it hit me that I was experiencing something most people could never imagine. The beauty of the moment was so incredible, I almost felt like I didn't deserve it. (Caitlin, Corsica questionnaire 2004)

Anthony used similar terms to describe the "specialness" of the entire visit:

> I felt like a very welcomed and even honoured guest, and with the songs that we had learned we had something to give back.... I felt as if I was in a privileged position; being able to get closer to the Corsican spirit that only a Corsican can really know.... I feel that we met Corsican people in a way that far surpasses any interaction that would have come about by being mere tourists. There was a real sharing and mutual respect that grew from the whole experience. (Anthony, Corsica questionnaire 2004)

Heidi, too, elaborated on the theme of making connections:

> Singing another culture's songs while immersed in that culture is also a powerful means of connecting with people. The Corsicans we met and sang for were obviously deeply moved and pleased that we respected and loved their music enough to come to their island and study it, and the Corsican singers who sang for us and with us connected with our group with enormous warmth and generosity. Singing together obviously creates harmony in more than one sense! (Heidi, Corsica questionnaire 2004)

For both parties, the impact of the encounter clearly transcended the purely musical. Dan recalls that, during the lengthy outdoor supper that followed another concert, a member of the Corsican group Barbara Fortuna

> made a toast... saying that we had really changed a lot of people's impressions of Americans and alerted them to the possibility that Corsica might not be such an

unknown quantity in the outside world. "The smashers of stereotypes" he called us. (Dan, Corsica questionnaire 2004)

In my Corsican feedback, the impact of "being there" was a prominent thread in its own right. Several participants offered surprisingly lengthy and evocative descriptions of their experience of place. Heidi, for example, wrote:

> I found it extremely meaningful to be studying Corsican music not only with one of the best Corsican singers in the world [Benedettu Sarrocchi], but *in Corsica*, surrounded by its open and generous people, its wonderful food and wine, its spectacular landscapes, villages of stone buildings, ancient churches, abandoned terraces and walls, plants and trees and gardens, the sea, the winds and the many scents they carried. (Heidi, Corsica questionnaire 2004)

The landscape and people made an equally profound impression on the youngest participant, Rosa (then aged fourteen), who also suggested that the impact of the experience would far outlast her physically "being there":

> I woke up every morning knowing that I was exactly where I wanted to be. I loved how welcoming people were despite the language barrier and the American reputation.... I loved the beaches, the donkeys, the wine festival, the old man who offered us cheese, the wind, the musicians we met, the group we became, the winding roads that you felt you were going to fall off at any second . . . and I *loved* the music. At other Village Harmony tours there have been a couple songs that stay in my head after tour is over. But with Corsica they're all still there, and I feel like they're going to stay there forever and everything I do is going to be somehow affected by this music that is always flowing in my mind.... I think that because of this experience, I'm going to be a happier person. (Rosa, Corsica questionnaire 2004)

Village Harmony in Bosnia

The "being there" theme took on a more pointed and sobering guise in the context of the Bosnian camp I attended in 2008, little more than a decade after the formal end of the war whose legacy was still all too apparent. This camp was led by Village Harmony veteran Mary Cay Brass, whose personal Balkan journey had begun when, at the age of nine, she was recruited into the dance troop of her Croatian neighbours in Minnesota. She went on to study ethnomusicology and, in the mid-1970s, spent two years in the former Yugoslavia on a Fulbright scholarship. A number of other participants had pre-existing connections with Bosnia, and some were also competent in the language. One had, like Mary Cay, lived there during the 1970s, first on a

Junior Year Abroad and a few years later on a Fulbright. Two of the older men (now retired) had spent time in former Yugoslavia as young men in connection with the Experiment in International Living, an organisation that runs home-stay and activity programmes for American youth in various countries around the world. Others had grandparents who had migrated to America from the Balkans or other parts of Eastern Europe and felt drawn to the region on that count.

Our party on this occasion included several members of the choirs led by Mary Cay in Vermont and Massachusetts. We were routinely introduced as an American choir for the purposes of this trip, so a Swiss woman and I— the only Europeans in the group—became honorary Americans. Prior to the trip, we had all been asked to circulate, by email, short letters of introduction so that we would know a little about one another by the time we met. Mary Cay also recommended books and films that would give us some useful background to the country.

We spent the first eight days occupying the Hotel Karalinka, a lodge-style hotel set in peaceful woodland near the town of Bugojno, and by day four we had already worked our way through twenty-five new songs. In addition to Mary Cay, who taught a selection of shape note and gospel songs, we had three Bosnian teachers. Branka Vidović, an ethnomusicologist and co-director of the Sarajevo Music Academy Ethno-Choir, taught us traditional village songs—songs about shepherds, mountains, and spinning wool; humorous songs about courtship; and wedding songs. These we sang in smaller single-sex groups in the traditional open-throated style. Tijana Vignjević, an award-winning choir director and orchestra teacher who studied conducting at Sarajevo Music Academy and who also acted as local organiser for our tour, focused mainly on arrangements of *sevdalinka* songs (soulful love songs from urban traditions with a strong oriental lilt) that we sang with accordion and clarinet accompaniment; included here were some pieces that I had first encountered in the context of the British circle dance scene in the 1980s. Maja Budimir brought more complex but exquisitely beautiful Serbian Orthodox church songs and arrangements of songs from the Islamic *ilahiya* tradition. These were drawn from the repertoire of the Pontanima choir, an interreligious choir based at the monastery of St. Anthony in Sarajevo. Established in 1996 by Ivo Marković, a Franciscan priest, the choir had opened its membership to people of all faiths and included in its repertoire vocal music from the Catholic, Orthodox, Jewish, and Islamic traditions, using its performances as a tool to promote post-war reconciliation. We later met and sang with the choir in Sarajevo.

The impact of the war was only too evident. Many buildings still bore the scars of shelling; others lay in ruins; graveyards presented seemingly endless vistas of memorial stones, not yet weathered; and sections of woodland still to be cleared of mines were cordoned off with blue tape. Tijana and Maja also talked about the effect of the war on their own lives. We sat outside on the terrace late into the night as Maja told us the story of how she had first made her way, with a young cousin, to relatives in Belgrade before leaving the country. Eventually she found herself in Bologna, where she won a scholarship and gained a degree, and from where she sent messages home via the Red Cross until she was eventually reunited with her mother more than four years later. Tijana told us about the girls' choir she joined (and later led) in Sarajevo that met to rehearse in a basement and functioned in part as a way of keeping young people away from the dangers of the street during the long years when the city was under siege. She also brought films about the war that we watched into the small hours, crowded around a laptop. Later, we drove deep into the mountains and spent a night (literally under canvas, for once) at a lakeside camp for children who had lost parents in the war.

People thanked us repeatedly for coming to Bosnia and taking such a keen interest in their culture. Far from being seen as uninvited guests riding roughshod over their territory or intruding on their still fragile lives in a voyeuristic way, we were generally cast as playing a part in the country's reconstruction and healing. We were invited to receptions with local dignitaries; television and radio crews appeared to document our visit; Alen, who served our meals at the Hotel Karalinka, was thrilled to take us to visit his mosque and meet the imam; ordinary people we met on the street invited us into their homes and neighbours came running with pots of coffee, plates of cakes, raspberries from their gardens, and bottles of homemade plum brandy. Everywhere we went we sang, and because we had learnt a number of popular Bosnian songs by heart, as well as some dance steps, we were often able to join in when our new friends struck up a tune (figure 8.6) (🌐 see web figure 08.18). People told us how important these songs had been in keeping up morale during the war. Sometimes they expressed gratitude for America's part in eventually helping bring the conflict to an end. Reference was made more particularly to the symbolism, in those days of George W. Bush's "war on terror", of Americans coming to a part-Muslim country. When we returned home, people would say, we could tell our compatriots that "Muslim" does not equal "terrorist."

For our final performance, on the steps of Sarajevo cathedral, we were part of a multi-choir extravaganza that in turn was part of the festival Baščaršijske Noći, and as the only choir from outside Bosnia-Hercegovina we were treated as guests of honour. At every concert our renditions of Islamic *ilahiya* songs, such as "Ej, Allahu, Pogledaj Me", had been greeted with approval and delight; this time we got a rapturous standing ovation before we had even reached the second verse. Lines such as "Rain will wash Bosnia / Lilies will flower in the early dawn / It will hold out to our children a bouquet of violets / And to me a dream of freedom and peace / The pain will pass when I close my eyes" (from another *ilahiya*, "Puhnut Će Behar") also had an obvious poignancy and communicated our empathy with our Bosnian hosts. At the end of the Sarajevo

Figure 8.6 Village Harmony camp participants singing with the late Omer Probić on a visit to his Sevdah Institute. Visoko, Bosnia, July 2008.
Source: Courtesy of Caroline Bithell.

concert, singers from the other choirs, to whom we had sent words and music in advance, joined us for "Oh, What a Beautiful City"—a song that we dedicated, of course, to Sarajevo.

Village Harmony and Other Travels in Georgia

In July 2010, I joined Village Harmony for their tenth singing camp in Georgia. Again, the majority of participants were from the United States, with young people in their teens or early twenties making up two-thirds of the group; three of us came from the United Kingdom and one from Switzerland. Our Georgian singing and dance teachers, some originating from Svaneti and the others from Kakheti, were all members of the group Zedashe. Our first week was spent in the Svan village of Ushguli, where we took possession of a newly opened rustic guesthouse and had the use of an old stone barn for our daily rehearsals. Later we stayed for a few days with the family and neighbours of a bagpipe-maker and player at the tiny village of Qvashta in the hills of Adjara, not far from the Black Sea and the Turkish border. During the final part of the tour, we were based in the historic fortress town of Sighnaghi in Kakheti, eastern Georgia, that is home to Zedashe and where Village Harmony now has its own retreat centre in the form of two renovated houses providing both rehearsal space and accommodation. (Several of the young people in our party stayed on after the singing camp for the month-long language camp that Village Harmony also ran from its Sighnaghi base.) Additional towns and villages were included in our concert schedule, with venues ranging from the rather grand Ilia Chavchavadze Theatre in the coastal city of Batumi to a small outdoor stage in the Kakhetian town of Akhmeta. This itinerary gave us the opportunity to immerse ourselves in sharply contrasting landscapes while absorbing the musical styles of the different regions and meeting with many different groups of singers and dancers (🌐 see web figures 08.19–08.26).

Our itinerary also included visits to numerous monasteries and churches. Christianity was introduced to Georgia in the first century, and the country formally converted in 337 CE, making Georgia the world's second oldest Christian nation after Armenia. The country is home to extraordinary complexes of cave monasteries, such as those at Davit-Gareja, dating from the sixth century; other important monastic centres like Gelati date from the twelfth century. The experience of listening to members of Zedashe singing medieval polyphonic chants in these settings and, later in the trip, singing these same chants ourselves featured prominently among the most powerful and transcendent moments that my fellow campers recalled months after our visit.

For co-director Patty Cuyler, the Georgian experience encapsulates all that Village Harmony stands for. Several key ingredients combine to make a profound and lasting impression that draws many participants back for return visits: an usually rich and varied palette of multipart song styles, dramatic unspoilt landscapes, the palpable presence of ancient spirituality that has been revitalised following Georgia's independence from the Soviet Union, and a degree of hospitality that most participants have never before encountered. A number of younger people who attended earlier camps have returned on Fulbright scholarships and are now reasonably fluent in the Georgian language, while one member of the teaching team for Village Harmony's own language course is an American college tutor who, after taking part in a singing camp, was inspired to give up her job back home and move to Georgia. As Patty explains it:

> Georgia's magic; it just feels like the homeland that's disappeared for people.... Being here, making music and being guests in Georgia, hearing the stories, riding through the countryside, seeing the mélange of rough natural beauty and the skeletal, stagnated remains of the Soviet era, the poverty and the wealth and the dignity of the people, just gives people, everyone, a new way of looking at life... everyone will say that their values shifted. (Cuyler interview 2010)

Our evening meals served as important focal points, not only for singing but also for learning about Georgian history and culture. In Georgia, the guest is seen as a gift from God and friendship between guest and host is cemented through the ritual of the *supra*, a lavish feast animated by eloquent toasts and impassioned singing. In Georgian culture as a whole, the *supra* fulfils an important psychosocial function, reinforcing and celebrating bonds between individuals and communities. Early on in the trip, we were initiated into the etiquette of the *supra* and the art of toasting by John Wurdeman, an American artist married to Zedashe member Ketevan Mindorashvili. John masterminded the logistics of our tour, acted as our guide at the historic sites we visited en route, and played a vital role as intermediary and translator at the tables we shared with our hosts in each new place. The speech that precedes a toast is often a highly poetic, deeply philosophical exegesis on a given theme, and the subjects of the toasts follow a ritual order. John skilfully drew us all into the spirit of the undertaking and we learnt how to make appropriate responses or raise our own toasts when invited to do so by the *tamada* (toast-master). Each night we drank to God and to Georgia; to our ancestors and children; to poetry and music; to our new friendship and to understanding between our countries; to love and to peace in the world. The heightened conviviality that prevailed at these times—the combination of sentiment, song, and copious amounts of good food and wine often giving rise to feelings of blissful transportation—was also, for many participants, a profoundly affective experience that left them with an enduring sense of gratitude and enrichment.

At the same time, the families and communities who hosted us benefited directly through the payments they received for providing us with board and lodging; this money was often to be invested in basic amenities such as indoor plumbing (as yet the exception in many Georgian villages). We also hired local drivers and their vehicles and bought musical instruments and handicrafts to take home. At a less tangible level, we were in some way reflecting back to our hosts images of themselves with which they may, in some respects, have lost touch. Some of the songs that are learnt on such trips, for example, are no longer widely sung in present-day Georgia but are now in the process of being revived by the Georgian singers acting as teachers. As well as consulting with the older generation of songmasters, many of the younger members of contemporary ensembles assiduously mine the archives and apply themselves to deciphering the transcriptions they find in old manuscripts; through their own performances, they then breathe new life into the songs of past generations. Some of the songs we sang in our concerts were therefore new to our Georgian audiences and, for older listeners, may have evoked memories of a bygone age. The spectacle of young people from a distant country performing the "old" songs and dances with such enthusiasm and evident enjoyment, it was suggested, also helped recommend them to younger generations of Georgians whose abandonment of their own cultural heritage in favour of the more novel distractions of the modern age is often lamented by their grandparents (▶ see video tracks 08.04–08.06).

The desire to interest the younger generation in maintaining local traditions was part of the story behind my return to Svaneti in the summer of 2011. In this case, an invitation was issued by the host community—in collaboration with the charity Ecologia Youth Trust, operating from the Findhorn Foundation in Scotland and working in conjunction with Tbilisi-based charity Braveheart Georgia, run by Madge Bray (from Edinburgh) and Georgian singer Nana Mzhavanadze—for a group of sympathetic foreign guests to join them for the celebration of the feast of Limkheri and to learn the pre-Christian songs and dances to be performed for the occasion. The project's website carried the statement:

> If managed carefully, the elders propose that the interest generated by this extraordinary invitation may serve to send a powerful message to their own young people—children who have been born into a modern Georgia and a new generation of "virtual" communications. They hope that this invitation will send out a clear message about the intrinsic value of roots, and about the spirit of a shared humanity—a birthright still intact here. (http://www.braveheartgeorgia.org/important.html, acc. July 2, 2011)

The majority of those who responded this time were from Britain and Ireland, and they included several community choir leaders and singers from dedicated Georgian choirs; others came from Germany and Finland. Most had a direct personal connection with Madge or Nana; in recent years, Nana has made regular visits to the United Kingdom and other parts of Western Europe to lead workshops and to appear in concerts with the ensemble Sathanao, to which one of the young Lakhushdi women driving the initiative also belongs. On this trip, we were housed with local families for the full two weeks and we took part in various domestic activities alongside our singing sessions. The profits from our visit were used to launch a cooperative (Union Lidbashi) to oversee the development of a sustainable community enterprise, in which projects aimed at preserving and transmitting the local heritage were combined with the goal of "helping inhabitants of mountainous regions of Georgia create a better touristic atmosphere" (https://www.facebook.com/Lidbashi, acc. June 19, 2013).[17] The cooperative's initial projects included making documentary films about local rituals, founding a heritage centre in the village, and establishing a new children's choir, as well as providing lighting for the village square, contributing to improved facilities in the homes of the host families, and financing urgent repairs to a bridge.[18] It will be interesting to monitor future developments here, in particular with regard to the desired revitalisation of local traditions[19] (🎵 ▶ see web figures 08.27–08.29 and video tracks 08.07–08.14).

OF REFASHIONING IDENTITIES AND LIVING DIFFERENTLY

In his contribution to a special issue of the *British Journal of Ethnomusicology* on Music and Meaning, Timothy Rice (2001) identifies a series of metaphors that may be applied to music. His examples include music as art, music as social behaviour, music as emotional expression, music as entertainment, music as commodity, and music as referential symbol. Veit Erlmann has suggested that "the essence of art no longer lies beyond the work of art, in a meaning, but in the interaction to which it gives rise" (1996b: 481). It is this metaphor—art or music as interaction—that has emerged most forcefully in this chapter.

The notion of community has, once again, been at the forefront throughout this discussion. Community itself is prefaced on the need for interaction and collaboration, for listening and understanding, for adapting and accommodating, and for working above all to maintain social health and harmony. Music, and more specifically singing, presents itself as an ideal tool to help promote such a state; and even without such deliberate intention, musical interaction may lead to the sense of being in community as one of its more predictable side effects. We have already engaged with the idea that music can do this kind of work not only for groups of people who come into regular contact and share many aspects of the wider culture (where, in Putnam's terms, it has a bonding function); it can also do similar work among strangers who may not even have a common spoken language (in which case, it serves a bridging function). The examples I have included in this chapter offer ample evidence of music in action, predominantly in its bridging capacity.

The liminal nature of the kinds of meetings and interludes I have described inevitably intensifies the affective experience. For travellers, the novelties they encounter at almost every turn put them in a receptive frame of mind and may predispose them to anticipate positive experiences. It is hardly surprising, then, that self-reported peak experiences—whether of personal euphoria or transpersonal connectedness—should figure so prominently. Of even greater significance is that fact that the work of music in this sense reaches beyond the immediate and most visible task of orchestrating face-to-face encounters in the moment. There are also long-term consequences for both individual travellers and the communities with which they engage. Things change: materially, psychologically, and existentially. These changes are more often experienced as positive than negative: greater happiness, satisfaction, confidence, creativity, and gratitude; a deeper understanding, a more refined sense of accountability; a renewed commitment to finding ways to incorporate greater integrity into one's day-to-day life, to achieve a healthier balance between work and leisure, to make more time for friends and family.

Camps and overseas travels, as prolonged "time out", give participants the time and space to experiment with living differently. Relationships with others and with the environment may be reconfigured, the self experienced in new ways. The Unicorn camp, Village Harmony tours, and choir exchanges of the kind I have described offer an opportunity not only to recreate community but also to revive, or be re-educated in, the art of festivity and to experience the healing power of collective joy. If we follow Barbara Ehrenreich's arguments, this is another level at which such initiatives have the potential to contribute in quite profound ways to the health and wellbeing of societies as well as individuals. Again, it is crucial to underline that, for many, such experiences are not merely a passing moment, a temporary high. They may have the force of a more permanent conversion, after which an individual will take concrete steps towards living differently. When people say (as they so often do) that discovering the Unicorn camp or Village Harmony, or going to Georgia or South Africa, changed their life, they often mean this in a quite literal sense. The path is not necessarily smooth: there are challenges and discomforts along the way. This in itself is one reason why such endeavours cannot simply be dismissed as the acting out of a tribal fantasy. Paul Stoller, alluding to the manner in which the modernist project is seen to have profoundly dehumanised society and caused many of its subjects to lose sight of what is most important, evocatively writes:

> Here and there, the wise ones find their way to a clearing—spaces where they fashion stories, laced with subjectivities, which restore some of that lost dignity. This ongoing process of restoration is central...to the contemporary human condition. (Stoller 2002: 229)

The sites and spaces in the landscape that the Unicorn camp temporarily occupies and to which Village Harmony takes its travelling groups are significant for the way in which they may also reveal metaphorical clearings where new insights and aspirations find a place to take root.

Thomas Turino has written of the way in which the performing arts serve as fulcrums of identity, allowing people to feel part of a community through the realisation of "shared cultural knowledge and style" as well as through the act of participating together. This creates a sense of "social intimacy", the signs of which "are experienced directly—body to body—and thus in the moment are felt to be true" (2008: 3). For Turino, too, the impact of these experiences beyond the original moment in which they occur is of paramount interest. He harnesses James Lea's terms of reference in proposing that "musical experiences foreground the crucial interplay between the Possible and the Actual" (Turino 2008: 16, referencing Lea 2001). In this sense, art itself may be seen as "time out":

> The arts are a realm where the impossible or non-existent or the ideal is imagined and made possible, and new possibilities leading to new lived realities are brought into existence in perceivable forms. (Turino 2008: 18)

George Lipsitz has pursued a similar line of thought in his writings on popular culture, again pointing to the realities that lie beyond a mere utopian fantasy:

> Culture enables people to rehearse identities, stances, and social relations not yet permissible in politics. But it also serves as a concrete social site, a place

where social relations are constructed and enacted as well as envisioned. Popular culture does not just reflect reality, it helps constitute it. (Lipsitz 1994: 137)

Simon Frith offers another variation on the theme of the interplay between the possible and the actual:

> Identity is always an ideal, what we would like to be, not what we are.... What makes music special is that musical identity is both fantastic—idealizing not just oneself but also the social world one inhabits—and real: it is enacted in activity. (Frith 1996b: 273–274)

What we would like to be need not remain a fantasy. The notion of identity as something malleable that may, to some extent, be refashioned has now become a familiar trope. Yet this does not mean, as Stuart Hall has been at pains to point out, that identity should be seen as "just a free-floating smorgasbord—you get up today and decide to be whoever you'd like to be". On the contrary, "identity is always tied to history and place, to time, to narratives, to memory and ideologies" (2008: 347). These elements may nonetheless be drawn from a greater or lesser choice of variables. The narratives and memories that an individual accumulates, and the ideologies he or she embraces, will become component parts of that person's identity.

These thoughts may be linked to the more pragmatic observation that not everyone feels at home with, or chooses to live their whole life within the confines of, the society into which they were born. As Ulf Hannerz puts it:

> They were perhaps never wholeheartedly for it ["their" culture] in the first place.... Presented with alternatives to the culture they have lived by, they might at times prefer to pursue these—whether or not they understand them in detail, and in their implications. (Hannerz 1996: 58)

They may not feel at home in their own skin, which may in any case hide a complex story of mixed ancestry, and this may in part explain the uncanny sense of homecoming they feel when they arrive somewhere else. For David Hollinger, the expectation that "individuals would naturally accept the social, cultural and political habits popularly ascribed to their communities of descent"—an expectation that he characterises as "deeply anti-individualist and anti-voluntarist"—was a serious stumbling block in the multiculturalism of the 1990s (2005: 220). It is for this reason that cosmopolitanism has recommended itself to so many contemporary cultural theorists as a more attractive proposition than multiculturalism. The voice of Kwame Anthony Appiah (2005) has been among the most energetic in arguing for the individual's right to choose, reinvent, and continuously reconfigure his or her identity (or identities), free from the tyranny of the established script of the society to which he or she ostensibly belongs. With equal force, Appiah has argued for our need to redraw the imaginary boundaries that have been erected between nations, cultures, and religions and remind ourselves of the powerful ties that connect rather than divide.

Cosmopolitanism has long provided a conceptual home for those whose horizons extend beyond the immediate skyline. Among the less satisfactory aspects of the classic, Kantian understanding of cosmopolitanism is the notion that the cosmopolitan, as a citizen of the world, is at home everywhere and nowhere. A cosmopolitan does not have to be proudly and resolutely rootless, however. Rather than always passing through, we may put down roots in different places and the friends we make in those places may become part of our elective extended family. Like many of the Village Harmony singers who have found their way to Georgia, we may be drawn to return and play a more integral part in the communities that have in some way adopted us. These kinds of "transethnic cultural relationships based upon affinity" can, as Richard Blaustein puts it, "supplement and even come to replace classical communal relationships grounded in kinship and territoriality" (1993: 271–272).

Alongside Mark Slobin's notion of "affinity groups" that lies behind Blaustein's observation, Turino's concept of "cultural cohorts" also recommends itself as a suitable descriptor for the translocal and transnational groups for which the Unicorn and Village Harmony camps serve as meeting grounds. The value of such cohorts, as Turino envisages them, lies in their potential to function as springboards for individual and social change, but "without requiring a transformation of everything at once":

> Cohorts allow people to begin where and with the "whos" that they are and, if so inclined, to begin working toward their vision of a satisfying life "part time," supported by others of like mind. (Turino 2008: 230)

Turino cites as an example the scenes that grew up around American old-time music and dance, whose revival in the 1960s was linked with the back-to-the-land ideologies of a counterculture opposed to the basic tenets of the dominant capitalist cultural formation. Because an initial musical interest opened windows onto other lives lived differently, these scenes provided both model and support for some of their members to make gradual but ultimately profound changes in the way they lived their own lives (2008: 115). Turino's conviction that the personal stories that emerge from what might seem like very circumscribed scenes or modest movements do, in fact, represent a significant force for social change is reflected in his adaptation of Leopold Kohr's mantra as the subheading of one of the final sections of his book: "Small Is Still Beautiful".[20] Here, he envisages a process of gradual expansion as links are formed between different cohorts and, in time, the networks that are thereby created gather sufficient weight and momentum to provide the foundation for broader cultural formations offering a viable alternative to the dominant formation. The counter-argument offered by Ulf Hannerz to the unfortunate (in his view) but pervasive idea that the media have a unique role as "the principal vehicle of culture production and distribution" might be applied just as well to the kind of cultural process Turino describes, which in turn may be mapped onto my own story: "The everyday and face-to-face may be small-scale; in the aggregate, it is massive" (Hannerz 1996: 28).

NOTES

1. For most of its life, the Unicorn camp has had a "no photography" policy. A small selection of images can be found on the website http://www.unicorncamps.com/. From 2013, campers were encouraged to post their own photographs on the camp's new Facebook page.
2. The speaker is not named in the film.
3. It is interesting to note here that the very first trip offered by Thomas Cook, founder of what is now one of the major package tour operators, was a day trip by train from Leicester to Loughborough to attend a temperance meeting. Cook saw travel not only as a democratic right but also as a means of keeping the masses out of the public house or alehouse.
4. The notion of front and back regions is borrowed from Erving Goffman.
5. In 2013, the camp moved to a new site on the Somerset–Wiltshire borders.
6. Compiled by tax collector and amateur folklorist Alexander Carmichael (1832–1912), the collection was originally published in six volumes. A single-volume English-language edition was published in 1992 as *Carmina Gadelica: Hymns and Incantations Collected in the Highlands and Islands of Scotland in the Last Century*.
7. The material acquired its name after Nickomo had been teaching the early chants for a year or two and realised that he had created a new sub-genre.
8. Tony Backhouse also refers to the need to reserve a place for "nonspecific spirituality, spirituality that doesn't necessarily attach itself to a label or a messiah" as part of his explanation for the appeal of gospel music to non-believers (quoted in Johnson 2003: 166).
9. The Harmonic Temple material also reaches a wider constituency through the dedicated weekend workshops that Nickomo and Rasullah lead in different parts of the United Kingdom and beyond. At the same time, another free-floating community is formed by the volunteers from across the UK who make up the choir for the performance CD that accompanies each new collection.
10. These podcasts are available for streaming or download on the Unicorn website: see http://www.unicorncamps.com/.
11. The term "interaction ritual" originated with Erving Goffman.
12. Bardsey, occupying an area of only two square kilometres but known as "the island of 20,000 saints" after the number of saints reputed to have been buried there, had a monastery dating back to 516 (demolished by Henry VIII) and was an important site of pilgrimage in the medieval period. Iona, often represented as the cradle of Scottish Christianity, also had a monastery founded in 563; the small graveyard next to the restored abbey that now occupies the site of the original monastery is believed to be the burial place of forty-eight medieval kings of Scotland, Ireland, and Norway.
13. Several NVPN members now lead singing holidays in various overseas locations. Examples can be found on the websites of many of the individual practitioners

listed on the companion website (see Who's Who: Practitioners Featured in the Book).

14. An archive of colourful diary-like accounts of exchange visits between Sedbergh and Zreče dating back to 2004 can be found at http://sedberghinternational.blogspot.co.uk/, acc. July 12 2013.
15. At the time of completing this manuscript, a full description of the trip, together with photographs and video clips, can be found at http://www.roughdiamonds.info/visittothedc.html, acc. July 12 2013.
16. Earlier discussions of Village Harmony's Corsican camps can be found in Bithell 2009 and 2012.
17. For a more detailed account of how this initiative came into being and how the cooperative operates, see Bray and Mzhavanadze 2013.
18. Union Lidbashi's Facebook page (https://www.facebook.com/Lidbashi) features a wealth a fascinating photographs of old Svaneti, alongside video clips of rituals as they are still performed today.
19. For a more detailed discussion of the part played by foreign enthusiasts and performers of Georgian polyphony in Georgia's own cultural renaissance, and more broadly in its strategic repositioning of itself in the contemporary geopolitical arena, see Bithell 2013.
20. The formulation "small is beautiful" was immortalised in the best-selling book by Kohr's student, British economist E. F. Schumacher, whose *Small is Beautiful: A Study of Economics as if People Mattered* was first published in 1973.

CHAPTER 9

The Voice of the Future

GATHERING THE THREADS

By way of drawing together the many threads that have been woven through my narrative, I first highlight some of the key themes and concepts that have recurred throughout this book.

Finding a Voice

We have seen how, in the context of a natural-voice-style singing group, community choir, or workshop, individuals may find their singing voice for the first time. They may also find their voice at a deeper level in the sense of having the courage to speak out and be heard. Finding one's voice may then become a metaphor for finding the "true" self. The experience of having one's voice witnessed by others is particularly powerful in the case of individuals who have more usually been excluded or overlooked: those once branded tone-deaf, homeless people, or political asylum seekers, for example. More experienced singers may discover different kinds of voices that display a hitherto unimagined range of qualities and timbres, and they may find ways of embodying some of these voices themselves, thereby enriching their own vocal palette. In a choir, members of a community find a collective voice, and this may be used to raise awareness or funds for causes they believe in.

Participation

The notion of active participation in music making has been at the forefront of this discussion, underpinned by the suggestion that it is participation, rather than consumption, which empowers and transforms individuals and helps to build communities. Focusing on the right to participate, and the many rewards that participation brings, casts other values or goals that may, in other contexts, take pride of place in a different light. For a community choir, achieving musical "perfection" may not be the only consideration, and working towards a public performance may not be the prime goal. We have seen that many of the songs favoured by natural-voice-style choirs come from traditions in which participation is a fundamental principle and are structured in ways that maximise their capacity to include all members of the community. Singing can also act as the key that allows people to become participants in lives lived elsewhere and, in the process, to arrive at deeper understandings of other people and cultures that reach far beyond the music.

Performance

Our insights into the kinds of activities in which community choirs (in the United Kingdom, at least) typically engage have taken us far beyond the notion of performance as something that happens on a stage in a specially designed concert hall or theatre. We have encountered a myriad ways of performing (with a small p) and of sharing music, and this has aided our understanding of the idea that, as Gary Ansdell puts it, "performing has shifted from being seen as just reproducing musical works to instead creating and sustaining social relationships through musicing" (2010: 168). Performance enables otherwise marginalised individuals to present themselves in a positive light, which puts them in the position of giving rather than receiving, and of doing rather than being "done to".

Community

The notion of community has also been at the heart of my discussion, principally in the guise of the community choir as a structure that may be seen to represent the community from which its members are drawn. In joining a choir, individual singers become part of a more intimate social community that may become a main source of friendship and support. Through the choir's activities, its members may come to feel more connected to their neighbourhood communities that, in turn, stand to gain from the trickle-down effect of the social capital that the choir generates. Individuals may become part of other communities with a wider catchment area or a different kind of membership when they travel beyond their own locality to attend a summer camp or residential retreat or take part in an overseas tour. These communities may operate at regional or national level, or they may take the form of more fluid transnational formations, and some may also have a virtual dimension.

Members of the NVPN and such organisations as Sound Sense form their own professional communities of practice. Community has also appeared as an aspiration or ideal. It may be imagined as something that has been lost, and its reclamation sought as part of the process of restoring social as well as individual health.

Networks

We encountered the "network" first and foremost in the name of the Natural Voice Practitioners' Network. Phenomena such as weekend workshops or the activities associated with a more discrete interest, such as Georgian singing, present themselves as a more open kind of network, and we have seen how individuals may belong to a series of intersecting networks. We have also seen the decisive part played by key individuals who act as the nuclei around which new networks form or as bridges between networks. In addition, we have seen how particular locations and events play a role as familiar, anchor-like meeting points for network members while also, at some level, appearing to embody core values. Finally, we have met suggestions of the way in which national and transnational networks may add to the sustainability of local networks, and vice versa.

Journeys

Metaphorical as well as literal journeys have featured throughout the book. We have seen how a non-singer or a "terrified" singer, or simply a lone singer looking for a way in, may progress to becoming a confident, happy, fully-fledged member of a choir. We have gained an insight into the different paths that have led individual voice practitioners to the natural voice approach. We have followed singers on their journeys to all manner of meetings, gatherings, festivals, camps, and alternative holiday destinations. We have also considered more epic journeys of self-discovery and journeys towards greater understanding of other people and cultures. Alongside these personal journeys, we have explored the journeys undertaken by different kinds of music that have travelled far beyond the borders of their place of origin.

Liberation and Transcendence

The theme of liberation (or emancipation), together with the related notion of transcendence, has appeared in many guises. We have seen how individuals may overcome personal limitations or the belief that they "can't sing".

Most significantly, we have seen singers being liberated from the need to read music notation. Emancipated from the world of Western classical and Anglo-American popular music through their discovery of parallel musical worlds, they are no longer limited by its preconceptions about what music is and how it should sound, or by any notion that the rules about music are universal and grounded in scientific certainties. More generally, they have transcended the constraints, conventions, and prejudices of their own society through engaging with other people in other places. Each layer of release has opened up new horizons: musical, social, cultural, and existential.

Empowerment

These different orders of liberation have often gone hand-in-hand with a sense of empowerment. Individuals who discover their singing voices have clearly been empowered in quite profound ways. Performing in congenial surroundings to supportive audiences has also appeared as a source of empowerment. Communities are empowered as more of their members become active participants and find ways of making a difference to the quality of their own lives and the lives of others. Host communities elsewhere in the world may also feel empowered as a result of the interest shown in their musical heritage, and this may encourage them in their efforts to preserve and revitalise their traditions.

Crossing Boundaries

In the emancipation process various boundaries have been crossed: between people of different social and educational backgrounds, between different ethnicities and nationalities, between different musical styles and tastes, and between ways of thinking and modes of operation that may once have been juxtaposed as marginal and mainstream. Central to our orientation has been the insistence that traditions or values that might be viewed as being in competition or ordered according to an established hierarchy may more usefully be construed as being simply different. At the same time, some apparent differences have been seen to mask underlying similarities or sympathies that unite more than they divide.

Opening Doors

As boundaries have been breached, new worlds have opened up. Most importantly, we have seen the doors cast wide open to singers who do not sight-read and to music from all corners of the globe. We have gained an understanding of the reasons for which people with diverse needs and backgrounds might step through these doors and where that might lead. We have heard how, through their singing activities, people have discovered other new interests, such as world music, circle dance, or camping, and new ways of spending leisure time, such as attending workshops and going on singing holidays. Some have also become involved with local charities, environmental issues, or political causes.

Liminality

The notion of liminality has lent analytical power to a series of contexts. The act of performance, time away from home, and the different environments in which that time is spent have all emerged as potentially liminal or transitional zones that offer opportunities to experiment with different identities, different ways of being with others, and different ways of living. The initial warm-up session in a choir meeting or workshop has been viewed as a liminal space that marks a transition from one state of mind and mode of activity to another. We have seen how language, too, may represent a liminal zone in which assumptions about intelligibility are suspended and meanings reconfigured. Performance and travel, in their liminal capacity, have also been seen to have transcendental qualities.

Communitas

The notion of *communitas*—which is related to that of community but with a specific overtone of heightened intersubjectivity that typically gives rise to a sense of bonding—has been encountered through the writings of a series of theorists who have drawn inspiration from the work of Victor Turner. The concept has lent itself well to enhancing our understanding of the ritual elements that are inherent in many kinds of performance and journeying and are deliberately incorporated into camps and festivities.

Transformation

We have seen the potential for change or transformation at many levels—not only musical, but also physical, psychological, social, political, and moral. We have encountered ideas from performance studies and ethnomusicology about the transformative potential of performance as a site for integrating and reconfiguring not only one's own subjectivity but also one's relationship with others and with the world. The force of such transformation is reflected in the frequent assertions of those who have taken this path that joining a choir or discovering a new kind of music, activity, or place has changed their life. In individual narratives, this sense of life-changing experience is often tied to a particular "eureka" or "lightbulb" moment that had the force of a conversion or sudden flash of enlightenment leading to a profound shift of consciousness.

Conviviality and Collective Joy

The worlds we have entered in my ethnographic descriptions have presented us with a profusion of scenes of singing, dancing, and feasting that capture the essence of collective joy, whose reclamation Barbara Ehrenreich sees as being so critical to the health of human society. We have also encountered Ivan Illich's use of the term "conviviality" to refer to a state of collective self-determination ("individual freedom realized in personal interdependence") in which individuals are brought into autonomous, creative, and harmonious interaction with one another and with their environment. Again, we have had clear glimpses into settings and spaces in which this vision has become tangible.

FALLACIES AND OTHER TRUTHS

In the course of our explorations, a number of assumptions about musical values and competencies founded, for the most part, on a limited cultural or historical perspective have been identified. Alternative (and not necessarily incompatible) perspectives have been introduced that suggest greater complexity and open up the field of understanding musical experience to different lived realities as well as different ways of thinking. We have also encountered a series of fallacies or misconceptions about music itself. These include some of the "lies my music teacher told me" (many more of which can be found in Gerald Eskelin's book of that name), together with suggestions of other "lies" (or partial truths) that we may have been told by the media, the music industry, or the "authenticity police". Here, too, responses have been offered that situate "music" in a more clearly defined social and historical context with regard to the development of ideas and practice. For ethnomusicologists these alternative positions are as much a norm as any other and need no further justification. It is, however, the dominant discourse that most influences the establishment and, to some extent, the popular view and that also adopts a protective position when the ground begins to shift. I therefore continue my review of the journey this book has taken us on by revisiting some of these fallacies, misconceptions, and assumptions.

"If you can't read music you're not a real musician"

This belief is deeply ingrained in Britain, North America, and other parts of the "modern" world but is, by definition, restricted to times and places where music is written down. The world is full of highly accomplished musicians who do not "read" music, and in societies where musical literacy is the desired norm, there will also be many people who are highly proficient at learning by ear. Sight-reading skills and a pseudo-scientific understanding of music theory do not, in any case, correlate with the degree of musicality with which an individual may be credited. Yet the idea that a musician is someone who has undergone advanced training in Western music theory leads on to the idea that there is a world of difference between "musicians" and "non-musicians". The extent to which this difference is overstated is illustrated by an example given by Rod Paton in a short report (published in the community music magazine *Sounding Board*) about his Lifemusic project. The context is a ten-week training course that attracted equal numbers of self-identified musicians and non-musicians:

> About half way through the course, the non-musicians requested if they might initiate a piece [based on group improvisation] and then compare this with a piece initiated by the musicians. The results were surprisingly (or unsurprisingly) similar with the exception that the musicians took longer to get started! But what was most noticeable was the way in which the group developed a remarkable sense of cohesion and togetherness, breaking down the (false) distinctions between those with training and those without. (Paton 2009: 10)

We may not wish to go as far as to argue that there are no distinctions whatsoever between formally trained musicians and untrained, or self-taught, musicians, but the idea that those who have undergone a particular kind of approved training are the only ones who may rightly claim the identity "musician" is clearly not tenable. Meanwhile, the lack of recognised qualifications remains a stumbling block for many natural voice practitioners who are often ineligible to apply for music-related posts to which they would otherwise bring considerable expertise.

Further normative assumptions about both musical learning and performance conventions were highlighted in questions posed by audience members at a concert given by the Georgian ensemble Sakhioba at St. Ann's Church in Manchester (in November 2011). How, the singers were asked, were they able to perform an entire concert programme without either scores or a conductor? The musicality and proficiency of the singers was not in any way in doubt: on the contrary, audiences across the United Kingdom were in awe of the group's virtuosic performances.

"The works in the Western classical canon represent the height of musical achievement and a model of the kind of music we should aspire to"

The belief that the Western art music tradition is somehow in the vanguard of an evolutionary progression towards ever-greater refinement has found itself on increasingly shaky ground. World music is moving in from the margins to take its place in the regular programming of major concert halls, and what may once have been dismissed as "folk" (or even "primitive") music is often revealed as a sophisticated form of expression based on a well-established musical grammar and science of sound that has developed over hundreds of years. In some cases, this clearly places the music in question closer to the Western notion of art or classical music, even if it is archived in and transmitted through an oral rather than a written tradition. The story of Western music history is also complicated by theories such as those of Marius Schneider, who built on Siegfried Nadel's ideas in proposing that Georgia might be identified as the cradle of European polyphony and its ancient singing traditions as the direct precursors of medieval art polyphony. The relabelling of the vocal polyphony of contemporary Georgia as "traditional" rather than "folk" goes some way towards rendering this idea more palatable. Meanwhile, Stravinsky referred to Georgian folk polyphony as "a wonderful treasure that can give for performance more than all the attainments of new music" (quoted in Levin 1989: 5).

The assumption that the latest arrivals in the Western art music canon represent the epitome of creative achievement is related to the further assumption that *the work is the music*. As we have established, however, music as work—a notion closely related to the notion of music as art—is just one metaphor among many, albeit the one that has dominated the field of Western music history. Among other metaphors that have emerged in these pages are music as process, music as participation, music as social interaction, music as communication, music as therapy, and music as advocacy. The metaphor of music as work has, in turn, given rise to the notion that meaning resides in the work. Again, we have encountered the idea that, whatever the composer's intention (if a single, identifiable composer even exists), meanings are constructed by performers and listeners in ways that relate to their own experiences, understandings, imaginings, and aspirations. A musical style or repertoire can take on different identities and assume different functions in any new setting in which it finds itself. If we see music as experience or action, rather than a *work*, then it is reasonable to assume that at least some of its meaning will rest with the individual *making* the music in a given time and place. The fact that, as we have seen, musical works are in many cultures somewhat slippery entities that do not exist in one definitive form but are recreated by performers in an infinite series of variations makes this alternative perspective easier to appreciate, alongside the notion that in the act of performance we enter into dialogue not so much with the work, or the "music itself", as with our fellow performers.

Musicologist Nicholas Cook has vented his exasperation with standard textbooks on music history that continue to equate Western culture with progress as they reiterate what is essentially a story of Western classical music in which all other forms of musical expression are relegated to the sidelines, their makers reduced to extras with, at best, the occasional walk-on part. In *Music: A Short Introduction*, he writes:

> That such thinking was commonplace at the turn of the twentieth century, the time when the sun never set on the British Empire, is only to be expected. That it is still to be encountered at the turn of the twenty-first is astounding, for it offers an entirely inadequate basis for understanding music in today's pluralistic society. It is hard to think of another field in which quite such uncritically ethnocentric and elitist conceptions have held such sway until so recently. (Cook 1998: 42–43)

"Singing other people's songs is theft"

The accusation that singing other people's songs is theft is based on the trope of cultural appropriation—extended here to the performance of music by someone who is not a direct culture-bearer—as an act of piracy or plunder; if the performer is European or American, they may also be deemed guilty of an imperialist rip-off. Earlier I introduced the argument that whether or not certain aspects of the tourist experience might be seen to rest on utopian foundations was in many ways beside the point. Similarly, we might argue that if the prospect of British singers learning songs from the African continent, for example, rings postcolonial alarm bells for some, that is in some ways beside the point and should certainly not be allowed to discredit any kind of cultural crossover. There are, of course, fundamental points about cultural imperialism that need to be made, and I do not in any way wish to diminish their moral import. But the politics and poetics at work here are again both complex and fluid, and we are not bound to carry the sins of past generations, like a ball-and-chain, for evermore—particularly if it means turning away from overtures of friendship in the present. The trope of musical appropriation as theft finds its counterpart in the trope of music as a resource for all humanity, and this latter trope is often, as we have seen, advanced by those once positioned as victims. In the stories I have told here, we have seen ample evidence of people behaving in ways that are sensitive and responsive, of mutual engagement rather than one-sided exploitation, of exchange rather than taking.

We have also seen how the musical choices people make are not simply random appropriations of what Deborah Root has termed "bits and pieces of...floating cultural exotica" (1997: 226). Often, they are part of relationships. The songs in a singer's repertoire, then, act as a record of human as well as musical encounters. In *Cannibal Culture*, Root makes a distinction between the sharing and borrowing that has always taken place across cultures and the kind of appropriation that involves "the taking up and commodification of aesthetic, cultural, and...spiritual forms of a society", which are then "neatly packaged for the consumer's convenience" (1996: 70). A story of appropriation in the latter sense might feature an ill-informed outsider who takes an object or idea from another culture without consulting its rightful owners and turns it to his or her own profit, recycling it in a distorted form. Those who then consume the derivative and exoticised product (as "authentic" artefact or "ancient wisdom") often know or care little about its place of origin and the lives of the people who created it. By contrast, we have seen how many of the "foreigners" who perform songs from Georgia, South Africa, or Bosnia, for example, have deep-rooted connections with those places and have worked intensively—musically and otherwise—with the primary culture-bearers who have also become their friends. Wider circles of singers in the West who have embraced songs from other parts of the world have become involved with social and humanitarian causes in those countries. Many of the stories I have told in these pages might, then, be better described—in Root's terms—as stories of sharing and caring.

In singing songs from different parts of the globe, community choirs are also performing the way in which they wish to position themselves in relation to the rest of the world. For Village Harmony director Patty Cuyler, this can be an act of cultural advocacy that, at the same time, enables listeners to experience music in a way that is revelatory:

> It has to be this channelling and a love, a respect for the music...that it's *not* about those notes. It's about finding that centre of understanding of what it is to be human, and the music is definitely a major voice from that essence of humanness that you need to find to live life properly, and choirs hunger for it.... If you can channel somebody else's [music] so that people feel that and are moved in a way that's almost, you know, almost orgasmic...they go "Woah! What happened?" [When] you get the chords just right and in the right mood, it's so different from reading a 1-4-5 on the paper then singing those notes. (Cuyler interview 2010)

For Mollie Stone, a conductor with the Chicago Children's Choir as well as a tutor in Village Harmony camps, the motivation is as much educational as musical:

> I teach world music because I love it and because I think it's the best way to get kids interested in the politics of the world and I want to create global citizens through music, not just global musicians.... We need to be teaching our kids to care about and value other cultures and traditions and the *best* way I have found to do that is through music. So I feel like we have an obligation to teach this music and learn it as authentically [as possible] and be advocates for it as much as possible, because otherwise we're going to produce a generation of people who don't care about other cultures and traditions. (Stone interview 2010)

These perspectives resonate in interesting ways with Polina Shepherd's reflections on her motivation to teach songs from her native Russian and Jewish traditions to singers in Britain. For her, it is important that other cultures be treated with respect, but beyond that, the songs themselves are "just a tool":

> I don't mind things being slightly stylistically incorrect, if you wish, if you want to judge it from that perspective, because these are Russian and Jewish songs sung in Britain by people who are not native to these cultures. So this is how it is; this is reality. *I* don't need to judge it.... It's about sharing, it's about opening, it's about freedom, it's about expression, about energy.... And it's wonderful, it's great, because we live in the world—we communicate, we exchange, and I think...the more you learn and the further you go from your own culture, the more open [as a] human being you become, the more of a free-thinker you become....This is probably the ultimate goal that I seek, you know, behind that singing.... I think it's about creating good energy in the world ultimately. (Shepherd interview 2011)

"People should stick to their own traditions"

The notion that people should stick to their own traditions is an obvious corollary to the notion that singing other people's songs equates to theft or is otherwise suspect (with the caveat that such sensitivities do not necessarily extend to the Western classical canon). It may also relate to a concern about the decline of home-grown traditions and the ignorance of the general public about their own national heritage (a concern that has been shared by composers who were at the vanguard of nationalist movements in classical music). Some answers to the question of why amateur singers in the United Kingdom may not find English folk songs an especially attractive option have already been suggested. For some, this material is associated with the dull and dreary routine of school music lessons, or with the clichéd image of the finger-in-the-ear session singer, or with Ewan MacColl's overly stringent insistence on authenticity. The discovery of African, Balkan, and other "foreign" material offered a way out of such impasses. The paucity of multipart songs was another stumbling block and some turned to non-English repertoire in their search for songs with robust harmonies that seemed better to represent the ideal of community.

Questions might also be asked about the relevance of songs from Britain's past to life in a society that has become not only more modern but also more multicultural. The songs themselves are often rooted in a particular locality and speak of a way of life associated with a particular historical period and class perspective. They cannot therefore be said to embody any kind of universal experience of what it means to be British. Singing songs from a distant part of the British Isles (with which the singer has no direct connection) about a way of life that existed a century ago (and for a relatively short time) is surely no more authentic, or relevant to life in contemporary Britain, than singing songs from, say, Bulgaria unless we define authenticity primarily in terms of language. David Oliver, speaking at a conference at Cecil Sharp House ("Out of This World: English Folk Song in the Community Choir Repertoire", May 15, 2011), reflected that only a small minority of the members of his community choir in Hexham had been born in Northumberland. By singing the folk songs of the region, he suggested, those who have now adopted the area as their home can "learn what it is to be Northumbrian". A similar argument has been made about how singing Bulgarian songs can teach us something of what it means to be Bulgarian. Yet one might well question the direct relevance of songs about drowned sailors and forthright fishwives amid a preponderance of tales of country folk who have never strayed far beyond the parish boundary to a generation inhabiting a world that, for the majority, has changed almost beyond recognition. These songs may serve an educational purpose by teaching us something about life as it once was, or they may offer themselves as a focus for nostalgia. How far they can instil a sense of identity—and, more to the point, whether that identity is a desirable one—is surely debateable. It is also understandable that this identity from the past may appear even more foreign than the present-day identity of a more distant place whose inhabitants one has, in fact, met.

English, Welsh, Scottish, Irish, and all manner of regional song traditions do, of course, occupy an important place in the national heritage. My point here is to challenge the argument that, as people who have been born or have chosen to live in present-day Britain, we should be confined to singing songs from Britain's past. Interestingly, though, just as their involvement in the English folk tradition led some singers to Bulgarian and other Eastern European folk traditions in the 1960s and 1970s, for others, a later fascination with music from other parts of the world inspired a renewed interest in their own heritage, together with the sense that they should have something of their own to show to or share with their overseas friends. In some ways this trend parallels a broader resurgence in the performance world, where English folk songs in particular have been recast as "our" contribution to world music. In addition to material gleaned from close-harmony groups such as Coope Boyes and Simpson, many choir leaders now make their own arrangements of English, Welsh, Scottish, or Irish songs, sometimes also carrying out their own research into the songs from their immediate locality. On the CD *New Songs for Old*, for example, members of Sue Harris's choirs perform her arrangements of songs from the Welsh Border region, which she sourced from the National Library of Wales and Cecil Sharp House, together with new songs ("that gave a sense of place in the area") which her research inspired her to write (Harris interview 2009). Ali Burns has also worked extensively with archives of songs collected in the late nineteenth century and speaks of the pleasure she derives from the project of resuscitating songs that have lain dormant for more than a century. Especially popular with choirs across the country are the Forgotten Carols workshops she offers in the months leading up to Christmas.[1] She describes her method of taking traditional texts and either rewriting existing melodies or inventing new ones as "reconditioning songs". "I think it's all part of reinventing our culture," she says, "re-exploring our culture" (interview 2008).

The appearance of a rapidly growing body of new songs by NVPN members and others composed specifically for community choirs is of particular interest. The NVPN's collection *To Grace the Earth* bears witness to the vibrancy of this new song-writing culture, as does the number of songbook-and-CD sets produced by individual members. The notes that often accompany these songs point to two especially striking features. The first concerns the subject matter chosen for the lyrics. Here, alongside songs that may be seen to have a loosely national identity in terms of the themes they address and the landscape they evoke, we find a significant number inspired by events elsewhere in the world or embodying what may be described as global concerns (such as environmentalism or human rights). The second point of note is the style of harmonisation: traditional choral-style arrangements take second place to a preference for polyphonic textures and some songs include voice parts and sections that can be combined in a variety of ways. Related to this is the frequency with which we find explanations of how the musical setting was influenced by exposure to rhythms and harmonies found in the music of other cultures. In some cases this was a deliberate choice. Helen Chadwick, for example, describes how she sometimes consciously incorporates patterns and procedures from other musical traditions into her work, explaining: "I just find some of the *forms* of traditional music so beautiful" (interview 2008). The songs that result may have English lyrics (often drawn from the work of Helen's favourite poets) but in their musical structure or harmonic choices they may be evocative of Corsican or Georgian music, for instance. In other cases the influence was unconscious at the time and recognised only in retrospect. Pauline Down tells of how the song to which she gave the name "Om Shanti" came to her on a visit to Bali, where the ever-present sounds of the gamelan "undoubtedly influenced the sounds and textures that appear in this little chant and the way that the simple melodic phrases are woven together" (note in *To Grace the Earth*, 2008: 35). For the song text, she adapted three traditional Balinese greetings and partings (giving one to each voice part). Some time after teaching the piece at a dance camp, she was surprised to discover it in a do-it-yourself songbook compiled by a camp participant under the title "Balinese Chant". When a transcription of a setting she had made of the Hallelujah appeared in a similar camp songbook as "Caribbean Hallelujah", she says, "it made me aware that I was obviously really influenced by African/Caribbean songs and sounds and the way things fitted—and certainly rhythms" (interview 2007).

What is pertinent here is not only the fact that exposure to a wider musical palette provides a songwriter with more options and that regular exposure to non-Western musical systems is likely to leave its mark. It is also significant that by incorporating musical features that are drawn from participatory traditions, the songs are, in a manner of speaking, predisposed to work well for community choirs. In considering whether there is something in the fabric of the music composed for community choirs that marries with the natural voice ethos, Pauline also points out that, since she has found inspiration in the sounds that already circulate in the natural voice world, the harmonies and rhythms she produces will to some extent appear familiar to the singers she is writing for. She reflects further: "I suspect that unconsciously I was coming up with stuff that had a sort of feel-good factor or was going to be accessible quite quickly—was going to be learnt by ear really easily" (interview 2007). All of this helps to explain the speed with which many of these new songs, and in some cases whole song cycles, such as Helen Chadwick's *The Blazing Heart*, Ali Burns's *The Raven*, and Kirsty Martin's *Four Directions*, have found their way into the repertoires of community choirs across Britain and beyond.

For some, writing new songs is not only a way of boosting the body of repertoire that is suited to natural-voice-style choirs but also a way of replenishing the British tradition. This was central to Ali Burns's motivation as a songwriter and an arranger. "I really started writing," she explains, "as a way of exploring my own culture and trying to put songs back into our culture of singing." At the same time, there were different levels at which she drew on "world music traditions...where singing has traditionally been part of everyday life". Harmony again features here. One of the reasons she never pursued a music degree, she reflects, is that "I just didn't want to end up using those harmony rules. I was much more interested in breaking those rules and looking at the ways that harmony from oral cultures has been organised and designated" (interview 2008). Elsewhere she sums up her overall aim: "I want to recreate the richness of harmony that makes songs of oral traditions around the world so satisfying and joyful to sing but with words that root the work firmly back in my own culture" (http://aliburns.co.uk/what-i-do/, acc. June 15, 2013). In the short introduction to her collection *Always the Singing*, she explains that many of the songs came to her while she was driving home after leading a workshop in a different part of the country. "This reinforces in my mind," she writes, "that it's the singers and the landscape of Britain that inspire me to write" (2008: 5). Kirsty Martin similarly speaks of being inspired by polyphonic traditions from elsewhere in the world, "but creating our own for the modern singer...we're writing these kind of modern folksongs" (interview 2008). Polly Bolton, herself a prolific songwriter, ventures:

> I'm sure that some of these songs, like Ali Burns' songs and Nick Prater's songs, will become part of the oral tradition in the way that folk music used to be—or already are, to a large extent....One likes to think that they will be sung for a great many years. (Bolton interview 2009)

If this is the case, then it means that future generations will no longer be faced with the paucity of multipart songs that has forced some to turn to more distant sources.

A QUIET REVOLUTION

In turning the spotlight on the various themes and stances outlined above and contributing to their reframing, the natural voice movement and related endeavours have impact far beyond the field of music. Those who operate in the intersecting worlds of natural voice practice, community choirs, and world song may not articulate the full range and complexity of the underpinnings, potential, and implications of their work in the way that I have treated them here. They are, nonetheless, clearly part of a bigger picture and a more powerful tide. The writings of cultural theorists such as Barbara Ehrenreich, Robert Putnam, Ivan Illich, and Ulf Hannerz have helped us understand how these phenomena can be be related to broader social visions and global trends and interpreted in the language of social anthropology, cultural studies, or political theory, for example. With specific reference to music, we have been able to situate these same phenomena as part of the kind of fundamental shift of consciousness called for or predicted by such scholars as John Blacking, Christopher Small, John Potter, and Nicholas Cook.

At one level, the kind of singing found in the world of community choirs and other open-access, singing-based activities is of cardinal significance in signalling a return to a "natural", universal, sociobiological norm: "If you can talk, you can sing." This back-to-basics impulse might also be identified in the more general bottom-up, do-it-yourself ethic espoused in natural voice and world song circles as part of the quest for an alternative in a society obsessed with consumption and the cult of the celebrity. This quest is taken a step further in the summer camp scenario and in visits to remote communities where a different kind of spirit seems to linger, evocative, perhaps, of a simpler past or a more authentic way of being in world. At each stage of the journey, there is a stripping away of assumptions, conventions, and constraints. In its overall trajectory, the natural voice movement may also be seen to mirror the course typically taken by a revival movement. It has its pioneers or burning souls, its message, and a vision of social change that builds to some extent on values from an idealised past. The fashion for community choirs has itself, on occasion, been referred to as a revival in amateur singing. To view the impulses behind such developments as essentially retrospective, however, would be misleading. As in any social movement, the apparent reclamation of beliefs and practices that might be associated with notions of a lost past is balanced by an injection of new energy inspired by visions of the kind of future that might lie ahead—not simply as a utopian ideal but as an achievable reality. In this instance, the greatest inspiration has been drawn from living examples found by taking a sideways rather than a backwards step. What is especially interesting in the natural voice case is the way in which the processes of decentralisation and democratisation have married with a markedly ecumenical and cosmopolitan spirit to make manifest a world in which those so often excluded from the main theme of history—the dispossessed and the colonised—may emerge from the shadows and take their place, side by side, at the feast.

As a translocal and transnational phenomenon, the natural voice movement has been significantly aided by new technologies and modes of communication that have themselves undergone a process of democratisation. With its preference for face-to-face encounters and for the age-old practice of mouth-to-ear musical transmission, the movement operates at the same time in a cutting-edge digital world, where music, as well as messages, is carried on electromagnetic waves and stored in easy-to-access clouds. Interestingly, Helen Chadwick comments that the advent of email was crucial in enabling her to "take the leap" and bring together choirs from across the country for the London Sing for Water extravaganza.[2] Now, a link in an email gives almost instant access to recordings of voice parts that a singer may learn (by ear) in advance of joining up with fellow members of a mass choir at this or other national events such as the Street Choirs Festival. Calls for help to the global community may result, in a matter of days, in the kind of multi-site manifestation that occurred when, in response to Russia's invasion of Georgia in 2008, groups of people across the world performed Georgian songs at the same moment, witnessed almost simultaneously by viewers in Georgia itself.

Having observed many aspects of the worlds I have written about in this book at close quarters and, on many occasions, as an active participant, it has been illuminating for me to take a step back and consider, through a different lens, the manner in which the UK natural voice network has evolved since being formalised in the mid-to-late 1990s. It has also been enlightening to try to untangle its multiple lines of descent from loosely knit pockets of activity scattered across the musical, social, and political landscape of the 1960s, 1970s, and 1980s. Certainly, the movement has travelled a phenomenal distance since Frankie Armstrong "wore thin" A. L. Lloyd's *Folk Music of Bulgaria* LP and Joan Mills felt her ears "light up" at the sound of the Aka and Bulgarian voices that had reached her via the recordings of Simha Arom and Marcel Cellier. The network's current growth spurt—not only in terms of direct recruitment to the NVPN but also with regard to the greater visibility of community choirs and an apparent renaissance in vernacular song-writing—is in many ways timely. Combined with increasing media interest in the benefits of singing and the broader embrace of songs from diverse cultures, it suggests that the movement as a whole is poised to realise its potential as a powerful force in contemporary British life.

One of the most pertinent features of the natural voice trend is the extent to which the musical traditions of other cultures not only provide a colourful repertory but also inform the ideological, methodological, and ethical principles on which the movement is founded. World songs may not constitute the majority repertoire for all of the choirs now associated with the NVPN. They may, nonetheless, be seen as the lynchpin that continues to lend coherence to the enterprise. The founding philosophy of the NVPN was inextricably bound up with a turn to songs from outside the national or Anglo-American repertoire, and these songs from the world's oral traditions possessed intrinsic qualities that made them a suitable match for the organisation's social as well as musical goals. Thomas Turino, in his concluding thoughts about the emancipatory potential of participatory music, suggests:

> It is not playing the mbira or panpipes or banjo that makes the difference; it is the *whys* and *hows*, the values and practices underpinning alternative modes of performance that are important for devotees and "multicultural educators" to understand, experience, and teach. (Turino 2008: 227)

These *whys* and *hows*, and the new understandings to which they give rise, may then be carried over into the ways in which other kinds of music are approached and experienced.

In surprisingly similar terms, John Blacking, writing in 1973, expressed his conviction that "ethnomusicology has the power to create a revolution in the world of music and music education, if it follows the implications of its discoveries and develops as a method, and not merely an area, of study" (1973: 5). In this regard, ethnomusicology has long since realised its potential as an academic discipline. Under the guise of "applied ethnomusicology" and "ethnomusicology at home", it has also taken steps to bring the revolution closer to home and into the streets. Those who are active as practitioners in the natural voice world are well equipped to play a complementary role that reaches into ever-more remote corners of local communities, while also consolidating a national profile. Their activities may, until now, have remained largely under the radar, but at each stage of the meta-journey I have described there have been signs of a quiet revolution.

In the British context, this pivotal point in the natural voice journey is shared by the wider community music movement, which is likewise undergoing an intriguing act of repositioning itself vis-à-vis the mainstream. Arriving at this juncture has not been without its dilemmas. In a 2011 report produced under the auspices of the Arts and Humanities Research Council (AHRC)'s Connected Communities initiative, George McKay and Ben Higham reflect on the "essential if sometimes uneasy relation" of community music to various publicly-funded schemes that have been put in place by the British government since the 1980s, related to reducing unemployment, fighting crime, supporting social inclusion, reducing anti-social behaviour, and encouraging health and wellbeing (McKay and Higham 2011: 8–9). The challenge facing the community music world has been to find a way of maintaining its independence from top-down strategies while also gaining the recognition and status it deserves and capitalising on new opportunities that enable more people to benefit. The radical, countercultural identity originally embraced by community music was such that, even twenty years ago, as David Price puts it in a 2010 article in *Sounding Board*, "most of us believed that working in formal education was tantamount to sleeping with the enemy" (2010: 12). A year earlier, Ben Higham (who founded Community Music East in 1985 and served as its director until 2009) had addressed the potential trauma of becoming mainstream, writing:

> The sacred walls of the alternative, revolutionary and community approach are creaking with opportunity and threat.... As we approach the limelight do we retain our revolutionary sheen? As we become increasingly involved in an outcomes-driven, contracting culture are we still delivering alternative experiences and services? Are we prepared to run income-earning businesses rather than purely grant-funded projects? (Higham 2009: 15)

The answer, he concluded, had to be yes. On the occasion of Sound Sense's twentieth anniversary in 2011, chair Catherine Pestano (also an NVPN member) would go on to write:

> We're no longer the outsiders, and a minority activity. We have gained recognition among a wide range of government departments, and ministers. We've helped to create new models of music education for young people, through our work on the Music Manifesto. Most importantly, I think we've done all that and much more with no loss of the core values that make a community musician: the sense of inclusion, the emphasis on creativity, and the key characteristic that community music tells a story: the story of the participants that make the music that we facilitate. (2011: n.p.)

For the NVPN, too, this balancing act is well within reach, and the future is ripe with opportunity.

A RIVER OF MUSIC

We may now recall John Potter's prediction about where the significant future developments in singing were likely to come from: "I would hazard a guess that what we now call world music is the well-spring from which new forms of vocal expression will flow" (2000: 1). As world music continues to assert its presence in the mainstream, it brings with it different voices, different sounds and structures, different ways of thinking about music.

I end my own journey through this book back where I began: in London, on the banks of the River Thames. This time I am here for the BT River of Music festival, the cultural curtain raiser for the 2012 Olympic Games. Spread across six "iconic" sites along the Thames, this "spectacular global summit of rhythm and song" is billed as "arguably the most ambitious musical event ever staged in the capital" (http://www.btriverofmusic.com/, acc. June 22, 2012). As a researcher, I am doing business as usual: casing the joint, taking photographs, making notes, chatting with other festival goers, catching as many of the acts as I can, soaking up the atmosphere. As a singer, I am appearing on the Africa Stage in the newly opened London Pleasure Gardens as part of Beninese superstar Angélique Kidjo's backing choir, alongside other amateur singers from Manchester World Voices Choir. As we step our way through the syncopated harmonies of songs like "Agolo" and "Tumba" that have long been part of the soundtrack in my living room while Angélique, in her inimitable style, works an adoring crowd of thousands, it occurs to me that the tables have been well and truly turned—or more appropriately, perhaps, the table has become well and truly round.[3]

Alfred Wolfsohn's unchained "voice of the future" continues to resonate and, as the kaleidoscope turns, positions shift and new constellations become possible. The voice of the future is also multicoloured and multivalent. It sings of many things, in many registers, and in many tongues. It reminds us that we live in a rich, vibrant, and diverse world. It reminds us of who we are—not only where we have come from but also who we want to be. It reminds us that we can converse across the language divide. And more than that: as a WaterAid volunteer put it in a short trailer made for Sing for Water 2008, "We can't all talk at the same time, but we *can* all sing at the same time."[4]

Several community choirs have adopted the creed of the Woodcraft Folk (popularly, if problematically, attributed to William Morris):

> This shall be for a bond between us: that we are of one blood you and I; that we have cried peace to all and claimed kinship with every living thing; that we hate

war, sloth, and greed, and love fellowship; and that we shall go singing to the fashioning of a new world.

If a new world is to be fashioned, then all should have a place in it. If we are to be part of a "big society", then everyone should be invited to the party. If singing helps to get us there, so much the better.

NOTES
1. Some of this material can be found in the collection *Raining Bliss and Benison*.
2. Helen refers in particular to the way in which email allowed her to "contact several friends around the country who run choirs with great ease and all at once. I would not have done it if it involved phoning or typing individual letters" (pers. comm. December 11, 2011).
3. Our London appearance followed an earlier performance at Manchester's Royal Northern College of Music, which was documented in a short film produced by Band on the Wall. See http://www.youtube.com/watch?v=6qsVvP8DGPE, acc. June 15, 2013.
4. See http://www.youtube.com/watch?v=BEolWXnGKVo, acc. June 15, 2013.

APPENDIX

NVPN Philosophy and Working Principles

From http://www.naturalvoice.net

As Natural Voice practitioners we believe that singing is our birthright. For thousands of years all over the world people have sung—to express joy, celebration and grief, to accompany work and devotion, to aid healing—without worrying about having a "good" voice or "getting it right". Song has been a part of life, a way of binding the community together. We aim to recreate the sense that vocalising, singing and singing together is natural and open to all.

Each person's voice is as unique as their fingerprint and, respecting that individuality, we aim to provide people with opportunities to express themselves vocally and to develop their full vocal potential. The voice we are born with is capable of freely expressing a full range of emotions, thoughts and experience—this is what we mean by the "natural voice". However, the tensions and stresses of daily life create physical and emotional blocks to the natural voice. We therefore focus on breath and bodywork as the foundations of healthy voice use.

We are principally concerned with the melodic voice—the voice as it moves from speech to melody—the voice that is instinctively used in folk traditions around the world. In this culture many people see themselves as non-singers because of previous experiences of criticism and judgement. Many are excluded from singing groups if they do not have music reading skills. Therefore, in our work we aim to counteract these experiences and to give people confidence in their melodic voice by providing a supportive learning environment.

We believe that vocalising, creativity and song should be accessible to all regardless of previous musical ability or experience. Therefore, creating a sense of an accepting community is an essential element of our approach in working with groups.

These underlying principles inform our work practice in the following ways:

(a) We provide a range of opportunities for people to explore their voices and enjoy song including running voice and song workshops, offering training, short courses and creative projects and by running community choirs. Within each context we work according to our guiding principles.
(b) We work at a pace and using an approach which recognises the needs of the less experienced and slower learners.
(c) We use demystifying and accessible language and strive to avoid technical language and jargon.
(d) The majority of music in the world comes from the oral tradition and we aim to teach songs as far as possible by ear recognising that this is the most accessible and effective way for the majority of people to learn and retain songs in the longer term.
(e) Vocal and physical warm ups are an essential element of our work. They ensure healthy vocal use by anchoring the voice in the body and breath and generally prepare the voice for action. They also allow opportunities for increasing creativity, practising listening to others and creating a sense of community.
(f) We are concerned with the enjoyment of singing and accessibility and so in our work the main focus is on the process of coming together to sing whilst at the same time developing people's vocal skills and, within the context of performance, aiming for the highest standards.
(g) Respect for individuals, traditions and creativity is essential to our work—therefore we take care wherever possible to acknowledge sources and song writers and set songs in the context of their history and culture.

REFERENCES

Abram, Simone. 1997. "Performing for Tourists in Rural France." In *Tourists and Tourism: Identifying with People and Places*, edited by Simone Abram, Jacqueline D. Waldren, and Donald V. L. Macleod, 29–49. Oxford: Berg.

Abram, Simone, and Jacqueline D. Waldren. 1997. "Introduction: Tourists and Tourism—Identifying with People and Places." In *Tourists and Tourism: Identifying with People and Places*, edited by Simone Abram, Jacqueline D. Waldren, and Donald V. L. Macleod, 1–11. Oxford: Berg.

Adzinyah, Abraham Kobena, Dumisani Maraire, and Judith Cook Tucker. 1986. *Let Your Voice Be Heard! Songs from Ghana and Zimbabwe*. Danbury, CT: World Music Press.

Ahlquist, Karen, ed. 2006. *Chorus and Community*. Urbana and Chicago: University of Illinois Press.

Aleksieva, Ekaterina, and Dinna Ancheva. 1991. *Ancient Magic in Bulgarian Folklore: Perls of Syncretic Folk Art, Village of Bistritsa, Bulgaria*. Sofia: Kalimana Publishing House.

Allain, Paul. (1997) 2004. *Gardzienice: Polish Theatre in Transition*. London: Routledge.

Altenmüller, Eckart, and Gottfried Schlaug. 2010. "Music, Brain, and Health: Exploring Biological Foundations of Music's Health Effects." In *Music, Health, and Wellbeing*, edited by Raymond MacDonald, Gunter Kreutz, and Laura Mitchell, 12–24. New York: Oxford University Press.

Alvin, Juliette. (1966) 1991. *Music Therapy*. London: Steiner and Bell.

Anderson, Benedict. 1983. *Imagined Communities: Reflections on the Origin and Spread of Nationalism*. London and New York: Verso.

Ansdell, Gary. 2010. "Where Performing Helps: Processes and Affordances of Performance in Community Music Therapy." In *Where Music Helps: Community Music Therapy in Action and Reflection*, by Brynjulf Stige, Gary Ansdell, Cochavit Elefant, and Mercédès Pavlicevic, 161–186. Farnham: Ashgate.

Appadurai, Arjun. 1990. "Disjuncture and Difference in the Global Cultural Economy." *Public Culture* 2 (2): 1–24.

Appadurai, Arjun. 1996. *Modernity at Large: Cultural Dimensions of Globalization*. Minneapolis and London: University of Minnesota Press.

Appiah, Kwame Anthony. 2005. *The Ethics of Identity*. Princeton, NJ: Princeton University Press.

Appiah, Kwame Anthony. 2006. *Cosmopolitanism: Ethics in a World of Strangers*. New York: W. W. Norton.

Armstrong, Frankie. 1992. *As Far as the Eye Can Sing*. London: The Women's Press.

Armstrong, Frankie. 1997. "Freeing Our Singing Voice." In *The Vocal Vision: Views on Voice*, edited by Marion Hampton and Barbara Acker, 43–49. New York: Applause Theatre Book Publishers.

Armstrong, Frankie. 2000. "Bodies under Siege." In *Well-Tuned Women: Growing Strong through Voicework*, edited by Frankie Armstrong and Jenny Pearson, 64–82. London: The Women's Press.

Armstrong, Frankie. 2004. "Giving Voice." *Natural Voice Practitioners' Network Newsletter* 2 (Autumn): 20–22.

Armstrong, Frankie. 2006. "Singing Praise." In *A Performance Cosmology: Testimony from the Future, Evidence of the Past*, edited by Judie Christie, Richard Gough, and Daniel Watt, 34–35. London and New York: Routledge.

Armstrong, Frankie, and Jenny Pearson, eds. 2000. *Well-Tuned Women: Growing Strong Through Voicework*. London: The Women's Press.

Armstrong, Frankie, and Darien Pritchard. 2005. *Handbook for Voice Teachers' Training*. Self-published.

Averill, Gage. 2003. *Four Parts, No Waiting: A Social History of American Barbershop Harmony*. New York: Oxford University Press.

Backhouse, Tony. 2004. *A Cappella: Rehearsing for Heaven*. Fourth edition. Bondi: École de Fromage.

Backhouse, Tony. 2010. *Freeing the Song*. New Zealand and Australia: École de Fromage.

Bailey, Betty, and Jane Davidson. 2002. "Adaptive Characteristics of Group Singing: Perceptions from Members of a Choir for Homeless Men." *Musicae Scientiae* 6 (2): 221–256.

Bailey, Betty, and Jane Davidson. 2005. "Effects of Group Singing and Performance for Marginalized and Middle-class Singers." *Psychology of Music* 33 (3): 269–303.

Barba, Eugenio. 1985. *Beyond the Floating Islands*. New York: PAJ Publications.

Barnwell, Ysaye M. 1989. *Singing in the African American Tradition*. Woodstock: Homespun Tales Ltd.

Barnwell, Ysaye M. 1993. "Becoming a Singer". In *We Who Believe in Freedom: Sweet Honey in the Rock... Still on the Journey*, by Bernice Johnson Reagon and Sweet Honey in the Rock, 255–274. New York: Anchor Books.

Barnwell, Ysaye M. 1999. "Notes on Performance." In *Continuum: The First Songbook of Sweet Honey in the Rock*, by Ysaye M. Barnwell and Sweet Honey in the Rock, xii–xiii. Southwest Harbor, ME: Contemporary A Cappella Publishing.

Barthes, Roland. 1977. "The Grain of the Voice." In *Image, Music, Text*, translated by Stephen Heath, 179–89. London: Fontana.

Barz, Gregory. 2006. "'We Are from Different Ethnic Groups, but We Live Here as One Family': The Musical Performance of Community in a Tanzanian *Kwaya*." In *Chorus and Community*, edited by Karen Ahlquist, 19–44. Urbana and Chicago: University of Illinois Press.

Bassnett, Susan. 1989. *Magdalena: International Women's Experimental Theatre*. Oxford: Berg.

Bebey, Francis. 1975. *African Music: A People's Art*. Westport: Lawrence Hill

Beck, R. J., T. C. Cesario, A. Yousefi, and H. Enamoto. 2000. "Choral Singing, Performance Perception, and Immune System Changes in Salivary Immunoglobin A and Cortisol." *Music Perception* 18 (1): 87–106.

Becker, Howard. 1982. *Art Worlds*. Berkeley and London: University of California Press.

Bell, Cindy L. 2008. "Toward a Definition of a Community Choir". *International Journal of Community Music* 1 (2): 229–241.

Bennett, Andy, and Richard A. Peterson. 2004. *Music Scenes: Local, Translocal, and Virtual*. Nashville, TN: Vanderbilt University Press.

Bernatzky, Günther, Simon Strickner, Michaela Presch, Franz Wendtner, and Werner Kullich. 2012. "Music as Non-Pharmacological Pain Management in Clinics." In *Music, Health, and Wellbeing*, edited by Raymond MacDonald, Gunter Kreutz, and Laura Mitchell, 257–275. New York: Oxford University Press.

Bithell, Caroline. 2007. *Transported by Song: Corsican Voices from Oral Tradition to World Stage*. Lanham, MD: Scarecrow Press.

Bithell, Caroline. 2009. "'Singing Out of Other Throats': Performing Corsican Polyphony from the Outside In." In *The Musical Anthropology of the Mediterranean: Interpretation, Performance, Identity*, edited by Philip V. Bohlman and Marcello Sorce Keller, 159–167. Bologna: Cooperativa Libraria Universitaria Editrice Bologna.

Bithell, Caroline. 2012. "Songs, Sounds and Sentiments in Translation: The Transnational Travels of Corsican and Georgian Polyphony." *Journal of Mediterranean Studies* 21 (2): 333–348.

Bithell, Caroline. 2014. "Georgian Polyphony and Its Journeys from National Revival to World Heritage." In *The Oxford Handbook of Music Revival*, edited by Caroline Bithell and Juniper Hill. New York and Oxford: Oxford University Press. First published on Oxford Handbooks Online, 2013.

Blacking, John. 1973. *How Musical is Man?* Seattle and London: University of Washington Press.

Blacking, John. 1987. *A Commonsense View of All Music: Reflections on Percy Grainger's Contribution to Ethnomusicology and Music Education*. Cambridge: Cambridge University Press.

Blaustein, Richard. 1993. "Rethinking Folk Revivalism: Grass-Roots Preservationism and Folk Romanticism." In *Transforming Tradition: Folk Music Revivals Examined*, edited by Neil V. Rosenberg, 258–274. Urbana and Chicago: Illinois University Press.

Boissevain, Jeremy. 1996. Introduction to *Coping with Tourists: European Reactions to Mass Tourism*, edited by Jeremy Boissevain, 1–26. Providence and Oxford: Berghahn Books.

Bopape, Matlakala, and Patty Cuyler, eds. 2004. *The Folk Rhythm: South African Folk, Church and Protest Songs*. Vol. 1. Marshfield, VT: Northern Harmony Publishing Company.

Bopape, Matlakala, and Patty Cuyler, eds. 2008. *The Folk Rhythm: South African Folk, Church and Protest Songs*. Vol. 2. Marshfield, VT: Northern Harmony Publishing Company.

de Botton, Alain. 2012. *Religion for Atheists*. London: Penguin.

Bourdieu, Pierre. 1984. *Distinction: A Social Critique of the Judgement of Taste*. London: Routledge.

Bradley, Philippa. 2008. "UK Festival Fever on the Increase." BBC Money Programme, July 11. http://news.bbc.co.uk/1/hi/business/7499708.stm. Accessed July 20, 2013.

Brass, Mary Cay, ed. 1995. *Village Harmony: Traditional Songs of the Balkans*. Plainfield, VT: Northern Harmony Publishing Company.

Brass, Mary Cay, ed. 1999. *Balkan Bridges: Traditional Music of the Former Yugoslavia and Bulgaria*. Brattleboro, VT: Community Music and Dance, Inc.

Bray, Madge, and Nana Mzhavanadze. 2013. "Two Woman Charity Helps to Preserve Life, Culture and Dignity in Upper Svaneti." *Georgia Today* 652 (February 22–28). http://www.georgiatoday.ge/article_details.php?id=10885. Accessed June 19, 2013.

Browne, Richard. 1729. *Medicina Musica or; A Mechanical Essay on the Effects of Singing, Music, and Dancing, on Human Bodies*. London: J. and J. Knapton.

Bungay, Hilary, Stephen Clift, and Ann Skingley. 2010. "The Silver Song Club Project: A Sense of Wellbeing through Participatory Singing." *Journal of Applied Arts and Health* 1 (2): 165–178.

Burbidge, David. 2004. "Voices in a Lakeland Landscape." *Natural Voice Practitioners' Network Newsletter* 1 (January): 7–8.

Burns, Alison. 2001. *Enchantments and Glamouries*. Castle Douglas: Little Egg.

Burns, Alison. 2005. *Raining Bliss and Benison*. Castle Douglas: Little Egg.

Burns, Alison. 2008. *Always the Singing*. Castle Douglas: Little Egg.

Campbell, Don. 1997. *The Mozart Effect: Tapping the Power of Music to Heal the Body, Strengthen the Mind, and Unlock the Creative Spirit*. London: HarperCollins.

Carmichael, Alexander. 1992. *Carmina Gadelica: Hymns and Incantations Collected in the Highlands and Islands of Scotland in the Last Century*. Edinburgh: Lindisfarne Press.

Chernoff, John Miller. 1979. *African Rhythm, African Sensibility: Aesthetics and Social Action in African Musical Idioms*. Chicago: University of Chicago Press.

Chorus America. 2009. *The Chorus Impact Study: How Children, Adults, and Communities Benefit from Choruses*. Washington, DC: Chorus America. http://www.chorusamerica.org/publications/research-reports/chorus-impact-study. Accessed July 20, 2013.

Clarke, Eric, Nicola Dibben, and Stephanie Pitts. 2010. *Music and Mind in Everyday Life*. New York and Oxford: Oxford University Press.

Clarke, Nickomo. 2002. *Ateh Malkuth*. The Harmonic Temple. Self-published.

Clarke, Nickomo. 2007a. "Barefoot in the Chorus." *Natural Voice Practitioners' Network Newsletter* 11 (November): 20–29.

Clarke, Nickomo. 2007b. *Deep Peace*. The Harmonic Temple. Self-published.

Clarke, Nickomo. n.d. *Uncle Zumpa's Bumper Book of A Cappella Belters*. Self-published.

Cleall, Charles. 1960. *The Selection and Training of Mixed Choirs in Churches*. London: Independent Press.

Clift, Stephen, and Grenville Hancox. 2001. "The Perceived Benefits of Singing: Findings from Preliminary Surveys of a University College Choral Society." *Journal of the Royal Society for the Promotion of Health* 121(4): 248–256.

Clift, Stephen, and Grenville Hancox. 2010. "The Significance of Choral Singing for Sustaining Psychological Wellbeing: Findings from a Survey of Choristers in England, Australia and Germany." *Music Performance Research* 3 (1): 79–96.

Clift, Stephen, Grenville Hancox, Ian Morrison, Bärbel Hess, Don Stewart, and Gunter Kreutz. 2008a. *Choral Singing, Wellbeing and Health: Summary of Findings from a Cross-national Survey*. Canterbury: Sidney De Haan Research Centre for Arts and Health. http://www.canterbury.ac.uk/Research/Centres/SDHR/ResearchProjects/CompletedPojects/ChoralSinging.aspx. Accessed July 20, 2013.

Clift, Stephen, Grenville Hancox, Rosalia Staricoff, and Christine Whitmore. 2008b. *Singing and Health: A Systematic Mapping and Review of Non-Clinical Research*. Canterbury: Sidney De Haan Research Centre for Arts and Health.

http://www.canterbury.ac.uk/Research/Centres/SDHR/ResearchProjects/CompletedPojects/SingingAndHealth.aspx. Accessed July 20, 2013.

Cohen, Mary L. 2009. "Choral Singing and Prison Inmates: Influences of Performing in a Prison Choir." *Journal of Correctional Education* 60 (1): 52–65.

Cohen, Ronald D. 1999. "Woody the Red?" In *Hard Travelin': The Life and Legacy of Woody Guthrie*, edited by Robert Santelli and Emily Davidson, 138–152. Hanover, NH: Wesleyan University Press.

Collins, Randall. 2004. *Interaction Ritual Chains*. Princeton and Oxford: Princeton University Press.

Conquergood, Dwight. 1985. "Performing as a Moral Act: Ethical Dimensions of the Ethnography of Performance." *Literature in Performance* 5 (2): 1–13.

Cook, Nicholas. 1998. *Music: A Very Short Introduction*. Oxford: Oxford University Press.

Cook, Nicholas, and Anthony Pople. 2004. "Introduction: Trajectories of Twentieth-century Music." In *The Cambridge History of Twentieth-Century Music*, edited by Nicholas Cook and Anthony Pople, 1–17. Cambridge: Cambridge University Press.

Csikszentmihalyi, Mihaly. 1988. "The Flow Experience and Its Significance for Human Psychology." In *Optimal Experience: Psychological Studies of Flow in Consciousness*, edited by Mihaly Csikszentmihalyi and Isabella Selega Csikszentmihalyi, 15–35. Cambridge: Cambridge University Press.

Csikszentmihalyi, Mihaly. 1997. *Finding Flow: The Psychology of Engagement with Everyday Life*. New York: Basic Books.

Curry, Barbara, and Hilary Davies. 2008. "'Choirs in Harmony' Visit to South Africa Easter 2008." *Natural Voice Practitioners' Network Newsletter* 13 (August): 13–15.

Davidson, Jane W., and Julie Fedele. 2011. "Investigating Group Singing Activity with People with Dementia and Their Caregivers." *Musicae Scientiae* 15 (3): 402–422.

Debord, Guy. 1977. *Society of the Spectacle*. Detroit: Black and Red.

Department for Education. 2011. *The Importance of Music: A National Plan for Music Education*. https://www.gov.uk/government/publications/the-importance-of-music-a-national-plan-for-music-education. Accessed April 7, 2014.

Down, Pauline. 2006. *Heartspun: Songs for Acappella Voices*. Self-published.

Eavis, Michael. 2011. Preface to *Destination: Music: The Contribution of Music Festivals and Major Concerts to Tourism in the UK*. London: UK Music.

Ehrenreich, Barbara. 2007. *Dancing in the Streets: A History of Collective Joy*. London: Granta Books.

Ellis, Alexander J. 1885. "On the Musical Scales of Various Nations." *Journal of the Society of Arts* 33: 485–527.

Eno, Brian. 2008. "Singing: The Key to a Long Life." *This I Believe*. National Public Radio (NPR.org). November 23. http://npr.org/templates/story/story.php?storyid=97320958&ps=bb1. Accessed July 1, 2013.

Erkomaishvili, Anzor. 2005. "A Song Dies When Young People Forget It." *Bulletin of the International Research Center for Georgian Polyphony* 6: 27–31.

Erlmann, Veit. 1990. *The Early Social History of Zulu Migrant Workers' Choirs in South Africa*. Berlin: Das Arabische Buch.

Erlmann, Veit. 1993. "The Politics and Aesthetics of World Music." *World of Music* 35 (2): 3–15.

Erlmann, Veit. 1996a. *Nightsong: Performance, Power, and Practice in South Africa*. Chicago and London: University of Chicago Press.

Erlmann, Veit. 1996b. "The Aesthetics of the Global Imagination: Reflections on World Music in the 1990s." *Public Culture* 8 (3): 467–487.

Erlmann, Veit. 1998. "How Beautiful Is Small? Music, Globalization and the Aesthetics of the Local." *Yearbook for Traditional Music* 30: 12–21.

Eskelin, Gerald. 1994. *Lies My Music Teacher Told Me: Music Theory for Grownups*. Woodland Hills, CA: Stage 3 Publishing.

Everitt, Anthony. 1997. *Joining In: An Investigation into Participatory Music in the UK*. London: Calouste Gulbenkian Foundation.

Featherstone, Simon. 2005. *Postcolonial Cultures*. Edinburgh: Edinburgh University Press.

Feld, Steven. 1994a. "From Schizophonia to Schismogenesis: On the Discourses and Commodification Practices of 'World Music' and 'World Beat'." In *Music Grooves*, by Charles Keil and Steven Feld, 257–289. Chicago: University of Chicago Press.

Feld, Steven. 1994b. "Notes on 'World Beat'." In *Music Grooves*, by Charles Keil and Steven Feld, 238–246. Chicago: University of Chicago Press.

Feld, Steven. 2000a. "A Sweet Lullaby for World Music." *Public Culture* 12 (1): 145–171.

Feld, Steven. 2000b. "The Poetics and Politics of Pygmy Pop." In *Western Music and Its Others: Difference, Representation and Appropriation in Music*, edited by Georgina Born and David Hesmondhalgh, 254–279. Berkeley and Los Angeles: University of California Press.

Finnegan, Ruth. (1989) 2007. *The Hidden Musicians: Music-Making in an English Town*. Second edition. Middletown, CT: Wesleyan University Press.

Fitzmaurice, Catherine. 1997. "Breathing Is Meaning". In *The Vocal Vision: Views on Voice*, edited by Marion Hampton and Barbara Acker, 247–252. New York: Applause Theatre Book Publishers.

Fowler, James H., and Nicholas A. Christakis. 2009. "Dynamic Spread of Happiness in a Large Social Network: Longitudinal Analysis of the Framingham Heart Study Social Network." *British Medical Journal* 338 (January 3): 23–27.

Freedland, Jonathan. 2011. "The Success of The Choir's Military Wives Suggests We're Losing our Taste for Malice TV." *The Guardian*, December 21.

Frith, Simon. 1996a. "Music and Identity." In *Questions of Cultural Identity*, edited by Stuart Hall and Paul du Gay, 108–127. London: Sage.

Frith, Simon. 1996b. *Performing Rites: On the Value of Popular Music*. Oxford: Oxford University Press.

Fryer, Peter. 1984. *Staying Power: The History of Black People in Britain*. London: Pluto Press.

Gabriel, Peter. 2007. "Q&A." WOMAD programme.

Garakanidze, Edisher. 2004a. Introduction to *99 Georgian Songs: A Collection of Traditional Folk, Church and Urban Songs from Georgia*, viii–xiv. Aberystwyth: Black Mountain Press.

Garakanidze, Edisher. 2004b. "Notes for Users of This Collection." In *99 Georgian Songs: A Collection of Traditional Folk, Church and Urban Songs from Georgia*, xv–xvi. Aberystwyth: Black Mountain Press.

Garakanidze, Edisher. 2007. *Kartuli Khalkhuri Simgheris Shemsrulebloba* [The Performance of Georgian Folk Song]. Tbilisi: Int'elekt'i.

Garman, Bryan K. 2000. *A Race of Singers: Whitman's Working-Class Hero from Guthrie to Springsteen*. Chapel Hill, NC: University of North Carolina Press.

Garnett, Liz. 2005. *The British Barbershopper: A Study in Socio-Musical Values*. Aldershot: Ashgate.
Garofolo, Reebee. 1993. "Whose World, What Beat: The Transnational Music Industry, Identity, and Cultural Imperialism." *World of Music* 35 (2): 16–32.
Geertz, Clifford. (1973) 1993. *The Interpretation of Cultures*. London: Fontana.
Gibson, Chris, and John Connell. 2005. *Music and Tourism: On the Road Again*. Clevedon: Channel View Publications.
Gibson, Chris, and John Connell, eds. 2011. *Festival Places: Revitalising Rural Australia*. Bristol: Channel View Publications.
Gilroy, Paul. 1994. "Sounds Authentic: Black Music, Ethnicity, and the Challenge of a Changing Same." In *Imagining Home: Class, Culture, and Nationalism in the Black Diaspora*, edited by Sidney Lemelle and Robin D. G. Kelly, 93–117. New York: Verso.
Gittell, Ross, and Avis Vidal. 1998. *Community Organising: Building Social Capital as a Development Strategy*. Thousand Oaks, CA: Sage.
Goodchild, Chloë. 1993. *The Naked Voice: A Singer's Journey to the Spirit of Sound*. London: Rider.
Goodman, Jenny. 2000. "When Communities Find a Voice." In *Well-Tuned Women: Growing Strong through Voicework*, edited by Frankie Armstrong and Jenny Pearson, 136–144. London: The Women's Press.
Graburn, Nelson. 1978. "Tourism: The Sacred Journey." In *Hosts and Guests: The Anthropology of Tourism*, edited by Valene L. Smith, 33–47. Oxford: Blackwell.
Graves, James Bau. 2005. *Cultural Democracy: The Arts, Community, and Public Purpose*. Urbana: University of Illinois Press.
Graves, Richard M. 1954. *Singing for Amateurs*. London: Oxford University Press.
Gridley, Heather, Jill Astbury, Jenny Sharples, and Carolina Aguirre. 2011. *Benefits of Group Singing for Community Mental Health and Wellbeing: Survey and Literature Review*. Carlton, Victoria: Victorian Health Promotion Foundation. http://www.vichealth.vic.gov.au/en/Publications/Social-connection/Benefits-of-group-singing-for-community-mental-health-and-wellbeing.aspx. Accessed July 20, 2013.
Grotowski, Jerzy. 1968. *Towards a Poor Theatre*. New York: Simon and Shuster.
Günther, Marita. 1990. "The Human Voice: On Alfred Wolfsohn." *A Journal of Archetype and Culture* 50: 65–75.
Hall, Stuart. 1996. "Introduction: Who Needs 'Identity'?" In *Questions of Cultural Identity*, edited by Stuart Hall and Paul du Gay, 1–17. London: Sage.
Hall, Stuart, and Pnina Werbner. 2008. "Cosmopolitanism, Globalisation and Diaspora." In *Anthropology and the New Cosmopolitanism: Rooted, Feminist and Vernacular Perspectives*, edited by Pnina Werbner, 345–360. Oxford and New York: Berg.
Hallam, Susan, and Andrea Creech, eds. 2010. *Music Education in the 21st Century in the United Kingdom: Achievements, Analysis and Aspirations*. London: Institute of Education, University of London.
Hannerz, Ulf. 1996. *Transnational Connections: Culture, People, Places*. London and New York: Routledge.
Harrison, Colin. n.d. *Songs from South Africa: The Book*. Self-published.
Hart, Mickey, with K.M. Kostyal. 2003. *Songcatchers: In Search of the World's Music*. Washington, DC: National Geographic Society.
Hart, Roy. 1967. "How a Voice Gave Me a Conscience." Paper presented at the seventh International Congress of Psychotherapy, Wiesbaden. August 21–26.

Higham, Ben. 2009. "Making the Most of Opportunity." *Sounding Board* (issue 3): 15.

Higgins, Lee. 2012. *Community Music: In Theory and Practice*. New York and Oxford: Oxford University Press.

Higgins, Lee. 2013. "Foreword." In *Community Music Today*, edited by Kari K. Veblen, Stephen J. Messenger, Marissa Silverman, and David J. Elliott, vii–viii. Lanham, MD: Rowman and Littlefield.

Hill, Moira. 2007. "Singing Is Political." *Natural Voice Practitioners' Network Newsletter* 11 (November): 18–20.

Hill, Moira. 2008. "BBC Choir Wars: A Response from the Chair." *Natural Voice Practitioners' Network Newsletter* 12 (March): 4.

Hilton, M. P., J. O. Savage, B. Hunter, S. McDonald, C. Repanos, and R. Powell. 2013. "Singing Exercises Improve Sleepiness and Frequency of Snoring among Snorers: A Randomised Controlled Trial." *International Journal of Otolaryngology and Head & Neck Surgery* 2 (3): 97–102.

Hollinger, David A. 2005. *Postethnic America: Beyond Multiculturalism*. Tenth anniversary edition. New York: Basic Books.

Holt, John. (1964) 1982. *How Children Fail*. Revised edition. New York: Da Capo Press.

Hood, Mantle. 1971. *The Ethnomusicologist*. New York: McGraw-Hill.

Horden, Peregrine. 2000. "Musical Solutions: Past and Present in Music Therapy." In *Music as Medicine: The History of Music Therapy since Antiquity*, edited by Peregrine Horden, 4–40. Aldershot: Ashgate.

Horn, Stacy. 2013. *Imperfect Harmony: Finding Happiness Singing with Others*. Chapel Hill, NC: Algonquin Books.

Hoskins, Chris. 2008. "Amazing Grace." *Natural Voice Practitioners' Network Newsletter* 14 (December): 10–12.

Hunt, Peter. 2001. *Voiceworks 1: A Handbook for Singing*. Oxford: Oxford University Press.

Illich, Ivan. (1971) 1976a. *Deschooling Society*. Harmondsworth: Penguin Books.

Illich, Ivan. (1973) 1976b. *After Deschooling, What?* London: Writers and Readers Publishing Co-operative.

Illich, Ivan. (1973) 2009. *Tools for Conviviality*. London and New York: Marion Boyars.

James, Jamie. 1995. *The Music of the Spheres: Music, Science and the Natural Order of the Universe*. London: Abacus.

Jameson, Fredric. 1998. *The Cultural Turn: Selected Writings on the Postmodern, 1983–1998*. London: Verso.

Johnson, E. Patrick. 2003. *Appropriating Blackness: Performance and the Politics of Authenticity*. Durham, NC and London: Duke University Press.

Jordan, Glenn, and Chris Weedon. 1995. "The Celebration of Difference and the Cultural Politics of Racism." In *Theorizing Culture: An Interdisciplinary Critique after Postmodernism*, edited by Barbara Adam and Stuart Allan, 149–164. New York: New York University Press.

Kalo, Laura C., with George Whiteside and Ivan Midderigh. 1997. "The Roy Hart Theatre: Teaching the Totality of Self." In *The Vocal Vision: Views on Voice*, edited by Marion Hampton and Barbara Acker, 185–199. New York: Applause Theatre Book Publishers.

Kane, Frank. 2003. "Learning Techniques for Georgian Singing Used by Georgian Choruses Abroad." *The First International Symposium on Traditional Polyphony* (Proceedings), edited by Rusudan Tsurtsumia and Joseph Jordania, 558–563. Tbilisi: Tbilisi State Conservatoire. http://www.polyphony.ge. Accessed July 20, 2013.

Kenny, Carolyn, and Brynjulf Stige, eds. 2002. *Contemporary Voices in Music Therapy: Communication, Culture, and Community*. Oslo: Unipub Forlag.

Kisliuk, Michelle, and Kelly Gross. 2004. "What's the 'It' That We Learn to Perform? Teaching BaAka Music and Dance." In *Performing Ethnomusicology: Teaching and Representation in World Music Ensembles*, edited by Ted Solís, 249–260. Berkeley and Los Angeles: University of California Press.

Kitzinger, Sheila. 1978. *Women as Mothers: How They See Themselves in Different Cultures*. London: HarperCollins.

Knight, Susan. 2011a. "Adult 'Non-Singers': The Phenomenon, Its Implications, Prevention and Intervention." Paper given at the Phenomenon of Singing International Symposium VIII. St. John's, Newfoundland. July 10–13.

Knight, Susan. 2011b. "Adults Identifying as 'Non-Singers' in Childhood: Cultural, Social, and Pedagogical Implications." In *Proceedings of the International Symposium on Performance Science 2011*, edited by Aaron Williamon, Darryl Edwards and Lee Bartel, 117–122. Utrecht: European Association of Conservatoires (AEC). http://www.legacyweb.rcm.ac.uk/ISPS/ISPS2011/Proceedings. Accessed July 20, 2013.

Koen, Benjamin D., ed. 2008. *The Oxford Handbook of Medical Ethnomusicology*. New York: Oxford University Press.

Kreutz, Gunter, Stephan Bongard, Sonja Rohrmann, Volker Hodapp, and Dorothee Grebe. 2004. "Effects of Choir Singing or Listening on Secretory Immunoglobulin A, Cortisol and Emotional State." *Journal of Behavioral Medicine* 27 (6): 623–635.

Kreutz, Gunter, Cynthia Quiroga Murcia, and Stephan Bongard. 2012. "Psychoneuroendocrine Research on Music and Health: An Overview." In *Music, Health, and Wellbeing*, edited by Raymond MacDonald, Gunter Kreutz, and Laura Mitchell, 457–476. New York: Oxford University Press.

Laušević, Mirjana. 2007. *Balkan Fascination: Creating an Alternative Music Culture in America*. Oxford: Oxford University Press.

Lea, James. 2001. "Charles Sanders Peirce: The Extraordinary Moment and Musical Affect." DMA diss., University of Illinois.

Léothaud, Gilles, Bernard Lortat-Jacob, and Hugo Zemp. 1996. *Les Voix du Monde/Voices of the World: An Anthology of Vocal Expression*. Centre National de la Recherche Scientifique and Musée de L'Homme: Le Chant du Monde.

Levin, Ted. 1989. Liner notes to The Rustavi Choir, *Georgian Voices*. Elektra Nonesuch 979224-2.

Lewandowski, Joseph D. 2007. "Capitalising Sociability: Rethinking the Theory of Social Capital." In *Assessing Social Capital: Concept, Policy and Practice*, edited by Rosalind Edwards, Jane Franklin, and Janet Holland, 14–28. Newcastle: Cambridge Scholars Publishing.

Li, Sicong, and Jane E. Southcott. 2012. "A Place for Singing: Active Music Engagement by Older Chinese Australians." *International Journal of Community Music* 5 (1): 59–78.

Libana. 1990. *Fire Within: Magical and Contemplative Rounds and Songs from Around the World*. Durham, NC: Ladyslipper, Inc.

Lindström, Dorota. 2006. "Sjung, sjung för livet! En studie av körsång som pedagogisk verksamhet och av deltagarnas upplevelse av hälsa och livskvalitet" [Sing, Sing for Life! A Study of Choirs as Educational Activity and of Participants' Experience of Health and Quality of Life.] Piteå, Sweden: Institutionen för Music och Medier, Musikhögskolan i Piteå. http://epubl.ltu.se/1402-1757/2006/43/LTU-LIC-0643-SE.pdf. Accessed July 4, 2013.

Linklater, Kristin. 2006. *Freeing the Natural Voice*. Revised and expanded edition. London: Nick Hern Books.

Lipsitz, George. 1994. *Dangerous Crossroads: Popular Music, Postmodernism and the Poetics of Place*. London: Verso.

Locke, David. 2004. "The African Ensemble in America: Contradictions and Possibilities." In *Performing Ethnomusicology: Teaching and Representation in World Music Ensembles*, edited by Ted Solís, 168–188. Berkeley and Los Angeles: University of California Press.

Lohrey, Amanda. 1998. "The Clear Voice Suddenly Singing." In *Secrets*, by Drusilla Modjeska, Amanda Lohrey, and Robert Dessaix, 173–274. Sydney: Picador.

Lortat-Jacob, Bernard. 1998. *Chants de Passion: Au Coeur d'une Confrérie de Sardaigne*. Paris: Les Éditions du Cerf.

Louhivuori, Jukka, Veli-Matti Salminen, and Edward Lebaka. 2005. "'Singing Together': A Crosscultural Approach to the Meaning of Choirs as a Community." In *Cultural Diversity in Music Education: Directions and Challenges for the 21st Century*, edited by Patricia Shehan Campbell, John Drummond, Peter Dunbar-Hall, Keith Howard, Huib Schippers, and Trevor Wiggins, 81–94. Toowong: Australian Academic Press.

Love, Roger. 1999. *Set Your Voice Free: How to Get the Singing or Speaking Voice You Want*. New York: Little, Brown and Company.

MacCannell, Dean. 1973. "Staged Authenticity: Arrangements of Social Space in Tourist Settings." *American Journal of Sociology* 79 (3): 589–603.

MacCannell, Dean. 1976. *The Tourist: A New Theory of the Leisure Class*. New York: Schocken Books.

MacDonald, Raymond, Gunter Kreutz, and Laura Mitchell, eds. 2012. *Music, Health, and Wellbeing*. New York: Oxford University Press.

Magrini, Tullia. 1995. "Ballad and Gender: Reconsidering Narrative Singing in Northern Italy." *Ethnomusicology Online* 1. http://research.umbc.edu/eol. Accessed July 20, 2013.

Magrini, Tullia. 2000. "From Music-Makers to Virtual Singers." In *Musicology and Sister Disciplines: Past, Present and Future*, edited by David Greer, 320–330. Oxford: Oxford University Press.

Marcus, George G., and Fred R. Myers, eds. 1995. *The Traffic in Culture: Refiguring Art and Anthropology*. Berkeley: University of California Press.

Marsh, J. B. T. c. 1881. *The Story of the Jubilee Singers with Their Songs*. New York: Dover Publications.

Martin, Kirsty. 2006. *Soulstorm*. Brighton: Springboard Music.

Martin, Peter J. 2006. *Music and the Sociological Gaze: Art Worlds and Cultural Production*. Manchester and New York: University of Manchester Press.

Maslow, Abraham H. *Religions, Values, and Peak Experiences*. New York: Viking, 1964.

Massey, Alexander. 2005. "Hip Wiggling and Knee Bending." *Natural Voice Practitioners' Network Newsletter* 4 (July): 8–9.

McGovern, Charles F. 1999. "Woody Guthrie's American Century." In *Hard Travelin': The Life and Legacy of Woody Guthrie*, edited by Robert Santelli and Emily Davidson, 111–127. Hanover, NH: Wesleyan University Press.

McGuire, Charles Edward. 2006. "Music and Morality: John Curwen's Tonic Sol-fa, the Temperance Movement, and the Oratorios of Edward Elgar." In *Chorus and Community*, edited by Karen Ahlquist, 111–138. Urbana and Chicago: University of Illinois Press.

McKay, George, and Ben Higham. 2011. *Community Music: History and Current Practice, its Constructions of "Community", Digital Turns and Future Soundings*. AHRC Connected Communities.

Mills, Joan. 2004. Preface to *99 Georgian Songs: A Collection of Traditional Folk, Church and Urban Songs from Georgia*, vi–vii. Aberystwyth: Black Mountain Press.
Mithen, Steven. 2006. *The Singing Neanderthals: The Origins of Music, Language, Mind and Body*. London: Pheonix.
Morrison, Ian, and Stephen Clift. 2012a. *Singing and Mental Health*. Sidney De Haan Research Centre for Arts and Health. Canterbury: Canterbury Christ Church University.
Morrison, Ian, and Stephen Clift. 2012b. *Singing and People with COPD*. Sidney De Haan Research Centre for Arts and Health. Canterbury: Canterbury Christ Church University.
Muller, Carol A. 2002. "Archiving Africanness in Sacred Song." *Ethnomusicology* 46 (3): 409–431.
Muller, Carol A. 2004. *South African Music: A Century of Traditions in Transformation*. Santa Barbara, CA: ABC-CLIO.
Murphy, David. 2007. "Where Does World Music Come From? Globalization, Afropop and the Question of Cultural Identity." In *Music, National Identity and the Politics of Location: Between the Local and the Global*, edited by Ian Biddle and Vanessa Knights, 39–61. Aldershot: Ashgate.
Natural Voice Practitioners' Network. 2008. *To Grace the Earth: Short and Easy Warm Up Songs by the Natural Voice Practitioners' Network*. Castle Douglas: Natural Voice Practitioners' Network.
Neuman, Daniel M. 1993. "Epilogue: Paradigms and Stories." In *Ethnomusicology and Modern Music History*, edited by Stephen Blum, Philip V. Bohlman, and Daniel M. Neuman, 268–277. Urbana and Chicago: University of Illinois Press.
Ninoshvili, Lauren. 2010. "Singing between the Words: The Poetics of Georgian Polyphony." PhD diss., Columbia University, USA.
Nyberg, Anders, ed. 1990. *Freedom Is Coming: Songs of Protest and Praise from South Africa*. UK edition. Glasgow: Wild Goose Publications.
Olseng, Ingrid. 1990. "Community Music Activity: Report on the Oslo Seminar (29 July–4 August 1990)." *International Journal of Music Education* 16 (1): 57–59.
Olwage, Grant. 2004. "The Class and Colour of Tone: An Essay on the Social History of Vocal Timbre." *Ethnomusicology Forum* 13 (2): 203–226.
Partington, Gitika. 2001. "A Study of the Musical Pathways of Members of the Natural Voice Practitioners' Network Who Use Music from Oral Traditions and Body Work as their Primary Learning Strategies." MA diss., University of Surrey Roehampton.
Paton, Rod. 2009. "Community, Music." *Sounding Board* (issue 2): 9–11.
Pavlakou, Metaxia. 2009. "Benefits of Group Singing for People with Eating Disorders: Preliminary Findings from a Non-clinical Study." *Approaches: Music Therapy and Special Music Education* 1 (1): 30–48.
Pavlicevic, Mercédès. 2010. "Crime, Community, and Everyday Practice: Music Therapy as Social Activism." In *Where Music Helps: Community Music Therapy in Action and Reflection*, by Brynjulf Stige, Gary Ansdell, Cochavit Elefant, and Mercédès Pavlicevic, 223–241. Farnham: Ashgate.
Pavlicevic, Mercédès, and Gary Ansdell, eds. 2004. *Community Music Therapy*. London: Jessica Kingsley.
Pestano, Catherine. 2011. "Sound Sense Celebrating 20 Years of supporting Community Musicians." February 22. http://www.soundsense.org/. Accessed June 15, 2013.
Peterson, Richard A., and Andy Bennett. 2004. "Introducing Music Scenes." In *Music Scenes: Local, Translocal, and Virtual*, edited by Andy Bennett and Richard A. Peterson, 1–15. Nashville, TN: Vanderbilt University Press.

Philpott, Chris, and Gary Spruce, eds. 2012. *Debates in Music Teaching*. Abingdon: Routledge.

Picard, David, and Mike Robinson, eds. 2006. *Festivals, Tourism and Social Change: Remaking Worlds*. Clevedon: Channel View Publications.

Pitts, Stephanie. 2005. *Valuing Musical Participation*. Aldershot: Ashgate.

Potter, John. 2000. "Introduction: Singing at the Turn of the Century." In *The Cambridge Companion to Singing*, edited by John Potter, 1–5. Cambridge: Cambridge University Press.

Potter, John. 1998. *Vocal Authority: Singing Style and Ideology*. Cambridge: Cambridge University Press.

Prana. 1991. *Prana Chants*. Second edition. Newcastle Emlyn: Prana.

Prater, Nick. 2005. *Heaven in My Heart*. Self-published.

Prater, Nick. 2006. *Everytime I Feel the Spirit*. Self-published.

Price, David. 2010. "It Was 20 Years Ago Today (ish)." *Sounding Board* (issue 3): 9–12.

Putnam, Robert D. 2000. *Bowling Alone: The Collapse and Revival of American Community*. New York: Simon and Schuster.

Putnam, Robert D., and Lewis M. Feldstein. 2003. *Better Together: Restoring the American Community*. New York: Simon and Schuster.

Rasmussen, Anne K. 2004. "Bilateral Negotiations in Bimusicality: Insiders, Outsiders, and the 'Real Version' in Middle Eastern Music Performance." In *Performing Ethnomusicology: Teaching and Representation in World Music Ensembles*, edited by Ted Solís, 215–228. Berkeley and Los Angeles: University of California Press.

Raspopova, Irina. 1996. *Irina Raspopova's Method of Voice-Training in Folk Styles of Russian Polyphony*. Leiden: Parallax Music Publishing.

Rauscher, Frances H., Gordon L. Shaw, and Catherine N. Ky. 1993. "Music and Spatial Task Performance." *Nature* 365 (14 October): 611.

Raynor, Henry. 1976. *Music and Society Since 1815*. London: Barrie and Jenkins.

Reck, David. 1997. *Music of the Whole Earth*. New York: Da Capo Press.

Rice, Timothy. 1988. "Understanding Three-Part Singing in Bulgaria: The Interplay of Theory and Experience." In *Selected Reports in Ethnomusicology, Volume 7: Issues in the Conceptualization of Music*, edited by James Porter and Ali Jihad Racy, 43–57. Los Angeles: Department of Ethnomusicology, University of California at Los Angeles.

Rice, Timothy. 1994. *May It Fill Your Soul: Experiencing Bulgarian Music*. Chicago and London: University of Chicago Press.

Rice, Timothy. 2001. "Reflections on Music and Meaning: Metaphor, Signification and Control in the Bulgarian Case." *British Journal of Ethnomusicology* 10 (1): 19–38.

Rise Foundation. 2009. *We Are Together Songbook*. London: The Rise Foundation.

Roma, Catherine. 2010. "Re-sounding: Refuge and Reprise in a Prison Choral Community." *International Journal of Community Music* 3 (1): 91–102.

Root, Deborah. 1996. *Cannibal Culture: Art, Appropriation, and the Commodification of Difference*. Boulder, CO, and Oxford: Westview Press.

Root, Deborah. 1997. "'White Indians': Appropriation and the Politics of Display." In *Borrowed Power: Essays on Cultural Appropriation*, edited by Bruce Ziff and Pratima V. Rao, 225–233. New Brunswick, NJ: Rutgers University Press.

Rosaldo, Renato. 1989. *Culture and Truth: The Remaking of Social Analysis*. Boston: Beacon Press.

Rosen, Charles. 1975. *Arnold Schoenberg*. New York: Viking Press.

Rosselson, Ruth. 2000. "Healthy Notes." *The Mirror*, September 28.

Rowbury, Chris. 2004. "We Are Not Here to Serve the Music." *Natural Voice Practitioners' Network Newsletter* 1 (January): 9.
Rowbury, Chris. 2009. "Preparing to Sing: Why Bother?" *From the Front of the Choir* (blog). February 1. http://blog.chrisrowbury.com/2009/02/preparing-to-sing-why-bother.html. Accessed June 20, 2013.
Russell, Dave. 1997. *Popular Music in England, 1840–1914: A Social History*. Second edition. Manchester: Manchester University Press.
Sacks, Oliver. 2008. *Musicophilia: Tales of Music and the Brain*. Basingstoke and Oxford: Picador.
Saguaro Seminar on Civic Engagement in America. 2000. *Better Together*. Cambridge, MA: John F. Kennedy School of Government.
Sampath, Niels. 1997. "'Mas' Identity: Tourism and Global and Local Aspects of Trinidad Carnival." In *Tourists and Tourism: Identifying with People and Places*, edited by Simone Abram, Jacqueline D. Waldren, and Donald V. L. Macleod, 149–171. Oxford: Berg.
Sarno, Louis. 1995. *Bayaka: The Extraordinary Music of the Babenzélé Pygmies*. Roslyn, NY: Ellipsis Arts.
Schippers, Huib. 2010. *Facing the Music: Shaping Music Education from a Global Perspective*. New York: Oxford University Press.
Schneider, Marius. 1940. "Kaukasische Parallelen zum europäischen Mittelalter." *Acta Musicologica* 12: 52–61.
Schumacher, Ernst Friedrich. 1973. *Small Is Beautiful: A Study of Economics as if People Mattered*. New York: Harper and Row.
Seeger, Anthony. (1987) 2004. *Why Suyá Sing: A Musical Anthropology of an Amazonian People*. Urbana and Chicago: University of Illinois Press.
Seeger, Pete. (1960) 2011. *Choral Folk Songs from South Africa*. Introductory notes and English lyrics by Pete Seeger. Edited by Robert DeCormier. New edition. New York: G. Schirmer.
Sheller, Mimi, and John Urry, eds. 2004. *Tourism Mobilities: Plays to Play, Places in Play*. London: Routledge.
Silber, L. 2005. "Bars behind Bars: The Impact of a Women's Prison Choir on Social Harmony." *Music Education Research* 7 (2): 251–271.
Sing Up. 2011. *Learning Across the Curriculum*. Sing Up 2007–2011: Programme Evaluation—Theme 4. http://www.singup.org/fileadmin/singupfiles/previous_uploads/4.Learning_Across_the_Curriculum.pdf. Accessed July 19, 2013.
Slater, David D. n. d. *Vocal Physiology and the Teaching of Singing*. London: J. H. Larway.
Slobin, Mark. 1993. *Subcultural Sounds: Micromusics of the West*. Hanover, NH: University Press of New England.
Small, Christopher. (1977) 1996. *Music, Society, Education*. Middletown, CT: Wesleyan University Press.
Small, Christopher. 1998. *Musicking: The Meanings of Performance and Listening*. Middletown, CT: Wesleyan University Press.
Smith, Melanie K. 2009. *Issues in Cultural Tourism Studies*. Second edition. London: Routledge.
Smith, Melanie K., and Mike Robinson, eds. 2006. *Cultural Tourism in a Changing World: Politics, Participation and (Re)presentation*. Clevedon: Channel View Publications.
Smith, W. Stephen. 2007. *The Naked Voice: A Wholistic Approach to Singing*. New York: Oxford University Press.
Solís, Ted. 2004. "Introduction. Teaching What Cannot Be Taught: An Optimistic Overview." In *Performing Ethnomusicology: Teaching and Representation*

in *World Music Ensembles*, edited by Ted Solís, 1–19. Berkeley and Los Angeles: University of California Press.

Solís, Ted, ed. 2004. *Performing Ethnomusicology: Teaching and Representation in World Music Ensembles*. Berkeley, Los Angeles, and London: University of California Press.

Southcott, Jane E., and Dawn Joseph. 2013. "Community, Commitment and the 'Ten Commandments': Singing in the Coro Furian, Melbourne, Australia." *International Journal of Community Music* 6 (1): 5–22.

Spintge, Ralph. 2012. "Clinical Use of Music in Operating Theatres." In *Music, Health, and Wellbeing*, ed. Raymond MacDonald, Gunter Kreutz, and Laura Mitchell, 276–286. New York: Oxford University Press.

Stebbins, Robert A. 1996. *The Barbershop Singer: Inside the Social World of a Musical Hobby*. Toronto: University of Toronto Press.

Stephens, Kevin. 2009. "Finding the Community in Choirs." *Sounding Board* (issue 5): 9–11.

Steptoe, Andrew, and Ana V. Diez Roux. 2009. "Editorial: Happiness, Health, and Social Networks." *The British Medical Journal* 338 (January 3): 1–2.

Stige, Brynjulf. 2002. *Culture-Centered Music Therapy*. Gilsum, NH: Barcelona Publishers.

Stige, Brynjulf. 2010a. "Introduction: Music and Health in Community." In *Where Music Helps: Community Music Therapy in Action and Reflection*, by Brynjulf Stige, Gary Ansdell, Cochavit Elefant, and Mercédès Pavlicevic, 3–16. Farnham: Ashgate.

Stige, Brynjulf. 2010b. "Musical Participation, Social Space, and Everyday Ritual." In *Where Music Helps: Community Music Therapy in Action and Reflection*, by Brynjulf Stige, Gary Ansdell, Cochavit Elefant, and Mercédès Pavlicevic, 125–147. Farnham: Ashgate.

Stige, Brynjulf. 2010c. "Practicing Music as Mutual Care." In *Where Music Helps: Community Music Therapy in Action and Reflection*, by Brynjulf Stige, Gary Ansdell, Cochavit Elefant, and Mercédès Pavlicevic, 253–274. Farnham: Ashgate.

Stige, Brynjulf, Gary Ansdell, Cochavit Elefant, and Mercédès Pavlicevic. 2010a. *Where Music Helps: Community Music Therapy in Action and Reflection*. Farnham: Ashgate.

Stige, Brynjulf, Gary Ansdell, Cochavit Elefant, and Mercédès Pavlicevic. 2010b. "When Things Take Shape in Relation to Music: Towards an Ecological Perspective on Music's Help." In *Where Music Helps: Community Music Therapy in Action and Reflection*, by Brynjulf Stige, Gary Ansdell, Cochavit Elefant, and Mercédès Pavlicevic, 277–308. Farnham: Ashgate.

Stokes, Martin. 1999. "Music, Travel and Tourism: An Afterword." *The World of Music* 41 (3): 141–155.

Stoller, Paul. 2002. "Afterword—The Personal, the Political and the Moral: Provoking Postcolonial Subjectivities in Africa." In *Postcolonial Subjectivities in Africa*, edited by Richard Werbner, 225–230. London and New York: Zed Books.

Storey, John. 2003. *Inventing Popular Culture: From Folklore to Globalization*. Oxford: Blackwell.

Storr, Anthony. 1992. *Music and the Mind*. London: HarperCollins.

Sugarman, Jane C. 1988. "Making Muabet: The Social Basis of Singing among Prespa Albanian Men." *Selected Reports in Ethnomusicology, Volume 7: Issues in the Conceptualization of Music*, edited by James Porter and Ali Jihad Racy, 1–42.

Los Angeles: Department of Ethnomusicology, University of California at Los Angeles.
Sugarman, Jane C. 1989. "The Nightingale and the Partridge: Singing and Gender among Prespa Albanians." *Ethnomusicology* 33 (2): 191–215.
Sugarman, Jane C. 1997. *Engendering Song: Singing and Subjectivity at Prespa Albanian Weddings*. Chicago: University of Chicago Press.
Susilo, Hardja. 2004. "'A Bridge to Java': Four Decades Teaching Gamelan in America." Interview by David Harnish, Ted Solís, and J. Lawrence Witzleben. In *Performing Ethnomusicology: Teaching and Representation in World Music Ensembles*, edited by Ted Solís, 53–68. Berkeley and Los Angeles: University of California Press.
Swetina, Barbara, ed. 1993. *Cantiones Sacrae: Sacred Songs, Rounds and Chants for Singing in Community*. Findhorn: Self-published.
Taizé. 1982. *Music from Taizé: Volume 1: Vocal Edition*. London: Collins.
Taizé. 1984. *Songs from Taizé*. Cluny: Ateliers et Presses de Taizé.
Taizé. 1986. *Music from Taizé: Volume 1: People's Edition*. London: Collins.
Taylor, Timothy D. 1997. *Global Pop: World Music, World Markets*. London: Routledge.
Taylor, Timothy D. 2000. "World Music in Television Ads." *American Music* 18: 162–92.
Thibaudat, Jean-Pierre. 1995. "Grotowski, un véhicûle du théâtre." *Liberation* (July 28): 28–30.
Timothy, Dallen J. 2011. *Cultural Heritage and Tourism: An Introduction*. Bristol: Channel View Publications.
Tomlinson, Gary. 2003. "Music, Anthropology, History." In *The Cultural Study of Music: A Critical Introduction*, edited by Martin Clayton, Trevor Herbert, and Richard Middleton, 31–44. New York and London: Routledge.
Turino, Thomas. 2000. *Nationalists, Cosmopolitans, and Popular Music in Zimbabwe*. Chicago: University of Chicago Press.
Turino, Thomas. 2008. *Music as Social Life: The Politics of Participation*. Chicago and London: University of Chicago Press.
Turner, Victor. (1969) 1995. *The Ritual Process: Structure and Anti-Structure*. New York: Aldine de Gruyter.
UK Music. 2011. *Destination: Music: The Contribution of Music Festivals and Major Concerts to Tourism in the UK*. London: UK Music.
UNESCO. 2011. "What is Intangible Cultural Heritage?" http://www.unesco.org/culture/ich/index.php?pg=00002. Accessed June 18, 2013.
Urry, John. 1990. *The Tourist Gaze*. Newbury Park, CA, and London: Sage Publications.
Urry, John. 1995. *Consuming Places*. London and New York: Routledge.
Veblen, Kari K., Stephen J. Messenger, Marissa Silverman, and David J. Elliott, eds. 2013. *Community Music Today*. Lanham, MD: Rowman and Littlefield.
Vella-Burrows, Trish. 2012. *Singing and People with Dementia*. Sidney De Haan Research Centre for Arts and Health. Canterbury: Canterbury Christ Church University.
Vella-Burrows, Trish, and Grenville Hancox. 2012. *Singing and People with Parkinson's*. Sidney De Haan Research Centre for Arts and Health. Canterbury: Canterbury Christ Church University.
Von Lob, Genevieve, Paul Camic, and Stephen Clift. 2010. "The Use of Singing in a Group as a Response to Adverse Life Events." *International Journal of Mental Health Promotion* 12 (3): 45–53.

Wan, Catherine Y., Theodor Rüber, Anja Hohlmann, and Gottfried Schlaug. 2010. "The Therapeutic Effects of Singing in Neurological Disorders." *Music Perception* 27 (4): 287–295.

Wang, Ning. 2000. *Tourism and Modernity: A Sociololgical Analysis*. Oxford: Pergamon.

Welsch, Wolfgang. 1999. "Transculturality: The Puzzling Form of Cultures Today." In *Spaces of Culture: City—Nation—World*, edited by Mike Featherstone and Scott Lash, 194–213. London: Sage.

Wenger, Etienne. 2002. *Cultivating Communities of Practice: A Guide to Managing Knowledge*. Boston, MA: Harvard Business School Press.

White, Mike. 2009. *Arts Development in Community Health: A Social Tonic*. Oxford and New York: Radcliffe Publishing.

Wood, Abigail. 2010. "Singing Diplomats: The Hidden Life of A Russian-speaking Choir in Jerusalem." *Ethnomusicology Forum* 19 (2): 165–190.

World Health Organization. 1948. Preamble to the Constitution of the World Health Organization as adopted by the International Health Conference, New York, 19–22 June, 1946; signed on 22 July, 1946 by the representatives of 61 States (Official Records of the World Health Organization, no. 2, p. 100) and entered into force on 7 April, 1948.

Wright, Stephen. 2008. *The Sounds of the Sixties and the Church*. Guildford: Grosvenor House Publishing.

Young, Laurel. 2009. "The Potential Health Benefits of Community Based Singing Groups for Adults with Cancer." *Canadian Journal of Music Therapy* 15 (1): 11–27.

Young, Rob. 2010. *Electric Eden: Unearthing Britain's Visionary Music*. London: Faber and Faber.

Zeserson, Katherine. 2005. "Voicing Heart, Mind and Body". In *Community Music: A Handbook*, edited by Pete Moser and George McKay, 123–138. Lyme Regis: Russell House.

Ziff, Bruce, and Pratima V. Rao. 1997. "Introduction to Cultural Appropriation: A Framework for Analysis." In *Borrowed Power: Essays on Cultural Appropriation*, edited by Bruce Ziff and Pratima V. Rao, 1–27. New Brunswick, NJ: Rutgers University Press.

Ziff, Bruce, and Pratima V. Rao, eds. 1997. *Borrowed Power: Essays on Cultural Appropriation*. New Brunswick, NJ: Rutgers University Press.

DISCS CITED

A Filetta. *Medea*. Naive, 2006.

Bruno Coulais/A Filetta. *Don Juan*. Original motion picture soundtrack. Auvidis, 1998.

Ensemble Organum, dir. Marcel Pérès. Guillaume de Machaut, *Messe de Notre Dame*. Harmonia Mundi, 1996.

Gasworks Choir. *Gasworks: The Best of the Gasworks Choir*. Gasworks Choir, 2005.

Global Harmony. *Songs for Today*. Global Harmony, 2002.

Rough Diamonds. *Lilizela!* Rough Diamonds, 2011.

Tavagna. *Tavagna Canta Malcolm Bothwell*. Sergent Major Company Ltd., 2002.

WorldSong. *WorldSong Live: A Decade in Harmony, 1997-2007*. WorldSong, 2007.

FILMS CITED

A Filetta: Voix Corses. Un Voyage Musical de Don Kent. Directed by Don Kent. Éditions Montparnasse, 2002.

Alive Inside. Directed by Michael Rossato-Bennett. Ximotion Media, 2013.
Baka: A Cry from the Rainforest. Directed by Phil Agland. River Films, 2012.
Baka: People of the Rainforest. Directed by Phil Agland. National Geographic, 1986; River Films, 2012.
The Alzheimer's Choir. Directed by Joseph Bullman. BBC2 Wonderland series, 2009.
The Virgin Queen. Directed by Coky Giedroyc. Written by Paula Milne. BBC Productions, 2005.
We Are Together. Directed by Paul Taylor. Rise Films. EMI, 2008.

INTERVIEWS CITED

Note: All direct quotations were reviewed with interviewees prior to publication and pertinent details updated where relevant.

Aman, Zaka. May 28, 2009. London, England.
Acquaviva, Jean-Claude. July 15, 2004. Calvi, Corsica.
Armstrong, Frankie. April 12, 2008. Cardiff, Wales.
Bevilacqua, Paul. October 21, 1994. Corte, Corsica.
Bolton, Polly. May 9, 2009. Clee St. Margaret, England.
Bothwell, Malcolm. July 23, 2004. Aléria, Corsica.
Bowker, John. August 10, 2007. Child Okeford, England.
Burbidge, David. September 9, 2007. Sedbergh, England.
Burns, Alison (Ali). August 6, 2008. Child Okeford, England.
Burns, Bernard. May 28, 2009. London, England.
Burton, Geoff. May 28, 2009. London, England.
Chadwick, Helen. February 4, 2008. London, England.
Chamberlayne, Ann. August 22, 2007. Conway, Wales.
Chandler, Nina. February 11, 2009. Oxford, England.
Clarke, Nickomo. August 10, 2007. Child Okeford, England.
Croose, Sian. November 5, 2008. Norwich, England.
Cuyler, Patty. July 22, 2010. Tsinandali, Georgia.
Daulne, Anita. February 9, 2009. Oxford, England.
Davies, Sally. February 7, 2008. London, England.
Down, Pauline. July 8, 2007. Menai Bridge, Wales.
Garratt-Adams, Katherina. July 20, 2011. Lakhushdi, Georgia.
George, Michele. April 1, 2008. Aberystwyth, Wales.
Gibb, Jules. February 1, 2011. Manchester, England.
Gordon, Larry. October 27, 2005. Tregarth, Wales.
Harman, Sarah. April 10, 2008. Cardiff, Wales.
Harper, Michael. August 7, 2008. Child Okeford, England.
Harris, Sue. May 10, 2009. Clee St. Margaret, England.
Hart, Su. November 5, 2011. Bury, England.
Jarlett, Dee. October 31, 2007. Bristol, England.
Jordania, Joseph. October 4, 2007. Portel, Portugal.
Kane, Frank. January 30, 2012. Findhorn, Scotland.
Knight, Bruce. February 26, 2008. Leamington Spa, England.
Martin, Kirsty. August 8, 2008. Child Okeford, England.
Mills, Joan. July 24, 2005. Llanrhystud, Wales.
O'Connell, Kate. August 9, 2008. Child Okeford, England.
Parlby, Sue. December 11, 2007. Cambridge, England.

Pasquali, Iviu. August 31, 1994. Alzi, Corsica.
Prater, Nick. August 11, 2007. Chile Okeford, England.
Rowbury, Chris. February 27, 2008. Coventry, England.
Roxborough, Jackie. August 9, 2007. Child Okeford, England.
Rozelaar-Green, Frank. April 13, 2008. Cardiff, Wales.
Shepherd, Polina. November 11, 2011. Manchester, England.
Stefanova, Dessislava (Dessi). February 6, 2008. London, England.
Stone, Mollie. July 23, 2010. Sighnaghi, Georgia.
Tugwell, David. July 22, 2011. Lakhushdi, Georgia.
Verney, Candy. January 12, 2008. Wortley, England.
Verney, Teresa. November 4, 2008. Norwich, England.
Walker, Roz. August 8, 2007. Child Okeford, England.
Walton, Margaret. July 24, 2007. Llanfairpwllgwyngyll, Wales.
Wells, Jane. November 5, 2008. Castle Acre, England.
Whitehead, Rowena. December 11, 2007. Cambridge, England.
Yule, Lynn. July 24, 2007. Llanfairpwllgwyngyll, Wales.

INDEX

Note: references to figures appear in italics.

Abram, Simone, 261
a cappella
    arrangements of popular songs, 220
    movement in Australia and New Zealand, 119–120, 170, 247
    singing, 11, 16, 225, 226
accessibility
    as guiding principle, 79, 87, 90, 125, 170
    of oral learning, 49, 50, 120, 122, 170, 246, 307
    and participation, 82, 188
    and sharing, 177, 186
    of songs from different cultures, 18, 126, 143, 169, 170, 177, 186, 187, 193
    of ways of working with the voice, 61, 65, 177
Acquaviva, Jean-Claude, 133–134
advocacy (cultural), 303–304
affinity groups, 36, 168, 291
A Filetta, 133
Africa
    appeal of songs from, 174–176
    music from, 92
    songs from, 14, 50, 151, 152
    writings about music in, 49–40, 52
African American singing traditions, 18, 71, 124, 169–173
    transformative power of, 127, 170, 173
Afropean Choir, 176, 177, 204n5
Agape Children's Choir, 181
agency, 2, 37, 201
Agland, Phil, 182
AIRS (Advancing Interdisciplinary Research in Singing), 233
Aka, 150, 166, 181–182, 204n6, 310
Alexander technique, 85, 89, 114, 197

Alilo, 199
Alive Inside, 236, 239
Alquist, Karen, 22
Alvin, Juliette, 90, 104n16
Alzheimer's disease, 19, 237, 238
Aman, Zaka, 191
aMaSing, 238
American Choral Directors' Association, 222
Ansdell, Gary, 295
anthroposophy, 87
anti-apartheid movement, 83, 174
    and songs, 159, 178, 181, 266, 267
Appadurai, Arjun, 35, 257
Appiah, Kwame Anthony, 290
appropriation, 34, 169
    cultural, 37–38, 43n15, 160, 200–202, 302–304
    of gospel music in Australia, 171, 172
    of "pygmy" music, 181–182
    of the songs of others, 29, 186
Armstrong, Frankie, 21, 71, 74, 81, 85, 89, 150, 216
    career of, 73–78
    as catalyst in other practitioners' stories, 82, 84, 85, 91, 95, 100, 187
    and Ethel Raim, 76–77, 116, 185
    as founder/mentor of NVPN, 16, 32–33, 47, 66
    and Giving Voice, 61, 64
    and influence/work in Australia, 33, 73, 78
    and language, 116, 154–155
    musical influences of, 73–75, 142
    and theatre work, 104n8
    and vocal and physical exercises, 110, 113–116

Armstrong, Frankie (*Cont.*)
   vocal philosophy of, 51, 53–55, 65–66, 67, 109
   and voice training weeks, 78, 81, 96, 99, 100, 104n7, 110, 185
Arom, Simha, 150, 310
arts-in-health movement, 238–239
Arts on Prescription, 239
art worlds, 32, 39
Associated Board of the Royal Schools of Music and Trinity Guildhall, 136
asylum-seekers
   as members of choirs, 208, 232-233, 294
   songs about, 217
   working with, 216, 243–244
Australia
   a cappella movement in, 23–24
   community singing in, 23
   Sing for Water in, 15
   See also Frankie Armstrong: and influence/work in Australia
authenticity, 160, 169, 191
   in Corsican singing, 279
   critiques and politics of, 29, 172, 200–203, 299, 305
   cultural and stylistic, 75, 144, 146, 180, 183, 204n4, 304
   in Georgian singing, 193–194, 195, 197
   in performance 122
   in South African singing, 179–180
   staged, 261, 262
   tourist's quest for, 259–260, 262
   of the voice, 46, 66, 68n8, 264
authentic voice, 16, 22, 54, 55. *See also* authenticity: of the voice
Averill, Gage, 26

BaAka, 202–203. *See also* Baka, Bayaka.
"Babethandaza", 108, 124, 178
Backhouse, Tony, 109, 129, 137n3, 163, 246, 247, 266, 292n8
   and Café of the Gate of Salvation, 170–172
   on repetition, 126
   teaching of, 120, 122
   on technique and style, 146, 147
Badoo, Ben, 93, 94, 100
Baez, Joan, 17, 126

Bailey, Betty, 239
Baka, 181–184, 204n10, 217. *See also* BaAka, Bayaka
Baka Beyond, 182
Baka Culture Camps, 183
Balkan song and dance, 85, 105n19, 163n2, 184–189
   appeal of, 26, 150, 152, 154, 186–189, 304
   author's introduction to, 3
   and Ethel Raim, 76, 116
   and Frankie Armstrong, 76–77
   and meaning for women, 187, 189
   in the United States, 29, 76, 105n19, 166, 184, 188–189
ballad tradition, of Northern Italy 157
"Bambalela", 42
Bangor Community Choir, 13, 65, 140, 151, 226, 228–230
Barba, Eugenio, 60, 101
barbershop, 25–26, 222, 230
Barfield, Kate, 81
Barnwell, Ysaye, 21, 96, 108, 124–127, 129, 137n2, 138n15, 140
   on congregational and communal singing, 125
   philosophy of, 125, 170, 174
   on repetition, 126–127
   workshops of, 123, 170, 178
Barthes, Roland, 46
Barz, Gregory, 23, 224
Baščaršijske Noći festival, 283
Bassnett, Susan, 101
Bayaka, 146, 164n4, 204n6. *See also* Aka, BaAka, Baka
BBC Radio 3 Choir of the Year, 98, 212, 213, 238
Bebey, Francis, 49
Becker, Howard, 32, 39
"being there", 5, 8, 281
bel canto, 68n8, 146, 217
Bell, Cindy, 2, 222
belting, 147
Bennett, Andy, 31
Best of the Gasworks Choir, 141
Bevilacqua, Paul, 157
Big Heart and Soul Choir, 88
"big society", 2, 313
bi-musicality, 168
Birmingham International Voices, 94

Bisserov Sisters, 185
Bistritsa Grandmothers/Bistritsa Babi, 3, 185
Blacking, John, 36, 68n3, 131, 308
  on ethnomusicology, 310
  on music and language, 50
  on unmusicality, 2
  on Venda music, 50, 52
Black Umfolosi, 97
Black Voices, 14, 230
Blatchford, Robert, 214
Blaustein, Richard, 291
blues, 73-74, 83, 92, 116
Boal, Augusto, 85
body work, 48, 57, 111, 114
Boissevain, Jeremy, 259, 261
Bolton, Polly, 71, 72, 126, 138n19, 308
  background/career of, 81–82
  on job satisfaction, 102–103
Bolton Clarion Choir, 84, 216
bonding, 237, 267, 298
  as function of warm-up sequence, 112, 114
  as function of multipart singing, 157
  and participatory music, 39
  through shared musical taste/activity, 36, 168, 189, 272
  as type of social capital, 40, 44n17, 288
Bopape, Matlakala, 180
Borjghali, 199
Bosnia, 40, 186
  Village Harmony camp in, 276, 277, 281–284
Bothwell, Malcolm, 134, 139n27
Botton, Alain de
  on travel, 262
  on religion, 269
Bourdieu, Pierre, 32
Bowker, John, 183–184, 263, 266
Boy Scouts, 3, 17
Bradley, Philippa, 258
Brahms, 132
Brass, Mary Cay, 129, 186, 281, 282
Braveheart Georgia, 287
Bray, Madge, 297
breath (in singing), 48, 62, 111, 113, 114, 118, 119, 137n5
Brighton and Hove Russian Choir, 99
Bristol Chant Group, 94, 267

British-Bulgarian Friendship Society, 184
British Choirs on the Net, 213
British/English folk revival, 54, 74, 81, 151
Brook, Peter, 58
Browne, Richard, 236
Brown, Sara, 140
BT River of Music festival, 312
Budimir, Maja, 282, 283
Bulgaria
  attraction to music of, 74, 82, 92, 151
  music of, 3, 184
  and vocal technique, 117
Bulgarian State Radio and Television Choir, 185
Bullock, Kathy, 71, 72
Burbidge, David, 67, 72, 91, 114
  background and training of, 83, 85, 97
  events organised by, 245, 273
  and Sedbergh– Zreče twinning, 275
Burgess, James, 93, 263
Burkina Faso, 177
Burns, Alison (Ali), 71, 81, 129, 220, 253, 266, 267
  background of, 96
  motivations of (as songwriter/arranger), 306, 307–308
  songs by, 141, 217
Burns, Bernard, 231–232
Burton, Geoff, 231
Bury AcaPeelers, 217
Bush, Kate, 185

Café of the Gate of Salvation, 137n3, 170, 171
call-and-response, 114, 115, 116, 120, 123, 124, 125, 126, 138n8, 171, 181
Cameron, David, 2, 209
Cameroon, 182
Campaign for Nuclear Disarmament (CND), 77, 83–84
Cardiff Community Music, 85
Cardiff Laboratory Theatre, 15, 55, 64, 68n4, 84, 85, 104n15, 151, 190
Carmichael, Morag, 11
Carmina Gadelica, 267, 292n6
Cecil Sharp House, 6
  Community Choir, 97, 161
celebration, 39, 42, 120, 215

Index [337]

Cellier, Marcel, 150, 310
Centre for Performance Research (CPR), 4, 15, 55, 60, 64, 84, 85, 97, 104n15, 192
Chadwick, Helen, 3, 62, 72, 100
    career of, 15, 84–85
    and Georgian singing, 190, 192, 195–196, 199, 204n16
    and Sing for Water, 12, 13, 15, 309
    songs by, 140, 141, 220, 306, 307
    as workshop leader, 89, 96, 104n15
Chamberlayne, Ann, 153, 226
Chandler, Nina, 151, 190
Chela, 199
Chernoff, John Miller, 50
chest voice, 74, 103n2, 186
chi gung, 114
Chilcott, Bob, 220
chimurenga, 176
Choir, The (radio series), 20, 213
Choir, The (TV series), 19, 209–210, 213
choirs
    amateur, 16, 99, 131, 162, 214, 221
    and British media, 19–20
    and charitable work, 243–244, 249
    classical, 16, 23, 99, 131, 221
    and/as community, 18, 91, 212, 223, 224–226, 230–233, 242–244, 248
    and cross-cultural activity, 242–244, 249
    and dress, 17, 43n9
    and exchange visits, 274–275, 288
    as family, 224–225, 232
    health benefits of, 237
    for health conditions, 238
    as life-changing, 14, 233, 239, 248, 249
    names of, 13, 221–222, 238
    non-auditioned, 16, 99
    open-access, 91, 99, 120, 131, 222, 241, 247
    political, 18, 84, 215–217
    and repertoire, 220, 222
    and social and psychological benefits, 24, 233, 237–238, 239, 247
    in Sweden, 238
    Welsh male voice, 18, 214
    world music, 17
    and "world" repertoire, 163
    See also chorus; community choirs; natural voice choirs
choral music, literature on, 22–23
choral singing
    in Britain, 214
    and congregational singing, 125
    renaissance of, 212, 219, 222
    in the United States, 23
choral societies, 16, 17, 24, 214, 221, 222, 242, 246, 248
chorus, definitions of, 23
Christie, Judie, 55
circle dance, 3, 230, 270, 298
    network in UK, 92–94, 96, 100, 105n18, 184, 282
    and South Africa, 178–179
Cirques Divers, 4
civil rights movement, 33, 83, 174
    songs of, 125, 266
Clarke, Nickomo, 95, 175, 225
    background/journey of, 92–94, 101, 179, 263, 267
    songs and collections by, 129, 141, 208, 266
    See also Harmonic Temple
Clarke, Rasullah, 93, 179, 267
Clarke, Sharon D., 212, 249n3
Clarion choirs, 214–215
Clarion movement, 214–215
Cleale, Charles, 118–120, 138n13
Coastal Voices, 140
collective effervescence, 240, 272, 273
collective joy, 9, 41, 137, 272, 288, 299
Collet's record shop, 75, 86
Collins, Randall, 273
commodification, 37, 200, 303
communitas, 168, 199, 240, 262, 268, 272, 298
community, 295–296
    building, 5, 219
    choir as, 23–24, 295
    collective singing as reinforcing, 83
    loss of, 40, 41
    restoration/recreation of, 34, 288, 295
community choirs
    definition of, 16, 222, 250n17
    gatherings of, 64, 245, 273
    names of, 13
    non-auditioned, 2

non-performing, 16, 50, 248
and performing style, 17
repertoire of, 17, 132, 140–141
suitability of songs from other cultures for, 142–143
See also choirs; natural voice choirs
Community Choirs Festival, 245
community music, 78, 85, 86
    definitions of, 87–88
    ethos of, 20, 53, 89, 231, 242
    international perspectives on, 27
    literature on, 2, 25–28
    in relation to NVPN, 31, 73, 87–89
    in the United Kingdom, 26, 311
Community Music Activity Commission, 87
Community Music East, 89, 311
community music therapy, 24, 27–28, 89, 90–91
    definitions of, 90
community of practice, 61, 101-102, 248, 296
community singing, 13, 19, 87, 119, 227
    in Australia, 23
    See also community choirs
Congo, 176, 177
Connell, John, 30, 262
Conquergood, Dwight, 203
consumption, 38, 308
    of the other, 37
    versus participation, 40, 260, 294
    of world music, 29
conviviality, 110, 136–137, 242, 286, 299
Cook, Nicholas, 161, 302, 308
Coope Boyes and Simpson, 267, 306
copyright, 83, 129–130
Côr Cochion, 84, 104n12, 216
Côr Gobaith, 208
Côr Ysbyty Gwynedd, 230–231
Corsica, 6, 112
    as focus of author's research, 4, 28, 29
    Village Harmony camp in, 278–281
    See also polyphony: of Corsica
Cortijo Romero, 91, 94
cosmopolitanism, 36, 290–291
    subdivisions of, 35
Coulais, Bruno, 133–134
Cradick, Martin, 182
creativity, 38, 89, 90, 111, 183, 272, 288
Critics Group, 75

Croatia, songs from, 140, 141, 185, 187, 208, 266
Croose, Sian, 88–89
Csikszentmihalyi, Mihaly, 239–240
cultural appropriation. *See* appropriation: cultural
cultural diversity, 5, 26, 201, 218
    celebration of, 2, 162, 218
    in music education, 27, 30
    postmodernism and, 33
cultural formations, 35, 291–292
cultural imperialism, 29, 38, 44n16, 161, 302
Cultural Olympiad, 163, 312
cultural process, 2, 36, 292
Cuncordu di Orosei, 62
Curwen, John, 23, 214
Cuyler, Patty, 180, 277, 278, 285, 303

Dalston Songs, 15
dance, 12, 16, 41, 42, 150
    Balkan, 29
    music and, 39, 80, 94, 179
    and singing, 11, 42, 50
    See also circle dance
Dance Camp Wales, 94, 96, 100, 105n24, 267, 270
Dances of Universal Peace, 94, 263
"Dancing in the Street", 12, 42
Dartington College of Arts, 84, 95, 97
Daulne, Anita, 176–177
Davidson, Jane, 239
Davies, Hilary, 71, 275
Davies, Peter Maxwell, 59
Davies, Sally, 97, 161
Deason-Barrow, Michael, 86–87, 217, 250n11
Debord, Guy, 41
democracy
    cultural 26, 88
    and social capital, 40, 223
democratisation, 5
    of music, 90
    of the voice, 1
    See also singing: democratisation of
deschooling, 110, 135
Diamond Choir, 71, 275, *276*
diaspora, 35
    African, 167
    Georgian singing, 166

Dick-Read, Grantly, 66
Digby, Suzi, 212, 249n3
discord, 150, 191, 252
dissonance, 145, 186, 188
Dolgellau Choir/Côr Dolgellau, 140
Don Juan, 133
Douglas, Colin, *228*
Down, Pauline, 4, 65, 71, 130, 228, 266
   and aMaSing, 238,
      and Bangor Community Choir, 140, 227, *228*
      and Côr Ysbyty Gwynedd, 230–231
      songs by, 71, 129, 306–307
Dr Foster's Travelling Theatre Company, 85
drone, 186, 188–189, 280
Durkheim, Émile, 240, 272, 273
Dutiro, Chartwell, 97, 227

early music, 86, 147, 150, 163n2
Earthsong Camp, 183, 263
East Lancs Clarion Community Choir, 81, 84, 207, 216
Eastwood, Christine, 140
Ecologia Youth Trust, 287
ecstasy, 23, 41, 46, 239, 272. *See also* euphoria; peak experience
Ehrenreich, Barbara, 41, 137, 272, 288, 299, 308
Eight Songs for a Mad King, 59
Ellis, Alexander John, 145
Ellis, Vivien, 185
Eno, Brian, 37, 226
epiphany, 96, 100, 263
Erkomaishvili, Anzor, 194, 195
Erlmann, Veit, 28, 36, 174, 288
empathy, 171, 210
   with hosts, 255, 283
   songs as route to, 143, 149, 200, 226, 256
empowerment, 5, 38, 79, 100, 200, 228, 297
   community music therapy and, 90,
   music as tool for, 120, 170
   natural voice ethic and, 2, 20, 67, 82, 86, 87, 125, 182, 264
   participation and, 294
equal temperament. *See* scale (musical): equal tempered
Erkvanidze, Malkhaz, 159
Estill Voice Training, 80, 106n27

ethnography
   new style of, 35
   as research method, 5
ethnomusicology, 30, 137, 310
   applied, 27, 310
   concerns of, 49, 133, 223, 298
   and ethnomusicologists, 167
   medical, 43n11
   and studies of community music making, 28
   and studies of "pygmy" music, 182
euphoria, 26, 29, 191, 239, 288. *See also* ecstasy; peak experience
European Choral Association—Europa Cantat, 218, 220
Everitt, Anthony, 25
Exaltation of Larks, 208
expanded sound, 26
Experiment in International Living, 282
exploitation
   of the other, 37, 200, 201, 302
   of "pygmy" music, 182
   tourism and, 259, 261

feasting, 42, 163, 272, 299
Feldenkrais Method, 78, 85, 114
Feldstein, Lewis, 224
Feld, Steven, 37, 181, 200
Festival 500: Sharing the Voices, 219, 220
festivals, 128, 180, 190, 199, 224, 245, 279
   in Britain, 257–258, 263, 271
   choral, 214, 217–219
   folk, 76, 77, 81, 116
   proliferation of, 262
   See also Festival 500; Giving Voice Festival; Glastonbury Festival; Koprivstica Festival; National Street Choirs Festival; Thames Festival; Three Choirs Festival
festivity, 41, 137, 288
   decline and suppression of, 41
   Unicorn camp as embodiment of, 272
field
   of artistic practice, 132
   as defined by Bourdieu, 32
   as research location, 6
Filip Kutev Choir, 185
Findhorn, 92–93, 95–96, 105n17, 128, 199, 287

finding a voice
    in metaphoric sense, 187, 200, 248
    trope of, 175, 228, 294
    voice work as aid to, 22, 57, 82, 91, 92, 153, 227
Finnegan, Ruth, 16, 25, 221
Fisk Jubilee Singers, 23, 126, 138n17, 138n19
    and reception in South Wales, 126
flow, 239–240, 268
folk music, 79
    of different nations, 17
    English, 6, 83, 97, 104n11, 151, 152, 304–305
    of South Africa, 180–181
Folk Music of Bulgaria, 74
Folkworks, 85, 104n14
Forres Big Choir, 224, 273
Freeing the Natural Voice, 21, 46, 56, 57, 137n5
Frith, Simon, 52, 131, 248, 290

Gabriel, Peter, 258, 261
Garakanidze, Edisher, 96, 129, 158, 169, *192*, 201
    and Georgian singing in the UK, 64, 191–196, 199
Garakanidze, Gigi (Giorgi), 199, 205n19
Gardzienice Theatre, 60–61, 62
Garnett, Liz, 26
Garofolo, Reebee, 38
Garratt-Adams, Katherina, 190
Gasworks Choir, 11, 102, 116, 141, 267
Geertz, Clifford, 5
gentrification, 47, 53
George, Michele, 21, 57–58, 63, 64, 68n5
Georgia, 20, 62, 63, 163n2, 166, 199, 201, 217, 232, 291, 301, 309
    language of, 159, 194
    Village Harmony camp in, 284–286
    See also Georgian singing; Georgian songs; polyphony: of Georgia
Georgian Harmony Association, 199
Georgian singing
    network, 31
    teaching methods for, 193–198
    in the UK, 64, 191–193, 199
Georgian songs
    appeal of, 151, 189–191, 198
    musical features of, 191
    and Sing for Water, 15
    See also polyphony: of Georgia
Georgian State Ensemble, 196
Georgieva, Eugenia, 99, 106n28
Ghana, 49, 122
Gibb, Jules, 15, 84, 96, 266
Gibson, Chris, 30, 262
Gilroy, Paul, 172
Girl Guides, 3, 17
Giving Voice Festival, 6, 55–58, 61–65, 84, 142
    artists appearing at, 61–63
    and relationship to NVPN, 63–65
Glanville, Sue, 274
Glastonbury camps, 93-94, 100, 105n20, 263
Glastonbury Festival, 105n20
global cultural flows, 35
Global Harmony, 42, 141, 222
globalisation, critiques of, 34
Global Music Exchange, 182–183
global village, 33, 257, 258
Glorious Chorus, 42
Gnawa, 93
Goodall, Howard, 19
Goodchild, Chloë, 22
Good Vibrations Choir, 187, 243
Gordon, Larry, 122, 277, 278
gospel, 81, 94, 174, 222
    appeal of, 95, 126, 169–170, 292n8
    in Australia, 109, 137n3, 166, 170–173, 204n4
    choirs, 212, 217
    singer, 14, 71, 86
    singing style, 125, 126–127, 147, 174
    songs in collections, 125, 129, 204n3, 266
    songs in repertoire, 140, 141, 164n2, 220, 222, 270, 277
    in South Africa, 174
    and Welsh male voice choirs, 18, 126
Gough, Orlando, 162
Gough, Richard, 55, 68n4
Graburn, Nelson, 259
Graceland, 200
Graves, Richard, 119, 120
Green Candle Dance Company, 97
Greenham Common
    Cruise Missile Base, 77, 84
    Women's Peace Camp, 77, 103n5

Greenwell, Judy, 185
Grotowski, Jerzy, 60–61, 62, 63, 68n6, 117
Grotowski Institute, 62
Gunn, David, 140, 141
Guria, 158, 159
Guthrie, Woody, 74, 77, 82–83

Hall, Stuart, 34, 203, 290
Hanley, Alex, 42
Hannerz, Ulf, 34, 36, 201–202, 290, 292, 308
happiness, 23, 34, 83, 233, 239–241, 288
   as collective phenomenon, 240–241
Harman, Sarah
   background/training of, 79, 84, 85
   on learning by ear, 123
   on teaching songs from other cultures, 142–143, 147, 151, 155
Harmonic Temple, 141, 225, 267–269, 292n7, 292n9
harmony
   and community, 150–151
   and health, 234–235
   interdependence of musical and social, 28, 112, 157, 225, 235
   rules of Western classical, 143, 144–145, 149, 187–188, 297, 307
Harper, Michael, 11, 12, 14, 86
Harris, Sue, 72, 81, 152, 170, 225, 306
Harrison, Colin, 93, 95, 101, 178–179, 263
Hart, Roy, 59–60, 62, 63. *See also* Roy Hart Theatre
Hart, Su, 182–193, 201
Heartsong camp, 128
Heaton Voices, 244
heightened speech, 115
Helen Bamber Foundation, 233
Henderson, Bill, 224, 273
Hidden Musicians, The, 16, 25, 221
Higgins, Lee, 26–27, 88, 231
Higham, Ben, 2, 311
Hill, Eleanor, 217
Hill, Moira, 83–84, *215*
Hodgson, Rose, 15
Hollinger, David, 35, 290
Holt, John, 135
Hood, Mantle, 167
Horn, Stacy, 23

Hoskins, Chris, 242
hospitality, 26, 231, 285
How a Choir Works, 211
Hullabaloo Quire, 54, 221, 225
hybridity, 33, 173

identity, 2, 40, 203
   and musical style, 26, 38, 124
   as performative, 26, 34, 149, 289–290
   performing arts as fulcrum of, 289
   (re)construction of, 39, 153, 290
   songs as part of, 18, 256, 305
"Ide Were", 12
"If you can talk, you can sing", 16, 47, 51, 107, 125, 258, 308
ilahiya, 282, 283
Illich, Ivan, 110, 135–137, 299, 308
imagined worlds, 35
improvisation, 70, 72, 227, 230, 300
   in Aka and BaAka singing, 182, 202
   in Corsican singing, 279
   in Georgian singing, 195
   in gospel singing, 125
   in South African singing, 180
   teaching of, 99, 118
institutionalisation, of music making and music education, 47, 53, 135–136
intercultural encounter, 61, 165, 168, 176, 249
   through tourism, 262
intercultural understanding/cooperation, 2, 147–149, 219, 256, 280–281, 303
interculture and interculturality, 35–36, 168
International Centre for Georgian Folk Song, 194
International Centre for Theatre Research, 58
International Choirs Meet, 245
"Internationale, The", 206, 216, 217
International Festival of Women in Experimental Theatre, 104n15
International Symposium on Traditional Polyphony (Georgia), 6, 199
Irinola, 197
isicathamiya, 28, 173
islands, as destination for singing holidays, 273–274

Jameson, Fredric, 33, 37
Jarlett, Dee, 141, 266, 267
  arrangements by, 11, 140, 276
  on job satisfaction, 102
  on warm-up exercises, 116
Jenkins, Karl, 65, 164n5
Joan Armatrading's Favourite Choirs, 213
Johnson, E. Patrick, 170–173, 203
Johnston, Anthony, 144
Jordan, Glenn, 33
Jordania, Joseph, 192, 193, 194, 195
journeys, 296. *See also* natural voice practitioners: backgrounds/journeys of; tourism
joy, 13, 23, 41, 94, 120, 227, 238, 243, 263, 269, 272. *See also* collective joy
Jung, Carl Gustav, 59

Kadenza Women's Choir, 84
Kahn, Susannah Darling, 42
Kane, Frank, 196–198, 201
Kartuli Ensemble, 196
Kartuli Khoro, 194
Kidjo, Angélique, 312
Killen, Louis, 74
Kinnersley Castle, 71, 78, 100–101, 104n6
Kisliuk, Michelle, 202–203
Kitzinger, Sheila, 66
Knight, Bruce, 95, 175, 266
Knight, Susan, 247
Kohr, Leopold, 291
Koprivstica National Festival of Bulgarian Folklore, 184–185, 187

Latin, 155–157, 268
Laboratory Theatre (Wrocław), 60
Lakeland Voice, 72, 245
Lakhushdi and Feast of Limkheri, 253, 255, 257, 286–287
Lanfranchi, Jean-Pierre, 134
language, 4, 97
  Georgian, 159, 194
  and music (origins), 50–51
  of songs in student recitals, 160
  and unintelligibility, 3, 29, 116, 152–159, 268
  and vocal quality, 116
Last Choir Standing, 16, 211–213, 218, 220
  critiques of, 20, 249n4

Laurieston Hall, 89, 95–96, 100, 101, 105n23, 128
  Harmony Week, 98
  Women's Singing Week, 96
Laušević, Mirjana, 29, 188–189
leisure, 17, 26, 40, 161, 256, 257, 288
Le Mystère des Voix Bulgares, 86, 150, 185
Lessac, Arthur, 56
"Let Love Rain Down", 11
Let Your Voice Be Heard, 49, 122, 129, 174
Lewandowski, Joseph, 223
Lewis, Jerome and Ingrid, 183
Libana, 129, 141
liberation, 296–297
Lies My Music Teacher Told Me, 47, 58, 299
Lifemusic project, 300
Lilizela! 71
"The Lily of the Valley", 126
liminality, 112, 168, 173, 175, 260, 288, 298
Lindström, Dorota, 238
Linklater, Kristin, 21, 55, 61, 62, 63, 64, 85, 114
  background/career of, 56–57
  on the natural voice, 21–22, 46, 57
Lipsitz, George, 289
Liverpool Socialist Singers, 207, 216, 250n10
Llangollen International Eisteddfod, 3, 218, 250n12
Lleisiau'r Byd/World Voices, 140
Lloyd, A. L., 54, 74–75, 103n4, 310
local and global, 2, 36, 162, 262
Local Voices, Worlds of Song, 64
Locke, David, 201, 203
Lohrey, Amanda, 23, 247–248
London Bulgarian Choir, 98, 188, 213, 224
London Olympics, 19, 162, 163, 312
London Russian Choir, 99
London Yiddish Choir, 99
Lortat-Jacob, Bernard, 23, 28
Love, Roger, 22
Lovenotes, 15
Lumko Institute, 179

MacCannell, Dean, 259, 261, 262
MacColl, Ewan, 75, 103n4, 304
Macedonia, Republic of, 186
Machaut, *Messe de Notre Dame*, 133, 139n23

Index [343]

Machlin, Evangeline, 56
Magdalena Project, 4, 89, 104n15
Magrini, Tullia, 17, 36, 157
Making Music, 162
Malik, Samia, 97
Malone, Gareth, 19–20, 209–211, 219
Manchester Community Choir, 208
Manchester World Voices Choir, 312
Mandela, Nelson, 178
Mapfumo, Thomas, 167
Marani, 197
Mariposa Folk Festival, 76
Marley, Bob, 167
Martin, Kirsty, 54, 96, 225–226, 266
  songs of, 71, 129, 220, 267, 307, 308
Martin, Peter, 38
Maspindzeli (London Georgian choir), 15, 98, 163, 199, 231–232
Massey, Alexander, 113
McKay, George, 2, 311
McLuhan, Marshall, 257
Medea, 133
Midsummer Festival of Sacred Dance, Music and Song, 96
Miller, Alice, 248
Mills, Joan, 85, 310
  and Edisher Garakanidze, 64, 193
  and Frankie Armstrong, 64
  and Giving Voice, 55, 56, 58, 61, 64
  on harmony, 150, 151
  on songs in foreign languages, 154
Milton Keynes, amateur musical activity in, 25, 221
Mindorashvili, Ketevan, 286
miners' strike (1984–1985), 83
Mithen, Steven, 50, 68n1
modes (musical), 189,
  psychological effect of, 235
  See also scale
Monger, Anne, 93, 178–179
Mongolian overtone singing, 63, 75
Montgomery-Smith, Chreanne, 19
Morgan, Sarah, 81, 104n11
Morris, William, 214, 312
mother tongue, 3, 154, 157, 160
Mouthful, 103
Mozart, 132, 160, 195
Mozart effect, 235
"Mravalzamier, Dato's", 11, 15
Muller, Carol, 37

multiculturalism, 168
  of Britain, 21, 162, 305
  critiques of, 34, 290
  in music, 58, 88
music
  as action or process, 39, 50, 100
  and the brain, 235–236, 251n22
  as bridge between cultures, 148, 149, 177, 180, 186, 218, 219, 275
  and community building, 288
  and dementia, 236
  as form of social engagement, 30, 132
  and healing, 235, 236
  and health and wellbeing, 28, 220, 233,
  as mediating social meanings, 26, 39
  and medicine, 234, 236–237, 251n24
  and memory, 235–236
  and metaphor, 287–288, 301
  as social capital, 30
  of the spheres, 234
  as tool for intercultural engagement, 30
  transformative power of, 30, 203, 236, 239
  as universal language, 50
  in Western societies, 47, 51
  See also choral music; folk music; Western art music; world music
musica humana, 234–235
musical worlds, 25
music education, 86, 110, 135–136
  in Britain, 52–53, 139n28
  and cultural diversity, 27
musicking, 39, 53
MusicLearningLive, 98
Music Manifesto, 136, 311
music therapy, 89–90, 234, 237
  definition of, 90
  Scandinavian tradition of, 27
  in the UK, 104n16
Muslim Women's Collective, 95
Mzhavanadze, Nana, 287

Nadel, Siegfried, 301
naked voice, 22, 55
Naked Voices, 102
National Childbirth Trust, 66
National Singing Programme, 19, 136

National Street Choirs Festival, 6, 206–209, 215, 216–217, 244, 273, 309
natural childbirth movement, 66–67
natural voice
 definitions of, 16, 46–47, 65–67
 movement, 32–33
 philosophy, 16, 21–22
natural voice choirs, 16, 17
 distinctiveness of, 130–133
 and performance, 241
 repertoire of, 71, 132
 See also community choirs
Natural Voice Dialogue, 130
natural voice practitioners
 backgrounds/journeys of, 21–22, 73–99
 and job satisfaction, 102–103, 243
 resources for, 71, 127–130, 139n21
 teaching methods of, 120–123
 training for, 16, 71, 99, 102
Natural Voice Practitioners' Network (NVPN), 1, 14, 15, 16, 31, 55, 296
 annual gathering of, 6, 69–72, 111
 as community of practice, 101–102, 296
 establishment of, 78, 93, 96
 membership of, 72
 philosophy of, 47–50, 57, 79, 109, 120
 and teaching style, 16
network (as descriptor), 31
New Age, 93, 183
99 Georgian Songs, 64, 129, 169, 193
Ninoshvili, Lauren, 158
"Nkosi Sikelel' iAfrika", 178, 179, 204n8
non-musician, 300
non-singer, 48, 116, 247, 251n31
Nordoff, Paul, 90
North American folk revival, 17
Northern Georgian Society, 199
Northern Harmony, 140, 141, 163n2, 185, 277
Norwich Women's Soul Choir, 89
nostalgia, 34, 151, 257, 305
 imperialist, 259
notation, 139n20, 180, 182, 214
 inflexibility of, 123
 lack of need for, 80, 130, 134, 297
 learning from, 120, 129, 133
 limitations of, 49, 122
Novalis, 237

Nyberg, Anders, 178, 179–180

Oakington Immigration Reception Centre, 243–244, 251n28
O'Connell, Kate, 95–96, 224, 266, 273
Odin Teatret, 60, 61
Ojay, Alise, 238
old-time music and dance (in North America), 291
Olomolaiye, Una May, 12, 14, 176–177, 213
Olwage, Grant, 51, 131
open-throat technique, 55, 77, 108, 116, 138n9, 186, 282
Open Voice, 208
oral tradition, 49, 61, 67, 82, 117, 120, 200, 220, 301
 characteristics of songs from, 123–124, 127
 and natural voice ethos, 124, 266–267
 and transmission, 18, 123, 125
Orbaum, Ali, 116, 141, 267
Organum, 133
ornamentation, 46, 75, 99, 117, 118, 180, 187
Orpheus McAdoo and his Minstrel, Vaudeville, and Concert Company, 174

paghjella, 157–158, 164n8
Pardo, Enrique, 85
Parkinsongs, 238
Parlby, Sue, 187–188, 190, 243
Parry, Alun, 206, 209, 217
participant observation, 6, 168
participation, 49, 87, 88, 90, 162, 294–295
 dynamics of, 26
 and musical style and structure, 50, 125
 politics of, 1, 25, 30, 110
 theories of, 26, 39–40, 132–133
Partington, Gitika, 72, 80–81
Pasquali, Iviu, 158
past, the
 consumption of, 37, 261
 nostalgia for, 151, 309
 as resource, 33
Paton, Rob, 300
Pavlicevic, Mercédès, 238

peak experience, 26, 191, 239, 288
People of Note, 12, 222
Pérès, Marcel, 133
performance
    and alternative identities, 28, 203
    in natural voice context, 50, 241–242, 248, 295
    participatory and presentational, 39–40, 100, 127, 132–133, 310
    place of, 24
    as social act, 28
    as transformation, 1, 189, 203, 298
performance studies, 168, 298
Pestano, Catherine, 311
Peterson, Richard, 31
Peters, Shirley, 77
Petts, Nick, 12
Phenomenon of Singing International Symposium, 6, 219
Philadelphia Folk Festival, 76
Philip Koutev National Folk Music and Dance Ensemble, 98
Pieśń Kozła (Song of the Goat), 60, 63
Pikes, Noah, 96
Pilpani family, 62
Pirin Ensemble, 185
Pitts, Stephanie, 25
Plato, 235
political choirs. *See* choirs: political
Polokwane Choral Society, 180
Polovynka, Natalia, 62
polyphony
    of Albania, 117, 132
    of Corsica, 62, 117, 133–134, 157–158, 278–279
    of Georgia, 62, 75, 127, 158–159, 166, 301
    of Russia, 117
    of Sardinia, 62, 117
    of Ukraine, 62, 117
Pontanima choir, 282
popular songs (Anglo-American), arrangements of, 17, 140, 141, 220, 266, 267
postethnicity, 35
postmodernism, 33–34, 37
    and postmodernity, 38
Potter, John, 48, 51, 67–68, 308, 312
Prana, 93–94, 266, 267
Prater, Nick, 72, 100, 102, 204n3, 225, 266
    on attraction of "other" musics, 150–15, 169–170, 174
    and gospel, 95, 170, 266
    musical activities of, 93–94
    songs and songbooks of, 71, 129, 140, 308
Prater, Susie, 42, 72
Preston People's Choir, 84
Priestley, Mary, 90
Prior, Maddy, 72
Pritchard, Darien, 78, 114
Probić, Omer, 284
Protestantism, 41, 53, 172
psychotherapy, 59, 85, 89, 90, 91, 270
Putnam, Robert D., 40, 223–224, 239, 241, 288, 308
"pygmy" music, 176, 178, 181–182
    See also Aka, BaAka, Baka, Bayaka
Pythagoras, 234–235, 236

Raim, Ethel, 76–77, 115, 116, 185, 189, 204n15
Rainbow Nation, 13
Raise Your Banners festival, 215–216, 220, 273
Rao, Pratima, 201
Rasmussen, Anne, 201
Raspopova, Irina, 117–118
Read, Jane, 273
Reagon, Bernice Johnson, 170, 173, 174
Received Pronunciation, 52
Reck, David, 51, 139n20
Reclaim the Night, 84
Red Leicester Choir, 207, 216
reggae, 167, 201
repetition, 123, 126–127, 156, 266–267
resources for choir leaders. *See* natural voice practitioners: resources for
revival movements, 34, 151, 309
    See also British/English folk revival; North American folk revival
rhythm, 127, 130, 144, 151–152, 153, 248
    in African songs, 49, 122, 124, 153, 173, 174, 177
    in Bulgarian music, 187, 188
    in Corsican music, 279
    as flexible/non-fixed, 122, 194
    as focus in warm-up exercises, 62, 111, 115, 116, 121
    in Georgian music, 194

in gospel music, 171
in new compositions, 152, 306–307
Rice, Timothy, 167, 287
ritual, 30, 39, 41, 151, 273
    dance as, 93
    need for, 269, 272
    in/of Georgia, 231, 255, 286, 287, 293n18
    Grotowski and, 60
    musicking as, 39
    revitalisation of, 34
    and traditional music, 180
    warm up as, 112
Robbins, Clive, 90
Root, Deborah, 303
Rosaldo, Renato, 257
Rosen, Charles, 145
Rosselson, Ruth, 237
Rough Diamonds, 71, *276*
rounds, 124, 129, 137n7, 164n6
Rowbury, Chris, 141, 211, 213
    background of, 85
    on function of warm-ups, 111–113
    on language, 154, 158
    on performance, 242
Roxborough, Jackie, 112, 150
    on African music, 175
    background/career of, 94–95, 105n22
    on language, 153
Royal College of Music, 86, 88
Roy Hart Theatre, 59–60, 61, 96
Rozelaar-Green, Frank, 196
Russell, Dave, 214
Russell, Janet, 81, 84, 216
Rustavi Choir, 194, 195, 196

Sacks, Oliver, 235, 251n22, 272
sacred dance, 93. *See also* circle dance
Sadovska, Maryana, 62, 64, 116–117, 138n10
Sakhioba, 300
Sage Gateshead, 103, 104n14
Salisbury Cathedral Choir, 86
salsa, 17, 161, 230
samba, 17, 161
Sampath, Neils, 261
Samzeo, 199
Sarajevo, 282, 283, 284
Sarno, Louis, 146, 164n4
Sathanao, 287
scale (musical), 68n3, 110, 145, 191, 235

equal tempered, 121, 130, 145, 121
planetary, 235
scene, concept and definition of, 31–32
Schechner, Richard, 168
Schippers, Huib, 29, 165
Schneider, Marius, 301
schooling, 110, 135
    and musical aesthetics and values, 51
School of Movement Medicine, 42
Seeger, Anthony, 29
Seeger, Charles, 167
Seeger, Peggy, 75
Seeger, Pete, 17, 74, 77, 82, 83, 141, 178
Seekers, The, 126
Setterfield, Ivor, 210–211
sevdalinka, 282
Shepherd, Polina, 99, 304
shiatsu, 89
Sidney De Haan Research Centre for Arts and Health, 6, 19, 233, 238
Sighnaghi, 284
sight-reading, 86, 120, 297, 300
    as barrier, 48
    opportunities not requiring, 56, 125, 170
    as requirement for classical choirs, 16, 131, 221, 222, 247
Silver Song Club Project, 19
Simmel, Georg, 223
Simon, Paul, 37, 200, 229
Singers Club, 77, 103n4
Sing for Water, 20, 25, 31, 140, 204n16, 241, 273, 312
    individuals associated with, 65, 88, 103
    at Thames Festival, 10–17, 42, 309
Sing for your Lungs, 238
singing
    and Alzheimer's, 19, 238
    amateur, 20
    benefits and rewards of, 2, 23, 24, 233, 236
    as birthright, 16, 47–48, 219
    and the brain, 23, 234
    changing perception of, 68
    and class, 51–52, 131
    and community, 48, 172, 183, 196, 200, 219
    and competition, 20–21, 40, 124, 211, 219, 279
    and co-operation, 124

singing (*Cont.*)
   democratisation of, 20, 54
   in foreign languages, 3, 29, 38, 116, 127, 152–155
   healing power of, 87
   and health and wellbeing, 19, 23, 71, 233–241, 251n25, 289
   holidays, 72, 91, 149, 245, 262–264, 273, 274, 275, 292n13, 298 (*see also* Village Harmony: summer camps)
   holistic approach to, 87
   and identity, 4, 256
   joy of, 66
   manuals and handbooks, 21–22, 118–120
   multipart, 4, 28, 49
   as natural act, 49, 54, 55
   as political act, 84, 217, 219
   and posture, 113–114, 118, 122
   reports on benefits of, 234
   social aspects of, 24, 132
   and social capital, 40
   and speech, 56
   style and environment, 146, 148
   and the Suyá, 29, 43n14, 163
   teaching of, 20
   technique, 52, 54, 198
   therapeutic effects of, 24, 153, 171
   as tool for transformation, 59, 103, 218
   and transcendence, 24, 28
Singing Estate, The, 210
Singing for Breathing, 238
Singing for Snorers, 238
Singing for the Brain, 19, 80, 238
Singing for the Terrified, 14, 242, 248
Singing Hospitals, 19
Singing in the African American Tradition, 124–125, 127, 129, 138n16, 140, 178
Singing on Prescription, 19
Sing Up, 14, 19, 81, 86, 136
Sistema England, 136
skiffle, 73, 92
Skinner, Edith, 56
Skotebi, 198
Skovoroda-Shepherd, Polina. *See* Shepherd, Polina
Slater, David D., 119
Slobin, Mark, 35, 163, 168, 291

Small, Andrea, 238
Small, Christopher, 110, 131, 132, 308
   on music education, 52–53, 134–135
   on musicking, 39
   on Western music theory, 145
Smith, Roxane, 11, *12*, 14, 65, 72, 140, 266
Smith, W. Stephen, 22
Snowman, The, 20, 43n7
SOAS World Music Summer School, 98, 99, 128
social capital, 2, 30, 40–41, 223, 223–224, 241, 295
   bonding and bridging, 288
Society for International Folk Dancing (SIFD), 93, 105n19
society of the spectacle, 41
Solís, Ted, 29, 167, 200
"Something Inside So Strong", 109, 141, 267, 276
song bank, 130, 136
songbooks, 94, 163, 249, 264, 307
   national, 18
   and songs by NVPN members, 71, 104n11, 129, 204n3, 220, 269, 306–307
   South African, 178, 181
   suitable for community choirs, 128, 129, 139n21, 181, 186, 193, 265
Songs for Today, 141
Songs of Heaven and Earth, 96
Songs of the Caucasus. *See* Maspindzeli
Sontonga, Enoch, 178
Sound Sense, 27, 87, 296, 311
South Africa, 24, 27, 28, 177
   attraction to music of, 94, 95, 173–174
   children's choir in, 238
   and choir exchange visits, 275–276
   songs from, 18, 42, 71, 83, 94, 122, 125, 129, 159, 178–181, 216
   treatment of songs from, 179–181
   Village Harmony camp in, 276
   See also folk music: of South Africa; gospel: in South Africa; songbooks: South African
spirituality, 37, 172, 269, 285, 292n8
spirituals, 14, 125, 126, 141, 151, 173, 174, 266
Spooky Men's Chorale, 15
Staelens, Yvette, 81, 104n10
Staniewski, Włodzimierz, 60–61, 62, 117

Stanislavski, Constantin, 75
Stebbins, Robert A., 25
Stefanova, Dessislava (Dessi), 98, 105n26, 106n27, 213
  on appeal of Bulgarian singing, 188
  on London Bulgarian Choir, 224
  teaching methods of, 117, 138n12, 188
stereotypes, 172, 177, 203, 281
Stewart, Dave and Liz, 72
Stige, Brynjulf, 90, 91, 132
Stokes, Martin, 30
Stoller, Paul, 289
Stone, Mollie, 303–304
Storey, John, 37
Storr, Anthony, 145
St. Peter's Catholic Seminary (Hammanskraal), 178–179
Stravinsky, Igor, 301
subjectivity, 203, 248, 273, 274, 289, 298
Sugarman, Jane, 28, 132, 167
summer camps, 270–271. *See also* Baka Culture Camp; Dance Camp Wales; Earthsong; Heartsong; Unicorn Natural Voice Camp; Village Harmony: summer camps
supra, 231–232, 286
Susilo, Hardja, 202
Suyá, 29, 43n14, 163
Svaneti, 62, 159, 253, 284, 286
Sweet Honey in the Rock, 96, 125
Sweet Mills Music Camp, 77
Swetina, Barbara, 96, 164n6
Swiss Bulgarian Choir, 98

Taberner, Stephen, 11, 15
Tabuni, 199
tai chi, 85, 114, 197, 198, 270
Taizé chants/songs, 94, 96, 105n21, 155–157, 163, 269
  as inspiration for Harmonic Temple, 267–268
  and language, 155–156
  as suitable for natural voice choirs, 164n6
Tavagna, 134, 280
Taylor, Timothy, 38, 158
Tbilisi State Conservatoire, 192, 199
teaching and learning by ear, 71, 108–109, 120–123
  benefits of, 246–247

temperance movement, 214, 292n3
Tempus Fugit, 62
Tenores Antoni Milia, 62
Thames Festival, 10, 42
Thatcher years, 84, 215
theatre, 55, 59–62, 78, 79, 97, 151
  and natural voice connection, 84–85
theatre anthropology, 61
Theatre in Education, 89
Theatre Zar, 60, 63, 142
Third Theatre, 101
Thomas, Ros, 141
Thornlie Primary Georgian Choir, 199
Three Choirs Festival, 217
Three Choirs Plus Community Choir, 217, 250n11
timbre, 46, 65, 75, 98, 116, 117, 121, 186
Tocqueville, Alexis de, 223
To Grace the Earth, 129, 220, 306
Tomlinson, Gary, 52, 131
Tonalis Music Centre, 86, 87
tone-deafness, 51, 53, 115
tonic sol-fa, 180, 214
TONSIL (The Ongoing Singing Liaison Group), 213
Torola, 198
tourism, 36, 268, 278
  alternative, 260
  cultural, 30, 166
  as escape, 259
  and identities, 260, 261
  musical, 30
  as neocolonialism, 259
  and quest for authenticity, 259, 260, 262
  package or mass, 259
  as pilgrimage or sacred journey, 259, 262, 274
  and post-tourist, 260
  and revitalisation, 261, 287
  and staged authenticity, 261, 262
  theories of, 259–262
  and Thomas Cook, 292n3
  as transformative, 262, 274
transculturality, 34–35
transformation, 298–299
  personal, 173, 239, 291
  through performance, 203
  through singing, 22, 54, 126, 218, 247
transnationalism, 34

Index [349]

transnational singing community, 18, 232
travel. *See* tourism
Trio Bulgarka, 185
Tugwell, David, 198
Tula Mama, 42
Turino, Thomas
    on cultural cohorts and cultural formations, 35, 291–292
    on performing arts and identity, 289
    on presentational and participatory music, 39–40, 125, 132–133, 310
    on repetition, 127
    on worldbeat and its appeal, 167, 169, 170
Turner, Victor, 168, 173, 240, 272, 298
twang, 147

UCL East European Choir, 99
Ulfah Arts, 95
UNESCO, 75, 182, 185
    and intangible cultural heritage, 166, 203n1
Unicorn Natural Voice Camp, 61, 92, 95, 100, 101, 142, 263–273, 289, 291
    attendees at, 263, 270, 256
    attraction of, 271–272
    ethos of, 258–259, 263, 265, 268, 271, 288
    and lifestyle, 270–271
    origins of, 93–94,
    and repertoire, 128, 265–267
    teachers at, 14, 15, 86, 94, 96, 98, 183
    as village/community, 252–253, 257, 264, 271
"Unison in Harmony", 267
universal peace dance. *See* Dances of Universal Peace
unmusicality, invention of, 52–53
Urry, John, 260
Ushguli, 253, 257, 284
utopia, 41, 257, 258, 272

Veda Slovena, 99
Venda, 50, 52
Verney, Candy, 274
Verney, Teresa, 91-92
Vidović, Branka, 282
Vignjević, Tijana, 282, 283
Village Harmony, 129, 130, 163n2, 180, 259, 303

Bosnia camp, 281–284
Corsica camp, 278–281
as family and community, 278
Georgia camp, 284–286
summer camps, 6, 98, 128, 143, 147–148, 180, 186, 276–286, 288, 289, 291
Virgin Queen, The, 98, 106n28
vocables, 158–159
vocal coaching. *See* voice work
vocal technique, 57, 62, 147
    in Bulgarian singing, 98, 117, 138n12, 187
    extended, 94
    in Georgian singing, 197–198
    in Russian singing, 118
voice
    anachronistic and bourgeois, 51
    effects of social conditioning on, 21
    as instrument, 45, 58
    liberation of, 54, 57–58
    as "muscle of the soul", 58, 61
    operatic, 146, 164n4
    placement, 55, 75, 121, 186
    political uses of, 21
    secret of, 23
    suppression of, 21, 57–58, 247–248
    therapeutic work with, 21, 91-92
    varieties of, 46
    See also natural voice
Voice and Speech Trainers Association (VASTA), 78
Voice Project, The, 89
Voices Now, 162
voluntary arts, 5, 85
    in the UK, 13
Vulcheva, Kalinka, 185

Walker, Roz, 42, 141, 190
Walton, Margaret, 151-152, 228-230
warm-up exercises, 48, 85, 107–108, 137n4
    function and rationale of, 111–118, 137n6, 147
    sources of, 137n5, 137n7
Warren, Iris, 56, 114
WAST Nightingales, 208
WaterAid, 13, 14, 42n2, 265
Watson, Faith, 15, 208
Weavers, The, 17, 74
Weber, Max, 41, 260

Weedon, Chris, 33
Wells, Jane, 88, 246
Welsch, Wolfgang, 34
Wenger, Etienne, 101, 248
Western art music
    aesthetics of, 46, 54, 68n8, 131, 146, 195, 211
    canon of, 24, 222, 304
    conventions of, 51, 133, 145, 188
    liberation from constraints of, 94, 144–145, 149, 186–187, 191, 297
    status of, 51, 161, 211, 217, 220, 301–302
    training in, 14, 19, 54, 86, 88, 91, 94, 98, 133, 134, 147, 221, 300
Western classical music. *See* Western art music
Western classical training. *See* Western art music: training in
Whitehead, Rowena, 71, 72, 95, 96, 175, 266
    on NVPN as professional home, 101
    and role/activities of community choir, 243–244
    and world music, 97
White, Mike, 238–239
Whitman, Walt, 82
Wing-It Singers, 97
Wolfsohn, Alfred, 58–59, 61, 312
WOMAD festival, 128, 229, 250n18, 258, 260, 261
Woman of Thirteen Shirts, The, 3
women's movement, 77, 79, 83, 95, 189
Woodcraft Folk, 312
Workcenter of Jerzy Grotowski, 60, 62
workshops, 1, 3, 4, 6, 13, 15, 84, 161, 209, 218, 264, 298
    clientele for, 102, 125
    experience of leading, 102, 177
    at festivals, 55, 62–65, 97, 104n15, 258
    as means of dissemination, 93, 127, 128, 193, 220, 292n9
    by NVPN members, 14, 54, 75, 87, 96, 98, 99, 154, 179, 225, 245, 266–267, 306
    as part of national scene/network, 31, 73, 128, 199, 220, 224, 232, 278, 296
    as part of practitioner's portfolio, 14, 47, 77, 176, 183, 197
    as part of practitioner's training and development, 70–71, 78, 81, 85, 97, 110, 128–129, 154
    songs suitable for, 66, 124, 142, 176, 200, 266–267
    as source of new repertoire, 77, 89, 128–129, 178, 179, 180, 183, 185, 199, 245
    as source of revelation/transformation for singers, 190, 191, 225, 230
    and teaching method, 18, 56, 110, 115, 117, 125, 137n4, 193–196, 197–198
    as turning point for practitioners-to-be, 82, 89, 95, 123, 170, 187
    by visiting overseas teachers, 97, 168, 185, 192–196, 197, 199, 247, 287
World Choir Games, 20, 210, 219
world music, 16, 67, 96–97, 229, 298, 312
    critiques of, 37
    in education, 29–30, 200
World Scout Jamboree, 17, 43n5
world song, 16, 141
    appeal/attraction of, 142–155, 166, 200
WorldSong choir, 14, 85, 141, 213
WorldSong Live: A Decade in Harmony, 141
Wortley Hall, 69–70, 100, 101
Wosien, Bernard, 92
Woven Gold, 232
Wurdeman, John, 286

X-Factor, The, 20

Yale Russian Chorus, 196
Yeomans, Helen, 42, 71, 72, 249n4, 267
yodel, 115, 146, 181, 187
yoga, 70, 85, 114, 198, 270
Youth Music, 14, 86
Yule, Lynn, 151-152, 228-230

Zagorche, 98
Zap Mama, 176–177
Zedashe, 284, 285, 286
Zeserson, Katherine, 103
Ziff, Bruce, 201
Zimbabwe, 49, 122
"Ziyamazumekisi", 12
zumba, 161–162
Zurmukhti, 199

Printed in Great Britain
by Amazon